ALISTAIR COOKE'S AMERICA

Alfred A. Knopf   New York

Manufactured in the United States of America.

CONTENTS

PROLOGUE
A PASSAGE TO AMERICA — 7

1
THE NEW-FOUND LAND — 23

2
A HOME AWAY FROM HOME — 61

3
MAKING A REVOLUTION — 93

4
INVENTING A NATION — 125

5
GONE WEST — 155

6
A FIREBELL IN THE NIGHT — 189

7
DOMESTICATING A WILDERNESS — 223

8
MONEY ON THE LAND — 247

9
THE HUDDLED MASSES — 273

10
THE PROMISE FULFILLED—THE PROMISE BROKEN — 303

11
THE ARSENAL — 335

EPILOGUE
THE MORE ABUNDANT LIFE — 367

ACKNOWLEDGMENTS AND INDEX — 393

For:
Stephen Hearst, who insisted on it
Michael Gill, who saw it through
and
Jane, who suffered it.

Prologue

A PASSAGE TO AMERICA

During the First World War, I was a small boy in Blackpool, a seaside town on the northwest coast of England, which was then the summer-time Mecca of the cotton workers of inland Lancashire. It had hundreds of boarding houses and a stretch of sand on which it was possible to drill thousands of soldiers, since it was six miles long and, at the low tide of the Irish Sea, as much as half a mile wide. The town accordingly became a vast cantonment, and pretty soon after the United States declared war in 1917 the "doughboys" arrived. We had seven of them billeted on us. (I learned much later that the men who wrote the American Constitution put in a clause expressly forbidding the billeting of any soldier in a private house. But the Founding Fathers, with their uncanny foresight, saw to it that this prohibition did not apply to England.) I thus had the experience, extraordinary in those days for a provincial middle-class boy, of encountering in the flesh the legendary tribe of "the Yanks," who were known to us only through the silent and often baffling antics of Buster Keaton, Mary Pickford, and William S. Hart at the so-called picturedrome.

The Americans moved in like a football team invading a hospital, for by the autumn of 1917 all the vigorous British conscripts had come and gone from Blackpool, and very many of them were already rotting on the fields of France. They had been succeeded by the last scrapings of the barrel, the old and the chronically frail and sick. All the "C3s," once confidently labeled as unfit for combat and assigned to the auxiliary service of the Royal Army Medical Corps, were now being desperately trained as warriors. To these brave crocks—most of whom would very soon go the way of their comparatively healthy predecessors—were added the "blue-jackets," a legion of the halt and the maimed who would today be categorized by the Pentagon as "impaired combatant personnel" but in those honest days were known as wounded soldiers.

The melding of these convalescents with the bouncing Americans was not easy. Cynical or crippled veterans of Ypres and the battles of the

Somme did not take warmly to eager-eyed youngsters from Iowa and Illinois who announced they had come to win the war so long and inconclusively fought by the British and the French. There was a climactic episode in which a Texan ran into a Lancastrian blue-jacket on Central Pier. They each have their own brand of dead-pan humor unfortunately not recognizable as such to the other. After some dry exchange, the blue-jacket tossed the Texan into the Irish Sea, and for a nervous week or so all the Americans were confined to their quarters. The mordant humor of this situation did not escape a wide-eyed nine-year-old, and so at a tender age I was witness to my first upheaval in Anglo-American relations.

I doubt that I harbored then any preconceptions at all about Americans. Everything about them was peculiar and fascinating. They wore Boy Scouts hats, an oddity that was never explained. All their ranks had identical table manners and, so far as we could tell, identical accents, thereby confronting the British officers with touchy problems in guessing at social station. They treated my mother with a New World courtesy that kept them strangers long after their British counterparts would have been close, if off-hand, friends. But they addressed children as equals, and I was treated as a sort of regimental pet. Since my own father, an artist in metalwork, had been drafted in his fortieth year into an airplane factory in Manchester, from which he came on leave only once a month, I had the luck of having seven extra fathers, and no doubt my inclination to take to Americans was incorrigibly determined then.

They were taller than our soldiers and uniformly paler, almost yellow. I now suppose that they came from the cities of the Eastern seaboard, or perhaps the South, where the burning sun is something you stay away from. At any rate, my father (who had not been to America either) explained to me that their biscuity complexions were due to the famous skyscrapers, which kept the sun off their faces the year round. Later on, after I had been subjected to the only American texts then compulsory in an English elementary school (*The Deerslayer, Hiawatha, The Legend of Sleepy Hollow,* and the totally incomprehensible *Tom Sawyer),* my mental picture of the United States, and of such scattered human life as it supported, became sharper but not, I regret to say, more accurate. First, there was New York, with skyscrapers and yellow men, and red men lurking in the suburbs. Then a long stretch of something called the prairie or pampas (we were never told exactly which) and through the middle of this uninhabited wilderness there flowed a wide river—"the wide Missouri," probably, since that was the subtitle of the only American song we were required to sing in unison. Later still, the musical *Show Boat* came to England and we knew then that the big river was the Mississippi, thrashing with steamboats and gamblers, who were nudged aside from time to time by a man in a white suit and a bushy white mustache who kept rushing to the stern and dropping a plumbline and shouting, "Mark Twain!" Beyond the Mississippi, it was said, there was another yawning prairie rising eventually to the only range of mountains in America, the Rockies; and at last you came on the Pacific Ocean and the only other American city, San Francisco, which we were told had been founded exclusively by Australian convicts.

There was very little in my excellent grammar school education to rip apart this tough patchwork of preconceptions, for in British schools in those days American history stopped abruptly with the outbreak of the Revolutionary War, on the principle that if they didn't need us, we didn't need them. But after the First World War, both the national prejudices I had imbibed and the personal memories of "the Yanks" that tended to contradict them began to blur together and fade as the inevitable reaction against Our Gallant Allies set in. Throughout the 1920s, America became known to us as a lurid society of licentious movie stars, ruthless gangsters, a boastful citizenry, and a grasping government called "Uncle Shylock," who was out to bleed old Europe white with demands for war reparations. Like most healthy schoolboys, I had no more social conscience than a puppy; so that while it was proper to defer to one's parents when they bemoaned the money-mad Republic across the seas and contemplated every American import, from canned beef to shirts with collars attached, as typical bits of "shoddy," these horrors paled for me and my friends before the heroics of Lindbergh, Douglas Fairbanks, and Bobby Jones; the country's reputation for beautiful and pliant females; the arrival of Fred and Adele Astaire; and the joys of American jazz.

This may seem like a very simple load of mental baggage with which a Cambridge graduate was to set sail for the United States in September 1932 after he had been awarded a fellowship for graduate study at Yale. But I believe that the preconceptions about another country that we hold on to most tenaciously are those we take in, so to speak, with our mother's milk; and after the showing of the *America* television series in Britain, it was made plain to me in many penitent letters, some of them from eminent persons, that the infection of these old prejudices is still widespread.

This is not the place to go into all the stages of my subsequent enlightenment, except as they seeded the long, unconscious gestation of this book. My fellowship was intended to train me in the expertise of American theater direction, so as to return and revolutionize the English drama. But one of the "obligations" of my tenure was to be given a car and tour, in the summer vacation, as many of the States of the Union as possible. It was more of an outrageous luxury than an obligation, at a time when bankrupt stockbrokers were pulling their sons out of Yale,

Photographs by Alistair Cooke. New York City, 1942, and New England.

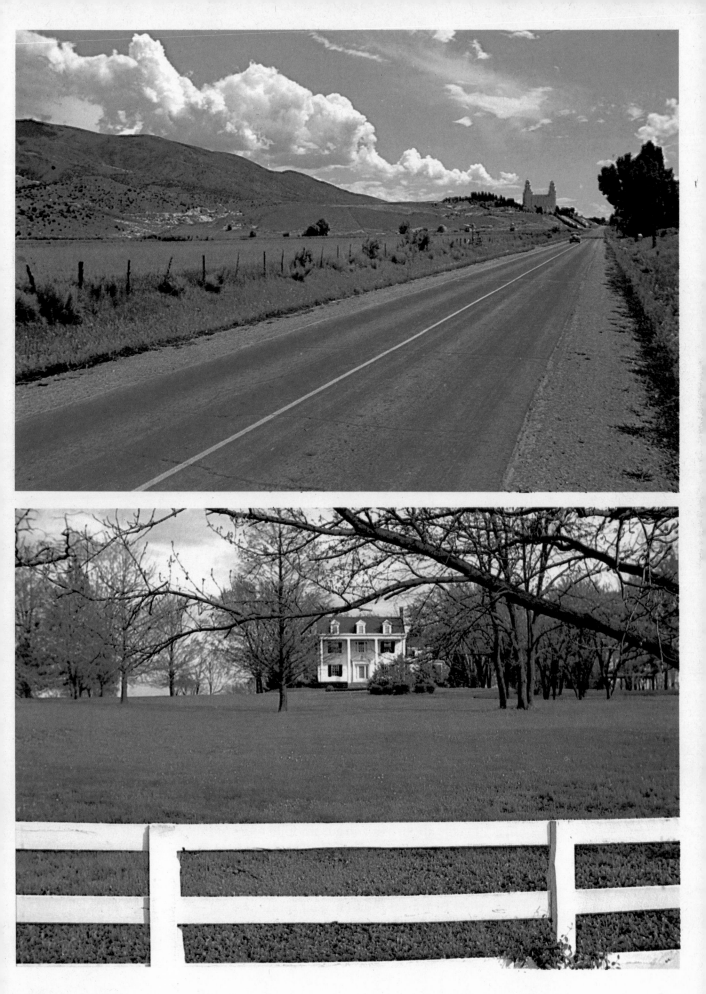

Utah and Kentucky.

and this first safari through America, in the midst of Roosevelt's Hundred Days, shook me out of my deep ignorance of politics. (In those days, a Senator was to me some sort of American with a toga, and for several years such vital mysteries as "judicial review" and "executive usurpation" were meaningless bits of jargon that the newspapers went on about.) But the upshot of this tour was to make the landscape and the people of America far more dramatic than Broadway; and when I returned to England, I weaned myself away from the theater during a tapering-off period as the BBC's film critic and then gave myself over to writing and directing programs about American life and history for a country that was then inadequately informed by a mere handful of correspondents in America, half of them in Hollywood. It was only a matter of time before I returned, on an immigrant visa, and found myself—to my astonishment—launched as a second-string foreign correspondent for the London *Times* and the BBC, required to write and broadcast knowing pieces on the criminal trial of a Tammany leader, the fate of a farm bill, and the indecisive thirteen-hour ordeal of a man waiting to jump from a hotel balcony. During thirty-five years as a foreign correspondent, I must have covered just about everything, from the public life of six Presidents to the private life of a burlesque stripper; from the black market in beef to the Black Panthers; from Estes Kefauver amid the snows of New Hampshire to Jack Nicklaus amid the azaleas of Augusta, Georgia; from Henry Kaiser's Liberty ships to Francis Chichester's *Gypsy Moth* sailing into Staten Island at one in the morning; from the Marshall Plan to Planned Parenthood; from Senator Joseph McCarthy's last stand to the massacre of Muhammad Ali by Joe Frazier.

I list this bewildering variety of assignments without foolish boast, because it is the stimulating duty of a foreign correspondent to cover everything. Whereas a domestic reporter, even at his best, graduates from general reporting and hops up the ladder to success towards a single specialty (sports, organized labor, the stock exchange, or the State Department), a foreign correspondent is required to act on the preposterous but exhilarating assumption that he takes all knowledge for his province and is equally at home in a textile mill, a political convention, a showing of abstract art, a proxy fight, or a launch pad at Cape Canaveral.

In all, I made about a dozen automobile tours of the country, as well as innumerable regional jaunts, and in one long and lonely drive through the late winter, spring, and summer of 1942, as an accredited "war" correspondent reporting from the American grandstand to an audience of embattled Britons, I found myself rediscovering—on re-tread tires at the compulsory thirty-five miles an hour—the whole American landscape, region by region, county by county. The theoretical purpose of this trip was to see and say what the war was doing to such wildly different specialties as steel production, long-staple cotton, the tattooing of sailors' forearms, and the manufacture of heels for ladies' shoes. But what I learned from this memorable experience was that in a continent of (then) forty-eight governments, a half-dozen radically different climates, a score of separate economies, and a goulash of ethnic ingredients, nothing that you say about the whole country is going to be true; and secondly, that the exciting way to learn about the history of this country, and the experience of settling it, is to dig it out of the landscape. It was more fun to come on sheepherders in Idaho talking a peculiar half-Irish, half-Basque lingo than to stay home and read a Congressional report on immigration. A fictional series on, say, "The Forty-Niners" cannot begin to convey the feel of their ordeal as much as a stroll through the graveyards in the foothills of the Sierras.

On all my trips, from the late 1930s on, I packed in an orange crate in the trunk of my car the federal guides to all the states I was likely to drive through. These had been written by penurious writers and local historians enlisted under the Writers Program of the government's Works Projects Administration during the Depression. America, which had had no guidebooks worth the name, suddenly had a library of the best; and it was these unsung historians who put me on to hundreds of places along the road that few tourists had ever heard about. So when the British Broadcasting Corporation first proposed to me the alarming project of recounting the history of the United States on television, I was given the courage, or gall, to attempt it because of two passing thoughts: one was that as a correspondent writing for an innocent audience of foreigners, I usually had to trace the most topical news story back to its historical beginning (you cannot assume, as *The New York Times* must, that its readers can instantly place the history of "interstate commerce" into the context of a sudden violation of it); and through my travels I had acquired something of what Theodore Roosevelt said every President should have, namely, "a sense of the continent." I might not, as many more learned men could, recall at once a well-articulated skeleton of the outline of American history. I had, of course, read a good deal of American history down the years, but when I think of some historic person or episode, I tend to think first of a place, some corner of that continental field that is forever American, because something charming or hideous or otherwise memorable had happened there. So I jotted down a long list of such places, most of them, I should guess, not much known to tourists or even to the standard history books: Catherine, Kansas (the first planting of Turkey Red wheat); Big Bone Lick, Kentucky (the dinosaurs' contribution to "the dark and bloody ground"); New Harmony, Indiana (the most touted of the "communes"); Pittsburg

Landing, Tennessee (the menace of the Union Army's plentiful reserves); The Humboldt Sink, Nevada (the cruelest ordeal of the Gold Rush); Newfane, Vermont (the epitome of native New England architecture); Livingston, Montana (the literal bottleneck in the continental wartime supply route to the Pacific); and so on and on. To arrange these memories of a nation's history from the landscape and not the books seemed the best I had to offer. There are rafts of formidable and brilliant historians. The papers and magazines are groaning with Cassandras. So without any preconceptions about how it would come out (I am not sure whether the United States is going to come out intact or not), I arranged the episodes in chronological order. Whether it was to succeed or fail, it seemed to me a good, though tortuous, thing to attempt: to try and say what is moving about the American experience over four hundred years at a time when that experience is either forgotten, badly taught, or shamelessly sentimentalized; and to recall what is tough and good about the American system of government at a time when that system is poorly understood and, in some high and low places, perilously close to corruption or betrayal.

The nucleus of this book is, of course, the scripts I wrote for the television film. But film has to be direct and immediate, at the expense of reservations and intellectual subtlety. Film as history is therefore inevitably oversimple (still, it is better to be oversimple than overwrought). Complicated issues, such as the scores involved in the making of the Constitution, have to be reduced to dramatic opposites—so that in the fourth episode, for example, the sort of Constitution that was to emerge turned into a clash between George Mason and Alexander Hamilton, with James Madison as the referee and eventual winner. The fourth chapter is considerably longer than the original script and, I hope, truer to the complexities of the seventeen-week debate. Similarly, the Spanish and French contributions, which had to be mercilessly condensed into a single episode, are here given their proper due. In all, this book is about four times the length of the spoken television scripts.

The first thing a foreigner has to try to take in about America—and it is not something automatically grasped even by all the natives—is the simple size of the place and the often warring variety of life that goes on inside it. In a motion picture of the 1930s, the hero was a young American from the prairie arriving in England to take up a Rhodes Scholarship. He settled for his first trip to Oxford into the snugness of an English "railway carriage" and found himself sitting opposite an English parson buried in his newspaper. As the gaping boy looked out over the small-scale landscape with its velvety pasture, the trim spinneys, and the checkerboard hedgerows, he could not restrain himself. "You know, sir," he said, "I guess the whole of England could be fitted into one corner of Nebraska." The parson looked up from his paper and crisply replied, "But to what *end*, young man?"

It is the classic English riposte to the classic American response on first seeing England. From Dickens on, the English have always remarked, with due condescension, on the American preoccupation with size, and the Americans have rarely let them down. And for good reason. If there was one conception more than another that white men had to forget when they came to America, it was of a guaranteed livelihood in a friendly landscape. They had to get used to the idea of a vast and dangerous country whose size alone guaranteed the possibility of success in one part of it after failure in another. The size of the country was the image of their salvation, just as brute size guaranteed sanctuary to the Indians—for a couple of hundred years.

What is consoling about the American concern with size is that once the insular Briton makes the crossing and is exposed to it he tends to share it with a gurgling childlike wonder. In Sussex, he might have been in the habit of driving twenty miles to dinner. But if, like me, he should acquire a friend in some such place as Alpine, Texas, and another in El Paso, he will brag till his dying day that he once drove 360 miles round trip just for a meal. Most people, I believe, when they first come to America, whether as travelers or settlers, become aware of a new and agreeable feeling: that the whole country is their oyster. They may, in fact, settle down in one place and stay there. But America can still fire dull imaginations with the prospect of a continent to explore. In my experience, the only people immune to this vision are those urban types to whom—as the late Fred Allen used to say—"everywhere outside New York City is Bridgeport, Connecticut." This parochialism is common in all the big cities of the East, but in New York City it amounts to a kind of insensate village pride.

There are, in fact, large regions of the United States that will challenge the hardihood of the most carefree wanderer. As I write this, a forgotten skyjacker is either living off roots and mountain-lion meat or, more probably, is frozen stiff on the slopes of the Cascade Mountains. The airplane passenger, on his first flight west, is invariably astonished to look down for hours on a landscape as seemingly hostile as the barren interior of Australia or the craters of the moon. But practically all of it may be driven across comfortably on cement highways and six-lane freeways. The determined adventurer has to make a special effort, if he wishes to imitate the pioneer, and penetrate the Great Basin in Nevada or the fastnesses of the Bitterroot Mountains or the High Sierras.

A famous American historian announced positively in 1893 that the frontier had disappeared three years earlier. But more free land was

Photographs by Alistair Cooke. Kansas wheatfield and Bryce Canyon, Utah.

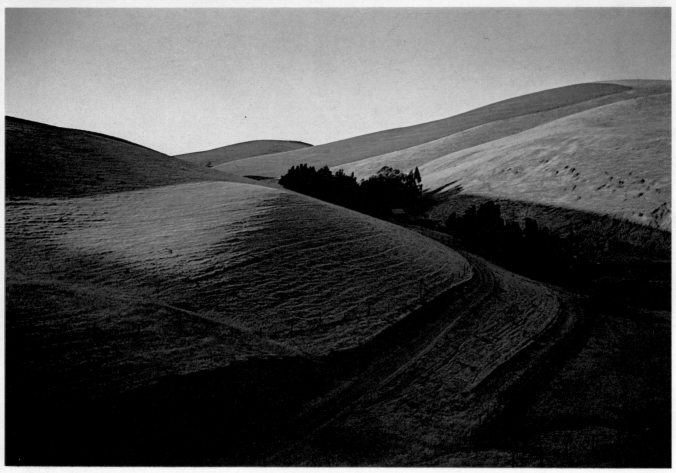

New Mexico and California.

homesteaded after 1900 than before, and so late as 1927 there were quantities of free government lands available. Undoubtedly, all the land mass of the United States has been mapped, and the prospects for a livelihood in any part of it are known. This is what we really mean by the end of the frontier, the word being taken to bear its original American meaning not of a state or national border but of the unknown land that lay to the west of a fringe of human settlements.

Before we begin to follow the history of the land and its people, it might be well to have in our mind's eye a picture of North America at once sharp and memorable. For a long time, Europeans and Americans alike were stuck with the picture of a giant ray with a shrunken tail curling into the Equator. The projection of Gerhardus Mercator, a Flemish mapmaker, did not allow the lines of longitude to converge at the poles, so the areas near the pole appear wider than they really are, and North America broadens out to the north like an open fan. This causes little confusion to most of us until we hear that the air route from London to San Francisco is shorter over the pole than it is via the Atlantic, New York, and Chicago. For our purpose, what we want is a picture of the terrain as the explorers saw it, then the people who settled it and walked across it, and then went by train, and only in our own time learned less and less of its sweep and character by flying over it.

Fortunately, the broad design was drawn for us, nearly a century and a half ago, by a Frenchman who saw only a little of it from the ground, but he has painted an incomparable big picture of this continent as it may be seen from the godlike height of a space ship. At the very opening of the first chapter of his monumental *Democracy in America*, Alexis de Tocqueville remarks that:

> A sort of methodical order seems to have regulated the separation of land and water, mountains and valleys. A simple but grand arrangement is discoverable amidst the confusion of objects and the prodigious variety of scenes.
>
> The continent is divided, almost equally, into two vast regions, one of which is bounded on the north by the Arctic Pole, and by the two great oceans on the east and west. It stretches towards the south, forming a triangle, whose irregular sides meet at length below the great lakes of Canada.
>
> The second region begins where the other terminates, and includes all the rest of the continent. The one slopes gently towards the Pole, the other towards the Equator.

Happily for us all, the United States is a stranger to that "first region" in the North, where there are neither "high mountains nor deep valley," where "great rivers mix their currents, separate and meet again, disperse and form vast marshes . . . and thus, at length, after innumerable windings, fall into the Polar seas."

The second region embraces what is now the United States. It is, Tocqueville succinctly observes, "more varied on its surface and better suited for the habitation of man." So, indeed, it is. Which is why the almost four million square miles of Canada house only twenty-one million people, and the three million square miles of the continuous land area of the United States (excluding the outposts of Alaska and Hawaii) support a population of over two hundred million.

When Tocqueville goes on to describe the land mass of what is now the United States, he sees it very much as an astronaut does:

Two long chains of mountains divide it from one extreme to the other: the Allegheny Ridge takes the form of the shores of the Atlantic Ocean; the other is parallel with the Pacific . . . the vast territory in between forms a single valley, one side of which descends gradually from the rounded summits of the Alleghenies, while the other rises in an uninterrupted course towards the tops of the Rocky Mountains. At the bottom of the valley flows an immense river, into which the various streams issuing from the mountains fall from all parts . . . the Indians, in their pompous language, have named it the Father of Waters, or the Mississippi.

This "grand arrangement" does not take in the Great Basin beyond the Rockies, or the higher range of the Sierras, but it does describe the three commanding features of the whole: the main mountain range of the East, the Appalachians (in his time called "the Alleghenies," because the northern ridge of the chain was most familiar); the largest mountain chain of the West, the Rockies; and in between a huge valley down which "fifty-seven large navigable rivers contribute to swell the waters of the Mississippi" along the twenty-five hundred miles of its course.

These features become very clear on a relief map and compose the big picture: a great quadrilateral, three thousand miles at its widest reach between the oceans, and about twelve hundred miles from the Great Lakes to the Gulf of Mexico. The prime asset of the United States is that it lies between the parallels of 26 and 55 N. Above these limits are bleak and unproductive lands, and below them are tropical forests and deserts and humid climates that debilitate the white man when its diseases do not enfeeble him. On the contrary, the United States spans the limits of the climates that white men can live and work in. The "prodigious variety of scenes" encompasses a widening littoral on the East Coast that goes from skiing country through temperate farmland to semitropical swamps and warm winter resorts; westward, over the Appalachians and across the broadest stretch of land, a huge and fertile prairie rising to the Great Plains; and on the West Coast, from north to south, virgin forest falling away to the green, damp England of Oregon, and down through all the various landscapes of California—Switzerland and Burgundy and Yorkshire and Scotland and Spain—to the desert and the balmy seashore of Lower California.

Although a third of the United States is too cold to maintain dependable agriculture, and a quarter of it is desert-dry, across the rest of the continent the North European was able to grow, and in undreamed-of abundance, every crop he had planted at home and many he hadn't, including maize, cotton, rice, and tobacco. And he was to find here half the world's coal, and more forest and mineral wealth than on any other continent.

The enviable richness of America's natural resources is a theme that Europeans like to dwell on whenever they are feeling peevish about some new American achievement like a moon shot or the fact that more than half the families in the United States have an annual income of $15,000. While the Europeans attribute America's bounty to the luck of her resources, Americans on the other hand like to ascribe it to nothing but character. It usually required a combination of both. As the dramatic history of this country, including the actual invention of a nation, will show.

1

THE NEW-FOUND LAND

Just when America was discovered by the human race is a large puzzle, and a matter of much jealous scholarship. The disputes flare up anew with every unearthing of a skull, a primitive burial ground, a charcoal pit, or a flint knife, and with every fresh scrutiny of an Indian artifact that suggests the symbols or graffiti inscribed in Egyptian tombs or Coptic churches. There are scholars who insist that we cannot know who first began to populate America until we have decided where the human being first appeared on the earth! As late as 1959, it was generally thought that the place was Asia.

In the summer of that year, Dr. Louis Leakey and his wife found two skulls, forty teeth, and a collarbone buried in a ravine on the Serengeti Plain, and thereby not only transferred the origins of man to Africa but set back the date of his appearance by over a million years. It is little wonder, then, that the question of when human beings first embarked for America, or strayed into it, is an open one.

There are eminent scholars who are convinced that America was first seen by Egyptians. There are others who assert the more or less plausible claims of the Greeks, the Etruscans, the Chinese Buddhists, the Hindus, the Japanese, even the Basques—and, of course, the Irish. There are prehistoric mounds in Indiana built, according to the Welsh, by the Welsh. The Mormons are still committed to the belief that the people we call Indians (after Christopher Columbus's error in thinking he had come on "the Indies") are descended from the Ten Lost Tribes of Israel.

But since this book is to be about the history of that part of North America that became the United States of America, we must leave these hassles to the archeologists and anthropologists and turn in relief to the present consensus that the first people who saw what we call America were following ice-age mammals who had stumbled east from Siberia into Alaska in search of more food in greener pastures. It was a trek supposed to lead them in time down to the grasslands of the American interior, on east to the Atlantic shores of Canada, south across the

A warrior of the Great Plains: Heap Wolves, a Comanche chief killed by the Osage in 1872, not long after W. S. Soule took this picture of him.

deserts, through semitropical America, and at last to the tip of Chile. Yet fifty-six miles of water separates the Chukchi Peninsula of Siberia from the Seward Peninsula of Alaska. It took sixteen years, two expeditions, and the life of Vitus Bering, a Danish navigator hired by Peter the Great in the early eighteenth century, to conclude that between the two jutting peninsulas, from which today the Soviet Union and the United States of America glare at each other most closely, there was no bridge of land. But there had been, so the accepted theory goes, in the prehistoric time when glacial ice sheets locked up much of our planet's water supply and lowered the level of the sea. Not until about ten thousand years ago, when one of these ice sheets started to melt, were Siberia and Alaska parted once for all by the waters. We can no more than guess how long Alaska entertained the human race, but the appearance of humans south of Alaska is unanimously fixed at a time not later than fifteen thousand years ago.

Unfortunately, American and Russian scientists have lately been pursuing a line of research that may well wreck the "consensus" that the first Americans came from Siberia. While I was at work on this book, I was introduced by Dr. Leon J. Salter to the findings of the American serologist Dr. William Boyd and the Russian anthropologist M. G. Levin. They declare that, while the predominant Asian blood type is B, American Indians run exclusively to A and O. Moreover, from "the southern edge of the last glacier at the Canadian border" American Indians "run an amazing 100% O blood" all the way to the Horn. None of them possesses B-type blood.

We had better simply say that long after man had settled in the land masses of Europe, Asia, and Africa, America was unknown to any human being, but that at some point—we now suppose about fifteen thousand years ago—humans began to range the length and breadth of the Americas. It is the popular belief, handed down to generations of schoolchildren, that Indians were of two main sorts: farmers living in villages or *pueblos*, and hunters—except, of course, in Mexico, where Cortés came on cities of high culture with complicated systems of government not unlike those known In Europe.

In the past forty years, however, anthropologists have done some very thorough digging into the life of the North American Indians and have discovered a bewildering variety of cultures and societies beyond anything the schoolbooks have taught. There were Indian societies that dwelt in permanent settlements, and others that wandered; some were wholly democratic, others had very rigid class systems based on property. Some were ruled by gods carried around on litters, some had judicial systems, to some the only known punishment was torture. Some lived in caves, others in tepees of bison skins, others in cabins. There were tribes ruled by warriors or by women, by sacred elders or by councils, or by fraternities whose rituals and membership were as unknown to the rest of the tribe as those of any college secret society. There were tribes who worshiped the bison or a matriarch or the maize they lived by. There were tribes that had never heard of war, and there were tribes debauched by centuries of fighting. In short, there was a great diversity of Indian nations, speaking over five hundred languages.

For at least a hundred and fifty centuries before "Yankee Doodle," the Indians' way of life composed "the American way of life." It is to most of us a long, dark chapter in American history. And though barrels of lost Egyptian and Asian manuscripts might testify to our ignorant chauvinism, it is the European discovery of America—and the experience of the whites who conquered the continent and settled it—that excites most of us.

So we begin with the simple, colossal question: Who was the first white man to discover America? (It was, incidentally, named after a Florentine businessman and promoter, Amerigo Vespucci, who promoted himself so well that he got his name attached first to South America, and then to the whole continent, though he took no part in the early voyages.) But the first? We simply do not know. The most plausible speculations involve Indian artifacts whose resemblance to the symbols of the ancient civilizations of the Mediterranean Basin can do no more than suggest expeditions of which there is left no trace. But it is certain that the Norsemen, Swedes, and Danes who swarmed over Europe in the tenth century colonized Iceland and Greenland and from there, in the first seven years of the eleventh century, journeyed to the southwest and came on some region of the east coast of North America. Finding "self-sown wheatfields and wild grapes, out of which a very good wine can be made," they called the place Vinland. Throughout the nineteenth century Icelandic scholars debated whether this attractive region lay on the coast of Rhode Island, Massachusetts, Labrador, Newfoundland, or Nova Scotia. The last seems the most likely, though if so its wine industry must have gone into a swift decline.

Lately there has been some powerful propaganda on behalf of the Phoenicians and the Jews, but the records of their voyages are, to say the least, well hidden in the womb of time. It seems sensible to bypass these scholastic brawls and fall back instead on the end of the fifteenth century and Christopher Columbus, and say at once that his first voyage is a decisive event in world history: it brought to the whole of Europe, in the following century, the first shock of recognition that the American continent existed; and it started the adventure that has never stopped since—the exploration, conquest, and settlement of this new-found land.

In 1453, there was a decisive turn in the centuries of warfare between the Christians of Europe and the Moslems of Asia. Their common market, bridge, and gateway was Constantinople, our Istanbul. In 1453, the Turks conquered it, and in so doing shut off the commerce between East and West, the exchange of the cloth, leather, wines, and sword blades of Europe for the silks, jewels, chessmen, and spices of Asia. All things considered, the stoppage was much harder on the court treasuries of Europe than those of Asia and, in one vital item, harder on all Europeans. That item was spices.

Some of the big jolts of history have been caused by the denial of a simple human need. A shortage of water. Lack of bearable living space for a large population cramped in a small country. A total absence of timber, which has plagued the Egyptians since the time of Solomon. But spices? Today only fastidious housewives and food critics for fashion magazines regard spices as fundamental to human survival. The vast majority of ordinary European householders look on nutmeg, cinnamon, cloves, paprika, basil, and the like as gilt on the gingerbread. And many of us, including the Latin nations and the inhabitants of most hot countries, have an incurable hankering after pepper. But in the fifteenth century these—and pepper more than anything—were what made food edible. Salt was available—and the only known preservative—but it didn't do much for food cooked in smoky, open fireplaces. Even in rich houses, the meals came putrid to the table. (Dysentery, by the way, seems to have been considered through most of the last five centuries a hazard as normal as wind and rain.) The spices deceived the palate, if not the digestion, as they sometimes still do.

Spices came from the Spice Islands, which lie east of Borneo and south of the Philippines. We know these islands as the Moluccas, and it is odd that this name should not be as famous in our history as London or Boston. Modern history, you could say, began with the problem of how to bypass Turkey and still get to the Spice Islands of Indonesia—or, more simply still, how to get pepper by sea.

There was a man who believed it could be done and that he had been providentially chosen to do it, although it should be said that his ambitions were a good deal more grandiose than merely the procurement of a cargo of pepper. To appreciate the visionary audacity of this man, to say nothing of his physical courage, we need to examine the only map of the world available to him. It conceived of our planet as a single continuous land mass in the shape—depending on the cartographer—of a pancake surrounded by an unknown ocean, or a giant prawn—a Florida jumbo shrimp—with its two ends enclosing a stretch of that ocean. Flat, in any case. The general belief that the earth was indeed as flat as a pancake implied that beyond the known lands, probably not far out into the ocean, there was nothing but the void of oblivion. Sail to the edge and

This may be a good likeness of Christopher Columbus, but there is no way to be certain. It was painted a few years after his death by the Italian Sebastiano del Piombo.

HAC EST EFFIGIES LIGVRIS MIRANDA COLVMBI ANTIPODVM PRIMVS
RATEQVE PENETRAVIT IN ORBEM

SEBASTIANVS
VENETVS FACI

No pictures of Columbus's vessels are known to exist, but these sixteenth-century Portuguese caravels, standing out to sea under full sail, are of a very similar type.

you would most likely drop off the earth into some unimaginable, reeling fate. The Portuguese had the best merchant marine of their time, but it took them seventy-five years to map the coastline of West Africa; they hugged the coastline, wriggling cautiously around all its bays and indentations, not caring to go too far beyond sight of land into the Atlantic, which they called the Sea of Gloom.

Geographers and mathematicians were beginning to agree that the earth was round, but there were not too many sailors who cared to believe it. There was, however, a superb one, who had spent much time with astronomers and mathematicians and had been a master mariner with the Portuguese. He was born to a working-class family in Genoa: Cristoforo Colombo, known to his future patrons, the Spanish, as Cristóbal Colón and to us as Christopher Columbus. A giant of a redhead, six feet tall at a time when the average virile male was about five foot four, he was also a fast-talking, obsessive egomaniac who combined in curiosity, romantic stubbornness, and sense of mission something of Galileo, Don Quixote, and John the Baptist. With his brother he had run a profitable map-making firm, but not profitable enough to enable him to launch his grand design: to outflank the infidel Turk by sailing west across the so-called Ocean Sea to reach the spices of the Indies. For, if indeed the world was a sphere, then by sailing west from Europe you would come to the Indies and in time to the farthest reach of the earth's mass, to China and then Japan, or to Japan and then to China. Nobody could say for sure which came first.

The theory that you could reach the Orient by sailing west had been mooted since Roman times. But it was one thing to talk about it and another to dare to prove it. Leonardo da Vinci had made drawings of airplanes several centuries before the Wright brothers, yet making sketches of an attractive fantasy is not the same as getting sponsors for an actual launch. But Columbus, fired by a majestic vision, was prepared to do more than simply prove that the earth was round. A Christian of almost maniacal devoutness, he also longed for the secular trappings of pomp and power, and, beginning with the Indies, he would convert every prince and pauper he encountered and have himself proclaimed governor of every land and island he discovered.

In the late 1470s he began to tramp round Europe, looking for a royal sponsor. And in the following ten years he found none. He was turned down by the King of Portugal; his brother had no better success with the kings of France and England. Three times Columbus watched and waited while King Ferdinand and Queen Isabella of Spain passed his proposals on to royal councils. They called in expert witnesses and three times concluded that the adventure was perilously impractical and ruinously expensive. He was finally led to say that "everyone to whom I spoke of this enterprise thought it a mere jest."

But what must have been the sharpest hurt was the skepticism of the Portuguese. The testimony of their ship builders, navigators, and ships' captains must have been as damning as it was conclusive. They could not, or would not, answer the question of where Africa gave out, whether there could be an alternative route to Asia other than by the north. Most· daunting of all was the mystery of the Atlantic, the visible part of the Ocean Sea itself. No one had any idea how wide it was or what really lay on the other side of it, except quite possibly perdition. Did the islands that whimsically dotted the maps of the Sea really exist? Were they supplied with grain and fruits for reprovisioning? Had they harbors for safe shelter?

Columbus had convinced himself, by calculations both shrewd and wishful, that he had the answer to all these vexatious questions. And the oftener his plan was rejected, the more dogmatic he became. Like many another evangelist, he compensated for public ridicule by growing paranoid. By now he had inflated his original request for a mere expense account into a set of extraordinary demands. He must be entitled Admiral of the Ocean Sea. He must have ten percent of all the treasure, the gold, the loot he scooped up along the way. The governorship of the Indies and of every country and island he discovered must pass through his eldest son to his heirs "for evermore."

It was too much for Ferdinand and Isabella. They said no once again. So early in January 1492 he left Granada, in disgust, "for evermore" and headed north for another appeal to France. But, on the plea of the Queen's confessor, one Juan Pérez (an unsung hero of American history), he was stopped on a bridge at Pinos, six miles north of Granada, and brought back: the Queen was disposed to change her mind.

For one thing, the seven hundred-year-old civil war with the Moors had at last come to an end, for in that same January Granada, the last Islamic stronghold, surrendered. For another, Ferdinand and Isabella were reminded that another Genoese, Giovanni Caboto (whom we know as John Cabot), had convinced Henry VII of England that the Spice Islands could be reached by sea. Thirdly, the court treasurer pointed out to the Queen that Columbus's expedition would cost no more than a couple of royal banquets. And since, like every other European monarch, Isabella was pinched for money after the Turks had cut off trade with the East, and was appalled, like the rest of Christian Europe, by the enormous inroads the Turks were making right on down into Africa, two urgent questions presented themselves, profane and sacred: Who could replenish the royal treasury? And who could save the world for Christ?

In his final eloquent plea, Columbus avowed that both answers could be found in a book recently printed for the first time, the *Travels* of Marco Polo in China, undertaken two centuries before. Columbus had read it, believed it absolutely, and in the year it appeared had started his trek for a sponsor. But now he recited its tempting revelations. The Orient, Marco Polo had written, was a land dripping with spices and paved with gold. And, more miraculous still, it was ruled over by a great Christian prince. If he could be reached, this prince would muster his legions and, allied with the glorious Christian monarchs of a united Spain, would surround and contain the infidel Turk.

Columbus reinforced the testimony of Marco Polo by solemnly recounting the long and ardent conversations he himself had held with the Almighty that confirmed these marvelous revelations. (As his contract was to testify, his visions did not cloud his instinct for ten percent.) His Christian argument prevailed. His contract, all its grandiloquent provisions indulged, was signed at Granada, and, with the royal blessing and a letter to be delivered to the Grand Khan of China (Cathay), he was commissioned to prepare for his expedition "for gospel and for gold."

There was a wrangling interval with the ship builders, who must have felt like an airplane manufacturer of the First World War being asked to raise the money to put John Glenn into space. They were not disposed to build ships that might sail off the edge of the earth. However, they bowed before a command from the Queen, and the royal treasurer underwrote the cost. Columbus needed three ships, but only two had to be built. The third, already in port, was owned by Juan de la Cosa, the man who eight years later was to draw the first map of the New World. It was bought for Columbus and became his flagship, the *Santa María*. Today it would not be acceptable as a Riviera yacht.

Only one hundred tons in weight and seventy-five feet long, the *Santa María* was not by a long shot one of the big ships of the time, but it was what was needed—a tough maneuverable tub, something between a freighter and a PT boat, sturdy enough to withstand roaring storms and agile enough to take quick shelter in the shallow channels of the imagined Atlantic islands. It was smeared with pitch against barnacles and had stones for ballast. It had a mainmast as long as the keel, one huge square sail, and a small topsail. The two accompanying ships, the *Pinta* and the *Niña,* were made over into square-riggers. They were all equipped with a gun or two against the unlikely risk of pirates, and among the more interesting provisions was red wine, the standard laxative, but to the amount of two and a half liters per man per day—which sounds like a very generous ration, though it could well have been meant to keep them all philosophical if the worst happened.

There were forty men—one Portuguese, another Italian, and the rest all Spaniards—aboard the flotilla, including a surgeon and the royal controller of accounts, sent along to keep tabs on Columbus's swindle sheet when he started to figure the cost of the gold and the spices he would accumulate. There was also a converted Jew who spoke Arabic, which was thought to be very similar to Chinese; he would be the interpreter. On the evening of August 2, 1492, the entire crew went ashore for confession, and on the next morning they set sail from Palos.

They sailed through August and September and came on none of those islands with which geographers had fancifully dotted the Atlantic. The crews grew weary, then anxious, then panicky. After a bout with the trade winds, which would slam at them on the homeward journey, they were close to mutiny. The captains of the two other ships at last signaled for a rendezvous and begged Columbus to turn back. He did his subtle best to reassure them by showing them the log, which he had faked to reduce the record of the miles they had gone from Spain. However, he must have had appalling apprehensions of his own, for he had miscalculated the width of the Sea of Gloom by about fifty percent.

He promised the captains that, if they were still in open sea forty-eight hours later, he would turn back. On the night of October 11, he swears, he "prayed mightily to the Lord." Whether by luck or divine intervention, on the following day he sighted, as he believed, the mainland of Asia or one of its offshore islands. We know it as San Salvador in the Bahamas. He went on to explore Haiti and then Cuba, which he soon decided was Marco Polo's Zipangu (Japan). He was a little puzzled by the absence of cities, but there *were* spices, and cotton, and weird birds, and coppery-colored natives, who kept assuring him—as the Indians did to all succeeding explorers—that inland, always farther inland, there were mountains of gold.

Till his dying day, Columbus never knew that he had not touched the Orient. For the present he was jubilantly convinced that he had, and like a good salesman he hurried back to Spain with what we should call display samples of the products of Japan: exotic plants, brilliant parrots, an alligator, prize natives got up like show horses, a little gold. His foreign sales exhibition was a brilliant success. For his second voyage he fitted out a fleet of seventeen ships, and there was a rush of fifteen hundred men—sailors, soldiers, youngsters on the loose—to explore the wonders of Asia, as well as a clutch of priests to sanctify the expedition and convert the potential slaves.

When Columbus landed again he paused only long enough to deplore the fact that the men he had left behind, having grabbed everything in sight including the native girls, had been massacred. He pushed on into Haiti, and here, in the stream beds, he did find considerable gold. He traced the coast of Cuba until it turned southwest and convinced himself he was now in southern China.

Once more he went home, taking with him this time the contractual five percent of the royal ration of gold. In spite of an oath of secrecy given to the controller of accounts, the magic word "gold" leaked out and very soon there was a more desperate rush of eager adventurers—"not a man," it was written, "down to the very tailors who does not beg to be allowed to become a discoverer." Now began the longest, most determined, and most brutal gold rush in history.

For centuries the Spanish have borne, with considerable ire, the weight of this shameful story. And perhaps we ought to throw in here the reminder that if the Spanish of the late fifteenth and early sixteenth centuries combined great physical courage, endurance, and intense religious zeal with devastating cruelty, they probably behaved no worse than any other Europeans would have done who got there first. British schoolbooks confidently describe the English sea dogs Drake and Hawkins as honest, dauntless men. But Drake's brutalities in sacking the cities of the west coast of South America are a byword among the learned, and Hawkins had spent many untroubled years in the Spanish slave trade. Yet we cannot ignore the exhaustive records of how the Spanish went on the rampage through Central America and Mexico exhausting whole populations in the mines, so that an honest sergeant recalling the cruelties of his life in Mexico lamented that "there was more gold than health." The marching orders prescribed a ruthless routine: round up the natives, prohibit their religion, enslave them, exhaust the gold, and move on—to more gold, silver, pearls. "Everything," wrote a chronicler, "at the Equator is rich."

As the later Cortés pushed inland, he came on cities with temples, pyramids, lighthouses, aqueducts, poets, and philosophers. The range and the customs of the native cultures were bewildering, to say the least, and less susceptible to roughshod suppression. So a simple murderous catechism was applied. After Columbus's first voyage, the Pope, a Spaniard, had drawn a line one hundred leagues west of the Azores and decreed that "everything beyond that which shall be charted by our beloved servants shall belong to Spain," as a part of Christendom. (After a thundering protest from the Portuguese, they too were included, as "our brothers," in the new dominion.) The King of Spain had proclaimed his title to it as New Spain. If, therefore, a kingdom or a tribe was hostile, it was no more than a Christian duty to suppress it, to topple its idols, and raise the Cross on the grounds that the natives were double traitors: to the Pope of Rome and the King of Spain, two deities of whom they had never heard.

If the natives were merely sulky or obstinate, they were terrified into submission by two horrors they had never encountered: the firing of monster machines called cannon, and the appearance of living monsters

Most Indian artifacts were stripped of their gold by Spanish conquistadors. But this brilliant headdress, formed of feathers and encrusted with pure gold, somehow survived.

called horses. Many brave priests were sickened by the conquistadors' outrages, and there is a heart-rending file of protests from them back to their superiors in Spain. One unforgettable story tells of a native king who would not renounce his religion and was about to be burned at the stake. As he felt the first fires lap his body, he was for the last time offered the rite of baptism. He refused, saying he feared that, if he accepted, he might "go to heaven and meet there only Christians."

Within fifty years of the first sighting of San Salvador, the Spaniards had plundered and conquered the whole of Central America and Peru, and shipped home glittering cargoes of rich and barbaric ornaments of gold and silver. Having spanned the width of Mexico, they knew that the land ran on to the north, and they now began to wonder how vast was its expanse and what treasures lay on it.

They had already probed far into Florida. A companion of Columbus on his second voyage, one Ponce de León, had heard from the Indians of Puerto Rico that to the north was not only abundant gold but also a fountain of youth, and in the spring of 1513 he landed a little north of Saint Augustine and promptly claimed the land for Spain. He sailed down and around the Florida Keys and up to the Gulf Coast, but found neither gold nor a fountain. After him, the Spanish made frequent, unauthorized, raids into Florida for slaves to work the West Indies; and they mounted several official expeditions to seek out the rumored piles of gold. They were all defeated by the native Indians, who had learned a lively detestation of the slave raiders, and on one of the last of these fruitless voyages the body of the commander, Hernando de Soto, was buried by his men in the Mississippi River to save it from desecration by the Indians.

But these setbacks did not disabuse the Spanish of their belief in a whole literature woven around the mystical legend that declared that somewhere in the New World there was that "terrestrial paradise," an actual Heaven on earth that would redeem the hard life of the true believer here below. In many Spanish books written by scholars and divines who had never been to sea, the most confident and bizarre accounts were given of the land to the north of New Spain. It was said to contain mermaids and volcanoes and fantastic animals. It was the place where Judas took his annual vacation from Hell. And the whole landscape sprouted outcrops of gold between the trees, which were hung with chains of precious jewels.

All these fancies came into focus with the supreme Spanish myth of Cíbola, "the Seven Cities of Gold." In 1540 another Spanish soldier set out to find them. Francisco Vásquez de Coronado is not the most illustrious of the conquistadors, and, indeed, the glamour of his reputation began to fade almost from the day he started his march to the north until it dwindled into the humble fame of a petty official in his fifties, retired on a small grant of land outside Mexico City. But he it was who first explored what today we call the American Southwest, and as a feat of endurance against depressing odds it is one of the great odysseys in the conquest of North America.

Of noble French and Spanish blood, Coronado was denied his inheritance in a considerable estate by an elder brother. Forced to make his own way, he sought favor at the court. He didn't find it until his middle thirties, when he met Don Antonio de Mendoza, who had just been appointed Viceroy of Mexico. Coronado sailed with him as a military aide and made an impressive reputation as a disciplined commander and a just administrator of Indian towns in several forays through Mexico. In his fortieth year he was appointed Governor of New Galicia.

Mendoza had Coronado in mind as the man who should confirm the existence of the Seven Cities and conquer them. But this would have to be a quite new kind of experiment in colonizing, for Pope Paul III, responding to nearly half a century of priestly protests about the enslavement and annihilation of the Indians, had just proclaimed that they were henceforth to be considered members of the human race and that anyone who enslaved them risked excommunication. Mendoza decided to send a reconnaissance expedition north, one that should have none of the trappings of a military invasion. It was led by a Franciscan friar, Fray Marcos, and going along with him as a guide was one of the most exotic and forgotten figures in American history: a Moorish Negro named Estebán, who had wandered around the fringe of the northlands and been received by some Indians as a welcome novelty and by others as a god.

Estebán was a florid and illiterate giant who nonetheless had an extraordinary gift for picking up both the dialects of the Indian tribes and an adoring harem of their women. He was quite fearless and proceeded with two greyhounds always at his heels—a braggart Emperor Jones who evidently hypnotized more tribes than he antagonized, until at last he was to come on one tribe that, refusing to believe he could be the emissary of any white ambassador, killed him. However, on this last journey he went impatiently ahead of Fray Marcos and penetrated into Arizona and Texas. Marcos, coming on behind, stood at last on a hilltop and saw what he was looking for, a collection of seven glittering cities larger than the capital of Mexico. The friar must have had powers of invention to rival Münchhausen's, or else he was the constant victim of wonderful mirages. For when he returned to Mexico he described in telling detail a trek through various landscapes peopled by submissive Indians and then the crowning spectacle—Cíbola itself, its rich pastures trodden by cows and partridges and camels, and then the first of the cities, its temple walls draped inside and out with precious stones, the "very wealthy" inhabitants wearing girdles of gold and riding on camels and elephants. It could be, it had to be, the delirious friar decided, the road to Cathay.

The written report of Fray Marcos thrilled Mexico City and Madrid and made him for a year or two the most famous man in New and Old Spain. Mendoza at once made Coronado captain-general of a land expedition to retrace the friar's journey and annex the cities of gold. In February 1540 Coronado, in gilded armor, set out from Compostela with two hundred and fifty horsemen, seventy Spanish foot soldiers, a thousand reliable (that is to say, tamed or friendly) Indians, baggage animals, sheep, goats, herds of cattle, and a train of priests.

Within the month Coronado had entered Culiacán, halfway up the mainland coast of the Gulf of California, which was then the northernmost outpost of New Spain. For another month he followed the river streams and continued with a tough advance party up into the mountains. Once through them on the eastern slopes, he saw ahead of him an unbroken horizon of desert and boulders and scrubland. It was formidable but it was, according to the Marcos report, the route to the Seven Cities. Coronado slogged across it, through Arizona and on into New Mexico, and at the beginning of July, in infernal heat, came into the first of the cities. It was a pueblo of adobe huts, in what has long been the Zuñi Indian country, and after a brief struggle the captain-general took this rude village. There were no camels or elephants or cows, no gold ornaments hanging from trees—indeed, no trees. Nothing but a continuous lunar landscape. Coronado pitched camp to rest and, heavy with disappointment, re-formed his forces and picked scouting parties to go to the east and west and find the glittering prize. The northwestern party was stopped by the apocalyptic deep of the Grand Canyon of the Colorado River. Another party found another collection of seven villages, as rude as the first.

During that first winter Coronado was disheartened enough to seize on the story of an Indian slave that far off to the east there was a rich and populous city known as Quivira. This, then, became the new El Dorado, and, fourteen months after he had started, Coronado marched on into Texas and then, encouraged by other native rumors, turned north again and on through Kansas. They came at last to Quivira, way to the north of our Dodge City. It was yet another miserable village, of the Wichita tribe. In a final venture, he sent out other scouting parties, and they returned and told the same story—rolling, inhospitable plains, small primitive villages. So at last he went back to the main body of his army, which had been limping along well behind the advance guard. We tear through this country today on paved divided highways, and it is impossible for us now to realize not only the arduousness of Coronado's march but the daily afflictions they took for granted. Most of his horsemen and foot soldiers wore about thirty pounds of armor. They rarely found a stream or lake to bathe in, and hemorrhoids and fistulas were as common as the common cold. Inevitably, the doctors they took along were surgeons.

Coronado had in two years gone up the Gulf of California, through Arizona and New Mexico and Texas, and wheeled into northern Kansas to the Nebraska border before he gave up. In the spring of 1542 he turned south again, marched down by a shorter route along the line of the Santa Fe Trail to the Rio Grande and then westward through the Zuñi country and wretched Cíbola, then through the mountain passages again and down the Gulf of California to Mexico City. He and his troop arrived there in the autumn, full of thought, empty of any riches, "very sad and very weary, completely worn out and shamefaced."

There are very few traces of this epic though shattering march. There is one, an immense mesa crowned by an Indian pueblo brooding over the boulder-strewn desert below. It is Acoma, in New Mexico, about forty miles west of Albuquerque. One of Coronado's scouts saw it and returned to the main camp to tell of "a great city in the sky . . . the strongest position ever seen in the world." Coronado decided to give it a miss—and wisely, for it was the stronghold of a hostile tribe that remained unconquered by the Spanish for fifty-nine years after Coronado's men saw it. Indeed, the Ácomas live on the crest there today as they have lived for over a thousand years.

Ácoma is the site of one of the last and most ferocious onslaughts the Spanish were to make, in defiance of the Pope's proclamation about the humanity of the Indian. The three-day and -night assault is celebrated in an epic poem, and certainly the Spanish took an epic revenge for the Ácomas' half century of resistance, killing six hundred and imprisoning as many, tossing the seventy warrior chieftains off the great cliff and binding to lifetime servitude another five hundred, mostly women and children. Those who could not be wooed out of their religion were literally thrown to the dogs or flogged into devotion to the Carpenter of Nazareth.

But, as usual, time softened the sting of these atrocities, and thirty years later a mild Franciscan priest, Father Ramírez, walked to the fortress barefoot and unarmed and, with the single weapon of a cross, converted the Ácomas.

There is also, another twenty miles to the west, a towering bluff, El

Overleaf: *Three hundred and fifty feet above the desert floor, the still-occupied adobe buildings of Ácoma perch on the edge of their red sandstone mesa.*

Morro. Indian guides led Coronado to it when his men were fainting from thirst. At its foot is a pool of pure water, and on its massive face, smoothed by the desert winds to the sheen of bones, is an inscription in Spanish done with the point of a sword by a grandee who came along sixty-odd years later to find, from Coronado's map, the same oasis. It says: "Through here passed the Governor Don Juan de Oñate, after his discovery of the Sea of the South, 16 April 1605." (By the Sea of the South he meant that he had been as far as the Gulf of California.) This Oñate set up the first Spanish government in the Southwest, and it is worth a passing thought—from an Englishman, anyway—that the Palace of the Governors at Santa Fe was built ten years before the Pilgrims landed on the Massachusetts coast.

But, even by Oñate's time the dream of extending New Spain through North America had been shattered once for all—and not in America or by its natives, but by the greatest sea battle of the sixteenth century. Philip of Spain's free access to North America depended, like Napoleon's or Hitler's, on mastering Europe by the conquest of Britain. And when, in the summer of 1588, the "invincible" Armada was first battered by the broadsides of the English sea dogs, then panicked by fire ships, and then scattered by a shift of the wind as far north as the Firth of Forth, Spain's grip on New Spain was frozen where it had first taken hold. The Atlantic thereafter became an open highway for the Dutch, the French, and most of all the English; and from then on Spain was powerless to prevent the planting in turn of New France in Canada and a new England in Virginia and Massachusetts.

For the next two hundred years these remote provinces of New Spain—today's Arizona, Texas, California, and New Mexico—slowly developed an outpost economy and a military government throughout a burning landscape half the size of Europe. The Spanish had introduced the two indispensable elements of life in western America, the horse and the cow. It was the horse that first terrified the Indian into submission; it was the horse that set him free, and freewheeling, from Mexico to the Canadian tundra.

The Spanish also left behind, in their branding signs and the embossing of saddles, a whole heraldry of ranching, and in conjunction with this they established the rodeo. The purpose of the rodeo was to round up, once a year, all the cattle that had run free or multiplied on the open range; to distinguish one man's herd from another, the yearling calves were branded with the owner's initials or some chosen emblems registered with the governor of each province. While the word "cowboy" is a direct translation of *vaquero*, much of the language of ranching, and the Spanish words for the kind of country it was done in, have passed over to the present-day practitioners and, indeed, to most children brought up in the Southwest: corral, mesa, arroyo, patio, adobe, mustang, sombrero, desperado, poncho, alfalfa, bronco. By small changes or abbreviation, other Spanish words were naturalized in English: "stampede" for *estampida*, "lariat" for *(la) reata*, "lasso" for *lazo*, "chaps" for *chaperajos*, which protected the wearer against the desert scrub called "chaparral" *(chaparro)*. The word "cinch," until fairly recently a common slang word for something quickly or easily done, derives from the Spanish word for the saddle girth, *cincha*. When it was securely fastened, it was said to be "cinched."

During the eighteenth century, the plundering life of the conquistadors gave way to the vigorous life of the *rancheros*. The last great military expedition came about through one of those paranoid rumors from which even the most civilized nations are not exempt. In the late 1760s Upper California—what we today call California—was part of New Spain, though it had been only vaguely explored, not settled. The only people known to live there were Indians rumored to be so fierce that the captain-general who had conquered all of Lower California said that to subdue them it would be necessary to hire sixty gorillas from Guatemala. The Spanish governors, secure down in Mexico, had no plans to colonize the north, until King Charles III of Spain received a report that Russians had been sighted in Monterey Bay in alarming numbers. They were heralds of a nightmare that has haunted California into our own time: the Russian menace. The Russians had been drawn there by the presence, in large schools, of the sea otter, which brought fantastic prices in the China trade. The skins could be exchanged for quicksilver, the absence of which in California had hampered the development of the provinces of New Spain; for at that time quicksilver (mercury) was the magic element for extracting gold and silver from their ores. But it was dreadfully obvious to the King of Spain that the Russians were intending to set up an empire in Upper California. In simple fact, the Russians wanted nothing more than the sea otter himself, a plump and comical beast, a Disney version of Colonel Blimp, who has the round brown face of a well-fed cat and swims on his back, his belly protruding, his whiskers bristling, his paws calmly folded across his chest. Indeed, when the sea otter was fished out, the Russians left.

But long before then King Charles had ordered military expeditions out of Mexico by land and sea, to build a chain of forts and hold the coast of California. As always, priests went along to lend a degree of humanity to the job of "pacifying" the natives. For this special mission, a Franciscan, Father Junípero Serra, was sent out to Mexico in 1767 and a year later started off with Captain Gaspar de Portolá on the conquering land expedition into Alta (Upper) California. If in the Spanish record there is one man more than another whose life could possibly redeem the

ferocity of the conquistadors, Father Serra is that man. He gave himself wholly to the barbaric Indians, and, for every fort built to protect the coastline he built a mission, so that the Russian menace bore some fruit in producing the twenty-one missions that are the Spaniards' main architectural legacy to California.

Altogether, Father Serra walked between four and five thousand miles up and down the coastline and the inland valleys on an infected foot he refused to treat, over scrub desert and through dense mountains, always stopping on saints' days to lay the foundations of a mission and ring a bell and cry, "Come, come and receive the faith of Christ." The route of his walk is today the route of the main north-south highway, and it is vividly marked in the spring by the blossoming mustard whose seeds the friar scattered as he went. Father Serra, who died in his seventieth year at Carmel, is the first and noblest of a great, though not greatly prized, American tradition: the priests, in the main Spanish and then French, who crossed the seas and tramped the enormous curve of wilderness from Lower California around to Montana to care for a few Indians and, later, trappers. Junípero Serra, De Smet, Ravalli, Megarini, Prando, Father Point. They accepted the terrible emptiness of the West as the good ground to work in, carried the barest essentials and lived out their Catholicism in the fearful innocence of its Founder.

Apart from the thousands of Spanish place names, the march across the American landscape from the eastern border of Texas, through the Southwest and up and along the nine hundred-mile sweep of today's California, there are one or two other relics of the Spanish empire in North America that ought to be mentioned, for I doubt that one American in a hundred is aware that they are part of the Spanish legacy. I refer to several of the basic American crops—oats, wheat, barley, and oranges. And it was the Spanish who took the rudest indigenous cereal of the Indians and made it the sustaining staple from the Canadian border to Cape Horn—namely, maize, everywhere in America called "corn," in accordance with the habit of all English-speaking countries in giving the name to their commonest staple crop, whether it is oats, barley, or—as in England—wheat. (When the Americans introduced the dry breakfast cereal to Britain, they had the tact not to market cornflakes in translation as "maize flakes"; had they done so, it is pretty certain that the custom would not have caught on.)

Of the other nations that explored the New World and were to challenge England for a claim to it—most notably the Netherlands, Portugal, and

By the late eighteenth century, the Spanish had created a stable, easy society in California, with estates built near such missions as San Carlos de Borromeo.

France—much the most impressive was France. She was also the first. If it comes as a surprise to hear that Spain had set up the first government in the West in Santa Fe eleven years before the Pilgrims stumbled on Cape Cod, a bigger surprise is available in the news that the French started their colonial experiment in North America a hundred years before the *Mayflower*.

Only twelve years after Columbus's first voyage, Breton fishermen started to work the cod banks off Nova Scotia. And, while the Portuguese and the English were ferreting along the North American coast from Labrador to Florida, trying to find the entrance to that waterway through to the Orient, the humble Bretons were pushing into the mainland and coming on Indians loaded with animal furs. Although the Bretons found to their delight that they could catch fish in those waters simply by hauling them up in baskets, they soon began to see the possibilities of a profitable fur trade. The Indians were as fascinated by bits of metal, axes, and iron kettles as the Bretons were by the furs.

This simple system of barter was the rude start of a fur trade that burgeoned when the fishermen penetrated the gulf and the river of Saint Lawrence. In time they abandoned the cod for the beaver and were soon trapping and skinning every animal in sight—and, incidentally, putting out the tentacles of the French dominion in the North. An empire could not, of course, be built and held by a scattered army of trappers and fishermen, however hardy. But in their way these rude Bretons were the poor man's conquistadors of the North. Their descendants helped form a new nation, reaching from the Atlantic to the Pacific, and they still live there securely nearly a century after Spain lost every big and little holding in the New World.

The French "kingdoms in the North" were made possible by four explorers—Verrazano, Cartier, Champlain, and La Salle—and, in the first place by a King of France who had the nerve to snap his fingers at the Pope. Francis I was born two years after Columbus landed at San Salvador and came to the throne when he was twenty-one. A violent athlete, with a passion for hunting, tennis, and women, by the time he reached his late twenties he needed all the revenues he could lay his hands on to satisfy the luxury of his court and the foibles of his mistresses. By then the French, the English, the Irish, and the Dutch had begun the systematic piracy of Spanish ships homeward bound with the loot of "the Indies." In 1522 Cortés celebrated the final conquest of Mexico by packing into a galleon a curator's collection of gold and silver objects and mosaic masks. The shipment was captured by the French on the last leg of its journey, off the tip of Portugal at Cape Saint Vincent. It exhibited in dazzling fashion the wealth of the Indies and egged on the fond suspicion of Francis I that perhaps a shorter route to similar treasure lay through the Far North of America. Francis was a blundering and profligate ruler but he has immortalized himself, in the history of America, by his sharp retort to a furious reminder from Spain that the Pope had proclaimed everything a hundred leagues west of the Azores as Spanish property: "We fail to find this clause in Adam's will."

Francis decided it was France's turn to discover the northern passage to the Indies. He chose his own Columbus in another Genoese, Giovanni da Verrazano, got the money for an expedition from the French silk merchants, and sent Verrazano off. Verrazano had no luck finding the elusive passage in the West Indies and sailed instead all the way up the North American coast. Chesapeake Bay turned out to be a bay. He paused to decide that the Hudson River was probably another, and he sailed on past Cape Cod, probed the coast of Maine, and continued on to Newfoundland and the Strait of Belle Isle.

This was a letdown, but Francis I did not give up. Ten years later Jacques Cartier, a wealthy citizen of St. Malo and an expert navigator, concentrated on the North and made two voyages there, following and naming the Saint Lawrence. Still no strait, no open way to China. But he found his Fray Marcos in a Huron chief, Donnaconna, who seduced him with tales of a northern Cíbola. It was an inland kingdom called Saguenay. It too was supposed to have mines groaning with gold and silver, to grow fragrant spices, to be populated by men bespangled with rubies who flew like bats. Cartier took Donnaconna back to France to sell this fantasy to the King, who was too excited by its gaudy promise to doubt it, so Cartier returned with his chief. But, just as the Caribs and the natives of Mexico had always promised gold over the next mountain range, Cartier was endlessly assured that Saguenay lay just across the next marsh, the farthest island in a waste of tundra. Like Columbus, Cartier thought he had better return with at least a few samples of the undiscovered mines. He took back quartz crystals.

After these fruitless searches, the French were too busy fighting among themselves to spare any more ships or money for another try, and for another fifty years the discovery of the interior of Canada (an Indian word meaning *pueblo,* or "village") was left to the fur trappers and traders. Instead of governors' mansions, trading posts rose between the present cities of Quebec and Montreal. Meanwhile, the French corsairs knew enough about the Bahama Channel and the Florida coast to be encouraged to try founding a colony in Florida. But they were beaten and pretty well annihilated by the Spanish, who in 1565 built at Saint Augustine the first of a line of forts going up as far as the Carolinas in order to protect their homebound ships from the pestiferous French pirates.

This unadventurous half century could well have marked the beginning of the end of French ambitions in North America, had it not been

In the manuscript of one of his New World journals, the great French explorer Samuel Champlain left this gory drawing—a group of presumably heathen Indians expiating their sins at the hands of two Spanish Inquisitors in Mexico. The French prided themselves on having much better relations with the Indians in their own territories of New France.

for the prosperous growth of the fur trade. Toward the end of the sixteenth century, it occurred—and to other Europeans as well as the French—that furs were a more tangible asset than rumors of gold. The summer haul along the Saint Lawrence was enormous, and France decided it was time to organize and monopolize it. And yet the belief in that sea passage through North America was so tenacious, so tantalizing to navigators and geographers and greedy monarchs, that the conquest of the fur trade and the establishment of New France were mere by-products of it.

Samuel Champlain was a sailor, a soldier, and a fanatical geographer who, in spite of the vague contemporary notions of longitude, loved to speculate about the width of America and draw imaginary maps of the whole continent, in one of them hinting at the existence of a Panama canal. After a two-year voyage to the West Indies, he was sent, in 1603, out to Canada, ostensibly to advance the business of a man who had been given a monopoly of the fur trade by King Henry IV, actually to map for the first time the convolutions and geographical relation of the Saint Lawrence, Saguenay, Ottawa, and Richelieu rivers. He was to trace their courses, note the prospects for farming and settlement of the lands they traversed—and, as a sideline and serious hobby, to see if any of these rivers flowed from the legendary inland sea.

Champlain was the first man to see that this vast expanse of marshland, plain, rivers, lily pads, and semi-tundra, and the many Indian tribes who inhabited it, could be made into a large self-sustaining colony only by Frenchmen who would come to America for keeps, learn about the new land, bargain and work with the natives, and settle. He set the example by founding Quebec as a base and from there investigating Lakes Huron and Ontario—and, by siding with the friendly Algonquins and Hurons, defeating the Iroquois, whom he rightly took to be the tribe most hostile to a white foothold. For the rest of his life, through the loss and renewal of trade monopolies, he was as busy as the beaver he sought to capture in fair dealing with the Indians who caught it. John Bartlet Brebner saw in him a true exemplar:

Nothing is more notable in the conduct of the French in North America than their success in getting along with the Indians and in living among them. It was Champlain who invented, as it were, the *coureurs du bois* [the fur traders in the woods] and the *voyageurs* [the traders on the plains] who carried French influence from the St. Lawrence to the Rockies and from Hudson Bay to the Gulf of Mexico.

The last phrase suggests a leap of French ambition far beyond the northern wilderness. And this brings us, by a comparable leap in time, to the French Coronado, Sieur de La Salle. The interval between the virtual settlement of Quebec and the appearance in Canada of La Salle, a

twenty-three-year-old emigrant, is about another sixty years. In that time
France became the political and cultural leader of continental Europe,
but New France almost expired. In the early years the colony suffered
from a politer but no less enervating form of the gang wars that harassed
Chicago in the era of Prohibition: ruthless squabbles over whose "territory" belonged to whom among monopolists and merchants who had
expected to make a quick million in the now legendary fur trade. But, in
the later years, New France had an open and declared enemy in the tribal
alliance usually called the Five Nations and known to the French as the
Iroquois League. For five years or so the Iroquois—with the help of the
Dutch—tried to drive the French traders and hunters into their stockades and to destroy their settlements. A new and, to the Iroquois,
obnoxious feature of Canadian life was the horde of Jesuit priests who, in
a burst of missionary zeal, had arrived and gone to work on saving the
Hurons and the other friendly Indians. Unfortunately they did not
regard the Iroquois as beyond redemption, and many of them suffered
abominably for their evangelical efforts in the back country. By 1663 the
young Louis XIV had responded to frantic appeals from the besieged
settlements and sent out an army of men, weapons, money, and colonists, and one able administrator, to stabilize the colony and convert it
into a royal province. But the Iroquois guerrillas remained unbeatable.

In the summer of 1665 there arrived, in the person of the Marquis de
Tracy, a first-rate soldier to dispose of them with almost Spanish ferocity,
in a campaign of "total warfare" that has come to seem intolerably
inhumane only in the last decade or so: to defeat not merely the enemy's
armies but to ruin his supplies, burn his villages, and cripple the life of
the noncombatants. Tracy waited until the crops of the Mohawk Valley
were ripe and then descended, with eight hundred veterans of wars with
the Turks. He crushed the tribes, burned the fields and villages,
destroyed the stores, and broke once for all the threat of the Iroquois.
Half of his men found the prospects of Canada promising enough to stay
for life.

The defeat of the Iroquois was timely; La Salle came along to Montreal
a year later to go into the fur trade, and had they still been on the warpath
they would doubtless have denied him the glory of his historic voyage
through the hinterland of America down to the Gulf of Mexico.

Like so many heroes, villains, and ordinaries of the seventeenth and
eighteenth centuries, La Salle is a hard man to fix as a recognizable human
type. The contemporary store of abstract virtues and vices has let loose
on him a shower of adjectives that still fail to pin him down. He is
described as audacious, diplomatic, overbearing, brilliant, courageous, a
man of "inexhaustible pride," "inflexible purposes," and "insatiable intellect," all of which sounds very impressive but still leaves the picture of a

faceless demigod. We can only try to snatch a hint of his mettle, his uniqueness as an undefeatable explorer, by tracing briefly the route of his enormous trip.

He prepared himself for it by learning a dozen Indian dialects and determining at all costs to make the Indians along the way his friends. He went back to France to get the money for enlarging the fur trade through to the rolling plains of the West, which had discouraged Cartier. He no doubt mentioned the usual aim of finding a passage through to the Orient, but he evidently took a dry Gallic view of it, for he named the rapids on the Saint Lawrence seigneury he had been granted—Lachine. His main aim was toward a French empire designed to conquer the hinterland of America and to keep the English, by now well planted in Virginia and New England, shut in east of the Appalachians.

There were several reconnaissance trips into the wilderness below Lakes Ontario and Erie. The last one, launched in November 1679, was that of the *Griffin*, the first ship to sail on Lake Erie. It went to Green Bay, Wisconsin, and loaded up with furs, with which La Salle hoped to placate his backers in Montreal, and it was never heard of again. La Salle, quite unaware of this disaster, went on around the west shore of Lake Michigan, built a fort at the mouth of the Saint Joseph River, portaged to the Illinois, built another fort to protect a tribe of friendly Indians, and then paused for the grand slide down the Mississippi. But by now he needed more supplies, and, having heard of the disaster to the *Griffin*, he raced—and "raced" is not too flip a word to describe a canoe-and-carry trip of a thousand miles in sixty-five days—back to Fort Frontenac, at Kingston, Ontario, to talk his jaundiced backers into providing more funds.

The next winter he did the whole trip back again by canoe and foot, only to find that the latest fort had been abandoned and his men had deserted. So he walked and canoed the thousand miles back again to Frontenac. This indestructible optimist got some more money and supplies and once more trekked the thousand miles back to the Saint Joseph fort. From there, leading twenty-three Frenchmen and thirty-one Indians, he started the long last lap down the continent's central watershed.

It was December 1681, and the rivers were frozen—a mere nuisance to La Salle, who had nearly starved in appalling weather on his first approach to the Illinois River. He made sledges for the canoes and the men pulled them across the Chicago River and down the Illinois, usually wearing out a pair of leather moccasins a day. They came at last to

Detail of Indians and an unlikely looking canoe is from a picture painted near Quebec in the eighteenth century by an amateur.

running water, and early in February floated into the Mississippi. The snow banks melted, the downriver current quickened, the early semi-tropical spring came in, high tides swirled around the fronds of live oaks against the shore, and the happy party paddled easily down the thousand miles and more of the great river and came to its mouth. There they divided into three groups, and each took a separate channel to the Passes, where the Mississippi debouches into the Gulf. Three days later, on April 9, 1682, they stood together on a small bluff overlooking the sea. La Salle raised a cross and planted the banner of France and annexed "this country of Louisiana," named at that moment after "the most high, mighty, invincible and victorious Louis the Great, by Grace of God, King of France and Navarre."

La Salle claimed nothing less than the whole Mississippi watershed. He then made the huge journey back to Quebec, pardonably proud in the knowledge that he had made friends and allies of all the Indian tribes he had come across and, by deliberately so doing, had fortified the claim of "Louis the Great" with the best kind of allies an empire builder can have, the natives on their own ground. But what he faced in Quebec was a new governor who loathed him and belittled his great expedition. Without money and without favor, he sailed home for France to make a personal appeal to the King to finance his planting of the southern capital of the new empire on the spot where he had raised the King's banner. Louis, who had been maliciously primed by the new governor, told La Salle that his voyage of discovery had been a vast waste of time, but ultimately thinking to twist a knife in the back of his chief enemy, the King of Spain, he relented and equipped La Salle with four ships, soldiers, and colonists of both sexes to build his fort on the Gulf and "control the continent."

La Salle sailed in 1684, and it ought to have been a triumphant return. But this last sorry chapter took nearly three years. La Salle, a tragic victim of the contemporary ignorance about longitude, overshot the Passes by four hundred miles, landed on the Texas coast, and began a march as forlorn as Coronado's—not to find a city of gold but merely to find again the majestic river whose length he had traversed! Nobody knows how many thousand miles his colonizers walked or in how many directions. They lived off the bison and the corn of Indians who were as vague about the Mississippi as they were about the Seine. La Salle, who had started with over four hundred men, by the spring of 1687 was down to forty-five—many dead, others having deserted. Two of his ships had been wrecked and a third gone back to France. In the last ship he took sail again, as he hoped, for Canada, got lost and was beaten by storms back into the Gulf.

He made one last try; he took twenty men on foot across a stretch of rolling prairie. Here, where two centuries later German and Polish farmers settled, there is a bronze statue of La Salle looking across to the stores and automobile sales lots of Navasota, Texas. For here, close by the Navasota River, still 350 miles from the Mississippi, La Salle's men could take no more. They murdered him and mooched off, leaving his naked body to the wind and the buzzards.

In time, of course, the French built the port of New Orleans. Yet they never domesticated the great watershed La Salle had claimed. As so often happens, a man aims at the bull's eye, but strikes on the periphery are what he is remembered by. La Salle had gone on his last voyage to France exalted by the vision of a French empire in the Mississippi Valley that would checkmate the ambitions of the English and the Spanish. What he actually accomplished, almost inadvertently, was to build a loose link of forts and bind them with the friendships of many tribes, so that when the time came, nearly a century after him, the French would be in a position to challenge the English conquest of the continent.

A French map of America of 1765 shows what an exclusive hold they had in the north, even though they were almost as vague about what lay to the south and west as the Spanish had been about what lay to their north and west. Being trappers and rivermen, the French did an incomparable job of mapping the entire nervous system of the rivers, but at any distance to the west of them they simply put in the names of Indian tribes—the Miamis, the Illinois, the Sioux. After La Salle they did not plant colonies on the English model—that is to say, thriving, static, self-governing settlements. They settled always close to the rivers, especially to "the Father of Waters," in way stations, or what we should call retail centers, for the downriver traffic bearing fur and hides and timber to the port of New Orleans. If they found a useful local product—salt, a mineral—they stopped and made a town. In one such, St. Genevieve, Missouri, they made a little Paris, planting their familiar vines and gardens, inviting remote French families with aspirations to gentility to send their children for the purpose of learning good French and attending a school of manners where they might acquire "the two elements of true politeness—grace and self-denial."

It must be obvious by now that Spain's imperial ambitions were arrested too soon for her to build, as the French did, in New Orleans, a full-blown capital city, which might well have been the capital of the United States if Napoleon had not sold for cash the huge interior that La Salle had claimed as Louisiana. But the French—and subsequently the Spanish—prospered there and for the better part of a century it was an overseas metropolis of an easygoing Latin type, where lawyers, bankers,

A hopeful promotion piece published by the French Mississippi Company in 1717 showed Indians trading gold and silver for cheap European goods at a nonexistent "Port of Mississippi." The following year, the town of New Orleans was laid out.

merchants, shippers, diplomats, and playboys maintained their quadroon mistresses in the terraced apartments of the Vieux Carré. But though the French Quarter of New Orleans retains—where it does not try too hard—some of the flavor of late eighteenth- and early nineteenth-century France, you will not find there many reminders of the great Frenchmen who created the towns of the Great Lakes and the Mississippi Valley. Only linguistic scholars are aware that the state of Arkansas is still pronounced Arkansaw because that's the way the French pronounced it. (The Arkansas River rises in country settled by Yankees and Germans and is consequently pronounced the way it's spelled.) The same is true of Chicago, which an Englishman has to learn is Shicago, not Tchicago.

Yet the French legacy to all of North America is incalculable and far-ranging. You have only to glance at the map, westward from Quebec twelve hundred miles to Duluth (named for Sieur Du Lhut), and then follow the names of the river towns down to Baton Rouge and New Orleans, to see how many places that we take for granted as Yankee establishments were founded by the French. There are many other places whose origin is not so obvious because of the gift of later settlers for fracturing the French names. Marietta, Ohio, was named after Marie Antoinette, and Narbonne turned into Jawbone. And an Irish railroad gang, coming on a lake in Arkansas that the French had named L'Eau Froid, struggled awhile and left it on the map as Low Freight.

It is not invidious to say that the French influence was far more benign than that of the Spanish. For one thing, the diligence of Huguenots who had been persecuted at home guaranteed not only their decent treatment in the new country but an actual compact with the Catholic Church that both religions would live "in all Christian harmony." There remain, of course, Catholic churches all the way down the Mississippi watershed. But the practical domination of the Church declined very rapidly after France lost her territory west of the Mississippi at the end of the French and Indian Wars. All the upriver French priests were recalled to New Orleans, where today there are more Catholics in a single parish than in most of the Southern states combined. When the priests were finally allowed to return, a missionary bishop found people who had not had the sacraments for forty years.

They had been seduced, he concluded, by the "diabolical writings" of Rousseau, Voltaire, Thomas Paine, and Jefferson. Later on, the sacramental wine was diluted forever in the invading flood of Methodists and Baptists, not to mention the more heathenish "Anglo-American population" deplored by the remaining priests as "infidels of a low and indecent grade."

But the main achievement, which Americans south of the Canadian border forget or never knew, is that the French were the first Western-ers. It is a thousand miles from Quebec to the western shore of Lake Michigan. First, they paddled the waters, then tracked the game on the surrounding lands. Then they organized the commerce of hundreds of tributary rivers and behaved most of the time not as interlopers but as cohabitors of a continent who had much to learn from the original Americans. They developed a breed unknown to the Spanish and the English: the trader-trapper, the water-borne businessman, living rough and mobile, learning from the natives all the vagaries of a new geography—new animals, humans, vegetables, and climate.

In the beginning no four-legged thing was safe from a Frenchman, and in the end no barren prairie, no mountain range was inaccessible to the *voyageurs*. They carried the fur trade two thousand miles inland to the Tetons (ribaldly named, by the way, for the mammary configurations of their peaks). They could live on the barest vegetation and the crudest shelter the plains or the snow-laden Rockies and Sierras could provide. It was French guides who staffed the expedition of Lewis and Clark. And when we trace the routes—especially the cutoffs—that pioneers as late as the gold rushers took, we come on names like Sublette and La Bonté, for, in terrifying places where no white man was supposed to have been, some Canadian popped up as a shaggy and cunning guide. Maybe only the French would have chosen to settle a landscape of marsh and rivers and lily pads. Certainly only the Scots of the Hudson's Bay Company, coming after, would have wanted to knot a lifeline across three thousand miles of tundra.

NEC SPE NEC METU

2

A HOME AWAY FROM HOME

One of Sir Francis Drake's more notorious exploits was the seizure of the rich Spanish city of Santo Domingo in the West Indies in 1585. In this contemporary map, Drake's fleet lies in the harbor. The Spanish eventually paid a ransom and Drake sailed away.

On a famous day in 1580, there was held in London a banquet in the Middle Temple, one of those "inns of court" which by Queen Elizabeth's time had become not only the law schools of England but the think-tanks and Establishment clubs, the meeting places of men who had the influence at court, and also the power and the money, to back, among other things, the English venture into the New World.

This feast was held to celebrate the return, from a two-year-and-ten-month voyage around the world, of the most unscrupulous of English pirates, a sea dog well trained by his kinsman, the slave trader Sir John Hawkins. Francis Drake was a Devon boy who went to sea in his early teens. He made daring voyages to Guinea and the Gulf of Mexico, and when he was twenty-four he received a regular privateering commission from Queen Elizabeth (whom the Pope had recently excommunicated) to sack Spanish ports and plunder Spanish treasure ships in the West Indies. He was so good at it that the Queen gave him the money to equip five small ships with a crew of one hundred and sixty-six men in order to attempt something no Englishman had ever done: enter the South Seas through the Strait of Magellan. On this astounding voyage he reached Brazil, put down a mutiny, withstood scurvy and dysentery, was tossed like a cork for fifty-two days in "a tempest . . . the like of which no traveller hath felt since Noah's flood," and ultimately found himself in the Pacific off the coast of Chile. Then he sailed north, harassing every Spanish ship he saw and ransacking the cities of Chile and Peru. He left the Pacific Coast only after going beyond San Francisco, proceeded to the Moluccas and Celebes and Java and then turned for home. He brought back so much altar plate and golden crucifixes and gleaming plunder that the *Golden Hind*, his flagship, could barely list into the home port of Plymouth. The Queen rewarded him with a knighthood. And his eminence as the best buccaneer of his age was celebrated in the Middle Temple, of which he was made an honorary member.

Drake's voyage excited the English, and not only the English court, with the vision that had finally ensnared Ferdinand and Isabella into financing Columbus: America as a land veined with gold and blazing with precious stones. The picture was filled in with much gorgeous detail by a geographer of Welsh extraction named Richard Hakluyt, who decided at an early age to devote his life to "globes, maps and spheres." Once Spain had been crippled at sea, geography became a mania with the Elizabethans, much as space movies have become since the first space flights. One of John Donne's most famous and bawdy poems—written, it should be said, before he became the Dean of Saint Paul's—describes the discovery of his mistress's body as a voyage to America ("And sailing towards her India, in that way, Shall at her fair Atlantick Navell stay"); and in another he hails his safe arrival with the triumphant line: "O My America! My New-Found-Land." Hakluyt, more of a researcher than a poet, burrowed into all the records he could find of the Spanish and French voyages and laid before the Queen a one-man encyclopedia of the wonders of America. It was, he assured everybody, a land "of huge and unknown greatness," though he himself had never been west of Bristol.

The English version of the Spanish El Dorado was more practical, and it had a wider appeal. In spite of that other myth, of Elizabeth's Merrie England, England was only just emerging as a European power. The Middle Ages were not far away: England was a land of farmers and shepherds resenting feudal taxes and tithes paid to large landowners, of mechanics and small merchants in small cities with enough slums to encourage the poor to get out of them. The Drake-Hakluyt story, as it touched the ordinary working Englishman, offered the miracle of a place to get away from it all, and it was naturally garnished with extravagant detail by every sailor in port. Ben Jonson and a couple of friends wrote a play that has a conversation between an intending emigrant, or maybe simply a goggle-eyed gossip, and a sea captain who in that year, 1605, had certainly not touched America. To the listener's doubts about whether Virginia was already inhabited by Englishmen, and whether any treasure had ever been found there, the sea captain goes off into this dithyramb:

A whole country of English is there, man . . . they have married with the Indians who are so in love with 'hem that all the treasure they have they lay at their feete . . . I tell thee, golde is more plentiful there than copper is with us . . . why, man, all their dripping pans and their chamber pottes are pure golde . . . and for rubies and diamonds, they goe forth on holydayes and gather 'hem by the seashore, to hang on their children's coates and sticke in their caps . . . And then you shall live freely there, without sargeants or courtiers or lawyers, or intelligencers.

When the time came, there was no lack of willing emigrants. It is hard to imagine a Scot, a Lancashire man, or even a native of barren Cornwall believing in chamber pots made of gold. But life was bleak for the common man, and he must have been greatly taken with these hints of a country with no recruiting sergeants and bailiffs, no spies, magistrates, tithe gatherers, or other such badgering types.

The men of substance who financed the colonies were not bemused by such fictions, but they saw the prospect of a breathtaking investment in a country that, unlike their own, had unbounded virgin land. Since all newly discovered lands belonged automatically to the Crown, the men who warmed to this enterprise had first to procure from James I a charter as a trading company. This was a joint-stock company, for individuals had learned to their cost in many lone trade ventures in Europe and the East that a private purse carried no authority abroad and was "cold comfort to adventures." So the men who jointly raised the money were such as Sir John Popham, a lord chief justice; Sir Thomas Smith, director of the East India Company; and Sir Ferdinando Gorges, governor of the fort at Plymouth. They were out to finance what they hoped would be profitable plantations in Virginia, guaranteed by the authority of the state.

Because of the commercial rivalry between the shippers of London and the provincial ports, two separate companies were organized, one for London and one for Plymouth. The backers got their charter, and while the document guaranteed such English rights as trial by jury and rights of inheritance, it left the trade and maintenance of the colonies to the backers—although, as the colony was to have the status of an overseas royal manor, it would be governed by a council approved by the Crown and its disputes would be settled by the English courts.

In 1606 three ships financed by the London Company set sail and went by the southern route past the Azores and the Canary Islands. They cruised in the West Indies and then went north, intending to settle discreetly north of the Spanish in Florida and south of the French in Canada. In April 1607 they came on Chesapeake Bay, and, after a month of inching their way past coastal Indian settlements, they entered the James River and moored in six fathoms off a wooded island, which they named after the King—Jamestown. Thirty-nine of the 144 who had sailed were already dead, and the weird noises the survivors heard from the woods, as well as the sporadic appearance of Indian scouts, quickened the labor of their first job, building a stockade.

While they were at it, they must have had very rueful second thoughts about the whole adventure. They were surrounded by a malarial swamp on the edge of endless dense forest. They found very few ingredients of the cornucopia promised in a poem written by Michael Drayton on the eve of their sailing:

Virginia,
Earth's onely paradise.
Where Nature hath in store
Fowle, Venison and Fish,
And the Fruitfull'st Soyle,
Without your Toyle,
Three harvests more,
All greater than your Wish,
And the ambitious Vine,
Crownes with his purple Masse,
The cedar reaching hie
To kisse the Sky,
The Cypresse, Pine
And use-full Sassafras.

They had been taken in by the promotional literature that advertised, as always, a paradise somewhere else. They were commanded by a few sea captains and relatives of the backers, but most of them were ordinary sailors, footloose bachelors, adventurers, poor farmers, slum people, the odd gentleman, and some convicts. (If you were eager to get to America, all you had to do was steal a rabbit or swipe a cloak, do a six-month stretch, and be shipped away.)

Their growing restlessness was not pacified by the opening of the sealed orders, which prescribed the names of the president and council that would be in charge. Among the names was that of one John Smith, who was immediately expelled by a majority vote for having been mutinous on the voyage over. A parson pleaded for him, and he was grudgingly reappointed, but the incident was a small omen of big troubles to come.

In the first place (and very nearly the last), the colonists hadn't the ghost of an idea of the first rule of settlement—to be self-sustaining. They lived off the supplies they'd brought over, and they exhausted them in seven months. Then they tried to barter with the Indians or filch food and land from them. It might have seemed to the colonists that this procedure had been laid down in the London contract, but to the Indians it was theft—so now it became dangerous to forage in the interior woods, even for timber. Shiftless as ever, they actually began to chop down the houses they'd built for firewood. They bickered and stole and, lacking medicines, they died.

The first two years, in fact, were dire, and, by the time there were only thirty-eight left of the 105 who had landed, they were down to living off the animals of the woods and cadging corn from the natives. At one stage they packed up to go home and were already afloat at the mouth of the river when by a providential fluke they met an incoming ship under the

John White sailed with the first colonizing expedition to Roanoke Island in Virginia in 1585. He produced a number of drawings of Indian life like this one, which were later engraved and published. After the colony failed, White himself led a second expedition in 1587, but was forced to sail back to England for more supplies. By the time he reached Roanoke again in 1590, however, all the colonists (including his daughter and granddaughter) had vanished without trace.

Their rype corne.

Their greene corne.

Corne newly sprong.

Their sitting at meate.

The place of solemne prayer.

The house wherin the Tombe of their Herounds standeth.

SECOTON.

A Ceremony in their prayers wth strange iesturs and songs dansing abowt posts carued on the topps lyke mens faces.

command of one Lord De La Warr. He was sailing in with a new load of supplies and more colonists, young men of "substance," though whether of much courage or character is another thing.

The colony now found a leader, or rather a man who decided to make himself one. He was none other than the once disgraced John Smith, henceforth to be known as Captain John Smith. He didn't have a central plan either, but he had the horse sense to see that the new country was nothing like the fantasy patented by Fray Marcos, Hakluyt, Drayton, et al.—and nothing like England, either. He forced everyone to work, on pain of being thrown out beyond the stockade and taking a chance with starvation or with the now hostile Indians. He announced a simple and startling rule of life, the stark Biblical prescription: "He that will not work neither shall he eat." It was a sentence that rooted itself early and deep in the American consciousness and was to make Americans, for a couple of centuries or so, distrustful if not contemptuous of inherited wealth; an early prejudice that has, however, long been overcome.

The settlers still didn't think of a subsistence crop. They started to make pitch and tar, as befitted a commercial enterprise, and Smith rehoused the population by splitting timber for clapboards, a quick and thrifty way of covering the outside of a house with overlapping layers of thin wood. They planted on assigned forty-acre lots, but the marshlands and the searing summers produced more mosquitoes than anything an Englishman would recognize as food.

In the end their salvation came from an Indian crop that grew like dandelions. It was tobacco, but of poor quality. During a truce with the Indians, which had come about through the marriage of one John Rolfe to Pocahontas, the daughter of an Indian chief, they were presented with the pick of a crop. Rolfe sent it to England, where Spanish tobacco was becoming a fashion, in spite of King James's celebrated *Counterblast* against the prevalent notion that tobacco was at once a pleasure and a medicine. The London Company, open to anything that might convert their colonial liability into an asset, sent orders to plant a company tobacco garden and to encourage private crops, to be shipped to England. The King's Council held a delicate session in which it tried to reconcile the plan with the King's detestation of "the scurvy weed." For a time, while conniving with the company, the Council issued word that the colony must persist in more respectable labor. Glassblowing was suggested, and tried. But the tobacco was burgeoning, and its growers found that the flavor was much improved if, instead of throwing it on the ground to dry, it was racked up in smokehouses. Graded by hand, it soon approached the purity of Spanish tobacco, and presumably King James looked the other way. (Ever since then, the British preference for Virginia tobacco has been absolute. During the Second World War, when transatlantic ships' bottoms were needed for the staples of life, Winston Churchill—pleading the cause of Christian civilization—was unable to convert his countrymen to switch to the product of the infidel Turk.)

After a decade of the Virginia experiment, the London Company was at last beginning to appreciate that a very different little England was in the making three thousand miles away. They sent over fewer of the types about which several visiting colonial governors had complained: "gentlemen unused to work, gallants and lascivious sons." Now small landowners were arriving and bringing along good laborers and servants. They brought to the colonists the industry and the confidence to move out of the stockade, to find better land, to build houses of brick, and a hospital, and a church. And it was in this church that popular representative government sprouted in the New World.

The London Company had come to the conclusion that the colonists were failing to rule themselves. Worse, the company itself was in debt to the tune of £75,000. So it got permission from the King's Council to elect a governor who should not go out to survey and come home and report, but stay. He was to be a single absolute ruler.

The colony had a succession of such, most of them severe but able. But then in 1619, they had the great good luck to acquire, in Sir George Yeardley, a governor who was lazy, inefficient, bewildered, kindly, and honest. He broke down and admitted that the government of the plantations and boroughs, instituted by his own local laws, was beyond him. He cried to London for help and was ordered to select two men from each borough and have them come to Jamestown. Twenty-two of them met there, in the Jamestown church, in July 1619. In midsummer Virginia, like four fifths of the American mainland, can be a steaming inferno, and most of the chosen twenty-two sweated through dysentery and various other ailments. One of them died. And in six days they quit. But what they did is worth the study of anyone proposing to found a government or to renovate, in the opaque jargon of our day, "participatory democracy."

They imposed the first kind of taxation in the New World by levying ten pounds of tobacco on every male over the age of sixteen—a rudimentary way of encouraging even "gentlemen unused to labor" to become able-bodied. They enacted a code of local laws to go into effect at once. And they named themselves the House of Burgesses. The later and grander House has been reconstructed to the original design on its old site in Williamsburg, and it receives much reverent attention in the tourist season as the first fort of American liberty, built by blue-eyed patriots howling to be set free from the abominations of British rule. Nothing could be less true. Yet it was the cradle of the American system of a two-house popular assembly, based in the beginning on the English Lords and Commons. It was the first self-governing body in America—though still responsible to the British Crown—and formed the kernel of the state governments and, in time, of the Congress of the United States.

The experiment was not greeted with wild applause either in London or in Virginia, where many people thought of it as "democratical" and so highly dangerous. But it was a remedy, of a sort, for the rule of one man. In the beginning, there were strict limits on what the Burgesses could do. They were to meet only once a year, and to follow and imitate in all things "the laws and customs of England." But in one thing London had given them a freedom that in those days was certainly not included in the liberties of Englishmen. The first Burgessmen, and the ones who came after, were to be elected "by the inhabitants." It was a fateful detail that the phrase was never defined. In practice an "inhabitant" came to mean every taxpayer—that is, every able-bodied male over sixteen—and servants, both free and indentured. In England, on the other hand, you had to own land or property to vote. In this fashion the colony got used to popular franchise, and a later suggestion from London that it be revoked in favor of propertied men caused a riot.

We shouldn't infer from this that these early Virginians were aflame with any notions about the equality of men or the justice of "one man, one vote." But they were devoted to the idea of equal rewards for industry, and "the inhabitants" would choose the men fit to make the local laws. When the elections for Burgesses were held, the planters were usually the overwhelming choice of the voters. As the plantations multiplied they became miniature colonies, and the men who ran them felt an equal responsibility for the government of the whole colony. Unlike their English counterparts, their prime concern was not to acquire land and wealth, and build houses on houses so as to leave "a luxurious living to idle generations." Virginia was to become the first state to abolish what Jefferson called the "pernicious" law whereby the eldest son automatically inherited the entire estate.

There developed inevitably a recognizable class system: at the top a small and hard-working class of landowners; a main body of yeomen who, once black slavery relieved them of hard labor, became a middle class; and at the bottom the indentured servants. But it was a very fluid system. The variety of social types who were plantation owners, and therefore generally Burgesses, was always a shock to the visiting English, one of whom made the sniffy comment, in 1662, that you couldn't expect much wisdom from the Burgesses, for "they are usually such as went over servants thither, and though by time and industry they may have attained competent estates, yet by their poor and mean education they are unskilful in judging of a good estate either of Church or Commonwealth." A man could arrive as a servant under contract to pay back his passage, as Adam Thoroughgood did, and in fifteen years own a plantation of 5,350 acres and be paying the passages of another hundred emigrants. But whether a planter was one of "mean and poor" education or, like the later William Byrd, a classical scholar, scientist, wit, and lawyer trained in England, he was, he had to be, a full-time farmer knowing all about the new soils and crops and methods of curing, and at the same time be able to mend farming tools, to know something of meteorology, and to be his own merchant, appraiser, shipper, and accountant. Byrd used to lament that he was kept from his books and paintings by the daily grind of tending "that bewitching vegetable, tobacco"; and, looking over his lavish and elegant estate of Westover, he remarked that "in the greatest fortune there is the least liberty."

The plantations, then, were neither villages nor entails attached to a lord of the manor. They were company towns in the country. And, thanks to the peculiar topography, they enclosed every stage of production from planting the crops to shipping them. For a glance at the coastline of Virginia and the Carolinas will show something that was a boon to the prosperity of the plantations once they had found their profitable crop. It was another thing that made the overseas experience quite different from life in England. What was unique about this coastline was its wealth of tidal rivers between fingers of fertile land. A man sent out from London reported that "no country in the world can be so curiously watered." And the visiting English, then as now, were fascinated by the idioms that grew out of the landscape: "creek" and "tidewater" and "the fall line," the point upstream where you can navigate no farther because of waterfalls or rapids.

The plantations were always laid out by a river that ran into the sea. There was no call to build towns or ports, no need for overland transport to harbors. Each landing stage was its own port, every lawn an assembly line. It was this lucky topography that produced the river plantation. By the late seventeenth century the system had spread down the long coast of the Carolinas, and by the 1760s the plantations were shipping out small fortunes in rice and indigo, the essential dyestuff of the time. Just before the American Revolution, South Carolina shipped to England more than a million pounds of indigo.

But it was tobacco that set the Southern pattern of a single luxuriant cash crop, grown on a large plantation housing a complete society that made everything for its sustenance. An ocean away from repairs, the first Americans by necessity developed their flair for gadgetry and invented the verb "to fix."

If you had been in such a place in the last quarter of the seventeenth

Aboard a Spanish slaver captured en route to the West Indies by a British warship, slaves huddle among bales and barrels. The watercolor sketch at left was made on the spot by a young English naval officer. Once in America, the more fortunate survivors of the journey might have ended up in the relatively sturdy brick-and-thatch slave quarters of a tidewater plantation (above).

century, you would have noticed another novelty that took hold as the root of Southern prosperity: the heavy labor was done by blacks. We are talking about slavery.

To the Portuguese goes the melancholy privilege of having started the European enslavement of African Negroes, in 1444, fifty years before Columbus. It was systematized under the kings of Spain "to lighten the burdens" of the natives of the West Indies. The English shipped the first blacks from Africa into Virginia—on a ship bearing the ironical name of the *Jesus of Lübeck*—twelve years after the settlement. In the first forty years, however, there were no more than three hundred blacks. All the lowly labor was done by white indentured servants. But tobacco called for labor battalions, and for more drudgery than skill, and when the Virginians needed slavery they made it legal. Once the Royal African Company gave a monopoly of the slave trade to England, the blacks were shipped in legions. By the 1680s they were coming in at the rate of sixty thousand a decade.

Obviously, the market for slaves was in the South, but the men who built the ships for the traffic were in the North, and the ports of Massachusetts, Connecticut, and Rhode Island made some famous fortunes out of it. It is interesting, in a morbid way, to recall that the first moral objections came from the North, but they were soon strangled by the ship owners' profits. The first realistic objections to slavery came in the South, and there was a long and strenuous campaign to stop it. But it was not waged in the conscience of the South. It was a fear of being outnumbered, a terror of insurrection. Yet the purchase of human lives was cheap, whether of black men for the fields of America or white children for the coal mines and factories of England. And when you can buy a tame laboring population with no say in the terms of its labor, you have solved all our plaguing problems of unemployment, wages, prices, and racial minorities.

On such a base there evolved in time, in South Carolina more than anywhere, a spacious society on the English country gentleman's model, with a plantation upriver and a town house, inhabited during a social season as regular as that of London or Bath, along the waterfront of Charleston.

If the other English settlements had been run on the Southern model, if—a very big if—the Northern lands and climate had been amenable to huge, profitable single crops, there could very well have been no American Revolution, and probably no American Civil War. For the Southern colonies did not resent their control by the King's Council, and in religion they remained more or less harmoniously Church of England—even though, after thirty years or so, dissenters bristled here and there and managed to form three parishes. These dissenters became dissatisfied with the King's vicars of Christ and applied for new parsons to come down from Boston, which by then was the American capital of dissent, more accurately, of separatism. Accordingly, three ministers were sent into the conformist South. Their arrival so outraged the majority that Virginia passed a law demanding conformity to the Book of Common Prayer, and the three wise men from the Northeast hotfooted it back to Boston. It was left for Germans and Ulstermen to introduce, very much later, nonconformist churches in a tolerable form. The Southern system, however, whatever its virtues and vices, did not produce a society so radically independent of Britain that it would portend a steady drift to republicanism. That was done in another and a ruder place, by sterner men to the north.

Two years after the Jamestown landing, a ship on its way to Virginia was wrecked on an island over five hundred miles due east of Charleston, South Carolina. The island had been known to English sailors for years, but not as a desirable resort. Shakespeare talks darkly about "the vex'd Bermoothes," and to Sir Walter Raleigh the mention of Bermuda recalled "a hellish sea for thunder, lightning and stormes." But in 1612, three years after the wreck, a shipload of men, women, and sailors settled there. Their charter belonged to the London Company, which, however, had enough on its hands in Virginia, so a subsidiary group took over the running of the new colony.

The settlers were astonished to come on three men, the only survivors of the earlier wreck, who were in bouncing health, who extolled the climate and had managed very cozily in a house they had built amid a garden of vegetables and a cache of seed pearls and ambergris. The colonists fought for a while over the local supplies of ambergris, which was greatly prized as a medicine and the essence of a fine perfume. It was ambergris that saved the island economy, and by the end of 1614 there were over six hundred settlers. For some time afterwards it was much easier to raise money in London by mentioning the tonic of Bermuda than the headache of Virginia.

But having paid our respects to the second English colony, we must now come to those "ruder and sterner" men who planted the third: those immortal Pilgrims who have managed to install themselves in the popular American pantheon as not only the bravest heroes of English settlement but the first. They were a new kind of emigrant, religious dissenters who had the courage of their beliefs and the luck to come after the Jamestown disasters. The Virginia Company of London wangled a charter from the Crown and was the Pilgrims' nominal and sympathetic sponsor. Unfortunately, the Company was losing thousands in Virginia, so it could offer no extensive financial assistance. But it did make it very

*A slightly fanciful nautical scene exactly contemporary with the embarkation
of the Pilgrims in 1620: "Departure of an East Indiaman," by Adam Willaerts.*

plain to these religious men that their only hope of a stable colony rested in sound financial backing, which involved negotiations as complex and tedious as anything known to the Securities and Exchange Commission.

I ought to stress at the beginning of a summary of the Pilgrims' story that there was no conflict in their minds between their resolve to worship God in their own way and their understanding of the need for capital investment. There was no shame in putting your money where your faith was. They were far better organized and equipped than the Jamestown expedition, though their troubles during the first winter have tended to mask this fact and to invest the *Mayflower* story with a heroic poverty and simplicity. Their voyage was subsidized by a modest loan of £7,000 to be repaid—which it was—with the fruit of their labors. The settlement of the later, equally idealistic, and even more expensive Massachusetts Bay Colony cost its promoters £200,000.

In 1608, the year between the Jamestown landing and the settlement of Bermuda, a small company of English people, some educated, most not, fled to Holland from their homes in Nottinghamshire, Lincolnshire, and Yorkshire after rough treatment both from their neighbors and the bishops. They truly believed that the simple faith of Christ had been corrupted by the Church of England, and they accordingly renounced it. They looked in the Second Book of Corinthians and read: "Come out from among them and be ye separate, saith the Lord." So they became "Separatists" and accordingly separated themselves, first to Amsterdam and then to Leyden.

They expected tolerance in enlightened Holland and they got it. They had to turn from farming to work at weaving and baking and other small trades, but they were free to worship in their own way. Yet, by a truth only deeply known to expatriates, they felt their roots withering after six or seven years. They no more enjoyed seeing their children become "Dutchified" than the parents of the young transatlantic evacuees in the Blitz enjoyed seeing their children become Americanized. They turned down a Dutch suggestion that they might like to go to America as new Dutchmen and found New Netherland. But the American experiment was much in the air, and for three years the two leaders of the expatriates, the only "gentlemen scholars" among them, John Robinson and William Brewster (William Bradford might also qualify), kept in touch with a prominent member of the Virginia Company who was also an old friend.

By the grace of luck or God, this man was Sir Edwin Sandys, a member also of the East India Company, a cosmopolitan scholar and business-man, a Middle Templar, and a lawyer with a brave concern for the legal rights of prisoners and the trading rights of small companies fighting monopolies. He was, as well, deeply sympathetic with the religious scruples of the Separatists—which is all the more surprising when you consider that he was the son of the Archbishop of York and had been knighted by James I, who had indeed made good his threat to religious dissenters: "I shall make them conform or I shall harry them out of the land."

There were many Channel crossings, and knotty and interminable discussions about financing and religious rights. One English Separatist in Leyden jumped the gun, got a patent for a Virginian plantation, and sailed off in the winter of 1618. Of the one hundred and eighty people aboard his ship, one hundred and thirty died in the jammed quarters. This calamity was well reported and discouraged many of the expatriates for life. But Sandys became the treasurer of the Virginia Company, which was eager to recoup its fortunes by letting out patents to groups of underwriters—and it was such a group that put up the money for the Separatists' venture. James I refused to grant them liberty of conscience, but promised they would not be molested for practicing their own faith. They would, in all secular matters, be responsible to the government of Virginia. It looked like a godsend, and eventually they prepared to plant themselves at the diplomatic distance of a hundred miles or more north of the Anglicans of Jamestown.

Two ships, the *Speedwell* and the *Mayflower*—which had been plying the Mediterranean in the wine trade—set off from Southampton. The *Speedwell* broke down. They put into Dartmouth for repairs and ten days later sailed again. They got a hundred leagues into the Atlantic and the *Speedwell* denied its name even more miserably by developing leaks. They turned back to Plymouth, where the *Speedwell* was abandoned. On September 16, 1620, the *Mayflower* went it alone.

The *Mayflower* was a good deal better prepared and equipped than the Jamestown ship. It had 149 people aboard, forty-seven of them officers and crew. At the most, there could not have been more than forty Separatists, thirty-five of them (including children) from Leyden, and sixty-six other sectarians, from London and Southampton. There were nine servants, fourteen indentured servants and artisans, three cooks, two gunners, a doctor, and a ship's surgeon. The ship, under the command of an old whaling captain, was well loaded with furniture and domestic utensils, with goats and chickens, with salted beef, vegetables, breads, and other staples, including hogsheads of beer. There was enough food, but it was typical of these early voyages that it was of the wrong sort. Although only one passenger and four of the crew died on the way over, the sixty-five-day voyage took a grim toll during the following winter on land, when over half of all the people who made the journey died of scurvy or "general debility."

"Virginia" was taken to run north through what is now New Jersey. But thanks to an incompetent navigator, the *Mayflower* missed even the northern limits of Virginia by a good two hundred miles. It beached at the end of a long peninsula that curves up into a fishhook—Cape Cod, in Massachusetts. William Bradford, the ship's Yorkshire chronicler, put it in an immortal passage:

> Being thus passed the vast ocean, and a sea of troubles . . . they had now no friends to welcome them, nor inns to entertaine or refresh their weatherbeaten bodys, no houses or much less townes to repaire too . . . it was muttered by some that if they got not a place in time they would turn them and their goods ashore [and return] . . . But may not and ought not the children of these fathers rightly say—Our Fathers were Englishmen which came over this great ocean, and were ready to perish in the wilderness, but they cried unto the Lord, and he heard their voice and looked on their adversities, Etc.

(The "etc." is Bradford's own.) A moving story from a man deeply moved, and in its drastically popular form it has moved three centuries of Americans and Britons to believe in the powerful myth that the South was settled by aristocrats and wealthy idlers who puzzlingly turned into Thomas Jefferson, whereas New England was founded by simple holy men who built a boat and cast themselves on the mercy of God—and somehow turned into Calvin Coolidge.

The Pilgrims deserve to be famous for two things. They survived. And they proclaimed the Mayflower Compact, a bolder assertion of their right to govern themselves than the Virginians' House of Burgesses. Since they had missed Virginia and were beyond the conditions of their patent, they snatched their liberty from an accident. Brewster and Bradford and other leaders drew up this "Compact," to create their own "civil body politic," and to abide by its laws. The Separatists were quick to sign it and get the first government in their own religious hands, for they had had plenty of trouble with both the other sectarians and the "wild and lusty" types, the seamen and unbelievers aboard. Once they had passed the first dreadful winter, they learned about American vegetables from the Indians and traded beaver pelts for corn. They shot turkeys and fished for clams and lobsters. And their settlement, on the mainland at Plymouth, was secure.

But the Pilgrims were not the ones who would secure Puritan New England. Left to themselves, they, like the early French, would probably have remained the lonely inhabitants of a trading post and fishing stations. The men were still in England who would make the radical departure, first from the Church of England and then from the government of England.

Paradoxically, they were nothing like so radical as the Pilgrims but stood halfway between the Church and the Separatists. It is useful to keep the name Puritans for them, for their great aim was to purify the Church, not to renounce it. They deplored its corruption, its incrustations of liturgy, the sale of livings to cynical men, its flirtations with the forms if not the creed of Popery. They didn't reject the Church, they felt it had rejected them. And certainly it was threatening them with persecution. They would go to America, they decided, and there restore the purity and authority of the Church. They would build a new England, and a better one.

Their unquestioned leader was a man who defies the Puritan stereotype both of his time and ours. He was no simple, unlettered, psalm-singing bigot. John Winthrop was to a manor born, Groton Manor, in Suffolk. His family had done very well in the cloth trade, at nearby Lavenham, the woolen capital of England. Winthrop went to Cambridge and became a successful lawyer, a drafter of parliamentary bills who earned the considerable income of £700 a year. In addition, he had the revenues from Groton, a small and comfortable world of its own, with rolling acres of woods and fields of wheat and rye and barley, and a company of servants and tenants. Hardly a place to desert for that wind-whipped northern coast and a bleak colony of traders and fishermen.

What made him leave was a combination of high principle, high prices, and low rents. He was politically conservative and an aristocrat by breeding, but he was also an inflexible Puritan genuinely appalled at the impurities of the Church and depressed, too, by the crookery that went on in the court of which he was an attorney: His Majesty's Court of Wards and Liveries, which administered—and sometimes annexed—the lands of the King's wards. In the 1620s, when Winthrop was in his thirties, and the father of seven children, the textile industry was hit by a severe depression, and the country by a general inflation. Prices were rising everywhere, but the rents of Winthrop's tenants were fixed by law. Then, we are unsure why, he lost his legal practice.

His own bad fortune coincided with a series of catastrophic public events. King Charles I, who had succeeded to the throne in 1625, a year during which London was beset by fear of the plague, wanted Parliament to put on the taxpayers the burden of a forced loan, a measure that was firmly resisted by two of Winthrop's Puritan friends. They were consequently sent to prison. In 1629 the King dismissed the last Parliament that would meet before the English Civil War.

This train of calamities was enough to convince Winthrop that God was visiting his wrath on a godless kingdom, for there was always in the Puritan's mind a strong, providential connection between earthly sin and heavenly punishment. He thought of moving to Ireland, but several meetings with other leading Puritans, and some thoroughly secular merchants convinced him that America was the place for "a city of God."

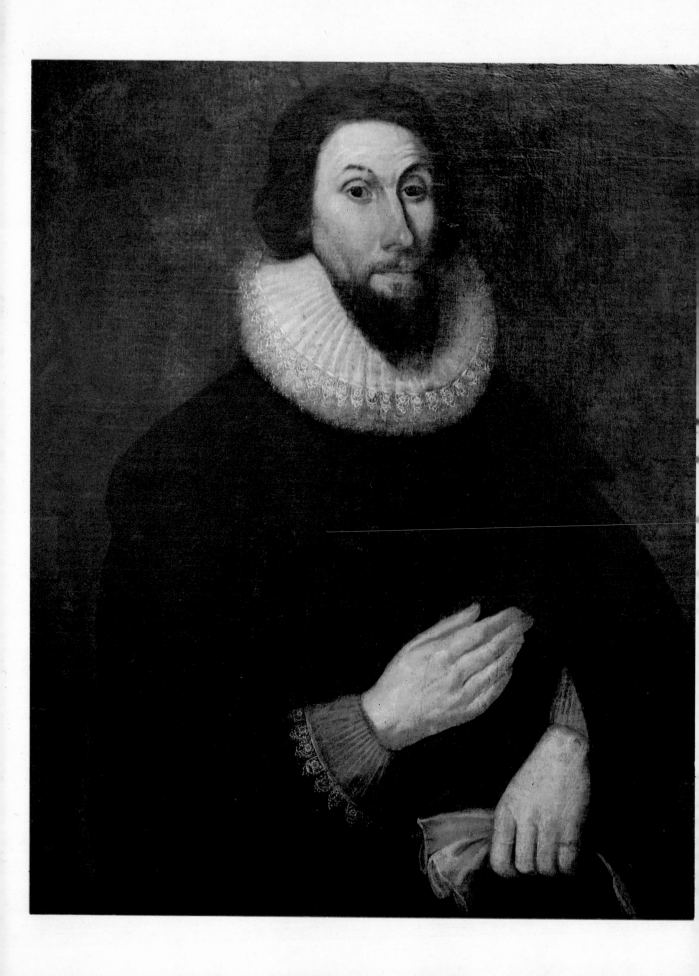

Within a year Winthrop and the Puritans were ready to sail with much the largest expedition that had gone to the New World. It was meant to be subsidized by the so-called New England Company, a new grouping of backers that got a patent from the old Plymouth Company, which had been recognized as the Council of New England. But the New England Company, after settling Salem in Massachusetts, felt uncertain about the validity of its patents and decided to have them confirmed by the King. The company was reorganized by substantial Puritans who secured a royal charter for "the Company of Massachusetts Bay in New England."

Between this charter and those of all the previous settlements, there was a crucial and liberating difference. And Winthrop was responsible for it. He was not alone in fearing that, if the new settlement failed to prosper, its charter would be revoked by the King and it would become a royal province. (This had happened in Virginia.) Winthrop argued that, since anyone who bought stock in the company could vote at its meetings, the control of the colony would be at the mercy of a shifting council based in England. The accommodating clause that was inserted was deceptively trivial. It said that the stockholders were not required to meet in a particular place—that is, England—and what it meant was, in the apt summary of Charles M. Andrews, that the settlers could be sure of controlling their own affairs "by taking company and charter along with them to New England, thus swallowing up the company in the colony. In this way the company would be under Puritan control and could be manipulated to serve Puritan ends, which, Winthrop argued, were the ends of God." What it came to mean, as we shall see, is that the governor of the Company could become the governor of the colony on the spot. Winthrop was chosen as the one and elected as the other.

He sailed, in March 1630, in the flagship of a fleet of four ships, carrying over five hundred men, women, and children, whom Winthrop tenderly thought of as a noble microcosm of the human family—*his* family, for he carried the company charter in his pocket. In Massachusetts he planted the first truly self-governing colony. If any one man can be called the Founding Father of New England, he is it.

While the Puritans were concerned in planting "a city of God," they also had to eat. Winthrop was the last man to see any conflict between prosperity and prayer. He epitomizes several bred-in-the-bone convictions that we don't today associate with Puritanism. He believed, for instance, that hunting with a gun was wrong only if you couldn't make a profit from the kill. He thought it would be wrong to move to New England unless the colony could guarantee a financial success. It was a man's duty to God to use his talents to the full. His material success would be the visible sign of God's blessing.

So, once arrived, the children of God raised cattle, and Indian corn and

John Winthrop, the first governor of the Massachusetts Bay Colony, cultivated an air of Puritan authority and rectitude for this portrait, which was painted in the 1640s.

vegetables for their own sustenance; but they looked to more profitable work later on and kept a long credit line out to the London merchants. They soon got busy in the fur trade, and at Marblehead they set up an industry that was as much their salvation as tobacco had been the Virginians'—"the sacred cod." (It soon replaced the royal coat of arms as an official Massachusetts emblem, and today it dominates the hallway of the lower house of the government of the state, the body that holds the purse strings.)

Winthrop had an almost inquisitorial concern for the saintliness of the rulers of the colony, but he was never fussy about the purity of the customer. His steady belief that virtue paid dividends made him rejoice whenever Yankee ships went off to deliver a cargo of codfish—even when the buyers were Roman Catholics, because they paid better than anybody. And when the English Civil War halted emigration, the Puritans—finding their work force frozen—apparently felt no qualms about going into the more profitable business still of building ships and loading them with fish and beef and vegetables for the sustenance of the slave-holding planters who grew a single crop of tobacco or sugar in the West Indies. (It was only the first of many noble American life styles supported by dubious means.)

Massachusetts, then, began to flourish by the business acumen of its founders. But it achieved stability, and ultimately independence, through a form of government that was severe but on the whole just. It was unquestionably more representative than anything the Puritans had known in England. Winthrop told an early meeting of the settlers why, by his lights, Virginia had failed: "Its main end was carnal, not religious. It gathered a multitude of rude persons and it failed to set up a right form of government." Like most Puritans before and since, Winthrop knew what was right for other people, and he was there to see that they got it. Yet to his great credit he set up a government growing out of the company charter that was later susceptible even to the pressures of democracy, a form of government that, in Winthrop's decided opinion, "amongst civil nations is accounted the meanest and worst." Samuel Eliot Morison has acutely remarked that the Massachusetts government fashioned the mold of "the standard American pattern" and was very similar to that of the typical American business corporation:

As a business charter, the corporation consisted of freemen (stockholders), meeting in an assembly called the General Court where were annually elected, on a stated date, the governor, deputy governor, and assistants (councillors). But transfer overseas turned the company into a colonial government. The freemen were now the voters, the governor and deputy governor the two chief magistrates, and the assistants doubled as governor's council and supreme court. By 1644, owing to a typical small-town dispute over a stray sow, the

83

In the mid-eighteenth century, Boston's squares and public buildings looked exactly like those of London. The Old State House (center) was supplanted soon after the Revolution by Charles Bulfinch's grand gold-domed structure now standing atop Beacon Hill.

general court separated into two houses, and Massachusetts Bay had something approaching a modern state government.

The franchise was confined to church members. This was a restriction vital to Winthrop's conception of planting "a government of Christ in exile" composed of *separate* "cities of God." For the essence of the Puritan system was the idea that every community, big and small, was a government in itself, a "congregation" of God's "elect," run by God's laws. And who was to elect God's elect? All the people, and only the people, who had been cleared by the select group that set up the church in each community, the original freemen and the assistants (*their* sainthood was presumed). They usually began by choosing a minister and then examining each colonist—his private life, his credibility about when he had felt he had become a true believer—before admitting him as a member of the congregation and a citizen voter. In other words, the "people" were allowed a say in the government only when they'd been certified by "God's elect."

What emerged was a mixed government that defies a single label familiar to us. It was a theocracy. It was an oligarchy. Yet in the first year after Winthrop's arrival it adopted some fundamentals whose denial was to cause, 135 years later, the final break with England: trial by jury, the protection of life and property by due process, freedom from self-incrimination, no taxes to be imposed on those who could not vote.

Looking back on it, I am bound to say that it also bears some striking resemblances to a Communist or other totalitarian government. The Party will tolerate you as a citizen, but you have no say in the government if you are not a Party member. Life is real and very earnest in a society being built from the ground up; and it cannot be sustained by consent but only by a rigid discipline imposed from the top. The rulers direct every function of society—work and worship and play, business and literature, and morals. In Massachusetts, discipline was reinforced by admonitions from the Old Testament, freely interspersed with the thoughts of Chairman Winthrop: "work for the night cometh"; "make with thine own hands all the things that thou needest"; "sow the good seed and the Lord will furnish the good harvest in His season"; "school the young in the laws of God, that they may truly worship."

The laws governing personal conduct were very strict. Prison for the smallest theft, for the singing of lewd songs, for drunkenness. The stocks for "raillery" near the church. Death for adultery. But suppose you were a good worker and an obedient citizen who said, as inevitably many new immigrants did, "I will obey the laws, but I have other religious principles and I want to practice my own faith." Well, that was an abomination. The Puritans had not come to America to practice religious tolerance, except of the things *they* tolerated. They came to set up a ring of holy cities, of congregations responsible under Winthrop to the General Court of the colony. And they never doubted that they had the one true prescription for the godly life. Consequently, they were as harsh on the new dissenters as their old oppressors had been on them. Baptists and Quakers were the Devil's agents. Quakers were the worst. They were accused as "radical meditators," consulting in mischievous silence the heretic known as their conscience. "If," said one minister, "they beat the gospel black and blue, it is but just to beat them black and blue." So it was done. A few were hanged, some were allowed to confess to their "diversionary" sins and become reconverted. Most were driven south to take haven in more tolerant settlements, in Rhode Island and Connecticut and Long Island.

This merciless prescription of what constituted the only good life was maintained on the usual totalitarian pretext that it was essential for good order. And it can be reasonably argued that neighborliness, at any rate, was essential to the common safety. For one thing, the Indians were there in the forest and, at long intervals, would emerge for a massacre. But the worm in the apple of neighborliness is gossip. Neighbors bound together by a bigoted conformity see villains in all eccentrics, religious or otherwise. Whenever the colony fell on hard times, as it did in the 1680s and 1690s, gossip and suspicion rekindled the horrors of witchcraft—an old story to the older colonists. Like Salem, Scotland and East Anglia also had their sporadic orgies of hangings and—a punishment never used in the colonies—burnings.

We should not shudder too smugly about these outbreaks. The tendency to see the eccentric as a menace to the community exists in a less pathological form in small towns all over the world. It is an impulse never conquered in America, perhaps because of the neighborliness essential to frontier life.

The worst outbreak of persecuting "witches" occurred after Winthrop was dead, and he would undoubtedly have thought of it as a grievous, though not outrageous, consequence of the system he had founded. I have possibly made him out to be a self-righteous tyrant. He was, however, a benevolent one, who wrestled as strenuously with his own views of justice and charity as he did with the souls of the relapsed. He was a scrupulous protector of the "body of liberties" he had drawn up in the first year. He was a passionately tender husband. In his incomparable journal there is no hint that he ever regretted the move from the spacious manor at Groton to a rude house in the colony. He extended representative government, irrespective of wealth or origin, throughout the colony. Any freeman, if only he were God-fearing, could achieve the highest post in the congregation.

Winthrop was, as well, the chief defender of the colony against several threats of parliamentary control, after England got a Parliament again in the 1660s. (The independence of the colony had been greatly helped by the lack of a strong central government in England before and during the Civil War.) He gave every waking moment, usually from an hour before dawn to midnight, to the guidance of the colony. The best proof of his skill and benevolence is the fact that he was twelve times elected as governor of the colony and died, in 1649 at the age of sixty-one, in office.

Between the two strong and opposing cultures of Virginia and New England, the only continuous highway was the sea. By land there lay five hundred miles of roads so primitive that the leading men of Richmond and Boston knew London better than they knew each other. Charleston, South Carolina, was as far from Boston as Vienna is from Plymouth; and those two cities are hardly more dissimilar than the societies created in the South and the North. The early model of New England could hardly have worked in the rest of the country, and neither could the early model of Virginia.

But the English, though often seized with odd delusions, are never obsessed for long with a single formula for salvation or society. They have tended to distrust magic remedies and hypnotic leaders and preferred moderate solutions that allow a lot of different types to be their dotty selves. So there came into being a string of Middle Colonies—New York, Pennsylvania, Maryland, Delaware—whose only original links were the English language, the English common law, and an itch to start afresh, for various reasons, in the New World. Like all middlemen—like Sweden always lying between two monolithic powers—they tended to neutrality and tolerance. Or, to put it the other way round, tolerant men tended to congregate in the hinterland that lay comfortably remote from the rigors of Puritan conformity and the uniformity of the Anglican, plantation South. Pennsylvania was founded because Charles II owed £16,000 to a dead admiral who, alive, had been grieved by his son's embrace of the Quakers and by his frequent wrangles with the Establishment. The King was happy to get rid of this son, William Penn, by settling the debt with a grant of land in America, very fertile and bursting with minerals, no less than three hundred miles long and one hundred and sixty miles wide! Maryland was set up because one of the King's ambassadors turned Catholic and wanted to make things safe for Catholics in America.

So through the late seventeenth and early eighteenth centuries, the various English spread themselves in the Middle Colonies and welcomed

As shown in this engraving, dated 1752, Baltimore was little more than a small coastal settlement where men could net fish in the shallows along the shore.

German Lutherans and Swedish Protestants, Moravians and Jacobites, Mennonites and Jews. By 1733 there were thirteen colonies settled along the Atlantic seaboard—in order of founding Virginia, Massachusetts, New Hampshire, New York, Connecticut, Maryland, Rhode Island, Delaware, Pennsylvania, North Carolina, New Jersey, South Carolina, and Georgia. Each had its own government, its own currency, its own trade laws and religious ways. They were, indeed, long before the Revolution, more like thirteen nations, enjoying or suffering every sort of relationship with the interior Indians from undisturbed friendship to murderous hostility.

It was the Middle Colonies that produced the most flexible societies, curiously classless and homogeneous, in which at the end of the day the parson and the tallow chandler, the baker, the bricklayer, and the banker seemed to reach instinctively for the same diversions: a little fiddle playing, a game of cards, the chanting of a ballad about the capture of the latest pirate, talk about politics and women and predestination, or a respectful reading of an admired sermon. Pennsylvania bred independent large farmers without slaves, and, although its establishment was Quaker, a dozen religious sects lived there without conflict or bigotry. In particular, the middle city of Philadelphia was probably the most civilized, by any modern definition, of colonial capitals. Here had developed a human type odd enough to make an English visitor write, in the middle of the eighteenth century, about a kind of scholar-citizen, politically alert, "whose learning is, however, always ingenious and useful."

Thus, three main cultures emerged from the English settlements. The planter society of the South, with a fluid aristocracy very open to labor and talent. The more egalitarian settlements of New England, controlled, however, by a Puritan oligarchy. And the greatly varied Middle Colonies, reaching from New York to the Virginia border, which were at once agrarian and mercantile and gave birth to the first cities, the first businessmen, a string of ports, and a range of trades from printer-publishers to skilled workmen.

These divisions were very clear to the people who lived within them, and provided the visiting English with a rough breakdown of the colonial system that could keep them from making elementary blunders in dealing with any one of the three types of society. But just as, today, Englishmen are always deaf to the social implications of the American accents they mingle with (even Peter Ustinov's mimic Americans —whether admirals, New England bluebloods, businessmen, or Hollywood agents—are always Midwesterners and usually sound like gangsters), so the English of the middle eighteenth century were, on the whole, deaf and blind to the subtle but strong and growing characteristics that were making Americans of these transplanted Englishmen. There were precious few Englishmen in Parliament or elsewhere who sensed the powerful drift of such strange American novelties as the town meeting, the abolition of primogeniture, the custom of electing rather than appointing officers in the state militias. Fewer still pondered the strangeness of some fundamental things noted by an admiring French immigrant: landowners without tenants, and farmers who had never heard of a peasant. If more Englishmen had sensed the possibility of a break with Europe that these characteristics portended, they might have echoed with a more ominous inflection Crèvecoeur's immortal question: "What, then, is the American, this new man?"

3
MAKING A REVOLUTION

It is fair to say that the vast majority of Americans have no doubts about the rightness of the colonists' break with England. The phrase "the American Revolution" causes a certain glow even in the most entrenched conservatives, who would never revolt against anybody except a new revolutionary and who, in the Revolutionary War, would most probably have been on the Loyalist side. This is because Americans are taught a very simple view of their revolution—that it was a straightforward crusade against a tyrannical Parliament and a hysterical king an ocean away. Of course, no revolution was ever so simple, certainly not this one. But patriotism, a bad historian, writes the most beguiling history, since it always offers a flattering explanation of a complicated story and satisfies our insatiable hunger for good guys and bad guys.

In the middle eighteenth century, the nation that was to rebel was hardly a nation at all but a string of separate, and separately governed, colonies reaching down the Atlantic seaboard fourteen hundred miles or so from northern Massachusetts (what is now Maine) through Georgia—in one place a royal colony, in another a barony, in a third a land-grant company. The laws of each were administered by a royal governor, or by planters, or by shippers, or by clergymen, or by Quaker "peacemakers." Their ways of work were dictated by different economies, by fisheries or by farming, by rice and indigo or by tobacco, or by turning molasses into rum and bartering it for English goods. Most of the colonials, if they had visited each other much, would have felt themselves to be in a foreign land. Like most nations living on the same continent, they quarreled a good deal. Who owned this river? Who had the right to the oyster catch in this bay? Where did the border lie between Pennsylvania and Maryland? (That caused such a rumpus that two of the King's surveyors came over to settle what threatened to turn into a border war. Their names were Charles Mason and Jeremiah Dixon.)

A puissant young king in his coronation robes: George III, painted by the Scottish artist Allan Ramsay in 1760, when the King was 22.

93

It has often been said that for a century and a half the strongest link between the colonies was their common allegiance to the King of England, which we certainly should not "belittle" (to use an Americanism of Jefferson's much ridiculed at the time in England). The colonists may not have made much of this allegiance, but, until the figure of George III was inflated by caricature into a tyrant, most of them would not have doubted that allegiance either. The stronger link was their inheritance of the English common law. But the strongest of all was the slowly growing knowledge that they had all shared the strange experience of living on a new continent and that, in the generations since 1607, they had changed from Englishmen, possessing interesting variations on the originals, into Americans.

The pull away from English institutions, and especially English law, took longer than the slow but more irrevocable departure from English folkways. But in the weaning of colonies and empires from the mother country there is usually a moment of organic change, an "episode" as the doctors call it, which is seen only later to have been decisive. Such an episode was the final attempt of the French, between 1754 and 1760, to confine the English colonies to the lands east of the Appalachians, and to hold the hinterland and prepare it for an American empire of their own.

For, while the English colonies were settling and prospering, the French were by no means abandoning their aim of establishing an interior empire based upon the Mississippi Valley. They were holding the Great Lakes and fighting the reinvigorated Iroquois and the Seneca; and in the South they were trading with the Indians and hoping one day to join the two ends of their settlements and outposts. They could do this only by securing control of the valley of the Ohio, the essential link between Canada and the Mississippi. For many decades they were busy quickening the trade of the lakes and rivers, and incidentally developing military mobility by building hundreds of bateaux larger and swifter than anything the English colonists knew. Forty feet long, nine feet wide, they could carry forty or fifty men, cannon, and provisions for a month or more.

Whenever England and France were threatening each other with war in Europe, or were actually at it, the French in Canada made sporadic and lethal raids on the frontier settlements of the New England colonies. And from time to time the New Englanders retaliated with northern expeditions (John Winthrop's grandson led one against Montreal). They always failed.

At the end of the 1740s, the French decided to stake out their main claim, literally. An expedition rolled down the Ohio River and buried lead plates at intervals to mark their territorial possession. At that moment, an English company of Virginia planters with a royal patent was surveying the same territory. The time had come, the French realized, to stop such English incursions. From the present site of Erie, Pennsylvania, down through western Pennsylvania and the Ohio all the way to the mouth of the Mississippi, therefore, they built a chain of impressive forts.

The vital link between the Mississippi and the Ohio Valley was the spot where the Monongahela and the Allegheny rivers met. The English already had a rude fort there, but in 1754 the French destroyed it and built Fort Duquesne. It was from this base that the French marched to their first open clash with the Virginians, who sent out a small force under the command of a newly commissioned, twenty-one-year-old lieutenant-colonel. He scarcely had time to build a primitive fort in a river bottom before the French overwhelmed him.

Luckily, the French were gallant enough to let the surviving Virginians go home disarmed. Their twenty-one-year-old commander, a country squire named George Washington, was humiliated but not cast down. As refreshed by the smell of battle as the young Churchill in a later river war, he wrote afterwards: "I have heard the bullets whistle and, believe me, there is something charming in the sound." It was to charm him for the next six years.

The following year the war was really on when Edward Braddock, a Scottish major-general in the Coldstream Guards, hacked his way with a much larger British and colonial force several hundred miles through the mountain wilderness to take Fort Duquesne. The French and their Indian allies ambushed and killed him, and routed his army. This disaster roused London to the realization that it had a full-scale war on its hands. A large expeditionary force commanded by a flock of English generals was sent over to pierce the French lines along the enormous reach of the rivers. But there were fewer lines than redoubts, at strategic clearings in a wilderness. It was not a kind of warfare to which the English had been accustomed, though it taught them something about the strange horrors they were to encounter in the Revolutionary War. They suffered atrociously in the mountains and the forests from the Indian guerrillas, and in the pitched battles they were up against superior generalship. At Fort Ticonderoga in upstate New York, three thousand Frenchmen under Montcalm stood off fifteen thousand British and colonial troops, and the Black Watch suffered the worst losses in the history of the regiment until the Second Battle of the Somme.

It took six years before Quebec and Montreal surrendered to the British and the fighting virtually ended in North America. Three years later, in 1763, Canada and her dependencies and the whole interior "empire" of France were transferred to the Crown of England. Florida

SECOND ENGAGEMENT

In 1755, on Lake George in upstate
New York, French troops and their Indian
allies attacked a British encampment.
They were driven off with heavy losses.

was taken from Spain, which had the misfortune to come in rather late and pick the wrong side. But the Spanish did acquire La Salle's vast, vague region of Louisiana.

The successful resistance to France's imperial effort, made by British and colonial troops, had been commanded from London. Though this did not serve to unite the colonies in an emergency, it made them see that, however independent they normally were of each other, they shared the peril of vulnerability to a single enemy. By England, their protector, they were therefore regarded as a single nation, the overseas blood ally. Once that protector had defeated the enemy and assured their security, they were the better able to make demands on him, the demands of a coalition of colonies with grievances held in common. And, out of the victory, the grievances were soon to accumulate.

First, the colonists had seen something of each other as recruits under the officers of the King. They noticed that the English officers bought commissions or were appointed; their own officers were elected. They fought better in the wilderness than professional soldiers accustomed to the battle lines of France and Holland. They took a new and confident view of themselves and they were, in many skirmishes, neither intimidated nor impressed by the superior British airs. There is nothing like what the infantryman calls "contact" to deflate the awe of a legend at three thousand miles.

The British soldiers, too, were impressed by the colonials, and when they got home they passed on the thought that if there were another threat the colonials would do very well on their own, especially up against the Indians.

This was a homely reflection on the main problem: how to protect the greatly expanded western frontier—an ill-defined region, to be sure, but not less than three fifths the size of the thirteen colonies combined. And, having arranged for its protection, how to administer it? For the government in Westminster, looking at the new map of North America, took stock of its huge holdings and began to doubt that they could any longer be managed simply as trading corporations that gave Britain preferential rights to their crops in exchange for manufactures and supplies.

It may seem ludicrous at this late date to simplify the British view in this way. But the colonies had been on a very loose rein to the old country and took something for granted that London had long overlooked: the rising power and effectiveness of the separate colonial governments. During the six years of war, the British got an education. And after the war, they suddenly came alive to the need to review their imperial system, to find some way of strengthening Britain's central authority over what was supposed to be a federal empire. They made the mistake of tightening their grip, asserting the supremacy of Parliament, and reminding the colonies that they were "subordinate and dependent" and must bow to all laws made for them in Westminster. (Exactly the same problem—of where the central authority ended and local authority began—was to frustrate the first government of the United States twenty years later.) Parliament began to pass laws compelling New England, for instance, to trade only with the British possessions in the West Indies. And it doubled the export tax the colonies would have to pay on European goods shipped to America.

These new restrictions were not inspired in the first place by a theory of imperial preference. They were practical responses to the huge cost of the French and Indian Wars, which saddled the British with whopping new taxes and doubled the national debt. Troops would have to be raised to form a more or less permanent patrol of the country beyond the Appalachians, and the British began to think that, at the least, the British in America should do something in their own defense.

This suggestion came as a shock to the colonists. The young men who had done the fighting expected to do what Americans have done ever since once a war is over: disarm, demobilize, forget the whole business, and get back to normal. But, partly because of the usual peacetime letdown in production for war, and partly because of the restrictions on their trade, things were not normal. There was a general depression in the 1760s, and many of the jobless and dispirited ex-soldiers felt the urge to pull up stakes and move on. Sitting in their inns and alleys back East, they must have thought with much yearning of the lands they'd fought in, of the millions of rich beckoning acres beyond the mountains. Like boys from Pittsburgh and Chicago who trained in balmy California in the Second World War, they saw the vision of a better life in the West.

From London's point of view, this prospect was full of hazards. The French and the Indians were beaten, but they were sulking and nursing their wounds in the Mississippi Valley still. And beyond them was New Spain, at least as a large shadow on the prairie. Parliament decided that, if it allowed the new lands to be settled, the English colonies would be spread too thin for their own safety. So it proclaimed that everything beyond the crest of the Appalachians was untouchable Crown property, strictly off limits. The young colonists had seen paradise through a door they had prised open and it was slammed in their faces. They felt cheated of their wartime inheritance.

The British then reminded them that, inheritance or not, it was a new frontier that would have to be defended. London gave the colonists a year to suggest ways in which this might be done. At the end of that time, London offered them a choice: either to raise their own patrol or to pay through taxation for the maintenance of ten thousand British soldiers. The colonies didn't want to do either, so Parliament, in 1765, in a routine session with little debate or indignation, passed a tax bill, the Stamp Act. It was simplicity itself, something none of us today thinks twice about, a means of paying the government through the retailer: a revenue stamp such as is stuck on a pack of cigarettes, a deck of cards, a bottle of liquor. This stamp was to be affixed to every legal document, colonial newspaper, deed, contract, ship's manifest, everything.

It was the first internal tax that Britain had ever imposed, and its effect was to unite the colonists in a fury. The revenue agents appointed to sell the stamps were about as popular as lepers. If they had any sense they quit their jobs or were soon persuaded to do so by mobs that tarred and feathered them, sacked their homes, and rioted—in Massachusetts, Virginia, New York, and North Carolina—outside the houses of the royal governors.

Within the year, a Parliament dazed by the viciousness of this response listened to an eloquent appeal by William Pitt the elder and repealed the Stamp Act. The rejoicing in America was evidently as widespread as the original defiance. Toasting the royal family was again a safe thing to do at public dinners. Philadelphia's official party to celebrate repeal was delayed until it could coincide with the King's birthday. "The repeal," wrote John Adams, "has composed every wave of popular disorder into a smooth and peaceful calm."

Not for long. For at this point the King of England, considered not as a symbol but as one of the leading dramatis personae, made his unfortunate entrance. George III is commonly regarded as a pathetic and egregious figure, and mad to boot. He suffers, like several other actors in the American Revolution, like Lafayette and Jefferson and Washington himself, from being known best by portraits painted in old age. But George III was only twenty-two when he came to the throne. He was as domestic and downright a monarch as George V, and considerably harder working. And before he was out of his twenties he had shown enough character and political adroitness to dictate the control of Parliament as few kings of England have done since the Restoration. But in the decade before the Revolution he overrode the prudent warnings of Pitt, who was now old and feeble, and handpicked a government that had the misfortune to employ in turn, as chancellors of the exchequer, two men very willing to press the King's view of the colonists as sulky wards ungrateful for their salvation from the French. One was Charles Townshend, a witty and vivacious man of disastrous political judgment. The other was Lord North, a timid and apologetic bumbler. Between them they sponsored repressive laws and new taxes that were to bring on the showdown. The restrictions of the West Indies trade were extended to all colonial shipping. Paper money could no longer be used as legal tender for debts. Import taxes were imposed on English paper, glass, and tea. The last tax, aimed at one of the two staple drinks of the colonies (rum was the other), caused organized boycotts of British imports, from Boston down to South Carolina. The boycotts were effective enough to make Parliament repeal, in 1770, all the new taxes except the one, on tea, which hurt most.

As any child knows—as any black child or man knows—it takes only so much continuous taunting to provoke a reaction out of all proportion to the original prod. Parliament ought to have been warned, but was not, by a small episode of insurrection that happened in Boston, on a snowy March day in 1770, outside the Customs House, the port of entry for British indignities and by now the detested symbol of Parliament's authority. It was guarded on that day by a single sentry. There is a great variety of versions of what happened: some toughs attacked the sentry, or he was showing off his swordsmanship and nipped a bystander in the arm, or somebody was beaten up. At any rate, a small crowd gathered and started to jeer at the sentry and throw stones and slivers of ice. He shouted for help, and more soldiers came running and lined up in formation to guard him and the Customs House. At some point the crowd grew scared, or bold, and one of the soldiers was clubbed and kicked to the ground. As he tried to get up, he slipped on the ice and his musket went off. So far that is what we should call the Establishment story. It is not disputed that after the first shot, the crowd charged and some of the soldiers panicked and fired. What happened next—as in most riots with political overtones—depends on the passion and the prejudice of whichever side you were on when you first heard about it. That, too, is history—not what happened, but what people convinced themselves *must* have happened.

Three civilians were killed and two, who later died, were wounded. One of them was a black, Crispus Attucks, who today has been resurrected as the first black hero of the United States. Bystanders made sketches, and the next day depositions were dictated to lawyers by every sort of person eager to put the only true account in the record. This so-called Boston Massacre was at once publicized in inflammatory broadsides and prints (the most famous, and also the most tendentious, was done by Paul Revere, the silversmith), which made sure that in time the echo of those first shots would ring all the way down to the Carolinas. The next night an indignation meeting was held in Boston's Old South Meeting House, a prime example of one of the most original and durable of New England colonial institutions: the church considered not only as a place of worship but as a court of law and a social center and the very hub of political life. Here more than a thousand aroused people stayed most of the night until the Governor agreed to withdraw the British soldiers to their barracks. This meeting house is the place, if there is any such, where

BOSTON, March 12, 1770.

THE Town of Boſton affords a recent and
melancholy Demonſtration of the deſtructive Conſequences of quartering Troops
among Citizens in a Time of Peace, under a Pretence of ſupporting the Laws
and aiding Civil Authority; every conſiderate and
unprejudic'd Perſon among us was deeply impreſt
with the Apprehenſion of theſe Conſequences
when it was known that a Number of Regiments
were ordered to this Town under ſuch a Pretext,
but in Reality to inforce oppreſſive Meaſures; to
awe and controul the legiſlative as well as executive Power of the Province, and to quell a Spirit
of Liberty, which however it may have been baſely oppos'd and even ridicul'd by ſome, would do
Honor to any Age or Country. A few Perſons
amongſt us had determin'd to uſe all their Influence to procure ſo deſtructive a Meaſure with a
View to their ſecurely enjoying the Profits of an
American Revenue, and unhapply both for Britain and this country they found Means to effect it.

It is to Governor Bernard, the Commiſſioners,
their Confidents and Coadjutors, that we are indebted as the procuring Cauſe of a military Power
in this Capital—The Boſton Journal of Occurrences, as printed in Mr. Holt's York Gazette,
from Time to Time, afforded many ſtriking Inſtances of the Diſtreſſes brought upon the Inhabitants by this Meaſure; and ſince thoſe Journals
have been diſcontinued, our Troubles from that
Quarter have been growing upon us: We have
known a Party of Soldiers in the face of Day fire
off a loaden Muſket upon the Inhabitants, others
have been prick'd with their Bayonets, and even
our Magiſtrates aſſaulted and put in Danger of
their Lives, when Offenders brought before them
have been reſcued; and why thoſe and other bold
and baſe Criminals have as yet eſcaped the Puniſhment due to their Crimes, may be ſoon Matter
of Enquiry by the Repreſentative Body of this
People—It is natural to ſuppoſe that when the
Inhabitants of this Town ſaw thoſe Laws which
had been enacted for their Security, and which
they were ambitious of holding up to theSoldiery,
eluded, they ſhould more commonly reſent for
themſelves—and accordingly it has ſo happened;
many have been the Squabbles between them and
the Soldiery; and it ſeems their being often worſted by our Youth in thoſe Rencounters, has only
ſerv'd to irritate the former—What paſſed at Mr.
Gray's Rope-walk, has already been given the
Public, and may be ſaid to have led the Way to
the late Cataſtrophe—That the Rope-walk Lads
when attacked by ſuperior Numbers ſhould defend
themſelves with ſo much Spirit and Succeſs in the
Club-way, was too mortifying, and perhaps it
may hereafter appear, that even ſome of thoſe Officers were unhappily affected with this Circumſtance: Divers Stories were propagated among
the Soldiery, that ſerv'd to agitate their Spirits;
particularly on the Sabbath, that one Chambers,
a Serjeant, repreſented as a ſober Man, had been
miſſing the preceeding Day, and muſt therefore
have been murdered by the Townſmen; an Officer of Diſtinction ſo far credited this Report, that
he enter'd Mr. Gray's Rope-walk that Sabbath;
and when required of by that Gentleman as ſoon
as he could meet him, theOccaſion of his ſo doing,
the Officer reply'd, that it was to look if the Serjeant ſaid to be murdered had not been hid there;
this ſober Serjeant was found on the Monday
unhurt, in a Houſe of Pleaſure—The Evidences
already collected ſhew, that many Threatnings
had been thrown out by the Soldiery, but we do
not pretend to ſay that there was any preconcerted Plan, when the Evidences are publiſhed, the
World will judge—We may however venture to
declare, that it appears too probable from their
Conduct, that ſome of the Soldiery aimed to draw
and provoke the Townſmen into Squabbles, and
that they then intended to make Uſe of other
Weapons than Canes, Clubs or Bludgeons.

Our Readers will doubtleſs expect a circumſtantial Account of the tragical Affair on Monday
Night laſt; but we hope they will excuſe our being ſo particular as we ſhould have been, had we
not ſeen that the Town was intending an Enquiry
and full Repreſentation thereof.

On the Evening of Monday, being the 5th Current, ſeveral Soldiers of the 29th Regiment were
ſeen parading the Streets with their drawn Cutlaſſes and Bayonets, abuſing and wounding Numbers of the Inhabitants.

A few minutes after nine o'clock, four youths,
named Edward Archbald, William Merchant,
Francis Archbald, and John Leech, jun. came
down Cornhill together, and ſeperating at Doctor
Loring's corner, the two former were paſſing the
narrow alley leading to Murray's barrack, in
which was a ſoldier brandiſhing a broad ſword of
an uncommon ſize againſt the walls out of which
he ſtruck fire plentifully. A perſon of a mean countenance armed with a large cudgel bore him company. Edward Archbald admoniſhed Mr. Merchant to take care of the ſword, on which the ſoldier turned round and ſtruckArchbald on the arm,
then puſhed at Merchant and pierced thro' his
cloaths inſide the arm cloſe to the arm-pit and
grazed the ſkin. Merchant then ſtruck the ſoldier
with a ſhort ſtick he had, and the other Perſon ran
to the barrack and bro't with him two ſoldiers,
one armed with a pair of tongs the other with a
ſhovel; he with the tongs purſued Archbald back
thro' the alley, collar'd and ſaid him over the head
with the tongs. The noiſe bro't people together,
and John Hicks, a young lad, coming up, knock'd
the ſoldier down, but let him get up again; and
more lads gathering, drove them back to the barrack, where the boys ſtood ſome time as it were to
keep them in. In leſs than a minute 10 or 12 of
them came out with drawn cutlaſſes, clubs & bayonets, and ſet upon the unarmed boys and young
folks, who ſtood them a little while, but finding the
inequality of their equipment diſperſed—On hearing the noiſe, one Samuel Atwood came up to ſee
what was the matter, and entering the alley from
dock-ſquare, heard the latter part of the combat,
and when the boys had diſperſed he met the 10 or
12 ſoldiers aforeſaid ruſhing down the alley towards
the ſquare, and aſked them if they intended tomurder people? They anſwered Yes, by G—d, root
and branch! With that one of them ſtruck Mr.
Atwood with a club, which was repeated by another; and being unarmed he turned to go off, and
received a wound on the left ſhoulder which

reached the bone and gave him much pain. Retreating a few ſteps, Mr. Atwood met two officers and ſaid, Gentlemen, what is the matter ? They
anſwered, you'll ſee by and by. Immediately after,
thoſe heroes appeared in the ſquare, aſking where
were the boogers? where were the cowards? But
notwithſtanding their fierceneſs to naked men, one
of them advanced towards a youth who had a ſplit
of a raw ſtave in his hand, and ſaid damn them
here is one of them; but the young man ſeeing a
perſon near him with a drawn ſword and good cane
ready to ſupport him, held up his ſtave in defiance,
and they quietly paſſed by him up the little alley
by Mr. Silſby's to King-ſtreet, where they attacked
ſingle and unarmed perſons till they raiſed much
clamor, and then turned down Cornhill ſtreet, inſulting all they met in like manner, and purſuing
ſome to their very doors. Thirty or forty perſons
moſtly lads, being by this means gathered in King
ſtreet, Capt. Preſton, with a party of men with
charged bayonets, came from the main guard to
the commiſſioners houſe, the ſoldiers puſhing their
bayonets, crying, Make way ! They took place by
the cuſtom-houſe, and continuing to puſh to drive
the people off, pricked ſome in ſeveral places; on
which they were clamorous, and, it is ſaid, threw
ſnow-balls. On this, the Captain commanded
them to fire, and more ſnow-balls coming, he
again ſaid, Damn you, Fire, be the conſequence
what it will ! One ſoldier then fired, and a townſman with a cudgel ſtruck him over the hands
with ſuch force that he dropt his firelock; and
ruſhing forward aimed a blow at the Captain's
head, which graz'd his hat and fell pretty heavy
upon his arm: However, the ſoldiers continued
the fire, ſucceſſively, till 7 or 8, or as ſome ſay 11
guns were diſcharged.

By this fatal manœuvre, three men were laid
dead on the ſpot, and two more ſtruggling for life;
but what ſhewed a degree of cruelty unknown to
Britiſh troops, at leaſt ſince the houſe of Hanover
has directed their operations, was an attempt to
fire upon or puſh with their bayonets the perſons
who undertook to remove the ſlain and wounded !

Mr. Benjamin Leigh, now undertaker in the
Delph Manufactory, came up, and after ſome converſation with Capt. Preſton, relative to his conduct in this affair, adviſed him to draw off his men,
with which he complied.

The dead are Mr. Samuel Gray, killed on the
ſpot, the ball entering his head and beating off a
large portion of his ſkull.

A mulatto man, named Criſpus Attucks, who
was born in Framingham, but lately belonged to
New-Providence, and was here in order to go for
North-Carolina, alſo killed inſtantly; two balls
entering his breaſt, one of them in ſpecial goring
the right lobe of the lungs, and a great part of the
liver moſt horribly.

Mr. James Caldwell, mate of Capt. Morton's
veſſel, in like manner killed by two balls entering
his back.

Mr. Samuel Maverick, a promiſing youth of 17
years of age, ſon of the Widow Maverick, and an
apprentice to Mr. Greenwood, Ivory-Turner, mortally wounded, a ball went through his belly, and
was cut out at his back ! He died the next morning.

A lad named Chriſtopher Monk, about 17 years
of age, an apprentice to Mr. Walker, Shipwright;
wounded, a ball entered his back about 4 inches
above the left kidney, near the ſpine, and was cut
out of the breaſt on the ſame ſide; apprehended
he will die.

A lad named John Clark, about 17 years of age,
whoſe parents live at Medford, and an apprentice
to Capt. Samuel Howard of this town ; wounded,
a ball entered juſt above his groin and came out at
his hip, on the oppoſite ſide, apprehended he will
die.

Mr. Edward Payne, of this town, Merchant,
ſtanding at his entry-door, received a ball in his
arm, ſhattered ſome of the bones.

Mr. John Green, Taylor, coming up Leverett's
Lane, received a ball juſt under his hip, and lodged
in the under part of his thigh, which was extracted.

Mr. Robert Patterſon, a ſeafaring man, who was
the perſon that had his trowſers ſhot through in
Richardſon's affair, wounded ; a ball went thro'
his right arm, and he ſuffered great loſs of blood.

Mr. Patrick Carr, about 30 years of age, who
work'd with Mr. Field, Leather-Breeches-maker
in Queen-ſtreet, wounded, a ball entered near the
hip and went out at his ſide.

A lad named David Parker, an apprentice to
Mr. Eddy the Wheelwright, wounded, a ball entered in his thigh.

The People were immediately alarmed with the
Report of this horrid Maſſacre, the Bells were ſet
a Ringing, and great Numbers ſoon aſſembled at
the Place where this tragical Scene had been acted ; their Feelings may be better conceived than
expreſs'd; and while ſome were taking Care of
the Dead and Wounded, the Reſt were in Conſultation what to do in thoſe dreadful Circumſtances.—But ſo little intimidated where they, notwithſtanding their being within a few Yards of the
Main-Guard, and ſeeing the 29th Regiment under
Arms, and drawn up in King-ſtreet ; that they
kept their Station and appear'd as an Officer of
Rank expreſs'd it ready to run upon the very Muzzles of their Muskets. The Lieut. Governor ſoon
came into the Town-Houſe, and there met ſome of
his Majeſty's Council, and a Number of Civil Magiſtrates ; a conſiderable Body of the People immediately entered the Council Chamber, and expreſſed themſelves to his Honor with a Freedom
and Warmth becoming the occaſion. He uſed his
utmoſt Endeavours to pacify them, requeſting that
they would let the Matter ſubſide for the Night,
and promiſing to do all in his Power that Juſtice
ſhould be done, and the Law have its Courſe ;
Men of Influence and Weight with the People were
not wanting on their part to procure their Com-

pliance with his Honor's Requeſt by repreſenting
the horrible Conſequences of a promiſcuous ...
raſh Engagement in the Night, and alſo urging
that ſuch Meaſures ſhould be entered into ...
Morning as would be agreeable ... their ...
and a more likely way of obtaining the ...
tisfaction for the Blood of their Fellow-T...
—The Inhabitants attended to theſe Sc...
and the Regiment under Arms being ... to
their Barracks, which was inſiſted upon by the people, they then ſeparated and returned to their dwellings by One o'Clock, at 3 o'Clock Cap...
was committed, as were the Soldiers who ...
few Hours after him.

Tueſday Morning preſented a moſt ...
Scene, the Blood of our Fellow Citizens ...
like Water thro' King-Street, and the ...
Exchange the principal Spot of the M...
rade for about 18 Months paſt. Our Bl...
alſo be track'd up to the Head of Long-...
through divers other Streets and Paſſages ...

At eleven o'clock the Inhabitants met ...
il-Hall, and after ſome animated Speech...
ing the occaſion, they choſe a Commi...
reſpectab; Gentlemen to wait upon the ...
vernor in Council, to requeſt of him the ...
ders for the immediate removal of the ...

The Meſſage was in theſe Word...

THAT it is the unanimous opinion of ...
ing that the inhabitants and ſoldiery ...
... ... to ſafety that nothing ...
ſionally be expected to reſtore the peace ...
and prevent further blood and carnage, ...
mediate removal of the Troops ; and that ...
ſore moſt fervently pray his Honor that ...
and influence may be exerted for their ...
val.

His Honor's Reply, which was laid ...
Town then Adjourn'd to the Old So...
ing-Houſe, was as follows,

Gentlemen,

I AM extremely ſorry for the unhappy ...
between the inhabitants and troops, and ...
for the action of the laſt evening, and I ...
ed myſelf upon that occaſion that a due en...
be made, and that the law may have its ...
have in council conſulted with the comm...
cers of the two regiments who are in ...
They have their orders from the Genera...
York. It is not in my power to counter...
orders. The Council have deſired that the re...
giments may be removed to the Caſtle. ...
particular concern which the 29th regi... is
in your differences, Col. Dalrymple ... commanding officer of the troops has ſignified ... the regiment ſhall without delay be placed in the ...
the Caſtle until he can ſend to the Ge...
receive his further orders concerning tro...
ments, and that the main guard ſhall be ...
and the 14th regiment ſo diſpoſed and laid ...
reſtraint that all occaſion of future diſturbance ...
be prevented.

The Bloody Maſſacre perpetrated in King-Street BOSTON on March 5th 1770 by a party of the 29th
Regt.

Unhappy BOSTON! ſee thy Sons deplore,
Thy hallow'd Walks beſmear'd with guiltleſs Gore.
While faithleſs P——n and his ſavage Bands,
With murd'rous Rancour ſtretch their bloody Hands;
Like fierce Barbarians grinning o'er their Prey,
Approve the Carnage and enjoy the Day.

If ſcalding drops from Rage from Anguiſh Wrung,
If ſpeechleſs Sorrows lab'ring for a Tongue,
Or if a weeping World can ought appeaſe
The plaintive Ghoſts of Victims ſuch as theſe;
The Patriot's copious Tears for each are ſhed,
A glorious Tribute which embalms the Dead.

But know, FATE ſummons to that aw...
where JUSTICE ſtrips the Murd'rer of ...
Should venal C——ts the ſcandal of ...
Snatch the relentleſs Villain from h...
Keen Execrations on this Plate inſ...
Shall reach a JUDGE who never ca...

Engrav'd Printed & Sold by PAUL REVERE BOSTON

The unhappy Sufferers were Meſſrs. Saml. Gray, Saml. Maverick, Jams. Caldwell, Criſpus Attucks & ...
Killed. Six wounded; two of them (Chriſtr. Monk & John Clark) Mortally

BUTCHER'S HALL

tte, of March 12, 1770.

going Reply having been read and f...
the question was put, Whether the...
...factory? Passed in the Negative. Only...
out of upwards of ...rs.
n moved & v...d that John Hancock,
amuel A...s, Mr. William Molineux,
...ps, ... Dr. Joseph Warren, Jo-
w, Efq; and Samuel Pemberton, Efq;
ttee to wait on his Honour the Lieut.
nd inform him, that it is the unani-
m of this Meeting, that the Reply made
the Inhabitants presented his Honor
ing, is by no means fatisfactory; and
less will fatisfy, than a total and im-
oval of all the Troops.
mittee having waited upon the Lieut.
greeable to the foregoing Vote; laid be
abitants the following Vote of Council
m his Honor.

r the Lieut. Governor laid before the
...e of the Town of Bofton, paffed this
and then addreffed the Board as follows.
...men of the Council,
efore you a Vote of the Town of Bof-
I have juft now received from them,
...se your Advice what you had ge...
Iffue upon it.

ncil thereupon expreffed themfelves to
...ly of opinion, "that it was abfolutely
his Majefty's ferv..., the good order
n, and the Peace of the Province, that
fhould be immediately removed out of
f Bofton, and thereupon advifed hi.
mmunicate this Advice of the Council
ymple, and to pray that he would or-
oops down to Caftle-William." The
alfo informed the Town, that Col. Dal-
r having feen the Vote of Council, faid
mittee, "That he now gave his word
at he would begin his Preparations in
g, and that there fhould be no unne-
until the whole of the two Regiments
ed to the Caftle."

above Report being read, the Inhabi-
not avoid expreffing the high Satisfac-
ded them.

afures were taken for the Security of
in the Night by a ftrong Military
Meeting was Diffolved.

h Regiment have already left us, and
egiment are following them, fo that we
Town will foon be clear of all the
The Wifdom and true Policy of his
Council and Col. Dalrymple the Com-
pear in this Meafure. Two Regiments
t of this populous City; and the Inha-
ly incenfed: Thofe of the neighbour-
actually under Arms upon the firft Re
Maffacre, and the Signal only wanting
a few Hours to the Gates of this City
oufands of our brave Brethren, and
eeply affected with our Diftreffes, and
ve are greatly obliged on this Occafion
nows where this would have ended, and
rtant Confequences even to the whole
pire might have followed, which our
and Loyalty upon fo trying an Occa-
ur Faith in the Commander's Affurances
ly prevented.

urfday, agreeable to a general Requeft
abitants, and by the Confent of Parents
s, were carried to their Grave in Suc-
Bodies of Samuel Gray, Samuel Ma-
...nes Caldwell, and Crifpus Attucks, the
Victims who fell in the bloody Maffacre
nday Evening preceeding!

Occasion moft of the Shops in Town were
he Bells were ordered to toll a folemn
were alfo thofe in the neighboring Towns
town, Roxbury, &c. The Proceffion be-
ve between the Hours of 4 and 5 in the
; two of the unfortunate Sufferers, viz.
...nes Caldwell and Crifpus Attucks, who
agers, borne from Faneuil-Hall, attend-
...merous Train of Perfons of all Ranks;
hel two, viz. Mr. Samuel Gray, from
of Benjamin Gray, (his Brother) on the
he Exchange, and Mr. Maverick, from
of his diftreffed Mother Mrs. Mary Ma-
Union-Street, each followed by their ref-
lations and Friends: The feveral Hear-
g a junction in King-Street, the Theatre
nman Tragedy, proceeded from thence
Main-Street, lengthened by an immenfe
e of People, ...h croud as to be obliged
in Ranks of fix, and brought up by a
n of Carriages belonging to the principal
f the Town. The bodies were depofited
ault in the middle Burying-ground: The
d Circumftances of their Death, the Dif
Sorrow vifible in every Countenance, to-
th the peculiar Solemnity with which the
neral was conducted, furpafs Defcription.

BOSTON, March 19.
Laft Wednefday Night died, Patrick Carr, an Inhabitant of this Town,
of the Wound he received in King-
Street on the bloody and execrable
Night of the 5th Inftant—He had
juft before left his Home, and upon
his coming into the Street received
the fatal Ball in his Hip which paffed
out at the oppofite Side; this is the
fifth Life that has been facrificed by
the Rage of the Soldiery, but it is
feared it will not be the laft, as feveral
dangeroufly languifhing of their Wounds.
...ins were attended on Saturday laft from
...all, by a numerous and refpectable Train
...ers, to the fame Grave, in which thofe
...g the fame Hands of Violence were in-
...laft Week.

The broadside was a favorite form of political propaganda on both sides of the Atlantic before and during the American Revolution. At left, a vigorously stated account of the Boston Massacre; above, a cartoon sold in London showing that not all British opinion favored the government policy of stern measures against the colonies.

the Revolution was conceived. For here was formed a radical underground to advertise the injustices, the latest tax, the latest misbehavior of the British soldiers or customs agents. The Old South Meeting House became so notorious as a cradle of sedition that one night, when the British heard there was to be a protest meeting, they packed the place with soldiers, and the speaker, one Joseph Warren, was forced to climb in through the window over the pulpit. It is still known as Warren's Window.

One thing must be clear by now: a revolutionary chain does not forge itself. It has to be secured by a conspiracy. The propaganda links between the colonial activists were established by what were called the Committees of Correspondence. These were inspired by James Otis, a Whig lawyer, Latin scholar, and customs agent of the British government who resigned to argue—in the Old South Meeting House—the people's case against the right of the British to search houses for smuggled goods without a writ. Otis was the first and certainly the most intellectual of the fathers of the Revolution. He was denounced in Parliament and also praised there, by Edmund Burke, for the "sagacity and force" of his arguments. He evidently had an effective apocalyptic manner; he came in his later years to pray that he might die in some swift and dramatic way. He had his wish. In his late fifties he was struck dead by a bolt of lightning.

The actual founder of the Colonial underground, and Otis's disciple, was Samuel Adams, a second cousin of John Adams, a florid and artful type. Tough, tender, and wily, he used to rough up his appearance and wear threadbare clothes on public occasions to show his bond with the common people. He had a genuine bond in the homely figures of his rhetoric: "A colonist cannot make a button, a horseshoe nor a hobnail but some sooty ironmonger or respectable button-maker of Britain shall bawl and squall that his honor's worship is most egregiously maltreated, injured, cheated and robbed by the rascally American republicans." Such Shavian snippets as these were circulated first in Massachusetts and then on into New York and in time through the South. Sam Adams was a genuine rabble-rouser, and the first man to urge what London was bound to consider a treasonable act—the calling of a Continental Congress of all the rebel colonies.

Among all the subsequent humiliations, there were two that most effectively rallied American popular indignation. They came as punishment for a one-night escapade in Boston harbor that has ever since been considered merely the most impudent example of colonial protest. It was that party, organized by Sam Adams, in which fifty men fussed out with feathers, their bodies and faces smeared with red ocher to resemble Indians, went down to the harbor and threw overboard a shipment of over three hundred chests of East India Company tea on which Lord North had mulishly required threepence a pound tax. There were less theatrical protests elsewhere: in Charleston, they let the stuff rot on the wharves, and from Philadelphia and New York they sent back full cargoes.

London sprang like a baited headmaster into a rage of retaliatory moves. The most fateful, I think, were the closing of the port of Boston to all commerce (imagine the port of London being closed by order of the United States Congress!) and the dispatch to Boston of four British regiments as a permanent garrison to serve under the command of a veteran of the French and Indian Wars, General Thomas Gage, who was also appointed Governor of Massachusetts. The second move was a fatal error. Taxes might outrage a man but they do not wound his manhood. What probably made the colonies feel most acutely that they were delinquents and outcasts from England was the sight on the streets—not unlike the appearance on a college campus of the National Guard—of whole companies of British soldiers. Gage was a soldier who knew only military discipline, but, when he was ordered to quarter troops in private houses and set up tents in parks and gardens, he said, "It is a great folly, which I fear the people will resist to the death, and soon." He was thinking of the people of Boston. If he had known how the South had been outraged by the closing of the Boston port, or guessed the strength and spread of the radical underground, he would have meant nothing less than the "American" people.

For the Committees of Correspondence ran over all those hundreds of miles of rutted roads down to South Carolina. The Southern end of the radical axis was over five hundred miles, and a whole culture, away from Boston. It was in Williamsburg, the capital of Virginia, one of the few Southern cities and much the most elegant. Twice a year, when the courts sat, the tobacco planters rode into Williamsburg to stay in their town houses. These periodic invaders included landholders as majestic as Lord Fairfax, the owner of five million acres, and small freeholders from the tidewater country. The Virginia planters, as we've seen, lived by land, and they, too, had a genuine grievance in being taxed by London not only on their land but on all the crops they shipped abroad. As everybody knows who has ever quarreled with a business partner or started a divorce action, one real grievance sprouts a host of fancies, and soon the planters were blaming London for their high cost of living. They lived high, no question; not perhaps as high as the Royal Governor (so highly esteemed, by the way, that throughout the Revolution his statue was regularly and meticulously cleaned as tribute to a nice man on the wrong side). But he set the style, and they increasingly complained that they were in hock to London for their carriages, their wines, their furniture, such beautiful baubles as still stand in the restored Governor's Mansion: candelabra from London; a handmade clock from Glasgow; a harpsichord made of walnut light as honey (London, 1762); wallpaper from Canton, which had to be shipped to London first and then, after a middleman's cut, on to Virginia. One way and another the planters were—by the 1770s—in debt to London to the tune of £2,000,000, twenty times the amount of money in circulation in Virginia at that time.

But the capital city was a hotbed of resistance for larger and more idealistic reasons. It is not surprising that in the more clubbable, less theological South, the cradle of sedition should have been not a church but a tavern, named after Sir Walter Raleigh. You could call it the Old South Meeting House of the Old South. It was there that the Virginians formed their Committee of Correspondence, there that they created the colonies' radical network—the Intercolonial Committees—and there that two men, more than any others, pushed the Virginians toward an open break with Britain.

One of these men was Thomas Jefferson, a young country squire living off the nineteen hundred acres his father had left him, a lawyer who distrusted lawyers and abandoned what he called "a talkative and dubious trade," a godly man who yet distrusted the clergy in politics. He had himself gone into politics in his twenties, when the troubles were first breaking out, as a member of the House of Burgesses. When dissent threatened sedition, and the Governor dissolved the House as an "insubordinate body," Jefferson and eighty-eight others went to the Raleigh Tavern and signed a pact not to import any slaves or wines or any British manufactures. The last straw for the Virginians was the day riders came clattering in with the news that Parliament had closed the port of Boston, and that Boston had suspended all trade with Britain. It was the Virginia rebels who had the nerve to proclaim themselves the first Provincial Convention, which amounted to declaring the first revolutionary legislature.

The Virginians needed and found their own breast-beater, their Sam Adams. Jefferson was not the type. A scholar, a rather wispy redhead and a meditative man, he detested what he called "the morbid rage of debate." But there was another man who lived by it: Patrick Henry, half Scotch, half Welsh (a formidable merger in itself), a people's lawyer with a smoldering eye, a querulous voice, and a marvelous gift of the gab. When he urged resistance to the Stamp Act, he roared—he must have sounded like something between John Knox and Aneurin Bevan—"Caesar had his Brutus, Charles the First his Cromwell, and George the Third—may profit by their example." On the verge of war, he proposed giving arms from a common arsenal to the Virginia militia, and, when somebody shouted that he was proposing a trade in death, he came through with another of his trumpet phrases: "I know not what course others may take but as for me, give me liberty or give me death!" (He lived to a fairly ripe old age.) He might have become known as the golden orator of Virginia but he had no national reputation until his biography was published, thirty years after the Revolution. Old John Adams was astonished to read about this newly concocted hero and said: "Well, if Henry was the Demosthenes of the Republic, then James Otis was its Moses and Isaiah."

Within a month of Virginia's proclaimed Convention, a Congress of the rebel colonists met in Philadelphia. The resort to arms was only a matter of weeks or days. Jefferson, speaking for the delegates, wrote: "Our cause is just, our union is perfect [sic] . . . if necessary, foreign assistance is undoubtedly available." (So it was. The French were to come in in the hope of reclaiming some of their empire; the Spanish, who theoretically owned everything west of the Mississippi, hoped to own everything east as far as the Appalachians.)

The first clash came at Concord, Massachusetts, a village beyond the Charles River west of Boston. The first "Provincial Congress of Massachusetts" had met there in 1774, making it naturally suspect as a storehouse for military supplies. In April 1775 General Gage heard that the farmers of Concord had taken to stockpiling firearms in secret. He sent out seven hundred British troops to destroy the stores. They had a brush with a company of rebels at Lexington and then went on to Concord, where a force ready to meet them found itself outnumbered and retired to wait for more men from the surrounding country. The British might well have made a brisk search and gone back to Boston. But they were under the command of a young officer, newly promoted and spoiling for blood. He kept his men waiting for hours till the reinforced farmers and "minutemen" (rebels sworn to be ready "at the minute") were too much for them and they started a slow retreat. Their rear guard was peppered all the way back, and by the time they reached Boston they were out of ammunition and, to the astonishment of Gage, shaken and demoralized. The account of this beating was lavished with much heroic detail by the rebels and fired the populace in many colonies with the inspiring thought that ordinary American farmers could put British regulars on the run.

This sad and muddled incident would surely not have been enough to create a heroic myth, but some of the expressions of it are memorable and moving. We should not forget that for quite a time the rebels thought of themselves as Englishmen abused, and in many engagements felt an uncomfortable sympathy for the other Englishmen who had been sent over to fight them. In Ridgefield, Connecticut, there is a plaque

sunk in the wall of a cemetery. It says: "In defense of American independence at the Battle of Ridgefield, April 27th, 1777, died Eight Patriots who were laid in this ground, Companioned by Sixteen British Soldiers, Living, their enemies, Dying, their guests."

The British arrived as a professional army expecting, with companies of German mercenaries, to fight European set battles. Not enough of them had learned, at first or second hand, the lessons of the French and Indian Wars. The Americans were at once too shrewd and too untrained to oblige them with an Old World war. First of all, as John Adams said, the colonial population divided up into one third that took to arms, one third that was either openly or secretly loyal to the British, and one third that didn't give a damn—not the best recipe for a disciplined national army. So against the army of British regulars there stood—besides some French volunteers, immensely valuable as professionals at the start—mainly a large, improvised force of farmers, mechanics, tradesmen, parsons, lawyers, grocers, hunters, trappers, con men, thieves, and hoodlums. "Never," their sorrowing commander was to lament when the going was bad, "such a rabble dignified by the name of army." How could they even hold off for six years, much less defeat, one of the crack armies of Europe?

For one thing, there was weaponry. The British for the most part used smooth-bore muskets that allowed a lateral error of three feet at a hundred yards range. The British infantryman was not trained to pick off single targets; he stood shoulder to shoulder with his fellows and they sprayed, shall we say, in the general direction of the enemy! The Americans had smooth-bore muskets, too, but as the war moved into the interior the British came up against the frontiersmen, who did not use guns for sport. Their very existence depended on shooting their food on the wing and saving their families by picking off Indians in night raids. They needed a weapon that was light and accurate and found it in the Pennsylvania flintlock, developed for them by German settlers in Pennsylvania who doubled the length of the barrel and grooved it to make the bullet spin and stay on line. (From this rifling of the barrel comes the word "rifle.")

This weapon did bloody damage to shoulder-to-shoulder infantry. A Pennsylvania Tory who had seen it at work wrote a letter to a London newspaper offering rather chill advice: "This province has raised a thousand riflemen, the worst of whom will put a rifle ball into a man's head at a hundred and fifty or two hundred yards. Therefore, advise your officers who shall hereafter come out to America to settle their affairs in England before their departure." This reputation for sharpshooting was magnified in England into a witch's curse, and there were some lively desertions among men drafted for service in the Colonies. It is, on the

A splendid radical orator and a true believer in the rights of man, Patrick Henry made his name and his fortune as a trial lawyer and a land speculator in his native Virginia.

109

whole, an all-too-true American myth: that legendary reputation for spotting the bull's eye which began with the embattled farmers and was sustained down the next century and a half by Wyatt Earp, Wild Bill Hickok, Annie Oakley, and Sergeant York. It is a romantic tradition that dies hard, and there is a lucrative industry in suggesting to sportsmen and country boys—and, unfortunately, to malcontents and psychotics also—that whether or not you are a fast man with a buck, you too can be a fast man on the draw.

A British commander sent home a short report that was read in the House of Commons. The gist of it was: "The Americans will not stand and fight." They were jack-in-the-box guerrillas who would fight like devils for a day and a night and then go home and harvest their crops on the weekend. They would return, not always in any discernible formation, and after a swift onslaught vanish into the country by night, and then again at some unpredictable time come whizzing in like hornets. What baffled and eventually broke the British was what broke the Roman armies in their late campaigns against the barbarians, and for so long frustrated the American army in Vietnam. Edward Gibbon said it in a single passage: "All things became adverse to the Romans . . . their armour heavy, the waters deep; nor could they wield, in that uneasy situation, their weighty javelins. The barbarians, on the contrary, were enured to encounters in the bogs." Or as William Pitt sadly commented, looking at his drawn battle-lines on an alien wilderness: "You cannot conquer a map."

There is a further, and less dramatic, explanation for the colonists' survival and victory. It was the consequence of one of the most perceptive deals in American history. When the war began it was fought for a time mainly in Massachusetts and the bordering North. It didn't take the men of Massachusetts long to know it and resent it. If it was to be a continental war, the South too would have to be visibly engaged. Virginia was rich and Massachusetts was chronically short of the money for arms and supplies (like the other colonies, it never managed to pay the soldiers for long). John Adams had the notion that if a continental commander could be appointed, and he was a Virginian, then the North and the South and the Middle Colonies would have a palpable, breathing symbol of a common cause. A good deal would depend, of course, on the chosen man. Adams used his great influence with the wartime Congress now formed, first to push the idea of a continental command and then to see that it went to the man of his choice.

He was that same officer who had heard "the bullets whistle" in the first brush of the French and Indian Wars: George Washington, the son of a father who had gone to school in England and had several large Virginia estates. Left fatherless at the age of eleven, the boy was shunted between two half brothers and picked up a little irregular schooling in the intervals of learning how to raise tobacco and stock and manage a plantation. He took to surveying in boyhood and decided that it was to be his profession, one that in those days sent a man roving for weeks on end, improvising his sleeping quarters, shooting wild turkey and chewing it on the bone. In the French and Indian Wars, he had suffered the horrors of Braddock's rout. He had horses shot from under him and went home to Virginia with a local reputation for being at all times unflappable. Then his health failed him, and he resigned his commission.

At the age of twenty-seven he married a very rich widow and settled on a majestic stretch of land, at Mount Vernon overlooking the Potomac. His wife had brought him the pleasant dowry of some profitable real estate, fifteen thousand acres near Williamsburg—what by today's exchange would be about a quarter of a million dollars—and one hundred and fifty slaves, whose condition, he confessed, embarrassed him. But he was an eighteenth-century man, and "emancipation" was a remote and strange doctrine. He assumed he would live out his days as a rich Virginia planter, but then, at the age of forty-three, he received the call.

I suspect most Americans would today be put off by his air of a prosperous landowner and real-estate operator in the guise of a rather down-the-nose British colonel. His most idolatrous biographers have been unable to find much evidence of charm, or even jollity, in him. He was imperious, massively self-sufficient, and he had decided ideas about the relations of rank and rank, class and class. He did not, for instance, like to be touched, and when he became the first President he laid down a rule that people coming to see him should remain standing in his presence. He arrived for his inauguration with a flourish of outriders and he shook no hands. Thomas Jefferson was greatly offended by the color and pomp of this ceremony and thought it "not at all in character with the simplicity of republican governments, and looking—as if wishfully —to those of European courts." As he took the oath, a bystanding Senator whispered to his neighbor: "I fear we may have exchanged George the Third for George the First."

Yet there were several things about him that made him the unquestioned leader of the new nation. A pervasive sense of responsibility, an unflagging impression of shrewd judgment, and total integrity. It can best be summed up in what the drama critics call "presence." But it was nothing rehearsed. It was the presence of nothing but character.

The war was only eighteen months old when it seemed that all was lost. The British captured Philadelphia, and many of the Congress took to the

---

Overleaf: *Beneath a lurid sky, American troops engage the British at Princeton, New Jersey, on January 3, 1777. After an initial reverse, Washington won the battle.*

mountains. They were a frightened and divided body of men—divided between genuine revolutionaries and sunshine patriots, between dedicated colonial statesmen and secret Loyalists, and a clutter of money grubbers selling arms or commissions, or merchants whose anxious interest was to see that Spain got the lands beyond the Appalachians so that trade would not go West. The word got to a delirious London that Washington was trapped in a frigid valley, and that the war was over. The first part was correct—but not the second.

In the bleakest winter, of 1777–1778, Washington was camped in Valley Forge, about twenty miles northwest of Philadelphia. He picked it for obvious military advantages. It lay between a creek and a broad river, and the hills were high enough to survey the main supply routes from the South into New England and the roads from Philadelphia that led to the gunneries and powder mills of the interior. He refused to go inland and leave the fertile Pennsylvania farming country as a granary for the enemy. He refused also to commandeer the villages, which hadn't enough food for the swarms of refugees from Philadelphia. So he chose this bare place, and his eleven thousand men built their tents with timber from the neighboring woods.

In the beginning life was bearable, even agreeable. The men were snug in their new huts, the generalissimo moved into a solid farmhouse. Mrs. Washington came to stay, so did some of the officers' wives. There were cheerful dinner parties and no lack of food and wine. But the party was short-lived. The winter snows came early, and by January there were oceans of mud. Congress wouldn't, or couldn't, commission supplies and told Washington to plunder the nearest farmers, which he refused to do. When the main stores ran low, the men started to forage for hickory nuts and the more edible local fauna. By March—when the countryside was blasted by blizzards—a third of them were down with typhus or smallpox and, of course, dysentery. Medical services barely existed, and the besieged army began to thin out alarmingly, if not from disease and actual starvation, then from desertion. Half of the living had neither shoes nor shirts. In the end, Washington was left with something over three thousand men, technically able-bodied, actually half starving.

To this implacable man the ordeal was grim but quite simple. Being an eighteenth-century gentleman-soldier with a puritan core meant that when the chips were down all the agreeable things of life—parties, good food, comfort, professional dignity—were baubles. The winds whistled and the food gave out and the fields stank with death and disease, and Washington's life simplified itself into one hard principle—duty. He had given his word that he would hold on with his army, however sick and bedraggled it might be, and he proceeded to do so. The spring came in and epidemic sickness flourished. But then the French formally entered

Probably the least-known life portrait of George Washington, this heroic painting by John Trumbull shows the general at Verplanck's Point on the Hudson in 1782. Finished in 1790, it was based on sketches Trumbull made on the scene earlier.

the war and poured in men, money, arms, and supplies. They lined up with Washington's ragged survivors and, to put it simply, the Revolution held. It was not won for another four years, and the third year was the darkest of all—but the obdurate, placid commander stuck it out.

When he died he was not yet a legend. To many of the revolutionary leaders the memory of him was of a man indomitable in war. But to others, to some of the governors, and the press, he was insufferable in peace: for signing a treaty that called for payment of all pre-revolutionary debts; for confirming the restrictions on New England's trade with the West Indies; for silencing his enemies in the press with public prosecutions; and for many other real and fancied iniquities. And when he left the Presidency the Philadelphia *Aurora* editorialized: "If ever there was a period for rejoicing, it is this moment."

But by now Washington towers over the generations of notable Americans as Shakespeare towers over the literature of England. About every thirty years some debunker starts to chip away at this monolith. He is rumored to have padded his army expense accounts. He is suddenly redrawn as "a promoter of stock companies, a land-grabber, an exploiter of mines and timber." However, as Calvin Coolidge once said, wheeling his chair around and looking up at the Washington Monument: "He's still there." So he is.

When the war was won, there must have been a deal of guilt in the fawning respect that important men, Congressmen in particular, showed toward him in public. They had quit and he had stayed. Perhaps only another soldier, and that the greatest, could truly gauge the fortitude it took to weather the military extremity of the bad years. At any rate, when Washington died and the word got to Europe, Napoleon himself was seen to bow his head. In the English Channel, the British fleet fired a salute of twenty guns.

The soldier-hero might rally the warriors and the patriotic third of the populace. But General Washington alone could not have sustained the morale of the embattled colonies had there not been also the powerful inspiration of other men, of two in particular, in maintaining the fiction of a new nation before the fact and in uniting behind it the educated classes, the merchants, the wobbling Congress, and other influential noncombatants.

Nothing kept alive the idealistic appeal of the Revolution more than the Declaration of Independence, the document that, at the beginning of the war, formally renounced the colonists' allegiance to the Crown and Parliament of England. And no other civilian in the country gave to that document a more steady or respectable authority than a Philadelphian, seventy years of age, who was rightly known as the Patriarch of the

Revolution. He was Benjamin Franklin, the fine flower of that "ingenious and useful" learning that so impressed foreigners visiting the Middle Colonies.

He was the son of a dyer from Banbury who had emigrated to Boston with three children. His wife died of her seventh child, and he married again and begat ten more children, the last of whom was our man. The small house of a soap boiler with thirteen children rattling around in it was a foolproof test of survival and young Ben survived without a second thought, tootling on a whistle among a swarm of children, one of whom was bound to die—and did—from congestion—"in a tub of suds." It never occurred to the youngest boy that his bawling home was an uncongenial cradle for a scholar. He enjoyed it thoroughly, talked with his father about the Deists, copied essays from *The Spectator.* At fifteen, under the influence of the freethinkers, he was printing a newspaper that took frequent slaps at Puritanism and its divines. At seventeen, he left Boston for Philadelphia to become his own man and set up his own printing shop. Printing was not then a humble trade. The printer was publisher, television network president, and government information officer; and, if he dared to risk violating his government license, he might be also the radical propagandist, because he was the man who owned the only means whereby people could be persuaded whether they were well or badly governed.

But this learned man was also the one whose learning was "the most ingenious and useful." More than any other in the long history of the colonists, he is the one most often instinctively recalled on many daily occasions of American life. A siren whines up Third Avenue in New York: Franklin organized the first volunteer fire brigade. The New York Public Library announces a microfilm room: he founded the first free public library. The middle-aged man who finds himself looking up from the newspaper to refocus on his wife is told by his oculist it is time for bifocals: Franklin was the first to wear them. The northeast wind drenching down from Maine: Franklin first spotted it as the characteristic storm signal for the North Atlantic seaboard. The latest heating system boasts it is an intelligent, inevitable development of the Franklin stove.

In an age of specialists, when the engineer thinks that Greek is fit only for doctors, and humanists shudder at computer programming, it takes a positive effort of good will to credit the seriousness of such a man, hopping from a meeting of the Philosophical Society he had started, or a tax debate in the Pennsylvania Assembly, to ponder the behavior of the electric kite and be led to invent the lightning rod, or to urge the reorganization of the colonial post office; then to parley with the Indians for their help against the French, to lay down the laws of a concise and elegant prose style; to descend on London to argue before the House of

Retreating toward Valley Forge in the autumn of 1777, Washington made an abortive attack on the main British camp at Germantown (above). Later, in a night-time skirmish at Paoli (right), British troops surprised the sleeping Continentals.

Commons for the repeal of the Stamp Act; next day to sail for France to run up for the King a report on Mesmer and animal magnetism; that night to write a love letter to Madame Helvetius. The mold has been lost of this American eighteenth-century archetype, the domesticated and urbane Leonardo da Vinci who finds no knowledge odd, the very opposite of a highbrow or trendy intellectual, for he was a man with the widest range of interests who had no preconceived hierarchy of their relative value.

He had one heavy quality. With systematic piety, he ticked off, on a specially prepared calendar, the virtues he would practice on assigned days of the week. Luckily, however, he was a happy hypocrite and his good intentions were cheerfully defeated by the pricking of the flesh. He might talk up the value of abstemiousness, but he advised all young sons to take old women for mistresses because "they are more discreet ... and so grateful."

He was so much the most familiar American in England that the cagey Staffordshire potters got out a statuette of him and sold it under three titles: B. Franklin, G. Washington (nobody knew what *he* looked like), and Old English Country Gentleman.

What makes him, after two centuries, not merely impressive but lovable is his absolute lack of arrogance and the steady goodness of his belief that in helping to create the American Republic he was founding a truer order of society. Once, when he came home, he opened a package and found that his wife had ordered some silver knives from London. He retired to his journal and sighed: "Alas, it is by luxury and the vanity of women that empires decay."

The other invaluable ideologue of the Revolution, almost forty years Franklin's junior, was Thomas Jefferson, that thirty-three-year-old Virginia lawyer-squire who was in the main responsible for writing the birth certificate of the United States of America, the Declaration of Independence.

It was worked out in Philadelphia by a committee of five, in a stuffy room over a stable plagued by horseflies, in the hot early summer of 1776, and adopted, in all its clauses except two, by a vote of twelve of the colonies now become states (New York waited awhile). The new "Congress," like most revolutionary governments, preferred to blame the rulers of the parent country and not its people, and a brave denunciation of slavery was deleted at the insistence of Southern owners and Northern shippers. It was published "to a candid world" on July 2 but dated on July 4. The signatures—fifty-six in all—came later.

The first signature, which is almost as large as that of a motion picture star, is that of a man from Massachusetts, John Hancock, who escaped capture by the British in the first battle of the War of Independence and then had his ship confiscated and burned. He wrote his signature in such a way, he said, that "the King of England can read it without his glasses." This whimsical act alone made him immortal, for an American handing out a contract for signature is apt to ask for "your John Hancock." After Hancock, the Declaration was signed by four of the five who drafted it (the fifth—Robert Livingston, an imposing owner of iron mines, being absent in New York): Franklin; John Adams, a Massachusetts lawyer who was to become the second President of the United States; the thirty-three-year-old Thomas Jefferson, who wrote out the final draft; and Roger Sherman of Connecticut, a lawyer who had started out as an apprentice shoemaker and whose habit of picking his teeth during the drafting sessions so provoked Franklin that he threatened the retaliation of "playing my harmonica."

Let us glance at some of the other revolutionaries who signed then or later. Philip Livingston, a New York merchant who organized the ban on importing British goods and who was in private "a breaker of hearts." Thomas Nelson, a Virginia planter, who gave the order to his own soldiers to blow up his splendid house as the British commander approached to occupy it. Charles Carroll of Maryland, an Irish-American Catholic squire, lawyer, and businessman who had the foresight to invest early on in such novelties as canal companies and railroads; he outlived all the other signers and died, at the age of ninety-five, the wealthiest man in America. Benjamin Rush, a Pennsylvania doctor, eminent in America and Europe as the pioneer of what we call psychiatry. John Witherspoon, a Scottish clergyman immigrant, the first president of what is today Princeton University, who was more American than the Americans except in his almost fanatical loathing of what he was the first man to dub "Americanisms." William Floyd, a New York landowner, whose house and extensive grounds are now the site of a nuclear research station; he was immortalized rather late in life—in death—by a motor expressway named after him on Long Island. And Jefferson's teacher and idol, George Wythe, the most eminent professor of law in the colonies, a rich man who died a little before his time had come (he was said to have been poisoned by his nephew, later charitably described as "an impatient heir"). The rest of the signers were a variety of lawyers, shippers, merchants, planters, who would not strike us today as revolutionary types.

But then, in the late eighteenth century, the idea of revolution itself was quite new, and neither its forms nor its practitioners could be recognized on sight. It was hardly possible for enlightened men in England, the heirs of a confident philosophy of universal order, to grasp the new shapes of society fashioned by "the American, this new man" or to feel the imminence of a radical break with their own forms of government. Alexander Pope had crystallized the general prejudice about government in a droll couplet: "For *forms* of government let fools contest, Whate'er is best *administered* is best." Like the Republicans of the early 1930s contemplating the ruins of the Coolidge-Hoover prosperity, the English felt that something must have gone wrong with "management," but that it could always be fixed. So the very prospect of a violent, let alone a successful, revolution was remote until it came hurtling into view. Furthermore, the men who defended the American revolt in the House of Commons did so on the wrong grounds. Very few, if any, of them sensed that two sentences written by Jefferson into the Declaration would shake the ordered world of their century.

The first was: ". . . that all Men are created equal, that they are endowed by their Creator with certain unalienable rights, that among these are Life, Liberty and the pursuit of Happiness." There was a lot of argument among the states over that phrase. And in the end many of the men who signed the Declaration, while letting "happiness" stand as a no doubt worthy general aim, went home and wrote into their separate state constitutions "life, liberty, and the acquisition and protection of property." This was not merely a tycoon's reflex. To most of them property was no dowry. It was the means of life they, or their fathers or grandfathers, had been forced to wrench out of a wilderness.

The second sentence was the stick of dynamite. Everybody knows it now, and at high school commencement exercises it is throbbingly recited as a noble, but self-evident, proposition. Yet it took a century or so for an Englishman (to be more accurate, a Scot—Lord Acton) to recognize in this one sentence the flame of a quite new revolutionary doctrine: ". . . that to secure these rights, Governments are instituted among Men, *deriving their just powers from the consent of the governed.*"

Let us forget for the moment (what we make a habit of forgetting today) the implication that there may be unjust powers—responding to the injustice of life itself—in which the governed have no say. But the idea that if you felt you were being unjustly governed, you—you being the butcher, the baker, the candlestick maker—had some "right" to resist or overthrow the government: this was a firebrand that was to blow up France and the German republic and imperial Russia and eventually the whole idea of empire. We have come to accept this right, and, looking back over revolutions from the Peasants' Revolt to the latest South American coup, we can make one fairly certain generalization about the cause of revolutions: when the people in power can neither keep the consent of the governed nor keep *down* the dissent of the governed, then there will be a blowup.

Mass-produced in Staffordshire, this porcelain figurine was also available labeled "B. Franklin" or "Old English Country Gentleman."

Gl Washington

4
INVENTING
A NATION

William Ewart Gladstone, a consummate politician and the patriarch of British prime ministers, called the Constitution of the United States "the most wonderful work ever struck off at a given time by the brain and purpose of man." Whose was the brain? And what was the purpose?

The brains were undoubtedly those of the colonial Establishment, yet these men varied greatly from state to state—being Quakers or freethinkers or yeoman farmers in Pennsylvania, Congregational divines in Massachusetts, Anglican lawyers and landowners in Virginia, heathen shippers and merchants in New York, and so on. We should also remember that it was comparatively easier in the eighteenth century for a man of energy and talent, or energy and cunning, to "establish" himself than in the great era of the industrial wage slave.

Their purpose was to invent a national government that would still leave the states with the sovereign powers they had grown used to. A laudable aim that proved, as we shall see, to be a practical impossibility.

The Revolutionary War did not end quite so summarily as we might gather from the pictures of Lord Cornwallis, the British commander, surrendering his sword at Yorktown on October 19, 1781. George III, for one, turned a blind eye on such a scene, simply finding it incredible that His Majesty's crack forces should have been defeated by the American "rabble" and that the thirteen prosperous if cantankerous colonies were lost forever. The American defeat coincided with his final failure to rule both the executive and legislative branches of the government at home, the last tenacious effort of a British monarch to rule both Parliament and people. He actually drew up two drafts of an instrument of abdication, in which he made no excuses and frankly admitted that "this patriotic endeavor [at royal rule] has proved unsuccessful." After that he made one or two fitful raids on the parliamentary power but then slipped, with remarkable sportsmanship, into an acceptance of his shrunken role. And when the colonies at last achieved their indepen-

With scarlet coats and freshly pipe-clayed straps gleaming, British troops march out of their defenses and lay down their arms after surrendering at Yorktown. Flanking the route were files of French soldiers (rear) and Americans. The British bands played "The World Turned Upside Down."

125

dence and sent over John Adams as the first American Minister to the Court of Saint James's, George III made the magnanimous concession to Adams's face: "I will be very frank with you. I was the last to consent to the separation: but the separation having been made, and having become inevitable, I have always said, as I say now, that I would be the first to meet the friendship of the United States as an independent power."

However, after the official surrender, the British still held New York. They also held, though loosely, some Southern ports and garrisons, as well as outposts in the wilderness above Ohio. But these were all doomed to yield, and in 1783 a peace treaty was signed at Paris. The British brought some bargaining strength to the table, since they had won brilliant naval victories in the West Indies and they held New York till the end. Obviously, though, they had to grant the total independence of the new nation called the United States of America. They yielded up therefore all the lands between Canada and Florida, as well as the disputed lands between the Mississippi and the Appalachians, but retained a share of the Newfoundland fisheries and navigation rights along the whole Mississippi.

For their part, the French hoped for a while to limit the expansion of the new nation by having both banks of the Mississippi and the whole lower valley transferred to Spain. In any event, they were satisfied to see the British stripped of her colonies, leaving a small, disheveled nation on a huge continent at the mercy of French protection. Spain wanted rewards far beyond her prowess as a fighting ally; she wrangled for Gibraltar and settled for Florida instead.

But now the peace conference was bedeviled by a word that haunts the defeated in every civil war: "reprisal." What was going to happen to the losers who lived on the old battleground, to the one third of a nation that had fought with the British or stayed suspiciously neutral or were known to have had a Loyalist brother or cousin or whoever? The treaty had expressed humane promises about compensation for seized lands and houses and other possessions. But the Congress was an infant with no authority to see that this was done, and the treatment of the Loyalists varied alarmingly from state to state.

The Pennsylvania Quakers, most of whom had refused to fight at all on principle, were understandably compassionate. South Carolina, considering that the British had dealt miserably during the war with many of her citizens on prison ships, was surprisingly generous. A stout, rebel New Yorker, on the other hand, writing to Alexander Hamilton in the middle of the war, boasted that "the spirit of the Tories, we have great reason to believe, is entirely broken in this state . . . I wish the several states would follow our example. Pennsylvania, in particular, would experience many good effects from a vigorous manly execution." Indeed, in most of the states the Loyalists had a brutal time. They lost their houses and businesses. They had no legal redress from assault and slander. They had to pay for the damage done by mobs to their homes. And in two states they were required to pay double and treble taxes. A protest against the riding of Loyalists on rails brought from George Washington the bland thought that to stop this quaint custom would be an interference with the liberty of the people!

At last they were forced into exile in great numbers—to Canada, to the West Indies, or back to England. The day the British evacuated Charleston, a hundred ships sailed down the bay jammed with Loyalists. The British commander at New York was so fearful of mob reprisals that he refused to give up the port until the last refugee was aboard. One of them made the forlorn note in his diary: "There will scarcely be a village in England without some American dust in it by the time we are all at rest."

I suppose you could say that it was bound to happen. The war had ended in a blaze of patriotism, and the people were so peacock proud that sooner or later the demagogues and the mob between them might well have menaced the lives of a population of "renegades." So, for a brief and heady time the patriots reveled in the fiction proclaimed by the revolutionary leaders, of a brave and indissoluble alliance of new states. Even so level-headed a man as John Adams wrote:

The second day of July, 1776, will be the most memorable epoch in the history of America. It ought to be commemorated as the day of deliverance, by solemn acts of devotion to God Almighty. It ought to be solemnized with pomp and parade, with shows, games, sports, guns, bells, bonfires and illuminations from one end of this continent to the other, from this time forward, for evermore.

But, as so many new African states discovered in the ecstasy of "Uhuru!," there is a morning after. Once the war and the celebrations were over, the indissoluble union began to dissolve. Like the victims of a hurricane or a blitz, the old colonists had learned that there is no livelier stimulus to brotherhood than physical danger. But once the storm had passed, they headed for home and went their own ways. They were drunk on the pride of their sovereignty, but not as Americans: as New Yorkers, Georgians, Marylanders, Vermonters—and so much so that they began to act like independent nations. The states hemmed in by other states were frantic to stake claims to the unsettled lands in the West. They developed their own money systems and levied their own taxes and ignored their neighbors. Some of them began to start their own

Overleaf: *Many Loyalists fled to Britain and made claims for their wartime losses. An inset in the portrait of Judge John Wilmot shows them being welcomed.*

relations with foreign countries. Georgia, with nobody's permission, fought its own little war with the Indians. Everybody wanted to raise his own crops, make his own products, without a thought of the national market. In some states they regressed to barter. They improvised their own boycotts of each other's goods, slapped tariffs on arriving cargoes, and shucked off the huge national debt as somebody else's business.

There were even old soldiers who had fought on the wild understanding that the victory allowed them to set up their own independent nation. The most dashing of these intending emperors was Ethan Allen, an early pioneer in Vermont whose ambition, before the war, was to defy the jurisdiction of the neighboring state of New York. He postponed this vendetta when the war started and made a warrior's name by making the British surrender the fort of Ticonderoga. He wrote to Congress to make it quite clear that he and his men were fighting for the independence of Vermont, as a separate nation. If he failed, he said, "I will retire into the desolate caverns of the mountains to wage war with human nature at large." He didn't. Instead, he schemed with the British to make Vermont a British province. He was lucky not to be tried for treason. As it was, he ended up having to escape from his beloved state to avoid imprisonment—a little matter of big debts—and left behind a brave name, a highly biased history of Vermont, and a fat pamphlet: *A Denunciation of the Prophet Moses and the State of New York.*

This hero is a gaudy, but not a farfetched, exemplar of the license that the several states enjoyed in flexing the muscles of their new-found "sovereignty." That sovereignty, and many other rights and powers, were conceded to each of the states by the Continental Congress because it hadn't the power to deny them. The Congress was the only national body once the war was over (the army, the navy, and the marine corps were almost instantly abolished as proof of the colonists' deep distrust of standing armed forces). It was up to the Congress, therefore, to devise the form of the national government, and it faced this task with early and encouraging alacrity. Only nine days after the Declaration of Independence was published, Congress appointed a committee to draw up Articles of Confederation, which would come into effect as soon as the states ratified them. It took only a month to draw up a debating agenda, but almost five years (until 1781) before the Articles passed into law as the national government.

Congress was to be the only central governing body, and each state was to have an equal vote in it. Congress was to manage foreign affairs, war, the national debt, a postal service, credit and borrowing, Indian affairs, and the appointment of national naval and military commanders. The states were required to defray the costs of defense, and of the central government itself, by contributing money to the value of the lands they owned. (There was a never-ending dispute between the states wanting to lengthen their borders on the lands that ran to the Mississippi, but they didn't want to be assessed too highly for them.) The Articles went into many other matters, including extradition of criminals, free exchange of state citizenship, the proper quota of troops Congress could call on from each state in proportion to its white population— a refinement the Southern states insisted on after an unholy row.

The Articles of Confederation are now seen by every historian to have been unworkable from the start (a fine example of the football coach's remark that "hindsight is always 20/20"). As an instrument looking not so much toward a noble and harmonious world as to the actual government of a scattering of small nations, it is quite as impressive as the Charter of the United Nations, another noble document of dubious practicality. The Articles presumed to set up "a firm league of friendship" that, in some hazy, undefined way, would serve as a practical substitute for Crown and Parliament. They suffered from the pious inhibitions and optimistic assumptions of later leagues of nations. Congress piously requested troops and money and never got them—it had no power to raise federal taxes to support the central government. Worse, it could not regulate shipping or commerce but only deplore the piratical depredations of the ex-enemy's navy, and the free and easy way in which the states taxed and boycotted each other's goods. The fatal weakness was that of the later League of Nations and then of the United Nations: Congress kept talking about an overriding authority that, in fact, it never possessed.

The upshot was that within four years of the end of the war the Union was close to bankruptcy, and the strong leaders of the new Republic were not in sight. For, as so often happens, it is only when the war is over that a nation realizes how much its strength and unity have been provided by its military leaders: in the main Eastern campaigns by George Washington; in the Western campaigns by George Rogers Clark, the military hero of the frontier who was condescendingly dubbed in the East "the George Washington of the West"; and at sea by Commodore John Barry, the outfitter of the first continental fleet, whom everybody, East and West, called "the Father of Our Navy." When hard times follow a war, the soldier heroes are usually forgotten; it is better than being blamed.

The Articles had been drawn up on the assumption that they would be carried out by men with a lifetime's experience in their own state legislatures. Unhappily, this experience was not much called on during the drafting process, which had to be done haphazardly and at intervals in the middle of an exhausting war, when most of the drafters were much too busy to weigh theories of centralism against the various powers the states had acquired. In the end, the influential men in the states came reluctantly to a common conclusion: they were not a nation, they were the Disunited States of America.

They agreed to meet and try and make the Articles work. For the meeting place they chose Philadelphia. It was one of the few large cities; it was in the Middle Colonies; and it was the place where the Declaration of Independence had been signed, and where Washington had received the command of the Continental Army.

In the spring of 1787 they went with laggard steps to Philadelphia. They were big men where they came from; some of them were morbidly sensitive to the powers and privileges they might have to give up in the revised draft of the Articles. The first to arrive was an eager, greatly concerned thirty-six-year-old scholar-politician from Virginia, James Madison. Nobody else appeared in the next ten days. Then they began to assemble in driblets and small delegations. Rhode Island never did show up. At last there was a quorum of seven states, and they began.

And who were "they"? The document they were to write begins with the grand phrase, "We, the People." But by any definition of "the people" *we* would accept, the people were not there. It is hard for us, hypnotized by the schoolbook passes that have been made over this famous convention, to appreciate that the men who created the United States, the so-called Founding Fathers, were, in some fundamental ways, not creating our society. Democracy, for instance, was not mentioned, being warily regarded as a menace to sound republican government. It is true that democratic practices had been growing in many states. The state legislatures were elected, and so were many governors. Still, it is fair to guess that many of the wisest men at the Convention—certainly George Washington and James Madison—preserved at all times an alert suspicion of democracy. Democracies bred demagogues, and they tended to concoct political parties, which the Convention had no intention of creating or even of sanctioning. It agreed with its chairman, George Washington, that "political parties provoke the mischief of associations and combinations."

But how about the People's people, the bloodshot boys who had rabble-roused the country into revolution? Where were the pamphleteers of the Intercolonial Committees of Correspondence? Where were Sam Adams and Patrick Henry? They were not present. Patrick Henry refused to attend, saying he "smelled a rat in Philadelphia, tending toward monarchy." A bitter truth, rediscovered lately by many African and Asian republics hailing their revolutionary leaders in the moment of independence, is that there is a permanent breed of men who love the bonfire but find the rebuilding something of a bore.

Thomas Paine is an interesting case of a man about whom it would be tempting to say that he got so exhilarated by agitation that he adopted it as a profession. This is unfair to a brilliant pamphleteer—whose *Common Sense* rallied the colonies like nothing else to the idea of independence —and a courageous libertarian. But he was sufficiently obsessed with the idea of revolution itself that, rightly or wrongly, he became suspect as a professional agitator in three countries. The very month that the Founding Fathers gathered in Philadelphia, Paine sailed for his native England with the model of an iron bridge he had designed. But in no time he was once more blasting away against the government: that is to say, against the government that was against the French Revolution. He published another incendiary pamphlet, *The Rights of Man*, and Pitt said, "Tom Paine is quite in the right but . . . if I were to encourage [his] opinions, we should have a bloody revolution." He was indicted for treason and was quietly helped (by the poet William Blake, of all people) to get out of England. Arrived in France, knowing hardly any French, he took his seat in the Convention, and, having become suspect to Robespierre and the Jacobins, he was thrown into prison. He had obviously hoped to become the first trumpeter of the French Revolution, but found they had their own trumpeters. He escaped the guillotine by a hair's breadth. He is a lesson to all columnists and writers of indignant books.

So who, then, were the men who were to be known ever afterwards as the Founding Fathers? Jefferson called them "an assembly of demigods." They were hardly that, but a superior lot, possibly the most enlightened, certainly the most civilized, revolutionaries the world has seen in the past two hundred years. They were fifty-five men, composing the elite of government, business, and the professions in their own states. The shippers and manufacturers and statesmen of the North, the planters, scholars, and statesmen of the South. More than half of them were lawyers. Twenty-nine were graduates of colleges of either Britain or America. The average age was forty-two, which in their time was just a little beyond the prime of life.

The first thing they did was to flout their instructions. They decided that the Articles of Confederation were hopeless as a prescription for a national government, so they abolished them and started from scratch to invent a nation. Perhaps the only two strong prejudices they held in common were against monarchy and a standing army. (Kings could command armies and manipulate parliaments.) But not being able to imagine a satisfactory substitute for a king as the executive leader, they toyed for quite a while with the notion of monarchy. The idea was quashed once for all when an army man who idolized his old commander proposed that George Washington be made king. The nominee himself snuffed it out with the withering denunciation of "an idea I must view with abhorrence and reprehend with severity." That was the end of that.

(He did not, however, view with abhorrence the first violation of the new Constitution. It was the act of ignoring the requirement of the dying Congress that the President should be elected. Washington was unanimously chosen as the first President of the United States. In deciding the proper title of address, the Convention fondled various honorifics: the Protector and His Excellency. Franklin thought "His Mightiness, the President of the United States" would be very fine. Well, they allowed his mightiness to appear as it was called for, and they settled for "Mr. President.")

The first weeks must have been at once intoxicating and bewildering. We have all played with the beguiling possibilities of "If I were king" or dictator; we usually end up by assuming absolute power to suppress the things we abominate. There was enough of this temptation riding through the delegations to pursue some famous red herrings. The South held a strong fear that there would be an attempt to proclaim, in the Constitution, the abolition of slavery. Abolition was proposed by one of their own, a Virginian, George Mason. And it was effectively defeated.

Where to begin? What was to be the basic form? A republic? An oligarchy? A syndicate? A parliament with an executive branch inside or outside? What was to be the system of commerce between the states? Who would devise and enforce a national code of laws? Who could emigrate to America? Who would patent inventions? What is treason? Should judges be appointed or elected? (The elected judge is another object of horror to the British. But on that question Franklin threw in the warning that, in the countries he had known where the bar associations appointed the judges, they simply kicked upstairs the most prosperous lawyers so they could divide up his practice—an expedient not unknown in Europe to this day.)

They spent eight weeks looking over ancient history and modern Europe for a model form of government to adopt. They found, Benjamin Franklin said, "only the seeds of their dissolution." But that was something. It convinced them, for instance, that a parliamentary system would not work. The country was already half the size of Europe and ran from the rock and near-tundra of Canada to the tropical swamps of Georgia and out, over the Appalachians, to the alien life of a vast river and the Indian lands. The states had had together the experience of a hundred and fifty years of separate governments. And the Convention had not met to decide grandly how large or small the powers, how much or little independence, it would give the states. As J. R. Pole has aptly put it: "The Convention had no power to 'give' anything to the states: the problem was how to take existing power away from them and yet secure their consent."

Very soon they made a decision that today would produce a frightful

In a painting done on glass during the period of mourning following his death in 1799, a slightly blue-jawed Washington is shown ascending into heaven. The work is by a Chinese artist and was apparently commissioned for the American trade.

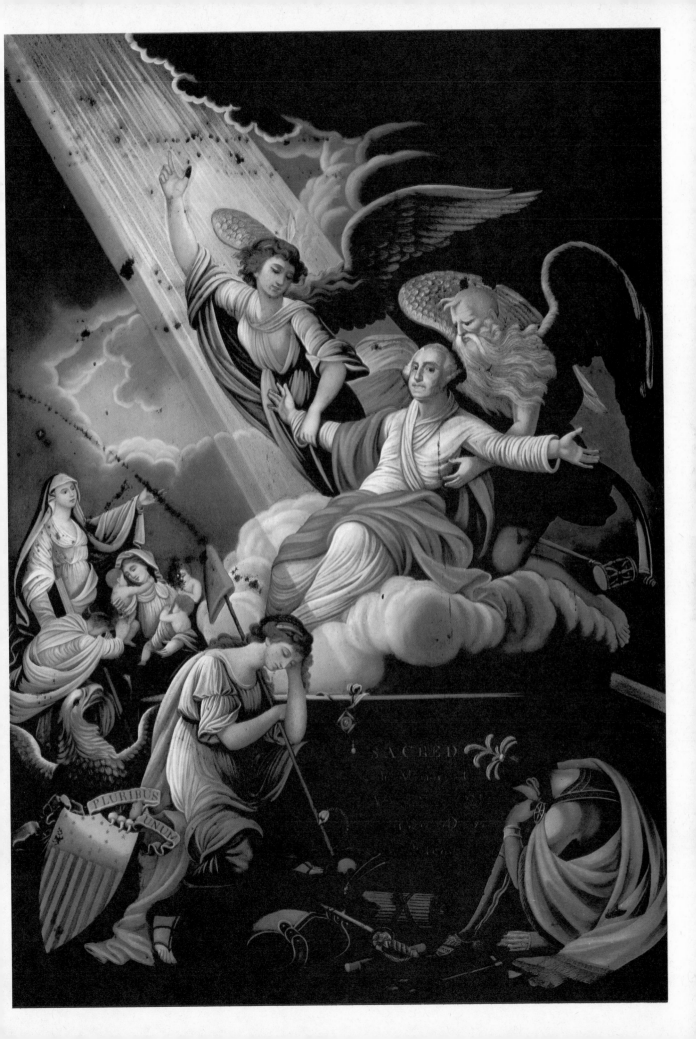

hullabaloo among the newspapers and the networks, not to mention "the people." Should they publish reports of their debates as they went along? It is and has remained a fundamental problem of diplomacy: whether, as Woodrow Wilson believed, such conferences should seek "open covenants openly arrived at," or, as Dag Hammarskjöld believed, "open covenants secretly arrived at." They came, after debating the rules of the convention, to agree with Hammarskjöld.

They began by agreeing to record all individual yeas and nays in the minutes until a Virginian pointed out that this would inhibit "a change . . . of conviction"—an objection unanimously sustained. The question of whether to publish came up on a motion to prohibit "licentious publications." But what is licentious and what is libertarian? By the end of three weeks they had agreed that nobody could make a copy of any entry in the Convention's journal, that only members could inspect it, and "that nothing spoken in the House be printed or otherwise published or communicated without leave." Powerful outsiders who heard about this rule seem to have accepted it without fuss as a necessary restraint, though one of them wistfully admitted that "I feel a strong desire and curiosity to know how it proceeds." But this ticklish question, like some others, was settled once for all by the sheer authority of George Washington's presence.

One day the delegates received copies of several resolutions and were routinely warned to keep them secret. One copy was found lying unclaimed on the floor of the hall, and it was handed to Washington. He thereupon called them to order and delivered a speech so scolding that nobody ever claimed the fallen paper. "I must entreat, gentlemen," he said, "to be more careful, lest our transactions get into the News Papers and *disturb the public repose by premature speculations*." (The italics are mine.) In consequence, what was recorded and what went on behind those closed doors was unknown to the public for sixty years. When the Convention was all over and Benjamin Franklin went through its doors for the last time, he was approached by an old lady who said: "Well, Doctor, what have we got, a Republic or a Monarchy?" "A Republic, madam, if you can keep it."

The Republic has now been kept for two hundred years, but not without considerable disturbance to the public repose. Anyone who has ever seen an American political convention, or for that matter lived long enough in the United States to follow the habits of newspapermen and television reporters, will be made aware every morning and every evening that afflicting the comfortable, disturbing the public repose, is a reporter's credo—and "premature speculation" is the lifeblood of political columnists.

The Convention sat for just under seventeen weeks, and the great debate, which ran through every discussion and dispute, turned on the crucial problem that had defeated the government of George III and vitiated the Articles of Confederation: the workable balance of power between the central government and the states. The gist of the debate can best be conveyed by isolating three men who, more than any comparable trio I can think of before or since, represent the two poles of the American political character and the archetype of the reconciler in between. This is not to say that these three men fought out the great debate in the flesh, and in Independence Hall. But to me they best concentrate the arguments and the prejudices that were contending for primacy in the minds of the fifty-five present: the urge to centralize authority in an elite, the urge to diffuse power among the states, and the balance valve.

Throughout all the debates there was one brilliant advocate of an overwhelmingly powerful central government. Alexander Hamilton, like other fervent nationalists—like Napoleon, like Hitler, like Lord Beaverbrook—was born elsewhere. Hamilton was born on the island of Nevis in the British West Indies. When he was eleven, his mother died and his father, a Scottish merchant, went bankrupt. He went to live with relatives and had to shift for himself by way of education and making a living, a fate that need invite no tears, for he was a very rare type—a precocious intellect that reveled in the worlds of business and politics. At thirteen he was running a mercantile business expertly in two languages. It is impossible to read his boyhood letters today without believing that you are in the presence of a man of affairs of extraordinary learning and maturity.

Some older friends were convinced that this genius should be given the benefit of a college education, and at sixteen he entered what is now Columbia University. By that time the revolutionary propaganda was at full blast, and in his eighteenth year he wrote two of the most closely reasoned, the most satirical and impressive, pamphlets on the colonists' cause. He fought bravely in the war but fretted at remaining for long a military aide to General Washington. He did eventually get a field command, but the war came to an end when he was only twenty-five, before he could fulfill his ardent ambition to be a military colossus.

He by no means monopolized the debates. But for a time he intimidated the debaters by his wealth of ideas, his flashing personality, his precocious knowledge of the history of governments. He was the supreme spokesman of the aristocratic principle. He wanted a lifetime

Overleaf: *The Founding Fathers worried about "democracy," but the American people quickly found politics a delight. Any election was a rousing event.*

chief executive, a lifetime senate recruited only from men of property, a central government that could absolutely veto the laws of the states. Indeed, he advocated—without much hope of success—extinguishing the states altogether.

At the opposite pole from Hamilton was a Virginian twice his age, a wealthy landowner with distinguished military and statesmanlike forebears who you would expect to have been an automatic seconder of Hamilton's ideas. He was George Mason, sixty-two years old, an uncompromising democrat about half a century before his time. He had organized the Ohio Company, whose surveys in western Pennsylvania brought on the French and Indian Wars. He was a prominent member of Virginia's "insubordinate" House of Burgesses and a Raleigh Tavern radical. He had drawn up the Virginia Bill of Rights, which went to the heart of the liberties the British had abused: searching without warrant, trying people twice for the same crime, suppressing free assembly. He called himself a radical republican and argued long, and fruitlessly, to have these assaults on individual liberty prohibited in the text of the Constitution. He argued to the end in favor of the weakest possible central government consonant with a confederacy. But since this was what most delegates believed they had tried and found wanting, he was beaten all along the line. So he concentrated on the rights of individuals, and argued for the inclusion of a bill of rights, and didn't get it.

Figuratively sitting in between these two was James Madison, an undramatic scholar, thirty-six years old, also from Virginia. A man destined at one time for the ministry, a Hebrew scholar apparently so innocent of practical politics that he was defeated for reelection to the Virginia Convention because he recoiled from the vulgar necessity of stoking the electors with the usual ration of rum. He was eventually elected to the Continental Congress, and when the war was over he went back to Virginia to study law and drum up on the side a campaign to prohibit a general tax for the support of any established religion.

Madison had thought about the defects of the Articles more profoundly than anyone present, and had already explored the perils of other confederacies. When he arrived in Philadelphia, he had with him an outline for a new system. It provided the groundwork for the so-called Virginia plan, which became the substance of the long debate. Its main point, which Madison was ready to illustrate to a fare-thee-well, was that you could never reconcile the sovereignty of each state with an "aggregate sovereignty" simply called a republic. He appeared armed with a study of confederacies ancient and modern, and he lectured the delegates at great length to prove that no confederacy had ever succeeded that set up a conflict of authority between the national and provincial governments. The main purpose of government, whether local or national, was "to act upon and for the individual citizen"—a new and vital concept. Another which enlarged a concern for "the individual citizen" to the protection of minorities was his awareness that a democratically elected government can encourage the majority to ride roughshod over the minority.

More than any other of the active debaters, Madison seized the principle that made the American Constitution durable; more than any other, he had the instinct of the balance valve, which yields steam protectively first to one side, then the other. His ideals were very well tempered by his survey of other systems and by a skeptical view of human nature. "If men were virtuous," he once reminded the Convention, "there would be no need of governments at all." He practically foresaw the rise of political parties as an inevitable exercise of human nature. Tactfully avoiding Washington's characterization of "associations and combinations," he maintained that you could not, and should not, try to suppress "factions," for they expressed the natural instinct for disagreement, and so were an expression of liberty. The trick would be to keep any one faction from becoming a tyrannous majority. And the way to do that was to leave as many powers as possible to the states and yet to have the national Congress represent all the variety of men, and interests, and factions in the whole country itself. In this willingness to admit the vast and often warring variety of state interests, Madison recognized the value of the "sectionalism" that to this day remains the root and branch of American politics. It has produced such uneasy coalitions as the modern Democratic party, which, considered as a national political party pretending to a single ideology, must often look like an impostor. But the freedom given to sectional interests within it— and within the Republican party, too—does prevent the national legislature from becoming the servant of any single ideology or "faction."

This system would guarantee a balance, however stormy, between national parties, or interests, inside the states. But suppose all the various interests, suppose even that the executive, the legislature, and the judiciary succumbed to the appeal of one powerful interest—the bankers, the farmers, the warmongers, say—what then? This hazard led Madison to the profound discovery that if the separate branches of government were made responsible to *separate constituencies*, then they would always tend to collide. This notion that collision is not only natural to governments but the source of their health was shocking to many of the idealists around him. But when he was challenged to say if the frailties of human nature were the proper elements of good government, he resoundingly replied that he knew no other: "Ambition must be made to counteract ambition. The interest of the man must be connected with the constitutional rights of the place."

As this central principle was worked out in the setting up of the new government, it became clear that, in Madison's view, both Hamilton and Mason were wrong. Give too much power to the provinces and they will swamp the central government (it had happened). Give to the national government the power to use force on a recalcitrant state, and you invite civil war. So there followed the triumphant theory that dictated the practicable balance of state and national powers: the national government shall not coerce the states or be their rival. Both exist to protect the American citizen.

So the men of Philadelphia boosted the pride, and the sense of reponsibility, of the little states by giving them equal representation in an upper house, the Senate; and they acknowledged the local interests of all the regions by giving them the widest representation—for a shorter term—in the lower house, the House of Representatives. And whatever powers were not stipulated in the Constitution were left to the states: they were to retain, as they do, the control of their own highways, education, banking, taxation, divorce, liquor laws, their own civil and criminal codes. It was a daring thing not to try and reduce the powers of the states. But to do so would have imperiled the whole Constitution by sending the delegates home in a huff. The states were allowed, as they had to be, to diffuse the opportunity for self-government, as also, we ought to add, for corruption.

It sounds like a shattering defeat for Alexander Hamilton, and so it was. When the Convention was all over, he confessed that "no man's ideas are more remote from the plan than my own are known to be." But he added, without a grudge, "Is it possible to deliberate between anarchy and convulsion on one side, and the chance of good to be expected on the other?" Hamilton had the pride of a Roman, and some Roman vices, too—arrogance, a prejudice in favor of men of property, an incurable distaste for "the mob." But he had also a great Roman virtue, that of magnanimity. He did not complain or recriminate because he had lost. To me Hamilton—not a fashionable figure in our day—represents the politician at his very best showing an absence of malice, "a steady willingness," in Mencken's phrase, "to believe that his opponent is as honorable a man as himself, and may be right." He swallowed his most passionate convictions and wrote more than forty brilliant proselytizing essays urging the states to ratify the Constitution. It was a close thing in some states. Virginia, for instance, voted 89 for, 79 against. George Mason and Patrick Henry voted against.

But in the end it was done. After seventeen weeks the weary fifty-five

What we now know as Independence Hall was the Pennsylvania State House when the Constitutional Convention met there in 1787. It looked like this about ten years later.

achieved the triumph of three principles that have sustained, however shakily, this federal republic on a continent. They are: compromise, compromise, compromise.

But some things in life cannot or will not be compromised. If it were not so, there would be no wars, no divorces, and "domestic tranquillity" would be the norm of American history. Perhaps the most familiar case to us of a social crisis that begins by defying compromise is the conflict between workers and employers. The "right" to strike is something claimed by all labor unions but never, as far as I know, conceded in federal or state law. Yet it is the main weapon of one whole body of citizens against the people who make their livelihood possible.

The mid-1930s was a period of incessant conflict of this sort. In the first seven months of 1937 there were nearly 1,500 strikes in the United States involving more than 670,000 workers. Twenty-four strikers and sympathizers were killed, and 490 injured. In one historic strike, 25,000 steel workers quit because the company ignored a new law that allowed them to join the union of their choice. Who, in such an issue, is to have the final say? It was settled in the end, not by the resistance of the company or the union, not by the President or Congress, but by a body of men, created by the Philadelphia Convention, that remains the one absolutely new thing in government invented by the Founding Fathers. To be accurate, the "absolutely new thing" was a function this body claimed sixteen years after its invention. The body is the Supreme Court of the United States; and the unique function was that of "judicial review."

Throughout their history, the colonies had been quite used to having their laws overturned either by the Crown or by the royal governors. In creating the judiciary arm of the government, the Founding Fathers were mainly concerned in seeing that the state legislatures could not encroach on the powers of the federal government. The federal courts were not specifically given the power to say whether the laws, of either the federal or state governments, were or were not constitutional. The Fathers simply laid down that the Constitution they were writing would be "the supreme law of the land." But once the state courts started to exercise a veto on state laws, the federal courts began to examine the validity both of state laws and of acts of Congress.

It is an interesting irony that the first case in which the Supreme Court asserted a right to declare an act of Congress unconstitutional was brought against the "Father of the Constitution" himself, James Madison, and initiated a historic power that our magnanimous loser, Alexander Hamilton, had urged on the Philadelphia Convention with no success. Congress had passed an act giving the Supreme Court the power to issue writs of mandamus (a court order commanding the performance of an act). In this case, one William Marbury had been made a justice of the peace by a previous administration, but his commission had not been delivered. He asked the Supreme Court to compel the new Secretary of State, James Madison, to give it to him. At the time the Court itself was under fire from the new Congress, which was of the opposite party from President Jefferson and spoke with horror of him and his followers as "Mad Tom radicals." When the Court announced it would hear the case, the Republican Congress went so far as to pass a law suspending the sessions of the Court for over a year.

Anyone who cares to go back and study the tumult in the first years of the nineteenth century between the Congress, the President, and the Court will marvel that the Constitution or any of its branches survived. But they did, the Court heard the case, and the Chief Justice, John Marshall, ruled that Marbury had a right to his commission, *but*—a fateful "but" in the history of the Republic—that Congress had no power to enlarge the jurisdiction of the Court. It could not, for example, authorize the Court to issue writs in the first place. In other words, the act of Congress that gave this power was *unconstitutional.*

Not for another fifty-four years did the Supreme Court presume to strike down an act of Congress as unconstitutional. But the power had been claimed. And for over a century the power to review both federal and state laws, and especially to declare that in some way or other they violated the right of an American citizen under the Constitution, not only grew; it became the sheet anchor of the American system. Madison may have been scolded in the first test, but his doctrine that the federal and state governments existed to protect the individual triumphed. In the day-to-day turmoil of living out the Constitution, Americans came to see that it had set up a President to keep an eye on Congress, and a Congress to keep an eye on the President, and a Supreme Court to keep an eye on both of them.

As a working foreign correspondent in the United States for thirty-five years, I came to realize, and never more than during some dangerous constitutional crisis, that the Court and the Court alone guards the rights of the citizen, whether he is a bum or a banker, the President or an infant. The justices' brief is the Constitution, not precedent. They sit most days of the year and look at the old stately document and decide whether you can, say, run an undertaker's firm and also hold stock in an insurance company (in the most recent judgment, you cannot); whether a public bus company can compel you to listen to piped music; whether a company of naked men and women pronouncing four-letter words on a stage are within their constitutional rights (at this writing, they are). The justices have defended the right of children to work in factories throughout the night, and then they have absolutely forbidden them to be forced to do just that. They have proclaimed the right to keep blacks and whites apart on trains and then, decades later, proclaimed the right of blacks to sit with whites on trains, in schoolrooms, theaters, restaurants, everywhere. They have interpreted the letter of the Constitution to say that there is no limit to the length of a railroad train, so long as the safety of the crew is provided for; that over a hundred thousand Japanese-American citizens can be rounded up in remote detention camps because they are of the same racial strain as a present enemy of the United States (a decision lamented ever since); that the individual's rights are imperiled when an oil company gobbles up its competitors.

Even from these few cases, you can see that the Constitution, like the Old Testament, can be cited to forgive one's enemies or to gouge an eye for an eye. Any visitor to Washington who is grateful to the Court for its role as the watchdog of the ordinary citizen would do well to drop into the old Senate Chamber where the Court sat for most of its existence and maintained its supreme power to decide the outcome of the political and social battles that engage the best and the worst passions of the American people. That chamber is haunted by memorable faces and single sentences that have buffeted, or kept on an even keel, the life of the American people:

Chief Justice John Marshall: "It is emphatically the province and duty of the judicial department and nobody else to say what the law is."

Justice George Sutherland: "The liberty of the individual to do as he pleases even in innocent matters is not absolute."

Justice John Marshall Harlan (speaking eighty years ago against all eight of his colleagues):"The Constitution is color blind."

Justice Oliver Wendell Holmes: "A Constitution is made for people of fundamentally differing views."

Chief Justice Charles Evans Hughes: "The Constitution is what the judges say it is."

So it is. Indeed, since a majority of the nine decides everything, the Constitution is what *five* judges say it is. That sounds ominous. For these nine men are human and of various character, and there is nothing rigid about the authority of the Constitution. It bends to the moral winds of the time. And if the judges are behind the times, and if ever their integrity as honorable men is seriously questioned, then the Court and the country will be in trouble.

But an odd and salutary thing very often happens when a man is appointed to the Court. Every President likes to have judges who share his general political and social views. The President commonly thinks he has installed a ventriloquist's doll on the Court; but gradually the man appointed begins to nestle into the realization that he is paid for life, he has never to seek election, he can be above the political battle. He can afford *to become himself*, a quite different character from the one the President ordered up. (Justice Frankfurter and Justice Warren are two late examples of judges who, once on the Court, appeared to change or modify their judicial philosophy, if not their character, to the chagrin and bafflement, respectively, of the Presidents who appointed them.) But however the Court acts, it will be a bad day for the United States if the mass of Americans come to lose their faith in it as their fair and final protector.

There might have been no workable Constitution, and no all-powerful Court, if the Founding Fathers had not listened, though rather late in the day, to an American who was not present in Philadelphia. He is the missing giant of the Constitutional Convention, Thomas Jefferson. He was in Paris as Minister to France, and he heard with alarm that George Mason had failed to impress on the Convention the vital need for a written bill of rights. He unceasingly nagged every influential man he knew until he got it. Looking around him in France, Jefferson was a daily witness to the old indignities and assaults on personal liberty that the Constitution had failed to prohibit. And he wrote home continually that it was not enough to presume the sanctity of those human rights whose violation was all too familiar to the Founding Fathers. You must, he wrote, "specify" those liberties and put them down on paper.

Within four years ten amendments came into force as the Bill of Rights. Since it has been lamentably shown, in polls and surveys, that only a small minority even of American students can identify more than a couple of them, they ought to be put down here:

I. Congress shall make no law respecting an establishment of religion, or prohibiting the free exercise thereof; or abridging the freedom of speech, or of the press; or of the right of the people peaceably to assemble, and to petition the Government for a redress of grievances.

II. A well regulated Militia being necessary to the security of a free State, the right of the people to keep and bear Arms shall not be infringed.

III. No Soldier shall, in time of peace, be quartered in any house, without the consent of the Owner, nor in time of war, but in a manner to be prescribed by law.

IV. The right of the people to be secure in their persons, houses, papers, and effects, against unreasonable searches and seizures, shall not be violated, and no Warrants shall issue, but upon probable cause, supported by Oath or affirmation, and particularly describing the place to be searched, and the persons or things to be seized.

Overleaf: *Painted by Samuel F. B. Morse in 1822, Congressmen and Supreme Court justices (among them John Marshall) gather, apparently for a joint session.*

V. No person shall be held to answer for a capital, or otherwise infamous crime, unless on a presentment or indictment of a Grand Jury, except in cases arising in the land or naval forces, or in the Militia, when in actual service in time of War or public danger; nor shall any person be subject for the same offence to be twice put in jeopardy of life or limb; nor shall be compelled in any criminal case to be a witness against himself, nor be deprived of life, liberty, or property, without due process of law; nor shall private property be taken for public use, without just compensation.

VI. In all criminal prosecutions, the accused shall enjoy the right to a speedy and public trial, by an impartial jury of the State and district wherein the crime shall have been committed, which district shall have been previously ascertained by law, and to be informed of the nature and cause of the accusation; to be confronted with the witnesses against him; to have compulsory process for obtaining witnesses in his favor, and to have the Assistance of Counsel for his defence.

VII. In Suits at common law, where the value in controversy shall exceed twenty dollars, the right of trial by jury shall be preserved, and no fact tried by a jury shall be otherwise re-examined in any Court of the United States, than according to the rules of the common law.

VIII. Excessive bail shall not be required, nor excessive fines imposed, nor cruel and unusual punishments inflicted.

IX. The enumeration in the Constitution of certain rights shall not be construed to deny or disparage others retained by the people.

X. The powers not delegated to the United States by the Constitution, or prohibited by it to the States, are reserved to the States respectively, or to the people.

It would not be a bad idea, and would save us from the spouting of much florid and impractical rhetoric, if a President were required on the day of his inauguration, not to make a speech, but to stand before the Chief Justice of the United States and recite the Bill of Rights. For most of the decent, and indeed the preposterous, claims to constitutional liberties that come up before the Supreme Court in our day are alleged violations of the Bill of Rights. The astuteness of including the Ninth Amendment has been proved elaborately down the centuries by the fact that sixteen other amendments have been added, and there will be more; for the persistence of men and institutions in tinkering with liberties we take for granted is unending.

Jefferson's incessant anxiety for the individual as against the states was certainly quickened by his living in France during the whole five years up to the brink of the French Revolution. But it was rooted in his memories of life in Virginia, which at a distance of three thousand miles wove in his mind a fantasy model of a prosperous republic inhabited by "God's finest creation"—the farmers. You might think of such a man, who disliked cities and idolized farmers, as a simple, rural, sentimental crank. On the contrary, he was a remarkable American eighteenth-century type, an upper-class, classless, inventive, scholarly, eccentric country squire. His house, Monticello, near Charlottesville in Virginia, was built to his own design, and it reflects, more than the elegant homes of most statesmen, the charm and the idiosyncrasy of his interests and his passions. He anticipated Le Corbusier by more than a century and a half by turning his house into "a machine for living," except that Jefferson's view of life and living made certain that it was never less than a home as well. Throughout the house we come on novelties of his invention: a twenty-four-hour clock; a revolving chair, in which he could move with the light always over his shoulder; a four-sided lectern that allowed a chamber-music quartet to play from the same stand. Jefferson designed his own furnishings, his own spectacles, his own medicine chest. He was an amateur of everything—of music, astronomy and meteorology, of architecture, anthropology, and gardening. He cultivated the famous Albemarle pippin, which—if anyone cares—was Queen Victoria's favorite apple.

He was a lifelong journal jotter and notetaker. He wrote reams of notes on the Greek and Roman authors, on contemporary French philosophers, on geology, on Hebrew manuscripts, most famously on his native state of Virginia, a curiously intense bit of writing that brings the same concern to bear on the varieties of trees, plants, and wildflowers in the state as on the locations of the known Indian tribes and the white's relations with his slaves. He also had a theory of currency, which he carried with the Congress against the bankers, and so became known as "the father of the dollar." His objections to the laboriousness of pounds, shillings, and pence anticipated by two hundred years the wisdom of the British government: the ordinary man or woman "is used to be puzzled by adding the farthings, taking out the twenties and carrying them on; but when he came to pounds, where he had only tens to carry forward, it was easy and free from error." He suggested that, since "everyone knows the facility of decimal arithmetic," it should be adopted in the coinage "to the great ease of the community."

If there is one notebook I'd give a great deal to have in the original, it's the one he carried around Europe, methodically putting down all the detestable things a republic must not have. "No public statues," a prejudice the American people have successfully overcome. No "titles of nobility . . . a very great vanity . . . which tends to prolong the artificial aristocracy of birth and wealth as against the natural aristocracy of talent and virtue." He went to London and visited the courts: no wigs on

judges. "We must not have men sitting in judgment who look like mice peeping out of oakum."

There is something comical, and maybe a little prim, about the earnestness of all this, but something, too, straightforwardly innocent in an age of powerful intrigue and far-ranging cynicism. He was shocked to hear of the Constitutional Convention's rule of secrecy and wrote at once to John Adams to deplore "so abominable a precedent." Jefferson seems to have had none of Madison's fear for the tyranny of majority opinion. Let everything come out, and the judgment of the common people will be sound. Over and over again, he writes of the essential "goodness and wisdom" of the common people. It forces us to wonder how many common people he knew, outside of the friendly farmers and the obedient servants and slaves who ministered to his serenity in his beloved Monticello. He disliked the hubbub of Washington, a place he called "that Indian swamp in the wilderness," and retreated as often as possible to the Blue Ridge and its systematic chores and pleasures. Until his old age, when he saw a disaster brewing between the slave states and the free states, and when he came to fear, of all things, the power of "the federal judiciary," he pictured life in America as a long pastoral symphony, a continuing Utopia of chivalrous and learned rulers walking hand in hand with good, honest farmers in—a favorite phrase—"perfect harmony."

Alexander Hamilton groaned to hear him. Three years before his death, Hamilton wrote: "Every day proves to me more and more that this American world is not for me." Maybe Hamilton could see a little farther into the future than Jefferson. He understood that the original mold of the Union, a civilized federation of states planted along the Eastern seaboard, had been broken. He saw over the mountains, where an unlettered generation of hunters, trappers, farmers, and their broods were hacking and sometimes slaughtering their way into rude settlements. These people had few, if any, links with the writers of the Constitution, and they would transform the Republic beyond the imagining of the learned men, the city-shrewd men, the paternal squirearchy of the eighteenth century. By 1804, the year Hamilton died, the French and the Spanish had yielded up the Mississippi Valley and the infinite lands beyond to the Anglo-Saxon mountaineers and frontiersmen. It was a prospect that ravished Jefferson and threw Hamilton into despair. "Democracy," he wrote, two days before he died, "is our real disease."

Every inch the young diplomat, Thomas Jefferson was painted by Mather Brown in London in 1786, shortly before he succeeded Benjamin Franklin as American envoy to the French court.

5
GONE WEST

Where the West begins is a question that has puzzled foreigners, immigrants, and Easterners for centuries. It has been answered for most of us by an emblem, by the stark appearance on the horizon of a one-street town that the movies have made into a stereotype. As late as the Second World War, it was possible to come on the genuine article at hundred-mile intervals through Arizona and Nevada and in the western foothills of the Sierras: a short row of wooden false fronts—a hardware store, a raddled saloon, the shell of the United States post office, the ghost of a newspaper office—standing alone under an encircling sky at the end of a dirt road that led nowhere.

Today the true ghost towns have been done over, with much facetiousness, by way of lurid saloon signs and synthetic gambling joints, as tourist traps; or they have been overlaid by the neat clutter of suburbia; or they have sunk without trace. There is one in Southern California—Bodie, eight thousand feet up in the Sierras—that the state has fenced off against "development" and disaster. Thus protected, it still remains a vivid memorial to the West of a century ago. The wooden false fronts are weathered into a coppery brown. They lean at threatening angles over a high boardwalk on a rambling dirt street that is sometimes as hard as cement and sometimes squelching with mud from the tumbling mountain rains. Drills, picks, and wagon wheels lie rusting in stubble grass below the old mine and mill up on the mountain, and inside the stores can be found the moldering domestic relics—the crockery, coins, wedding licenses, lanterns, rocking chairs, stoves—of a century ago. Bodie—a misspelling of one W. S. Body who found gold there in 1859—struck it rich in 1876. For four years the place was roaring with life and death: one killing a day, fifty-six saloons and gambling joints, twelve thousand people brimming with sap and mischief and vice. By 1883 it was mostly abandoned, and in 1932 a fire browned it off. Today, it is a graveyard up among the rolling cumulus clouds. It is as forgotten and forlorn as the Plains of Troy. But it is unforgettably what we all like

Vast herds of buffalo—more properly bison—were one of the glories of the Great Plains. The Indians, as in this 1840 painting by A. J. Miller, killed them for food and hides. But with the coming of the white man the slaughter increased radically, and by the end of the century only two wild herds were left between the Atlantic and the Pacific.

155

to think of as the West. Because the West is always a stretch of particular landscape, beginning with the eastern rise of the Rockies and going through to the Pacific. And it is also a state of mind: the idea still of El Dorado, of getting away from it all, of leading a new and luckier life under that "big sky," of being—as the song says—"bound for the Promised Land."

But where the West begins depends when you asked the question. In the nineteenth century Charles Dickens got no farther than St. Louis, nine hundred miles short even of the Rockies. He went home convinced he had seen the West, and he declared it to be a fraud. In the seventeenth century the West began practically at the Atlantic seashore. It was synonymous with "the frontier," that inland danger line where the colonial settlement ended and the woods and the Indians started. In the coastal towns of Massachusetts, a fond father, seeing his daughter off on a journey of only fifteen miles to visit relatives in another settlement, wrote in his diary: "I did greatly fear for Abigail's safety, as she is gone into Duxbury. It is her first journey into the West, and I shall pray mightily for her early return."

In the time of Jefferson and Hamilton, the West was anywhere beyond the crest of the Appalachians. Hunters and scouts had nosed along the eastern ridges for decades, searching, in this dense haystack of mountain and forest, for the needle of a trail. It was found in 1750 by an Englishman who had gone out as an agent for a Virginia land company. Thomas Walker, a doctor, found a gap, at 1,665 feet, on the border of what are today the states of Kentucky, Tennessee, and Virginia. It was a natural gap beyond which the Indians had beaten out, to the south and west, a great system of trails. Dr. Walker, a loyal Tory, named it after the Duke of Cumberland, but it was left to a veteran of the French and Indian Wars named Daniel Boone to make it a highway into the promised land so many of his brothers in arms had glimpsed, and then had forbidden to them.

Boone was a Pennsylvanian who had been a wagoner in Braddock's ill-fated expedition against the French at Fort Duquesne. After the war he started roaming, first into Florida and then into "the West." If it was the ideas of such as Jefferson that invented the new nation, it was the hardihood of such as Boone that shaped and secured it. He was an undefeatable hunter, explorer, and surveyor for several land companies, and he deserves the title of the first Westerner.

Buried in the shady cleft of an overhanging slab of rock in the Great Smoky Mountains there is a hut, built of split timber, that is about eight feet wide and four feet high. It would serve as a rather cramped kennel for a mastiff, but it has, in fact, been lately authenticated as a hideaway of

In 1820, the year of his death, Daniel Boone was a tough and soured old man. His brave days of exploration were long since over, he had lost title to most of the land he claimed, and he was living in a cabin in Missouri when an itinerant artist named Chester Harding made the long journey into the backwoods to paint this portrait.

Daniel Boone. In places like this, Boone would rest awhile before going out by day into the mountains, living the essentially stealthy and self-sufficient life of a rover—hunting, trapping, camping, surveying, killing an Indian scout when need be, surveying, and resting again. He disappeared for as long as two years at a stretch. Some men, some with whole companies, disappeared altogether. No wonder the phrase "gone West" became a synonym for death, a meaning it retained in England throughout the First World War. (I remember being puzzled, as a small boy, to be told that an uncle had been killed in France and then to hear the grown-ups saying that most of his pals had "gone West," too.)

Boone tried again and again to beat a westward trail into a new colony, into the rolling, open country of Kentucky. Before he made it he had been "adopted" by an Indian tribe and escaped; he had seen a brother killed and families massacred; he nearly died in a blizzard, and another time came close to drowning. At the end he was swindled out of the tracts of land he had cleared and laid title to. But, in March 1775, he rounded up a party of thirty woodsmen and started from eastern Tennessee to clear a continuous road west that families of pioneers might safely use. The woodsmen went through the narrow Cumberland Gap, picked up woodland paths, joined trails beaten down by wandering bison, skirted Indian encampments, rolled away rocks, and hacked down forest and brush and posted guide markers at difficult sites.

This so-called Wilderness Road was nearly three hundred miles long and ended at the Ohio River at Louisville. It would be another twenty years before it was graded so it would be fit for wagons. But Boone's grinding, Herculean feat of trail-blazing was glorified in ballads and tall tales. It enticed over one hundred thousand people to go into the new territories of western Tennessee and Kentucky within fifteen years. Thirty years after them, by 1820, the population of the United States had doubled, and the overflow of the native young and new arrivals from Europe made the Cumberland Gap the main Southern highway to the West, as it is today in the form of a six-lane Interstate.

They were mostly unlettered folk, hunters, disappointed farmers from Europe or the East, trappers, old army scouts, French and Indian Wars veterans still unadjusted to home and hearth, the adventurous, the tough, the footloose, and—we must believe—a nucleus of sturdy and honorable men who took along with them Daniel Boone's three essentials:"A good gun, a good horse, and a good wife." They needed also good health, good luck, and an ax. And one other thing—salt.

Salt was the only preservative for the traveler's food. Before the Revolution salt had to be shipped at great price from the West Indies. The first pioneers carried it laboriously over the mountains by pack horse. (Boone, by the way, was able to freewheel all the way between

Leading his pack horse, a traveler picks his way through the first rocky pass on the extreme easter. edge of the Appalachians. From this point, northwes of Philadelphia, trails le. in a southwesterly direction along the lines o the mountain ridges, finally breaking through into Kentucky and Tennessee at the Cumberland Gap.

Florida and Kentucky because he was blessed with an animal instinct. It was said he could smell salt at thirty miles.) You could get it from the rare salt creek or, better, from the standing water of a brine lake. Kentucky held out a special inducement, for people who wanted to settle, in the form of a huge brine lake, located, appropriately, in Boone County. The pioneers who smelled out the salt there were not the first. A million years ago dinosaurs, mastodons, and sloths came galumphing in, attracted by the salt. When a Virginian named James Douglas went through there in 1773 he saw the whole valley as a graveyard of gigantic bones—teeth weighing ten pounds each, eleven-foot tusks, thigh bones five feet long. His party made tent poles of mastodon ribs and took their supper using vertebrae for chairs. They called the place Big Bone Lick. The fame of this find spread to the East and to Europe. Expeditions came hustling in. The Royal College of Physicians collared quite a pile. And, of course, so did Jefferson, a collector of bones as of everything else. But his were destroyed by a simple, and no doubt powerful, servant who pounded them into fertilizer on the assumption that they were—just a bunch of old bones.

In between the mastodons and the Boones came the bison and deer and hordes of other game, all attracted to the salt lick—and in pursuit of them, from hundreds of miles away, Indians of many tribes. It was the finest hunting ground they had heard of, and the several tribes murdered each other to hold it. Understandably, it became known as "the dark and bloody ground." It was to be darker and bloodier still when the white man came, for the break into the West meant moving into the open lands of the original Americans.

When it was plain that the white man had come to stay, there were three things he could do with the natives. He could, as William Penn did, treat them as separate nations to respect and live with. (This Christian approach would work with some tribes and not with others.) He could treat them as a potential threat, skirmish and parley and hope for a continuing truce. Or he could treat them as annoying primitive obstacles to the extension of civilization. This view, it is no secret, prevailed among all but the most enlightened pioneers. Two hundred years ago very few people had doubts about the sharp difference between a civilized man and a savage. The phrase "the human race" was not yet in the language. The authors of the Declaration of Independence had presumed without a second thought that equality applied exclusively to white men. So also with the Declaration of the Rights of Man, which the more philosophical of the revolutionaries had taken up with enthusiasm. It did not extend to the red man, except in the mind of Jean Jacques Rousseau, who—never having seen one—called him "the noble savage." He was not noble to the pioneers. They were not philosophers or humanitarians. The schoolbooks tend to stress the twenty-four-carat integrity of the families inspired by the prospect of free land. But apart from the old soldiers of two wars, and the mountain boys who had also known the Indian as the enemy, there was in any large company of pioneers a generous quota of prodigal sons, land jobbers, cattle thieves, criminals on the hop. They pulled up stakes for the usual wild variety of human motives, and, after an ambush or a scalping or two, they were inclined to think of the red man mostly as a fiend. Samuel Eliot Morison, with his usual sense of reality, has said it harshly and truly: "These children of nature, white and red, could no more be made to respect a treaty than dogs can be kept from fighting by the friendship of their masters."

The first big trek to the West thus brought the first extensive threat to the Indian on his own lands, whether the white man dug in or moved on. And the discovery of a salt lick often separated the settlers from the rovers. A thousand gallons of water from a brine lake could be boiled down to twenty pounds of salt—which was enough to persuade young men with growing families to make a clearing and settle in. Here they would at first hunt for their food, then plant a crop, raise a few hogs, make a home. The ones who did this were mostly of English and Scotch-Irish (Ulster) stock, with names like Marshall, Johnson, Lincoln, Jackson, McGee, McCoy. They were only a couple of hundred miles from the elegance of Williamsburg, but they started life like an African tribe. In time they hoped to match the modest prosperity of the small farmers of the East, with a grain crop and a few vegetables, a cow or two, a whiskey still, and in the fullness of years a schoolhouse and a doctor and a lawyer on horseback.

The more restless or easy-going types, who could take the Indians or leave them (dead or alive), moved on to the rivers and mulled over the prospect of other ways of life less confining than that of a mountain farmer's. They came to know the amphibious pioneers, Frenchmen mainly, who traveled cheerfully up and down the natural highways of the American interior, the first Americans to discover and exult in the fact—which to this day amazes Europeans who leave the Eastern seaboard—that North America is a land of a thousand rivers.

Even at the beginning of the nineteenth century, the many great rivers, running ultimately north and south, sustained a flourishing trade between Canada and the Gulf of Mexico. And, for the enterprising pioneer with no family to worry about, there were careers opening up in the marketing of furs, skins, turpentine, tar, lead, grains, rum, and whiskey. The Missouri, the Illinois, the Wabash, the Ohio, all flowed into the vast current of the Mississippi down through the glamorous abstraction of Louisiana into the port of New Orleans. And we should recall that in 1803 Louisiana was not the compact little state of the Deep South that we know today. In 1803 Louisiana was an unmanned, undefended empire embracing the whole watershed of the Mississippi and comprising the present states of Louisiana, Arkansas, Oklahoma, Missouri, both Dakotas, Iowa, Nebraska, Kansas, Minnesota, Colorado, Wyoming, and Montana—a third of North America.

It will be remembered that the British had acquired everything east of the Mississippi after the French and Indian Wars, and in turn the Americans had won it from the British in the Revolution. Nobody ruled the huge territories to the west, but in 1801 the paper title belonged to Spain. There was an irregular chain of trading posts and a few garrisons hundreds of miles apart. Only a tiny percentage of settlers had chosen to go to Louisiana, even the sophisticated back East had only the blankest or most romantic notion of how it looked and what was there.

In 1801 Spain ceded Louisiana, for protective services rendered, to Napoleon in a secret treaty. Jefferson, now the third President of the United States, got wind of it. He knew that Napoleon was busy with plans to invade Britain and crush the old enemy once for all, but when he heard that a French expeditionary force had landed at Santo Domingo to suppress a native revolt, he divined a sinister connection between this move and Napoleon's designs on the American continent. Jefferson, indeed, was throughout his life a fascinating combination of a true *naïf* and a shrewdly paranoid lawyer. Left to himself with his gadgets and his gardens and the superb view he enjoyed around his circle of mountains, he could dream up the most chivalrous fate for the human race. Confronted with an enemy, a talebearer, or the odd movement of a fleet, and he could leap like a foxy lawyer to the protection of his client. He followed the battles in Santo Domingo on a map, and he learned without wincing overmuch that the flower of the French infantry was either wilting under heat and malaria or being cut down by a black general who was also a master of guerrilla warfare, Toussaint L'Ouverture.

In January 1803, Jefferson sent precise instructions to Robert Livingston, then Minister to France, to make a deal with Napoleon. Then he shipped off James Monroe as an envoy extraordinary (of the Harry Hopkins—Henry Kissinger type) to help him. Offer Napoleon $10,000,000 for New Orleans and Florida, or $7,500,000 for New Orleans alone. If he refused, secure a guarantee of perpetual navigation rights. If he would not go even so far, then Monroe was to "open confidential communication with the ministers of the British government," a threat that Jefferson ostentatiously advertised for the benefit of the French minister in Washington. In April Livingston, who had been making regular calls on the unyielding French Minister of Foreign Affairs, went along to the Ministry. Old Talleyrand came limping in on his club foot and said: "What would you give for the *whole* of Louisiana?"

The staggered Livingston blurted out an off-the-cuff price of $4,000,000. It was much too low, and Livingston retired to wait for Monroe to sail in.

Jefferson had suspected that the Santo Domingo campaign was meant to be the rehearsal for a grander exercise—for nothing less than the physical conquest of the Louisiana Territory and, in time, of the United States. "The day that France takes possession of New Orleans," Jefferson wrote to Livingston, "we must marry ourselves to the British fleet and nation." Luckily, there was no need. Napoleon had sent thirty-five thousand of the crack infantrymen of Europe to put down a rabble of unorganized natives, and he had lost twenty-four thousand of them. What hope, then, for crushing a continent of savages *and* the Americans, who fought with similar guile? Santo Domingo was Napoleon's Vietnam. He withdrew and decided against any further adventures three thousand miles from home. And before Monroe was off the boat, he had sold Louisiana to Livingston for the ridiculously low price of $16,000,000.

There is a cheerful-looking bust of Jefferson in the Cabildo in New Orleans, where the territorial transfer was signed. It ought to bear the inscription, "Thomas Jefferson chuckled here." For although a President cannot conclude a treaty with a foreign nation without the "advice and consent of the Senate," Jefferson had advised and consented with nobody. He never mentioned a word of the Louisiana Purchase to Congress until it was settled. His comment on why he kept it secret is a wonderfully barefaced bit of gall, worthy of Franklin Roosevelt at his blandest:

This Treaty must of course be laid before both Houses. . . . They, I presume, will see their duty to their country in ratifying and paying for it . . . the Executive, in seizing the fugitive occurrence which so much advances the good of their country, have done an act beyond the Constitution. . . . It is the case of the guardian investing the money of his ward in purchasing an important adjacent territory, and saying to him when of age, I did this for your good!

Of course it was unconstitutional. It was outrageous. But, in the end, even a majority of Jefferson's enemies accepted it for the most reliable of American reasons: it worked. Jefferson had more than doubled the existing territory of the United States (a one hundred and forty percent increase, to be exact). And for four cents an acre! He decided at once to measure and survey the Purchase with a military expedition led by his secretary, a veteran of several Indian campaigns named Meriwether Lewis, and a soldier friend, William Clark, the younger brother of General George Rogers Clark, the "Washington of the West." They had the luck to pick up as a guide an Indian girl, a sixteen-year-old Shoshone

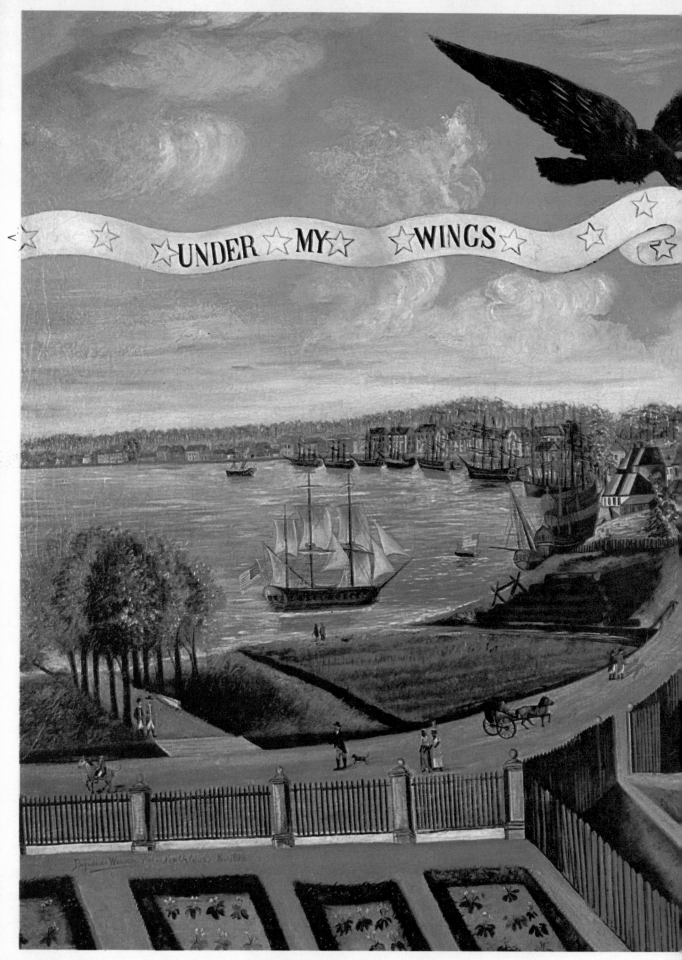

In 1803, the year of the Louisiana Purchase, Boqueto de Woieseri painted this patriotic view of New Orleans. It is now in the Chicago Historical Society collection.

named Sacajawea; her husband, a French-Canadian, would be guide, interpreter, and go-between. In the only threatening encounter they had with Indians, Sacajawea herself literally got between Lewis and a menacing chief, who, astoundingly, turned out to be her brother.

They started from St. Louis, in the spring of 1804, in a long flatboat, and by the time they got through North Dakota were threading their way in six canoes and two keelboats into country totally unknown to white men, except possibly to lone and unsung French-Canadian rovers. Jefferson's orders were, as always, crisp and all-embracing. They were to open up a river route for a continental fur trade, to study the Indian tribes, their languages and customs, to be nice to them on all occasions, but to convey the message that they now belonged to the Great White Father back in Washington. Lewis and Clark were blithely required to do for the whole lateral stretch of the continent what Jefferson had done for his familiar Virginia. To list and describe all the birds, trees, plants, flowers, fish, weather systems, geology along the way. To map all the interior river systems, march over the single range (as Jefferson imagined) of the Rockies, to come to the headwaters of the Columbia River, formally claim the whole continent for the United States, and so float sweetly in triumph to the Pacific. When they saw it, at the end of November 1805, after eighteen exhausting months, it was as if the first two men had landed on the moon.

Lewis died only four years later, and Clark in 1838. Neither of them could have doubted the blessing they had bestowed on their countrymen. But Sacajawea lived into her nineties, and must have been a very embittered old lady—for the great expedition had doomed the hope that her people would keep their native land. For a short time this hope had been enlarged into an actual constitutional right. But in 1830 it was overridden by, of all "usurping executives," the President of the United States. It was perhaps an inevitable act of the first President to be born in the colonial back country.

I had better say at once that what follows is not wholly fair to Andrew Jackson, since it bears solely on his decisive part in banishing the Indians from the East. It does not take in the good fortune of the Republic in having him, like Madison, where he was at the right time. With a large population crashing through the Appalachians, and starting to tackle an America as strange and challenging as the Atlantic seaboard had been to the Englishmen two centuries earlier, the United States could not afford, either for its growth or stability, to have an Eastern President, however learned or humane.

But here we are looking for the original trauma that explains Jackson's unqualified hatred of the Indians and the British. He was born of Irish immigrants in the pine barrens of the Waxhaw settlement on the border

During their epic overland journey, Lewis and Clark kept careful notes on almost everything they saw. These drawings by William Clark show how the Chinook Indians of the Columbia River Basin strapped infants between boards until they were about a year old, in order to produce a fashionably flat skull.

old man

Head of Flat head Indians on the Columbia the head broad at top, narrow

Note The highest tide at Fort Clatsop rises to 12 feet 4 Ins. The most common tide is from 8 to 9 feet and as all other parts of America rise twice in 24 hours something later every day —

Young man   Woman

of the Carolinas, on soil so poor that his father took two years to raise a crop and died of exhaustion at twenty-nine, when Andrew was two years old. He was only eight when the Revolution broke out, and in his early teens the British descended on the Waxhaws to burn and pillage. At thirteen he was a soldier, fought and was captured in a skirmish, and was scarred for life by a saber blow from a British officer. He was put with his brother in a prisoners' stockade, got smallpox, and within the year lost both his brothers and his mother. She had been a nurse to the Carolinians kept on British prison ships, had come home with tales of brutality and neglect, and herself died of "ship fever," cholera. At fourteen, he was alone in the world. He studied law and in time became a county judge, but much of his life was spent protecting the new settlements in Mississippi and Florida from Indian attacks, and in patrolling the settlers' trails through to the West, tramping in silence "for two days and nights, never daring to shoot game or kindle a fire," and resting always back to back, with a rifle cocked. When he commanded expeditions against the Indian tribes of the South, his natural suspicion and distrust of the red men was inflamed by finding, on the captured rifles that had killed his men, the imprint of British manufacturers. The subtle, strong alliance between the British and the Indians in the short War of 1812 galvanized his native belligerence. A cunning and brave soldier, an impetuous man (he was wounded twice in duels and killed a man in another), by the time he had helped win the war of 1812 he had come to suspect all Easterners, to distrust all bankers, to hate the British, and to loathe George Washington.

The great Indian ally of the British in 1812 was a Shawnee chief, Tecumseh, and to him the war was by no means the "foolish, unnecessary" war it is called in textbooks. It was the last hope of an Indian confederacy and of their claim to lands in the interior. Before the war Tecumseh had traveled from the Gulf of Mexico to the Great Lakes, pleading for a united Indian nation to make a stand against the white man. The coalition failed in a single battle in 1811, at Tippecanoe in Indiana. After that, the best hope of the Indians lay with the British, and after them there was none.

The white men who manned the (postwar) U.S. Army trading posts gave assurances that the Indians' rights to their own lands were absolute. But those lands kept shrinking as the whites moved westward. When they came into the flat lands beyond the mountains and down into the Mississippi delta they knew what they wanted their West to look like: an empire of cotton, not an Indian camp ground. So in 1830 the great cotton states of Mississippi, Alabama, and Georgia outlawed the tribal kingdoms, and President Jackson pushed a bill through Congress ordering all the Indian tribes, whether farmers or hunters, peaceable or

At the age of 78, shortly before his death, Andrew Jackson became the first President to have his picture taken. The year was 1845 and the daguerrotypist was probably Daniel Adams.

hostile, to move west of the Mississippi. And they started to move away, the Choctaws, the Creeks, and the Chickasaws. There was a brave pause while the Cherokees appealed to the Supreme Court and Chief Justice John Marshall upheld their claim that there was no constitutional right to remove them from their ancestral lands. Jackson called this decision "too preposterous," and, in what is surely one of the most shameless and arbitrary acts of an American President, he simply ignored the Supreme Court and ordered the army to "get them out." And so, in what is truly called "the trail of tears," thirty thousand Cherokees were persuaded or chained, gently led or viciously driven, as far west as Oklahoma, and along the way a quarter of them died.

This imperious ruling came to apply wherever the white man cared to explore. But in what we know as the Far West there were tough tribes whose blessed possession of the horse would enable them to hunt for their food, go on warring among themselves, and put off the day, for another sixty years, when the white man would subdue them all.

In the meantime, the Far West was an exploitable wilderness for the white land pirates who had the stamina to knock around in it. Among them, of course, were roving French-Canadians so remote from any fame or notice in the East that it was not until the 1850s that a new kind of pioneer came on the trails and cutoffs they had blazed. One of the most astonishing accomplishments of these Westerners, isolated by two thousand miles from the trans-Appalachian pioneers, was the creation of an international fur trade that in the first two decades of the nineteenth century drew bales of pelts from the waters of the Columbia and the Snake, the Rockies and the Cascades. They set their traps and they prospered mightily throughout the vast and brutal territory supposedly known only to Lewis and Clark and the native Indians. They stumped across the Plains on foot and into the Rockies for a very practical reason. They went after the beaver, not for himself but for what he could be made into, for by a whimsy of fashion, the beaver hat was the racy headgear in New York, Vienna, London, Boston, Philadelphia, and Paris. Until the silk hat supplanted it, it was· at the heart of a roaring business.

The British and the Americans each got into the fur trade after their own peculiar fashion. The British followed a straightforward class system. At the top, management—the English and the Scots, who did the hiring and kept the books. Below them were the canoeists, usually French-Canadians. And below them, the trappers—that is to say, the Indians. (By the way, three different grades of Indian tea were shipped out from England, to accommodate the superior and inferior tastes of these three classes.) The Indians caught the animals and delivered the pelts to the British posts for a dollar a throw. The British then sold them in the international market for ten dollars a throw.

In came the Americans, with no preconceptions about a system or a hierarchy. They set their own traps, paddled their own canoes, and employed the Indians to catch the beasts at three or four times the British wage. So the Indians deserted the British companies in large numbers, running the risk of being sued for breach of contract, a formality pretty difficult to proceed with in that sort of country. Several tribes were actually condemned "for personal disloyalty to the Crown." The Americans, however, didn't give a damn about loyalty or whether an Indian would be corrupted by money. They were happy to pay three times the going price and collar the market.

Though this lucrative trade collapsed in the 1830s, it went on long enough to introduce the forerunner of the American trade fair: the institution of the rendezvous, a regular annual gathering where all the bargaining and the buying were done. In wide pastures at the foot of the mountains, the Indians gathered with their pelts and the buyers came in with axes and kettles and dollars and various seductive trinkets, including whiskey. Gradually the rendezvous gave way to trading posts protected by stockades, but these first Western forts were privately owned. Only much later were some of them bought up for hard cash by the United States Army.

When the beaver trade declined, many of the old trappers and scouts retreated to British Columbia or slogged back to St. Louis to hire themselves out as guides along the Oregon Trail. But the Far West held other tempting prospects for adventurous men, especially within the large confines of northern Mexico. This region, it is easy to forget today, enclosed Texas (until 1835), and Arizona, Nevada, California, and Utah (until 1848). Government in these huge Mexican outposts barely existed except in California, and an ambitious man of any nationality could purchase a land grant and, with sufficient industry and panache, make himself the rough-and-ready lord of all he surveyed.

Such a hopeful seigneur was Johann August Sutter, a roving soldier of fortune of Swiss parentage. After speculative pauses in Missouri and the beaver trade and the shipping business to Hawaii, he undertook to found and rule his own California colony. The Mexican governor gave him forty-nine thousand acres along the Sacramento River on the condition that he would turn it into an impregnable Mexican outpost. The Mexicans had been frightened by the arrival of the Russians in pursuit of the sea otter and by their fortified settlement north of San Francisco. The disappearance of the sea otter and the subsequent order of the Czar to

Overleaf: *In 1837 artist A. J. Miller made this sketch in Fort William (later Fort Laramie), a trading station in what is now eastern Wyoming.*

withdraw all his subjects from California coincided fortuitously with the arrival of Sutter. He picked up the abandoned fort and all its chattels and livestock (seventeen hundred head of cattle, over nine hundred horses, and nine thousand sheep) and, as conversation pieces, muskets dropped by Napoleon's men along their retreat from Moscow. He removed them to his estate, which became a very grand rendezvous for sailors, trappers, and hunters. He built the promised fort and brought over Hawaiians and hired Indians to look after the cattle and grow wheat on his spreading lands. He started a distillery and a tannery and a blanket factory. He must have felt that he was already the first Swiss emperor of the West. To celebrate this agreeable feeling, he would parade the garrison and fire off a salute of guns to greet one of the rare Yankee visitors. "My holdings are extensive. In truth I have not beheld them in their entirety. I named my new home New Helvetia in honor of the ancient Roman title of our fatherland . . . the venture to the north improves steadily . . . and Sutter's Fort may still live in history." He lived to rue those words.

"The venture to the north" was a sawmill he had built fifty miles away in the foothills of the Sierras on the American River. In his boundless flat valley of the Sacramento there was only the live oak, and it made poor lumber for building. To the north, on the other hand, was pine. But the venture was not only intended as a useful adjunct to his ranch. It was a hedge against the looming possibility of political change and the loss of his vast estate altogether. For when the Americans of northern California rebelled against Mexican rule in 1846, Sutter had a premonition, unfortunately correct, that the Mexicans would soon lose California to the Union, and that the title to his lands would be declared invalid.

So Sutter saw himself as a prosperous lumber merchant, and as his subordinate in this enterprise he hired a Scottish carpenter, James Wilson Marshall. On the morning of January 24, 1848, Marshall was performing one of his more tedious chores, inspecting and cleaning out the tailrace of the sawmill, through which a strong current ran and deposited gravel and other debris on a bed of mud. Mixed in with it, that morning, he saw some foreign bodies the size of small peas. They gave off a peculiar dull glitter, and Marshall sat down on the river bank and, as he later said, "began to think mighty hard." He gathered up some particles and went off through a rainstorm to show them to Sutter. They had already made a breathtaking guess, and they locked the doors, took out some apothecary's scales and the *American Encyclopedia*, and tried the tests. There was no doubt about it. It was gold of extraordinary purity.

They swore each other to secrecy, and Sutter sent a messenger to the American military governor at Monterey demanding, with no reasons given, clear title to his estate. The Governor regretted he could not oblige, because California was not yet American territory, only an occupied Mexican province. (It became a territory eleven days later!) It was this mischance that ensured that Sutter's empire would be overrun by frantic gold seekers, that he would be cheated of all his lands and die expostulating in poverty.

Within a week the secret was out, but was warily disbelieved. Word didn't reach the East for six months, and Congress at first was inclined to put it down to some "Yankee invention got up to reconcile the people to the change of flag." But through the spring and summer of 1848 the rumor raced through the *vaqueros* and teamsters of California and out to Hawaii and down to Peru and Chile. The sailors of the coastal trade deserted, and so did the new American garrison at Monterey. Its governor reported to Washington that the reports "can scarcely be too exaggerated for belief." The Director of the Mint officially authenticated some nuggets as yielding "98 and two-thirds percent on 100 parts."

Finally, in December, President Polk told Congress that the most fanciful rumors fell short of the fact. The official word hypnotized Europe and, in London, deeply depressed Karl Marx, who, momentarily cheered by one of those "periodic convulsions in trade," now saw the cornucopia of a gold reserve to steady it. "All manifestoes," in the words of Marx's biographer, "were made inoperative, all proclamations vain, all revolutionary hopes futile."

You could go by ship from the eastern ports of Europe and around the Horn, a tedious and expensive route but one that appealed to New Englanders wishing to take pianos and furniture, along with the Bible recommended by the president of Harvard, to make a civilized mark on rude California. This was also the preferred route of gamblers, politicians, and prostitutes. But it cost the huge sum of $500 (today closer to $4,000 or $5,000). There were three alternatives:

1.   By sea to Panama, across the isthmus by land, and so to San Francisco by ship. This was a dreadful shortcut. Panama was a host to cholera. The land journey was up rivers steaming with yellow fever and then overland by mule, mosquito, and dysentery, with ticket scalpers at both ends of the isthmus.

2.   Down to Mexico and across its bandit-ridden deserts, a route that appealed mainly to veterans of the Mexican War.

3.   Overland through the Southwest from trails in Arkansas or Texas, the obvious preference of men dwelling in the Mississippi Valley and of Southerners used to long journeys on mule and horseback.

But as the grand prospect opened up before adventurers hot from Europe, before stubborn Northern and Southern families used to making their way with their hands, and before impatient youngsters willing to risk everything for speed, there was yet another way. And it has become

the classic route: the overland walk across the midcontinent. The starting point was St. Joseph, Missouri. The railroad was not to reach the Missouri River for another ten years, but Easterners went by train as far as possible and then transferred to the steamboat. St. Joseph was the northern and western terminus of the steamboat. It received all the heavy river traffic of the Ohio, the Mississippi, and the Missouri. There were sometimes as many as twenty-five steamboats tied up along the riverfront, and in 1849 it thought of itself, with a population just over three thousand, as one of the most thriving and populous river cities. Yet in the first year of the gold rush, over fifty thousand emigrants went through. As they were to discover, it was the place where civilization ended and the Middle Ages began. For there now lay ahead of them a two thousand-mile walk.

St. Joseph consequently was the supply center, the outfitting post, and the launching pad of the forty-niners. First, you had to have mules or oxen, both if you were lucky. The oxen were better on the early stretches of the prairie because they could get their feed wherever they browsed. But in the most precipitous mountains the mules could maintain any foothold they chose, and it was decidedly their choice. Not for nothing did the idiom "as stubborn as a Missouri mule" come into the language. If you had mules of your own already broken in, so much the better. If you didn't you had to buy what was available, and many a family sank its savings in the purchase of a few. Since the supply base was far from home, there was a good deal of sharp practice.

The next requirement was a wagon, a strengthened regular farm wagon, high-axled and caulked for fording the many streams the wagon and its occupants—the usual ratio was five persons to one wagon—would have to cross. Into its rear trunk were packed a shotgun and a pistol, horseshoe nails, axes, all the paraphernalia of a repair kit.

By the time they'd arrived at St. Joseph, most of the California-bound would have bought and read an "Emigrant's Guide to California," published in a dozen languages and supposedly written by old Western scouts. (The most popular was one concocted by a Saint Louis newspaperman who had the good sense never to leave his state.) These guides generally agreed on the necessary staples: one hundred and fifty pounds of flour, twenty-five pounds of bacon, twenty-five pounds of sugar, twenty-five pounds of salt, fifteen pounds of coffee. If you had a little extra cash, you could also afford some bags of cornmeal, rice, and prunes. Except for the prunes, then, it was an exclusively starchy diet. (A bottle of petroleum seems to have been the sovereign remedy against petrifaction of the bowels.)

Then there was the portable kitchen—pots and pans, a water barrel and water jug, a lantern, candles, bars of lye soap—and, packed away in

Muddy but still hopeful, a forty-niner pans a stream in the American River region at the height of the Gold Rush. This photograph was taken about 1850.

177

chests, the personal belongings: an overcoat, eight shirts, two pairs of boots, an oilcloth cap, a rubber knapsack, and the favorite accompaniments of the late-night show, the mouth organ and the jew's-harp. According to your social or financial standing when you started, you might also throw in a bedstead, some mattresses, mirrors, corsets, logbooks, sentimental keepsakes. With a final check on the most hopeful item of all—the pick and pan for the fortune you would take out of the goldfields—the cargo was complete.

They waited for the snow to melt from the prairie, and for the spring rains to raise enough forage for the animals. Then they took the ferry and started the long trek "across the wide Missouri." We picture them as straggling trains of sturdy families and weatherbeaten adventurers facing the future with no plans other than the maps of the westward trails. But they learned fairly soon that it was a risky business to cross the plains without some sort of organization for general discipline and for the particular hazard of an Indian attack. By the time they reached Council Grove, even the smallest companies found it prudent to elect a captain, a quartermaster, and lieutenants. As it happened, the forty-niners struck a remarkably docile period in the history of the Indian wars, and the Indians in the main appeared to act as guides, often to proffer mules and food and in other ways assist the survival of the white man.

But the standby military organization was a godsend in other ways, providing as it did a roster for the daily chores and a firm discipline when hunger and exhaustion transformed family encampments into bear pits. Many seagoing Yankees formed joint stock companies before they left, and later improvised written constitutions for their mutual protection. The most famous and successful example of self-government was the Charlestown Company, formed in the East, which subscribed its equipment and expenses, formed a committee to study the metallurgy of mining, and drew up a remarkably farsighted constitution that held them unscathed through sore trials, provided for the pooling of such gold as they might dig, and an equal, audited distribution when the company returned East.

For the first few weeks, the forty-niners had mostly a halcyon time, remarking in their journals on "beautiful country, grass, water, & wood plenty," and adding the fairly routine annoyances of "laid up today to repair the wagon that was broke yesterday—axle tree." They were amused by, say, the appearance of an Indian encampment and "an Iowa chief with seven wives, much children" who visited their camp and demonstrated skill with "the bow and arrow." Another day, and "water and good pasture" (they often christened such places Sweet Water, Bear Rock, Soda Springs). So they went, at about fifteen miles a day, in manageable teams of seven or eight wagons.

Such units would have to be self-sustaining when the going got rough, but over the first five hundred miles or so, staying close by the grass and the shade trees of the well-known rivers—the Little Blue, the Platte, the North Platte—different companies could follow the known trails in packs. When they were far from salt licks, and their bacon went bad, God provided protein on the hoof in the shape of the bison, always called in American English the buffalo. A big but infrequent problem was the fording of the very wide rivers. A few river men made a living by ferrying the timid at outrageous prices, but most people floated their wagons and mules and hoped they would not add to the surprisingly high casualty list of deaths from drowning.

As the timber gave out, and the shade, as they went beyond the Great Plains and the land crumpled and rose toward the foothills of the Rockies, the companies tended to crowd together into single trails through narrow defiles. There is a famous one, discovered by a French-Canadian trapper named Sublette in the 1830s, through South Pass, Wyoming. There, so enormous and so continuous was the traffic that went through in the summers of the 1850s that the forty-niners' wheel ruts are still frozen in the rocky soil.

Once through these rocky patches the wagons would fan out again. But in northern Wyoming the flat land and the wide horizon are deceptive. The route appears a safe and easy middle way between the towering peaks to the south and the north, but it is all uphill. And here, at nine thousand feet, up in the clouds where the storms are brewed, they were assaulted by ferocious rains and hail and slowed by ground so boggy that many wagons were abandoned. Here even the most cautious companies discovered they were overloaded. Not even the Charlestown Company had figured the feasible balance between the weight of their supplies and the weight the animals could bear. Families had taken along what they would need in a new home, artisans took the tools of their trade. As they went on and up to the brown midsummer crest of the Rockies, they all learned with bitter reluctance that the critical ratio, the survival ratio, was the number of human mouths to one ox or mule. Now the crawling companies began to dump stoves, bedsteads, trunks, bellows, dishes, kettles, harness, spades, plows, mirrors, brooms, boiled shirts—anything that added an ounce to the hard limit of twenty-five hundred pounds per wagon. They have left us sarcastic songs about their ordeal, which like most folk songs suppress the pain in the jollity of the tune:

> There's not a log to make a seat
> Along the River Platte,
> So when you eat you've got to stand
> Or sit down square and flat.

"Mirage on the Prairie or Traders' Caravan" was the title A. J. Miller
gave to his view of a wagon train slowly vanishing into the limitless plains.

It's fun to cook with buffalo chips,
Take one that's newly born.
If I knew once what I know now,
I'd have gone around the Horn.

Once across the Rockies their spirits picked up again, but not for long.
Moving south and west they had ahead of them the rolling desert land of
Utah, and once across Utah they had another three hundred and
fifty-mile walk following the Humboldt River, which begins in grass and
bright, rippling water and ends in the bone-bright wilderness that is now
the western reach of the state of Nevada. The desert landscape here
constantly unfolds a green horizon, but when you come to it you find a
scrubby carpet of creosote and mesquite and cat's-claw, some of it
poisonous, all of it arid. And now they came on a phenomenon that most
of them had never seen. The Humboldt slowed and turned a yellow
milky-green, the sure sign that it was impregnated with alkali. The cattle
that drank the water died; the humans boiled it and nevertheless had
continuous dysentery.

By this time they had been together for three or four months. It was
August and normally one hundred or one hundred and ten degrees in
any discoverable shade, and the nerves began to snap. People went mad:
one man shot his brother because he could no longer stand the sound of
his voice, another man tried to strangle a partner for the crime of twirling
a luxuriant mustache. This was, they thought at the time, the nadir of the
trek. Certainly, brotherly love gave out.

Something else gave out that the people who knew about it dreaded to
mention, and the people who didn't discovered too late. The river itself,
foul as it was, dribbled and spread into a fetid marsh and at last dried up
under the burning sun. It was something they could not credit. They had
never seen rivers that simply evaporated and left a scum.

Beyond the end of the Humboldt was nothing but alkali desert,
sixty-five miles without any water at all. They could make it in fifty-two
hours. But the parched animals were used to rest at the "nooning." They
couldn't let them. They had to push on, and when the animals collapsed
they left them to die. One man wrote later that you could not possibly
mistake the trail through the Humboldt Desert because it was littered at
intervals of only thirty yards or so with rusting shafts, bags of putrid
bacon, and the skeletons of mules and oxen and the corpses of humans.
Some people died of starvation, of thirst or dysentery, and some people
died—of just having had it. They crossed sticks and laid them over the
body: "Tom Walmsley, born Yorkshire, died this spot, August 10th,
1849." It occurred to some charitable people who could still muse as
they staggered that you couldn't get word back to a man's family that he
had died nowhere. So they created place names, and wherever the trail

turned or there was a new vista they marked a stick and planted it. And the word got back to Geneva or Glasgow or Philadelphia or Frankfurt that the son had died in Endurance, Nevada. I have an old, yellowing automobile map that still peppers the wilderness of Nevada with such names as Fortitude, Desolation, Last Gasp.

For those who survived the ghastly ordeal of the Humboldt there was the sudden miracle of tumbling water again, and tall shade trees and rising hills. But these blessings were a warning of the last huge hurdle. Some Europeans had never heard of it. They thought the last great mountain range was the Rockies. But rearing up beyond the foothills was the great granite fortress of the High Sierras. The later parties learned well that they must get through the Sierras before early September, when the heavy snows began. They had heard fearful, true anecdotes about impatient companies that had been tipped off to smart shortcuts. Some of these daredevils froze in snow-blocked passes. A train that had refused to break up into manageable teams, a company of four hundred, with a hundred wagons and many cattle and mules, went far south to race across Death Valley. They lost or killed and ate all their animals, wandered for weeks in an ocean of sand and out into scarlet canyons and emerged at last, half crazed and gnawing, as their rescuers recalled, "on poor ox meat but little better than basswood bark, and the marrow in their bones run and looked like corruption."

This was the time when the freewheeling companies no longer scorned the prim precautions of the companies that had kept to a strict military discipline. The Charlestown Company came through unscathed. Like the rest who made it before the snows, they tumbled down the western foothills into deep grass and around the golden buttocks of mountains with live oaks dotted over them as in a medieval tapestry. And they came at last to the American River. They called the last stops Pine Vista, and Cool, and Lotus. But it didn't turn out to be Lotus Land for most. The rich diggings had been seized early on by those California ranchers who were to become the founding families, the "Nobs" of San Francisco. They retired to that shanty town on nine wind-blown sandy hills and replaced its tents with shacks and then, as the gold poured in, with mansions on what is still called Nob Hill.

These were the few who had the luck and the muscle and the guile. Many others were bilked out of their strikes and gladly exchanged a bag of gold dust for a ship's passage home. The rest pounded up and down the river valley hoping to grab a little land and sell it a year later at an inflated price. Or they turned into retailers for the stage-coach line that came down from Oregon with eggs at two dollars apiece. Or they stayed on as artisans and saloon keepers in little villages to which they gave either grim or hilarious names, according to their mood, their luck, or

Bierstadt

their sobriety: Brandy Gulch, Chinese Diggings, Humbug Canyon, Knock'Em Stiff, Rich Bar, and Poverty Hill. Sutter's huge acreage was invaded and his livestock burned when he tried to hold off the invaders. Marshall, like Daniel Boone, was swindled out of every claim. He was intimidated by armed guards posted by the Nobs. And when he went to court, he found the Nobs sitting there as judge and jury. He died in total poverty thirty-seven years after his discovery and was buried within sight of his sawmill. Five years later, the state made belated amends by erecting a statue of him made of bronze.

It is a tremendous story. It took courage, or stark insensibility, to walk two thousand miles across the empty continent. But historically it was a freak. The forty-niners were what you might well call "sudden adventurers." Their aim was not to settle Mr. Jefferson's open West. They looked on the American continent as a vast intermediate nuisance between them and a fortune. The "gradual settlers," the families pushing the frontier steadily west, from the Appalachians and slowly on through "the dark and bloody ground," were still the real pioneers—the best of them neither adventurers nor scoundrels but small, grim people of a puritanical strain who journeyed only to find good soil and achieve nothing more than "their useful toil, their homely joys and destiny obscure."

I think of a family who started a farm on rocky soil in Kentucky: a dim, shiftless, rolling stone of a husband married to an illegitimate girl from the Virginia mountains. He tried five or six farms and kept moving on, a man afflicted, we'd say today, with a character neurosis who thought that by picking a new place, like a movie actress who keeps picking a new husband, he would somehow change the plot. He didn't, of course.

They plodded into Indiana and did a little better. In time, they had a barn and a few animals, a little corral, a rail fence, and they planted corn and flax and beans. But then the neighbors went down with "the milk sickness," picked up from cows that chewed on snakeroot. Our farmer's wife died. So the vagabond father and his dour son moved on to a new state and new ground, the son passing from an almost animal boyhood into a bleak manhood. Yet, out of that frail woman and her listless husband and the poorest ground, there came something strange and wholly admirable: the slow-moving son who seized the Republic and held it through its first cataclysm—Abraham Lincoln.

Overleaf: *In an 1850 photograph, San Francisco Bay is choked with ships, many of them derelict. Passengers and crew alike often went straight to the gold fields.*

6

A FIREBELL IN THE NIGHT

For more than three centuries the Negro in America has been in turn slave, lackey, tenant farmer, hired help, licensed clown and entertainer, who gave to America his cheap labor and his powerful, melancholy music. His lowly status has relentlessly mocked and only very recently challenged the monotonous American declaration that all men are created equal. The Negro has less schooling, worse health, more infant mortality, double or triple the unemployment rate of the whites. He is a permanent invalid in American society. And the places he lives, whether in the town or the country, are its casualty wards.

Let us look over some words that Jefferson put down at the end of a day during which he had seen a planter abusing a slave while the planter's small son stood by:

The whole commerce between master and slave is a perpetual exercise of the most boisterous passions, the most unremitting despotism on the one part and degrading submissions on the other. Our children see this and learn to imitate it. . . . The parent storms, the child looks on . . . and puts on the same airs in the circle of smaller slaves. . . . And thus nursed, educated and daily exercised in tyranny, cannot but be stamped by it with odious peculiarities. The man must be a prodigy who can retain his manners and morals undepraved by such circumstances.

The blacks of today are not likely to be deeply moved by this passage, except to be soured by the thought that Jefferson went on living out his life at Monticello with his own slaves, who were benevolently treated and attended to his wants without visible rancor or hate. No white man can deride this bitter reaction, for it keeps forcing us to think of what we have suppressed for centuries: the most continuously shameful contradiction of the American heritage.

But it also has to be said that men of all sorts belong always to their own time. Not many whites suffered Jefferson's torments (which must often have been quickened by the memory of a slave killed by his nephew). Few philosophers of the Enlightenment shuddered at the

The sorry truth behind the romance of the antebellum South: a bedraggled family of slaves in a Georgia cotton field, with even the children carrying picking sacks. Reproduced from an old stereograph photo.

hanging of a boy for a petty theft. The most humane Greeks in their golden age never doubted that humankind existed in two natural orders, a lower order that labored so that the higher might think fine thoughts and cultivate the arts and sciences.

Today the word "slave" calls up the image of a black man or woman, sold in Africa, by black men, to British or American shippers and put up on an auction block at some port in the West Indies or the American South and then delivered for life to a planter. But the slaves were not always Negroes. In the beginning the laboring whites and blacks under contract were lumped together under one word, "servant," although pretty soon they split up. The vagabond whites, the unskilled, and the shiftless became useless for heavy labor—because they made themselves so—and acquired odd menial jobs away from the fields. The best of the whites became craftsmen, gunsmiths, cabinetmakers, silversmiths, and so on.

And the best of the blacks? It is not possible for us to say what the best of the blacks might have become, for they had no chance to show it. In a warm climate, as Jefferson grimly noted, "no man will labor for himself who can make another labor for him." It never had to be asserted, it was universally assumed, that the Negro was a lower species whom God, in His wonderfully mysterious way, had endowed with a capacity for unremitting heavy labor. That the Negro was considered by civilized men to be exempt from the ordinary decencies can be simply inferred from a very precise drawing of a slave ship submitted to the House of Commons in the early eighteenth century to prove that the seagoing accommodations for slaves were not only ingenious but humane. Here people slept in orderly piles, two or three men on top of each other, an arrangement at once neat and thoughtful, to which, as Charles Dickens wrote in another satirical context, no Christian could possibly object.

Before the slaves arrived they had already forfeited their lives to an as yet unidentified owner. When they were shipped to Catholic Brazil, they could hope to work out their freedom by manumission; they could have no such hope in Protestant North America. They would be set to work on a rice or indigo or tobacco or cotton plantation and watched from dawn to dusk by an overseer. Their whole lives were spent within the confines of the master's domain, and they knew every sort of master, the vile and the chivalrous, the feckless, the good-natured, and the humdrum employers of a labor gang.

The moral or emotional attitude of the owner was not always the determinant of the slaves' treatment. A callow owner might have abundant acres, with a surplus of crops that *somebody* had to eat up. Many plantations were badly managed, not out of malice, but because the owner was always in debt. Even in the golden time of the Cotton

Kingdom, there was a good deal of shabby gentility among planters whose own diet and amenities were not much superior to those of their slaves, though enjoyed in larger rooms. On wealthier plantations in Georgia and the Carolinas, the better slave cabins, reserved for the servants of the big houses, might be built of brick. They were one-story, single-room affairs, built by the slaves themselves, with a fireplace and interior annexes contrived by partitions or brick parapets. Here one, two, or possibly three families were born, lived, bred, and died. The laboring slaves had wooden huts in the woods and the fields beyond. The working routine was sixteen hours a day, Sundays off always, and sometimes Saturdays also. Once a week, they were given four pounds of pork apiece and eight quarts—a peck—of corn. They kept their own poultry and grew their vegetables and chopped their fuel in the woods. At Christmastime, and on family anniversaries, they might be given big helpings of coffee and molasses and tobacco, and calico for clothes.

By the time of the American Revolution, half the population of Virginia were black slaves, and in the Carolinas it was two blacks to one white. These figures enlivened, even in the debates of the Constitutional Convention, the old self-protective argument against slavery —namely, all morals aside, the fear of being outnumbered. And by the end of the eighteenth century, there was another historical shift that made some worried planters begin to think again about "the peculiar institution."

The long high noon of the Southern economy was fading into an early twilight. Able young men were decamping to cross the Appalachians. The competition of the West weakened the demand for the crops of the coastal South, and much tobacco land had been worn out by overplanting. Many small planters could make ends meet only by selling off their idle slaves. And the ones that stayed were often a burden on a failing planter: they were susceptible to epidemics (the women, it was often complained, were "poor breeders"). But on one thing most of the Southern coastal planters, if not the Northern shippers, agreed. There were more than enough slaves already on hand. In 1808 the importation of slaves from Africa ceased to be legal.

But it was a ban rarely to be enforced, because in 1794 something had happened that made slaves more desirable than ever. That something was a small invention that produced the Cotton Kingdom. In the autumn of 1792 a young man fresh from Yale College arrived in Savannah, Georgia, and took a boat up the river to the plantation of the widow of General Nathaniel Greene, who had been given it as a reward for gallantry in the Revolutionary War. The young man's name was Eli Whitney. He was the son of a Massachusetts small farmer, on his first Southern journey, going to his first job as a schoolmaster. To a boy accustomed to the winter chores of a snowbound New England farm, his first sight of the South seemed as exotic as a glimpse of Siam; he was impressed and moved by the strangeness of the trees and flowers, the birdsong and the primal life of the bayous. He had struck up an acquaintance with a Southern professor at Yale, and through him he now found himself going to spend a few weeks, before his teaching started, as the house guest of the old soldier's widow.

Whitney was a recluse, an inquisitive brooding type we should call a loner, whose mania was carpentry and mechanics. As a boy he had amazed his family by going off to a carpenter's shop for days on end and reappearing with wheel rims, polished axles, needles, finely ground knives, metalwork, clocks, a fiddle—all of his own construction. He rigged up his own telescope and hygrometer. When a device for measuring the movement of the planets broke down, he talked the college authorities out of shipping it to London and repaired it himself. The president of Yale proudly told his corporation that "the College has been saved Fifteen Pounds by a student who is a remarkable artist."

One evening, sitting at the widow's table and overawed by the Lucullan fare—the muscat grapes and pecans, the rice birds, the little lobsters, the nectarines and peaches, the Madeira and German wines—he listened to some planters reciting a bitter lamentation about the tedium and cost of cleaning their short-staple cotton. It took twenty slaves a whole day to pick and clean twenty pounds of cotton. The problem was an old and nagging one: you had to separate the obstinate seeds from the precious lint before it could be spun, and the one way to do it was by hand. The only machines ever developed simply crushed the seeds and pressed them deeper into the lint. The Southerners talked wistfully about the marvelous spinning machines they used up North, fed by imported long-staple cotton—seventy spindles moved by a single water wheel and run by children. Until the Southerners could figure out how to clean their own Sea Island and green-seed cottons swiftly and cheaply, they could not hope to compete.

Young Whitney had never seen any species of cotton. But he was fascinated by the problem, and in the next few days he settled into a little workshop the family had rigged up for him and tried out various shapes of cylinders, pulling draw-knives over them—but nothing worked. How long it took him by trial and error to arrive at a solution we do not know. But he later recalled, in a letter, the day on the plantation when he had happened to see a cat sitting by the fence that enclosed the poultry yard. It had one paw out through the fence and held it there like a pointer, poised and waiting for a strolling chicken. The paw darted forward and missed the chicken but retrieved a pawful of feathers.

Whitney saw in this a principle of friction and separation, and he applied it to his experiments and came up with a simple box, the cotton gin. Inside it was a suspended wooden cylinder that revolved at the cranking of a handle. The cylinder was encircled with evenly spaced metal spikes that clawed at the deposited raw cotton, shed the seeds behind the cylinder, and let the pure lint come foaming up in front. Whitney calculated that a hand machine like this could do the work of ten slaves, of fifty slaves if it was driven by water. Like so many fundamental discoveries, like the propositions of Euclid, it was so simple that it seemed incredible nobody had thought of it. Once demonstrated, it was indeed so simple that any wheelwright could make it, and it was Whitney's misfortune that most of them did. Trying to monopolize it was like taking out a patent on a shoelace. He did take out a patent, but the accumulating variations obliterated his claim to ownership. Not until he was in middle age was he paid for the use of his gin in the Carolinas and Tennessee. From Georgia, where it was first used, he received next to nothing.

The device gave a gigantic lift to the fortunes of the Southern planters. It caused the arable South to expand into a landscape of cotton, and men who had once kept fifty slaves bargained and bartered for hundreds. At about the same time, another simple experiment turned the hot, wet delta lands of Louisiana into more fortunes and yet another recruiting ground for black slaves. Before, and after, the Revolution all the sugar made in the United States was produced for the household by the householder tapping trees for their sap. Within a year of Eli Whitney's first patent (1794), a bustling little Frenchman, Jean Étienne Boré, invited the people of New Orleans to his plantation outside the town, where he had set up in a shed some rude machinery and some vats. He was apparently something of a Barnum, and he wished to offer a public demonstration that sugar cane could be boiled off into crystals. Toward nightfall, as the vats were cooling off, the first crystals appeared. Boré invited the city fathers to come close and make their inspection, and then he appeared to proclaim, to resounding cheers from the crowd: "It granulates!"

So a sugar empire began to stretch west across the rich lowlands. The next question was how to get the great harvests to the North?

The Mississippi has a powerful downstream flow and whirling currents. Many planters had tried and failed to pull boats upstream with teams of horses plodding along the banks. Then, in 1811, New Orleans built the first high-powered, light-draft steamboat and solved the problem of upstream navigation. They started shipping cargoes of raw sugar

Overleaf: *In an 1861 painting by Adrian Persac, the Olivier plantation in Louisiana breathes calm and prosperity. The plantation's own sugar mill is at right.*

up the Mississippi for refining as far as St. Louis, Louisville, and Cincinnati. Not until the Civil War was over did New Orleans refine its own sugar, but, twenty years after the first steamboat went up the river, New Orleans was the sugar capital of North America. It was also the capital port of King Cotton.

So now the South settled into its golden age. The sugar boats sailed north, and on the return journey picked up the cotton from new plantations started along the shores of the Mississippi itself. The first stop the steamboats made was at Natchez, a town that had been ruled successively by the Indians, the French, the British, and the Spanish, and was only recently American. Before the coming of the cotton gin, it had been a frontier capital and a rough one, a landing place for the flatboatmen taking aboard their rafts skins and hams, and tobacco and grains and whiskey. It was a rowdy way station for pioneers going into the new lands and a boomtown for land agents and fly-by-night real-estate men. Land was cheap and money was easy to make, and lose. The farmers hereabouts had tried and failed to grow indigo. They had found tobacco didn't pay. But after the cotton gin the land bloomed, and so did the new rich. They came from the South and also from the North, and from Scotland and Ireland. They built new houses on the models that the French and Spanish had left them, but the grandest mansions—happily—followed the austere and graceful fashion of the Greek revival. It is characteristic, however, of the mid-century cotton tycoons that although they apparently admired and retained the classical forms outdoors, indoors they displayed all the gaudy and funereal contortions of early Victoriana: mantles of Carrara marble and bronze chandeliers from Italy, giant matching mirrors from Paris, sideboards and enormous slabs of mahogany for drawing-room doors from England. It was a far cry in more senses than one from these ostentatious showplaces in Natchez to General Greene's plantation outside of Savannah, and from the new fortunes to the old. But across the eight hundred miles that separated them you would have seen the same crop, the same raw source of wealth, the same lifeline, the same legions of the blacks.

Whitney's invention had given a new lease on life to the whole Southern system. Two years after he had landed at the Greene plantation he got his first patent for the gin, but, growing disheartened with the endless wrangling over his exclusive rights, he went back to the North and was soon intrigued by other mechanical problems. Watching craftsmen lovingly make and repair firearms, he was exasperated by an obvious fact that had been true since the first gun: that every weapon was a unique item, and if one part broke the gun had to go back to the maker and be doctored like an individual patient. He began to wonder why you might not look on a gun as the product of a mold, or as an assembled product of many molds. He tinkered for a while with jigs and patterns in automatic machines and at last produced a series of uniform parts. If this could be done on a large scale, he realized, then unskilled workers could do what had previously been done only by craftsmen.

This idea came to the notice of the government just when the Napoleonic wars had stopped the importation of arms from Europe and when the United States itself feared a war with France. The Treasury was so much in need of a savior that it saw one in Whitney. On his reckless promise to deliver ten thousand muskets in two years, he was to be paid the astounding sum of $134,000—which would make it, at today's reckoning, the first million-dollar contract. We ought at this point to cue in a rush of heroic music and say that he delivered. He did not. Nearly three years later there was no musket, and he was a joke in New England and something of a fraud in Washington. But Whitney had seen a labor problem where formerly there was none, and he had aired the method of solving it. Within ten years a man named Hall, subsidized by the government in one of its ordnance factories, produced the assembly line product.

The production of interchangeable parts—screws and threads for muskets, tackle blocks, and planking for ships—had already been accomplished in England and France. Yet these were still being handled by skilled men, and Whitney's standardized parts could be fitted by drones with no other skill. He had, in fact, introduced in his factories a wholly new system: division of labor, a system unwelcome in Europe since it threatened the craftsmen and the long tradition of apprenticeship.

What made Whitney's system a godsend was the growing shortage of skilled workers as the people grew footloose and abandoned the traditional assumption that a family of mechanics would go on for generations learning one trade and one trade only. Tocqueville was to remark, in the 1830s, on the astonishing mobility of Americans, how they seldom lived in the house they were born in, how they moved around and tried their hands at many things. Whitney's principle of mass production through uniform molds transferred the skill from the man to the machine. His factory system entailed small teams doing only one task of an assembly routine, and it was sufficiently revolutionary to be called first "the Whitney system" and then, in Europe, "the American system." It led to the Colt revolver and the sewing machine and the flour mill and the card-making machine. It marked the turning point, for the Northern states, between handicrafts and industry. It germinated all the fruits, and the ills, of mass production; and it revolutionized the conception of human labor in the Western world and—in our century—in Africa and Asia as well.

But that, as they say, is *our* problem. The historic fact is that, while the South was spreading cotton and sugar and tobacco and expanding the empire of slavery, the North was committing itself to men and machines and spreading them through the Northwest Territories. Eli Whitney's nagging ingenuity gave a tragic guarantee that the North would welcome the Industrial Revolution and the South would reject it, that the North would go one way and the South another—and that sooner or later they would collide.

As the pioneers flooded into the Western lands, and old territories turned into new states, not only machines followed them but independent farmers who were soundly against slavery. With them it was not simply a matter of principle. They had gone West to work free land for their own prosperity. They did not intend to compete with slave labor. So the awkward question came up: what would happen when the two streams of settlers flowed together *on the same ground?*

"This momentous question," wrote the aging Jefferson, "like a firebell in the night, awakened and filled me with terror. I considered it at once as the knell of the Union." The bell was rung by Missouri's request in 1819 to come into the Union as a slave state. Missouri had been settled by slaveholders, but it lay north of the horizontal line that divided the free states of the North from the slave states of the South. If Missouri were let in as a slave state, a Northerner would look at the map and see a precedent, an invasion, at best a buffer state. In the event, the Congress bowed to Missouri but to maintain its custom of balancing one free state and one slave, it also admitted Maine as a free state. In the same act, it prohibited, from then on, all slavery north of the line of latitude 36° 30'. It is known as the Missouri Compromise line. It was destined to be also a battle line.

This geographical balance lasted, precariously, for about thirty years. But it was thunderingly upset by the United States' war with Mexico, in 1848, out of which the Union acquired vast new lands, most of them south of the Missouri Compromise line: Texas, Territory of New Mexico, California, and Utah well to the north. They had their own strong traditions. Texas had slavery, California had not, and the two territories would test the power to legislate either system. This massive challenge to the compromise greatly aggravated the enmity between the North and South. It quickened the agitation in the North to keep slavery out of all the new states and territories, and it united the Southerners in a kind of self-protective defiance. The new Westerners in the North were

---

Industry was the North's great strength. At this Cold Springs, N.Y., foundry alone, 3,000 cannon and 1,600,000 projectiles were made for the Union Army.

confirmed in their prejudices, many of them gross and bigoted, about the brutality and peonage of the South. Not all Northerners by any means believed the fire and brimstone propaganda of the Abolitionists, which had been brewing for a quarter of a century. Anti-Abolitionist mobs beat up a Bostonian in 1837. In the same year, in Illinois, a clergyman was killed.

The issue came to a head, as great issues tend to, first in the United States Senate and then in the Supreme Court. The House passed a proviso prohibiting slavery in the territories taken from Mexico and made it apply to Texas, where many slave-owning Southerners had died in the cause of bringing their republic into the Union. The Senate defeated it. What had the Senate to offer on its own account? In the main it had the patriarchal figure of Henry Clay, a bony, awkward Virginian who had gone into Kentucky, become a successful lawyer, turned at twenty-two to politics and given fifty years of his life to a failing campaign to abolish slavery. In 1850 he stood on the Senate floor to make the last speech of his life. He was seventy-three, worn down to the bone and the dewlaps, and he was wracked with arthritis. He talked for two days, and he came up with a solution that fair-minded men, if they had been in a majority, might have accepted with good grace.

On the seething issue among Southerners—the harboring of thousands of fugitive slaves in the North—Clay proposed that they should all be returned to their masters. Let California be admitted as a free state. Let Texas retain the slave system it had always had. And give to the territories of Utah and New Mexico the freedom to decide when, if ever, they should legalize slavery. This compromise was voted and grudgingly accepted by both sides.

Then there set in one of those terrifying, and rationally unaccountable, decades in American life when all the ingenuity, vigor, and hot blood of the country seem to concentrate into opposing channels of fear and self-righteousness. Of course, there were fair-minded men of considerable influence in every part of the country, but they retreated into the quiet desperation of hoping for the best. They were drowned in a boiling sea of rhetoric and provocation. In defiance of federal law, the Abolitionists increased their help to fugitive slaves and got at least fifty thousand of them away by an organized underground. And there was that strange, brave egotist from Connecticut, John Brown, who raided a federal arsenal with the intention of arming Southern slaves. He was caught, tried, and hanged, but his name, if not his soul, goes marching on in a song that was in its day a fearful battle cry. All of this was enough to taunt the Southerners to the point where they talked of secession and meant it. It was left to the Supreme Court, of all healing institutions, to shatter the hope of compromise.

In 1854 and 1855, at the height of the political turmoil over slavery in Kansas and Nebraska, the Missouri painter George Caleb Bingham produced a series of genre scenes dealing with campaigning and voting. This one, dated 1854, was called "The Verdict of the People."

A Negro slave, Dred Scott, from the slave state of Missouri, had lived for some time in the free state of Illinois. He had done so with his master's permission, but when he went home again he sued to have himself declared a free man. The Supreme Court ruled that whether or not it could be argued that a Negro was a citizen, a slave was not. The laws of Missouri were binding. In a word, the Court said that Congress was powerless to exclude slavery from a free state. From that moment on, the two nations—for that is what in fact, and in feeling, they had become—fell almost resolutely apart.

On December 20, 1860, a state convention in South Carolina dissolved "the union now subsisting" between it and the other states. By February 1, the rest of the Deep South followed: Mississippi, Florida, Alabama, Georgia, and Louisiana. Eight days later these six seceding states met in Montgomery, Alabama, formed their own Congress, adopted a constitution, and proclaimed "the Confederate States of America." They were quickly joined by Texas.

In March a new President, Abraham Lincoln, on his own initiative declared secession void and promised to "hold, occupy and possess" all government property. He quickly kept his word. The day after his inauguration he ordered a shipload of troops to land on Fort Pickens, an island fort in Pensacola Bay off the coast of Florida. It was held by forty Union troopers who had escaped there in January, when Southern forces had seized government forts on the mainland. The reinforcements had agreed with the Confederacy to stay on their ship so as not to appear to be raising a dramatic siege. Undoubtedly Fort Pickens would be immortalized in all the schoolbooks if Lincoln's landing order had been obeyed. But there was an unaccountable delay in delivering the order of March 5, and the troops landed, without incident, on April 12, only a few hours after a similar episode far to the north had carried the nation into war.

There was another island fort, Fort Sumter, built on a sandbar in the mouth of Charleston harbor, off the shoreline of South Carolina, the first and most militant of the seceding states. At the end of February the fort's commander warned Washington that he was dangerously short of supplies and in April Lincoln ordered a fleet to go and relieve the Fort Sumter forces. The commander of the Confederate forces invited the garrison to leave. It refused, and at four thirty in the morning of April 12, 1861, the Southerners loosed their fire. In the afternoon of April 13 the Union forces surrendered—and the war was on.

In the slavery debates before the war, various orators and newspapers had picked up a tremulous slogan from the Bible: "A house divided against itself cannot stand." Two years before he became President,

Lincoln had added his own hard gloss: "I believe this government cannot endure permanently half slave and half free. I do not expect the Union to be dissolved; I do not expect the house to fall; but I do expect it will cease to be divided. It will become all one thing, or all the other."

But for two months or more, no such sharp division was made. Virginia first voted against secession and then, five days after Fort Sumter, seceded. Arkansas, Tennessee, most of all Virginia, were neither of one mind nor the other. They all had whole regions where there were no slaves. Eventually Arkansas and Tennessee—its eastern part unwillingly—joined the Confederacy. So did Virginia, but its mountain people were stubborn enough to hold out and form a separate state, West Virginia, which remained loyal to the Union while her people split their allegiance—and their fighting forces—in the ratio of three to one for the Union. North Carolina was the last state to go with the South; and the border slave states—Kentucky, Maryland, Delaware, and Missouri—overcame much hot propaganda to secede and stayed within the Union, hoping against hope to keep cool and neutral.

In many places, among innumerable old Southerners and border state people, the tug of opposing loyalties was never relaxed. "A house divided against itself" had a piercing relevance to the army regulars. They had an immediate duty to decide which side to be on. Two brothers were major generals with the opposing armies. The commander of the Confederate Navy had a son killed in the Union Navy. Mrs. Abraham Lincoln's three brothers died for the South. And we have only to look over the places where the battles were fought and guess the local loyalties of the troops to see that no war is more wounding to the young than a civil war, which turns the homeland into alien country and a map of bloody family feuds.

In the beginning the Northerners thought—as one side always does—that the war would be over "by Christmas." The North had twenty-two million people against the South's nine million. The North had the steel to make its guns and matériel; the South had to buy them from France and Britain. The North had twenty-two thousand miles of unified railroads, and the South had only nine thousand miles of track of various gauges. New York alone produced twice as many manufactured goods as the whole of the South. And so on. Why, then, did it go on for four years?

Few great wars can have swung so sluggishly, so uneasily, between one side and the other. Only in the naval war did one side, the North, establish an early supremacy and hold it. The blockade of the Southern ports froze the sea passage of Southern supplies very early, extended down the East Coast and round into New Orleans, and kept even the South's warships out of their own bases. And in the summer of 1863, the capture of Vicksburg ensured the North's total control of the Mississippi on the Confederacy's western flank.

On land, the record is one of massive and inconclusive thrusts and setbacks. Neither side was at all prepared in any professional military sense, but it has been an American characteristic, from the Revolutionary War to the Second World War, to flout the old professionalism and improvise its own ways of war. The Civil War introduced so many radical tactics—including trench warfare, the night raid, wire entanglements, hand grenades, flame projectors, land mines, armored ships and trains, torpedoes—that it provided the standard manuals for Sandhurst and Saint-Cyr, as well as West Point, even up to the Second World War. (If these academies had learned their lessons better, they would have appreciated by 1914 at the latest the inefficacy of the cavalry charge and the bayonet.) There was only one great engagement in the first year, at Bull Run, and like almost every battle thereafter it was indecisive. For a time, for a long time, the South held the advantage of position, if not of penetration, on the eastern front, while in the West, the Union asserted and usually held the advantage.

There are several battles among which the experts argue in picking out the "typical" engagement. Gettysburg is the popular favorite, as being the last and deepest advance of the South. Shiloh is another, often called "the half-victory," because the Southerners showed their daring in a night raid, because the sagging Northerners were able to call on tough, fresh reserves from across the river, and because the Northerners were then too exhausted to pursue the scattering Southerners.

Personally, I should choose the Battle of Antietam, of September 1862. Not for Lee's brilliant forked invasion of Maryland, with protective maneuvers to the south and west; not for McClellan's countermove to throw three forces at Lee's left, right, and center; not even for the typical Northern blunder of mounting these attacks one at a time instead of simultaneously; nor even for Lee's systematic defeat of all three. But for the all too typical situation in which the Southerners held, the Northerners slumped back in exhaustion to wait for their reserves, and the Southerners then withdrew, having no reserves at all.

Antietam did not set a pattern but it revealed one that foredoomed the South. The South had at the start a huge granary to dip into. For two years it kept the upper hand in cavalry battles, because it could call on a whole society of horsemen. Its generals were at once more adroit and better disciplined, and they developed exceptional skill at fighting along interior lines. But ultimately it came down to the great disparity of resources, of men and matériel, that we mentioned at the start. The South had the audacity, but the North had the reserves.

For all these disparities, camp life on both sides was equally primitive.

Going off to war in their new uniforms, they proudly posed for a daguerreotype portrait. For some, it was the last record. Private Edwin Francis Jennison (top right) of the 2nd Louisiana Cavalry died at the Battle of Malvern Hill in 1862.

Country boys, until they were talked into a little elementary hygiene, into the magic of carbolic soap, dropped in the plaguey summers like swatted flies. Amputation was the sovereign cure for a badly wounded limb. And if you survived after that, you had one chance in four of dying from infection. But it is one of the maddening facts of war that it can galvanize an embryonic specialty into life. The young science of neurology was forced into startling growth during the Civil War by the unprecedented opportunity to observe the effect of gunshot wounds on the nervous system. Philadelphia, in 1863, set up the first hospital, headed by S. Weir Mitchell, to treat soldiers suffering from "nervous disorders." Various "anti-aesthetic agents" were being rapidly developed in Boston, and the first printed use of the modern word is recorded, under the date 1863, in the Oxford Dictionary of American English: "Dr. Morton attended the principal battlefields, and administered anaesthetics with his own hands." For the last two years of the war, the battlefield use of anaesthetics became routine—among the Northern armies. For while high-minded men and women in the North formed something called the National Sanitary Commission to start veterans' pensions, organize nursing wards at the front, and provide for the human problems of the men going home, for the Southerners there was only the compassion of scattered families, and the hope that the next raid would capture not only food and ammunition but some of the drugs and the chloroform Abraham Lincoln had barred from shipment to the Southern armies.

There was another resource of the South that it may now seem hectoring or sentimental to harp on. This was the Southerners' tenacious conviction, however wrongheaded or unholy, that they were fighting for a principle. Not slavery. Slavery alone could not have united landowners and frontiersmen, merchants and mountain farmers, poor whites (and even black soldiers). The Southerners had a homeland in a sense that the North did not: even today, when the textile cities of the South and the soft-drink factories break up the old agrarian uniformity, the South is still a separate culture—with a literature, an idiom, a diet, mores, a pervading sense of irony, and tragedy—quite alien to the continental American culture in which a Maine potato farmer and an automobile salesman in San Diego are almost equally at home. The Southerners wanted neither land nor conquest. They wanted to prove that their homeland was unconquerable. The names of the places where they tried and ultimately failed to do so still toll through the American memory like an elegy: Vicksburg and Antietam, Bull Run and Chancellorsville, Manassas and Chattanooga and Fredericksburg, Cold Harbor and Shiloh and Gettysburg.

I once met a very old man with a long, chiseled face and a snowy mustache and a blazing eye. He was a New Englander of rather fearsome dignity and reserve. Yet, when he came to put down his entry in *Who's Who in America,* he couldn't help beginning with: "Born March 8th, 1841, Boston. Captain, 20th Massachusetts Volunteers, wounded in the breast at Balls Bluff, in the heel at Fredericksburg, in the neck at Antietam." He survived to become the most distinguished jurist, in his old age, in the English-speaking world. He was Justice Oliver Wendell Holmes. I still find it hard to believe that I once met a man who was wounded in the American Civil War, when I think also that his comrades in arms have been dead for over a hundred years. Their only lasting memorial is the sepia photograph they had taken when they first put on their uniform.

To fuse the unity of the South there was a single commanding hero, another thing the North lacked. He helped the South to fight with a single-minded passion. Robert E. Lee was the son of Washington's cavalry leader, a dashing improvident charmer whose wild speculations left his family bankrupt and himself a dying exile in the West Indies. Young Lee was brought up, by his invalid mother, as the scion of a once "land poor" Virginia family. From about the age of twelve it was his job to "carry the keys," that is to order the food, watch over the dwindling moneys, and more or less bring up his six brothers and sisters. He retained only adoring memories of his vanished father and almost as a filial duty went through West Point. He was put in the engineer corps and saw no fighting till the war with Mexico in 1846, when he was in his fortieth year. He was bright and gentle and professionally known for his ability to match the enemy in surprise but also for a rather regrettable tolerance of his subordinates' contrary ideas. He had one last sortie in the Comanche country and then, like George Washington, he retired. Unlike Washington, he went home to an ailing wife and little money.

When the slavery issue came to a boil, Lee made it quite clear where he stood. He freed his own slaves and wrote: "Slavery is a moral and political evil in any society, a greater evil to the white man than the black." There are some problems of conscience, however, that cannot be so cleanly solved, and when the war started Lee faced an acute moral conflict. It was always a shock to recall that Lincoln offered him the command of the *Northern* forces. He could have taken it on principle because he firmly believed that secession was unconstitutional. But through five generations all his loyalties and his affections were with Virginia.

He spent a day and a night pacing around the bedroom of his house and looking down the slope of the hill that is the last short stretch of Virginia before the Potomac River and the North begins. At the end of this agony, he came downstairs and wrote a letter to his son, in which he said he believed in the Union and could "anticipate no greater calamity"

Seated on pews dragged out of a Virginia church, General U. S. Grant (in front of trees) and his staff officers hold a conference during the Wilderness Campaign of 1864. Lincoln had made him commander-in-chief shortly before.

With horses, troops, and the smoke of cannon fire faintly visible in the distance, this is one of very few actual battlefield photographs taken during the Civil War. It was made by the famous war photographer Alexander Gardner on September 17, 1863, at Antietam, Maryland, probably for the use of magazine artists preparing wood engravings of the scene.

Confederate soldiers lie where they fell, in a shallow trench at the foot of Marye's Heights, after a large Union force seized the hill during the Battle of Chancellorsville on May 3, 1863. But the North's moment of triumph was brief. Robert E. Lee's brilliant generalship subsequently turned Chancellorsville into a major Confederate victory.

than its dissolution. "Still, a union that can only be maintained by swords and bayonets ... has no charm for me [and] if the Union is dissolved ... I shall return to my native state and, save in defense, will draw my sword no more."

The monumental serenity and gentleness of Lee have provoked many sentimental plays and reams of idolatrous prose. But there might be a fine play in the second moral—and political—conflict he had to resolve: that of never drawing his sword "save in defense" and yet accepting the command of the Southern forces. In any case, he went back to Virginia to fight for a principle that, ironically, Lincoln himself had enunciated better than anyone, thirteen years before Secession. "Any people, anywhere, being inclined and having the power, have the right to rise up and shake off the existing government, and form a new one that suits them better."

The nub of the conflict between North and South was the definition of "any people, anywhere" (how about the people of Virginia?). To Lincoln, it came to mean exclusively "the people" of the United States. The South took him at his earlier word and presumed that any region as closely knit by culture and economics as the South could claim to be a "people" free to assert the right of self-determination. But Lincoln, in his first proclamation of the war, had declared the "combination" of the Southern states to be illegal. And to this day, the historians and popular sentiment have overwhelmingly agreed with him. Yet, it seems to me, we have all been bedazzled by the Gettysburg Address, a small masterpiece of rhetoric of very dubious logic. Its most famous phrase is very close to political nonsense. Quite apart from the anarchy implied in any government "*by* the people," there remains the ticklish question of how many people or states or ethnic minorities constitute a "people" who may justly wish to govern themselves. Woodrow Wilson held no such bland assumptions about the whole being more sovereign than its parts when he created nations out of ethnic minorities yearning to be free of government by the Austro-Hungarian empire. I'm afraid we must conclude, with Justice Holmes, that the winner is always right.

A few days after Fort Sumter, Lee left his house on the hill and never went back to it. And within a few more days it was a camp and then a graveyard. The Secretary of War, to whom Lee had written a note rejecting the Northern command, saw to it that no one would want to live there again. He ordered that soldiers' graves should be planted close to the house. Later the place was confiscated by the government and became a military cemetery. It is now Arlington, the national military cemetery.

I don't suppose there is a more beautiful, bleak view in all America

Eleven days after he surrendered to Grant, Robert E. Lee stands on the back porch of his house in Richmond. He was reluctant to pose and did so only upon the urging of photographer Matthew Brady, an old friend.

than the one from the porch of Lee's portico, through the fat-bellied Doric columns, looking over the graves of the murdered Kennedy brothers, across the river to the white marble temple that enshrines the memory of yet another murdered President, Abraham Lincoln. He is the man who more than any Northern soldier—more than Grant, the Iowa farm boy—was Lee's moral and political antagonist.

It is difficult, and in some quarters thought to be almost tasteless, to talk sense about Lincoln. But we must try. For the holy image and the living man were very far apart, and keeping them so does no service either to Lincoln or to the art of government. Like all strong characters, he was well hated, and like most frontiersmen who have come to high office—like Harry Truman and Lyndon Johnson—he was ridiculed for his directness and country manners. The London *Times* called him "the Baboon." Lincoln had a gangling gait, a disturbing fondness for rough stories, and a maddening habit of being, in a kind of tooth-sucking way, wiser and sharper than you. (To make it worse, most of the time he was.)

Like all strong Presidents he enraged the Congress by sweeping and arbitrary acts that went, much of the time, beyond the Constitution—or in any case beyond the balance of presidential and Congressional authority that is inevitably tipped in the President's favor in time of war. Indeed, until he was dead Lincoln was never wildly popular. When the war started he used the executive power solely—to proclaim an insurrection, declare a blockade, suspend habeas corpus, expand the army, order emergency spending—and for a year or two he had a dreadful time getting Congress to approve his conduct of the war. Congress would not ratify his acts till the summer of 1861, and it was only two years later that a Supreme Court bolstered with Lincoln appointees upheld him by the whisker of a 5 to 4 majority. Proclamations were his favorite weapon, whereby, most notoriously, he threw thousands of people into jail without trial, on suspicion of treachery or disloyalty. The debunking temptation must nonetheless be resisted. Because he was not a saint, there is no obligation to see him as a tyrant or a hypocrite. He allowed the fiercest freedom of criticism in Congress, in the press, and in public protest meetings. He handed out appointments irrespective of party or military status. He learned very quickly about war, spotted the character flaw in a likable general and fired him, and in the end picked the best. And he was so lacking in egomania that he could tell his generals that "when you are in the field, you are the Union." He had an extraordinary feel for the humanity of quite inhuman people and tolerated them long enough to get them to do what he wanted—contractors, war profiteers, wheeler-dealers, the scum of the Republic. He dignified the trade of politician like few men before or since.

By some brain chemistry that has never been explained, Lincoln

On April 9, 1865, the day of the surrender at Appomattox, Lincoln sat for photographer Alexander Gardner. This extraordinary portrait, which shows plainly the toll of the war years, was the result. Lincoln was never photographed again; five days later he was shot by John Wilkes Booth at Ford's Theatre.

transformed in middle life his whole style of speaking and writing. His early speeches are frontier-lawyer baroque, stuffed with the fustian of his time. We know that he steeped himself in the subtleties of Shakespeare, the cadences of the Bible, and the hard humanity of Robert Burns. And somehow, and conspicuously during the war, he became what he always must have been: a shrewd, honorable frontiersman of very great gifts. Not the least of these was his ability to express a hard, unsentimental truth in the barest language every tinker and tailor could understand:

I have found that when one is embarrassed, usually the shortest way to get through with it is to quit talking or thinking about it, and go at something else.

I have no prejudice against the Southern people. They are just what we would be in their situation. I surely will not blame them for not doing what I should not know how to do myself.

If I could save the Union without freeing any slave, I would do it; and if I could save it by freeing all the slaves, I would do it; and if I could save it by freeing some and leaving others alone, I would also do that.

He exemplified better than any statesman until Churchill the Churchillian line: "The short words are best, and the old words are the best of all."

He is admired, of course, because he led the winning side. He is revered because he wrote—when the South was sure to lose—the Emancipation Proclamation. We often overlook the fact that this stirring document was intended to apply only to the Southern states, and not the slave-owning border states; Palmerston's verdict is still fair comment—that Lincoln undertook "to abolish slavery where he was without power to do so, while protecting it where he had power to destroy it." But the overwhelming aspect of his reputation is that he was assassinated, and so he was canonized, because a halo descends on all the murdered Presidents, and on Lincoln most of all.

At the end of the war, the South was beaten, and—much worse—it was devastated. The Cotton Kingdom was destroyed, the plantation system with all its evils, and its virtues, was debauched. Four million slaves were freed, but with nowhere to go. The land, simply the natural richness of the land and the man-made culture of the South, was defiled. In a single long march of sixty thousand men, from Atlanta three hundred miles to the sea, General Sherman destroyed every town, rail yard, mansion, and crop across a swath of sixty miles. It was a systematic atrocity that haunted Sherman for the rest of his life and made him howl at a graduating class of the Michigan Military Academy fifteen years later: "I am tired and sick of war. Its glory is all moonshine. It is only those who have neither fired a shot nor heard the shrieks and groans of the wounded who cry aloud for blood, more vengeance, more desolation. War is hell."

But the Union was restored. And at what a price! Germany, after the Second World War, was hardly so badly off as the conquered South. It was not only conquered; it was now to be punished. It took the strenuous efforts of General Grant to prevent Lee and other Confederate generals from being brought to trial for treason. The Northern politicians were fearful that if the Southerners were restored to their rights they would form a Democratic majority and leave Congress at the mercy of men lately traitors. So several Southern states were put under military command and many sections were patrolled by Negro federal troops. South Carolina was denied its entire white representation in Congress. Alabama had its governor removed and the government jobs of all ex-Confederates were filled by Negroes; Negroes dominated the state legislature in the proportion of three to one. In other states, Negroes—both able and practically illiterate—made up half the membership of state legislatures.

There were Northern idealists who thought they were seeing in this amalgam the dawn of the equality of man. But throughout the South both the blacks and the whites were puppets manipulated by Northern businessmen and salesmen, who descended on the conquered province like locusts. When the reaction came—and it came swiftly—the Negroes were brutally swept from such power as they had and from all the voting booths—and they didn't enter them again for many decades. The Negro was once again, if he was lucky, a hireling, never to be trusted as an equal. He had been pitied and despised, and on many plantations charitably indulged. Now he was feared. These memories were kept fresh in the South for many generations and planted the trauma from which we are only now painfully beginning to recover.

The Negro might once again be the creature of the Southern white, but, even after the scalawag and the carpetbagger had gone, the whole South—white and black—would remain for another eighty years the poor brother of the Union, the creature of the Northerners in Congress who fixed the tariff and the railroad freight rates. Not until the late 1930s would the South move out of worn land and single crops into valleys and industries fertilized by public power. By that time the South had a population of poor whites listless from malnutrition and other generations of blacks cowed by the doctrine of "white supremacy." And over them both by then stood a raw plutocracy, with the best of the old planter types gone to seed or gone to their shrunken acres.

Overleaf: *The desolate aftermath: scorched and broken, the brick walls of Gallego Mills in Richmond stand in a field of rubble. As capital of the Confederacy, Richmond held out grimly until the very end of the war. But as Grant marched in, and evacuation was going on, the city was swept with fire.*

7
DOMESTICATING A WILDERNESS

Walt Whitman, lying paralyzed in old age on a bed in Camden, New Jersey, spoke for all of us who have been there and back when he recalled his romantic image of the West:

Those towns . . . like ships on the sea . . . Eagle Tail, Coyote, Cheyenne, Agate, Monotony, Kit Carson—with ever the ant-hill and the buffalo-wallow, ever the herds of cattle and cowboys . . . bright-eyed as hawks, with their swarthy complexions and their broad-brimmed hats, always on horseback, with loose arms raised and swinging as they ride.

The impulse to go back once and for all, to settle in the open spaces or beyond them, is still strong and never stronger than after a war. I doubt that there have been many such disillusioned decades as the one after the Civil War. In the South the idea of representative government had become a tragic farce in the puppet governments of freed slaves and renegade whites set up by an unholy alliance of Northern reformers and calculating money grubbers. In the victorious North a million soldiers returned to scarce jobs and gouging profiteers. For the employed townsman there was a twelve-hour day. The European immigrants started to roll in again, city populations doubled, and the frontier spawned lawlessness. It was too much for some people, and most of all for God-fearing idealistic types, who broke away and in country places founded communes—equality-of-women communes, free-love communes, political and religious communes.

There was a great model already in existence, a community at once religious and intensely practical but also rumored to make a fetish of polygamy, the main cause of its being ceaselessly persecuted. But its followers thought always and only that it had planted the Kingdom of God in the wilderness.

They appeared, in the 1840s, an astonishing body of people, led by a second Moses, that walked into the West a thousand miles beyond the settlers, over the crest of the Rockies, and in a desert basin founded the first successful Western community. They called it the City of the Saints. To the rest of us it is known as Salt Lake City, Utah. But to the Mormons it is Rome and Mecca, the capital of the world.

It was a society conceived in the nightmares of Joseph Smith, a fifteen-year-old boy in a small town in New York State. He was aroused, he said, by a vision in which both God and Jesus Christ appeared and told him categorically that all existing and previous religions were fraudulent. After that, the Angel of the Lord came to him regularly and told him he was the chosen of God to found the one true church. He was to unearth a set of golden plates and translate them, and there he would have his holy guide. The fact is that he translated, at least set down, *something*, which became the remarkable substitute Bible known as the Book of Mormon.

Between the vision and the reality stretched seventeen years, and for the faithful they were as frightful as any in the history of American idealism. Smith tried to plant the church first in New York and was persecuted. He and his flock moved on into Ohio and were persecuted again. On into Missouri, where they were beaten, imprisoned, raped, and forced into bankruptcy by the burning of their banks. For the Mormons were not only holier than thou, they were thriftier. Their prosperity was as nauseating as their polygamy, so, always, their banks were burned. They went on into Illinois, where the rumors started that the chosen of God were in fact nothing but wholesale adulterers. Again mobs set fire to their houses and farms, and their banks, and dragged Joseph Smith from jail and shot him. Among his survivors was a quite fearless autocrat named Brigham Young, who decided now to fulfill the prophecy of the dead leader that they would one day build the true temple and the holy city "up in the mountains where the Devil cannot dig us out . . . where we can live . . . as we have a mind to."

Thus, one year after the murder of Smith, Brigham Young and his Apostles, so called, began their tremendous walk on into Nebraska and across the Rockies in Wyoming and into the Great Basin, ultimately to look down on the white flats of the Salt Lake Valley. And Young said, "This is the place." (Some people hold that Smith envisioned a final move to another country. If so, his vision was realized, for when the Mormons arrived in Utah, it was the northernmost province of Mexico.) The "place" was a belt of land reaching three hundred miles down through what is today central Utah. They found it as desert and they made it over into the most fertile stretch of the West, because of the immediate assumption, by Brigham Young and his High Council, of absolute power.

Six days after their arrival, Young put out a set of decrees. Land would be neither bought nor sold; it was assigned to each settler according to his particular skill, and if he failed to make it productive it would be taken away from him. Water and timber resources were to be held in common. The first thing to be done, in the two months left before the fall, was to dig irrigation ditches. Water would be allotted according to the condition of your soil and the needs of your crops, a system that still holds. Next, organized farming expeditions were sent out, each one staffed with a doctor, a carpenter, a miller, a blacksmith—all of them farmers as well. As they spread their crops, they spent days at a time away from the settlement, then weeks away as the winter set in. If their allotted land proved barren they were still not allowed to desert it; they had to try through the growing season to make it fruitful. Obviously some failed, some died in the winter snows, and others existed on thorns and grasses. But against the odds of nature and the interference of government scouts, against cheating whites and warring Indians, they sowed and they reaped. It took half a century to make the desert bloom, but in the end it was done. The Church still receives a regular share of the income from the land and organizes the agriculture—the herds, the feed, the sale of crops. In the depression of the 1930s the Mormons were the only American farm cooperative that steadily refused all help from the federal government. They stuck to their grim belief that the Lord alone giveth and the Lord taketh away.

In all other civil and criminal matters, the law was the law proclaimed by the High Council of the Church, including a precise code of punishments for such things as vagrancy, theft, disorderliness, and adultery. The last word reminds us of the Mormons' own "peculiar institution," which everybody is impatient to know about, for nothing bothers a man with one wife more than another man with many wives who doesn't even feel guilty. The simple truth is that polygamy was another of Joseph Smith's orders received from on high. He was commanded in a vision to establish a superior order of marriage, and polygamy was it. Once arrived in Utah, the High Council declared it to be a fundamental tenet of Church doctrine. Subsequently, many Mormon leaders shrank from it, but many more practiced it, and the record, curiously, testifies that there was little jealousy, few disturbed children, strong fidelity inside the families, and very harsh penalties for adultery.

Harsher still, however, was the treatment of the Mormons by the federal government so long as they kept up the practice. The railroads finally intruded on their isolation, and once Utah became an American territory the Mormons were forced to mingle and trade with malicious "gentiles" (the Mormon word for non-Mormons) who carried appalling tales to Washington. In time, the federal government refused their territory statehood and overrode the authority of their courts. Congress made polygamy a federal crime and prepared to confiscate all the property of the Church. In the end they had to give in. In the 1890s, fifty years after they had settled, President Cleveland signed an act proclaiming Utah as the forty-fifth state of the Union. Such polygamy and extramural shenanigans as now exist in Utah are undertaken with the same legal risks as in any other state of the Union.

To this day in Utah, the Church's hold on the social and economic life of the faithful is strong. The Church owns most of the office buildings, theaters, real estate, insurance firms, and banks: a religious monopoly of secular life that is hardly typical of the general run of Americans who domesticated the wilderness. To move at all, the majority always has to be prodded by a fear or inspired by a symbol—and, in the decade after the Civil War, the inspiring symbol was that splendid mechanical beast called "the iron horse."

A century ago, the railroad engine was as magical as a space ship. It stirred the American people with the idea that, once the Civil War was over and the Union was secure, it would be possible to unite the continent in fact as well as in sentiment and political theory—and the railroad train was what would do it. But this was quite an order. The Eastern railroads had extended tentacles only as far as Nebraska, while, at the Western end, existing railroads were running north and south, well to the west of the huge wall of the Sierras. In between was an unbridged gap of seventeen hundred miles or so.

To close this gap was a dream shared equally by businessmen and by romantics. The businessmen goggled over the vision of a continental network of towns and deliveries and customers. The romantics were fetched by the prospect of reliving in comparative comfort the trials, and the spectacular discoveries, of the scouts and hunters, the Mormons and the gold seekers. And by 1865, certainly, there had been a generation or two of footloose and first-rate artists who had touched the imagination of the East with paintings that composed a marvelous continental panorama. They started with the familiar East, but then the curtain went up on the blue Appalachians and, beyond, an ocean of prairie and scudding convoys of buffalo pursued by flotillas of redskins; then the land soared up to the famous Rockies and dipped again to another crumpled plain and semidesert, and then true desert, till the fabulous Sierras unloosed their cascading waterfalls; and over their watershed the continent tumbled in glory to golden valleys and the Lewis and Clark wonder of the sailless Pacific.

Until the war was over the transcontinental railroad was a giant enterprise stalled by much bickering between a reluctant Congress and the Army, which had clamored for it. If it had been left to the government it would have taken another twenty years to complete. But it was a commercial venture, and it was fortunately fed by the adrenaline of competition. There were two railroad companies, the Union Pacific in the East

Still some 150 miles short of the point where they would join with the east-bound Central Pacific line, workmen of the Union Pacific use an ingenious jury rig to lower heavy stones for an abutment over the Green River in western Wyoming.

and the Central Pacific in the West, panting to best each other in slamming down a record mileage of track. And although Congress, once it roused itself to the project, had stipulated that the Central Pacific should stop when it reached the California border (Congress was packed with Easterners), it decided in 1866 that the two companies should build hell for leather and meet wherever they met.

So now began a race that is typically American: in its conception, heroic; in its promotion, flamboyant; in its *dénouement*, comic. Yet, when it was done, it caught the breath of all but the most cynical.

First, the Eastern company sent out location parties, tracing the line and shooing off, or picking off, the Sioux and the buffalo and other busybodies. Then came construction gangs, working in shifts and grading the land by as much—in the flat East—as a hundred miles at a stretch, and behind them the track-laying crews, each consisting of ten thousand men and as many animals. For a single mile of track they needed forty cars to carry four hundred tons of rail and timber, and ties, bridgings, fuel, and food—and it all had to be assembled in a depot on the Missouri River. But the Union Pacific had the twin advantages of comparatively flat land and a continuous supply line back to the East Coast. It was quite different for the Central Pacific, which had to fetch most of its materials, except timber, by sea, twelve thousand miles around the Horn; and that included the locomotives. And whereas the Eastern gangs were recruited from immigrant Irish, from the defeated Southern whites, and blacks, the Western crews came mostly from China. The Union Pacific, it was said, was sustained by whiskey, the Central Pacific by tea.

While the Easterners were racing through the prairie, the Westerners were stripping foothill forests, painfully bridging and tunneling and inching up the mountains. Working summer and winter, it took the Central Pacific two years to hurdle the formidable barrier of the High Sierras. A thousand miles and more back East, the Irish gangers frequently fainted from the midsummer heat, but the company officials were revived by the thought that the government had promised a subsidy of $16,000 *per mile* of track. Once they started to climb the Rockies, it went up to $48,000 per mile, with wide stretches of free land bordering the track thrown in.

With the Westerners over the Sierras, and the Easterners over the Rockies, the two armies slogged along the sage toward each other. The graders actually passed each other along distant parallels in the hope of extra pay for establishing their own line an extra mile or two. When they came in sight of each other, the Irish trusted to their fists, but the Chinese had a preference for pick handles, and after a few cracked skulls the Irish took to gunpowder and fired their charges in the faces of the oncoming coolies. The Chinese reciprocated, but the sport was unprofitable, what with burial costs, compensation claims, and the like, and it was stopped.

On May 10, 1869, the tracks met at a place in Utah they christened Promontory Point. The crews had laid 1,775 miles of track in just over three years. Five days later a special Central Pacific train, loaded with company bigwigs, engineers, and state dignitaries came puffing in from California in a rainstorm. The Union Pacific train bogged down in floods and came shrieking in three days later, complete with its own company directors and official guests, and three companies of infantry and a regimental band. It promised a gallant and decorative ceremony. But in the course of their labor the crews had collected a more colorful assortment of interested parties: saloon keepers, gamblers, whores, money lenders, odd-job rovers. And these, with the cooks and dishwashers from the dormitory trains, made up the welcoming party.

Five states had sent along gold and silver spikes, and they had all to be exhibited and applauded. But the chosen symbol was a golden spike. The great Governor of California himself, Leland Stanford, stood ready to drive it into the last sleeper, a piece of California laurel. The band stopped its tootling. There was a prayer. The telegraph operator, high on a pole, finally connected with San Francisco and New York and was ready to flash the first coast-to-coast commentary. It was a single sentence: "Stand by, we have done praying." Then the Governor of California flexed his biceps, lifted the hammer, gave a mighty swing at the spike—and missed. But the faithful telegraph man had already tapped out the news, and New York fired a hundred-gun salute, Philadelphia rang the Liberty Bell, and a San Francisco paper announced the "annexation of the United States."

The country might take to the railroad as a novelty and a tourist fashion, but the companies saw it as a chain of missing links between the Great Plains and the people who would want, or could be urged, to settle it. Following the success at Promontory Point the railroads were spurred to spread branch lines out south of the central line. And the first community they attracted was not a community at all but the land pirates known as cowboys. The line that started this was one that ended at Abilene, Kansas. Here in the spring of 1867, while the continental line was creeping across the plains, there came a twenty-nine-year-old livestock trader from Chicago named Joseph McCoy. He looked at the railroad and he looked at a map, and he got an idea. He knew there was lush grassland all the way to southern Texas. What would be simpler than to connect a cow with a railhead and make a fortune and, incidentally, add beef to the diet of millions in the East? A methodical man, he decided first to buy the town, which was no more than a few cabins and a saloon on four hundred and fifty acres. Luckily, they were owned by another

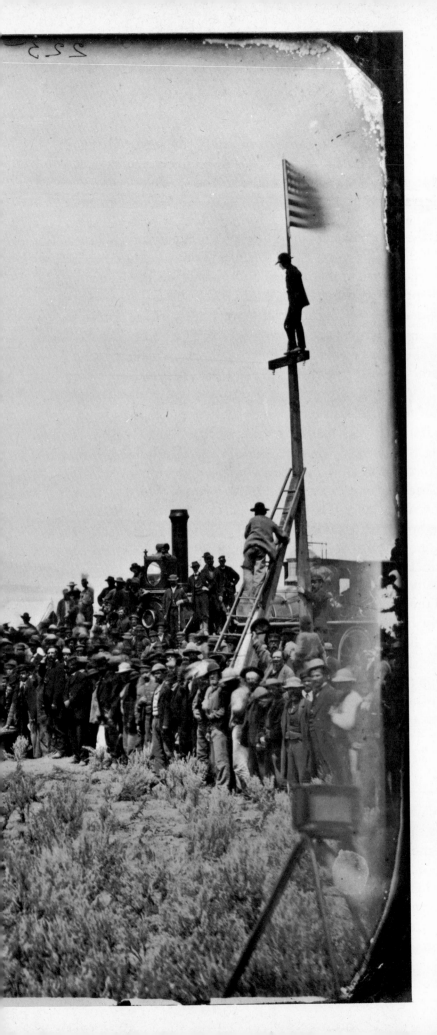

At Promontory, Utah, a flag snaps in a stiff breeze as workmen, dignitaries, and hangers-on celebrate the completion of the transcontinental railroad.

man from Illinois, Tim Hersey, and he sold the lot to McCoy for five dollars an acre. (Mrs. Hersey, a God-fearing pioneer, had one day opened the Bible at the book of Luke and she read there, in chapter 3, verse 1, "The Tetrarch of Abilene in the province of Judea." She liked it, and so she christened a town.)

McCoy now spent the considerable sum of $5,000 getting out advertising circulars and sending riders down to Texas to promise the cowboys a safe trail and a fair price at the railhead. The result was the Chisholm Trail. It started not far from the Gulf of Mexico, in southern Texas, with a breed of rawboned, half-wild cattle with long horns, whose ancestors had come over on Columbus's second voyage. By the end of the Civil War there were about three million of these longhorns, and they roamed no farther than the grass and water they needed. Their normal fate was to be slaughtered for tallow and hides, and on their home ground they could be sold for no more than four dollars a head. But at the end of a thousand-mile trail was Mr. McCoy's bait of forty dollars a head, so feeder lines began converging on San Antonio and then joined to run directly north through largely unsettled country and Indian territory. The trail was blazed by horses and oxen pulling plows, which together cut a wide furrow in the land. The herds moved, two or three thousand at a time, in loose order, with a few picked bulls or steers in the lead—at about a mile an hour. With luck, a herd took three months to arrive at Mr. McCoy's stockyard in central Kansas.

It was never a monotonous journey. Resentful settlers squatting along the trail passed their own laws to forbid the cowboys' passage or, failing that, pestered the herds with planted ticks or alarmed them with fires set in the long grass. Equally resentful Indian guides exacted heavy tolls for crossing their lands, at worst led the herds off into quicksands and vanished. The longhorns were temperamentally as nervous as cats, which was why the cowboys' plaintive lullabies and night herding songs came into being, not as a romantic bit of minstrelsy. The longhorns were apt to stampede at the first crack of a thunderstorm or the first high wail of a coyote. And a serious stampede could mean a per capita loss of ten pounds in weight, or a loss of $10,000 to $20,000 on the herd at the railhead.

A hundred days after McCoy had posted his offer, the village of Abilene heard a thunderstorm of hooves coming up from the south. It was the start of the cowboy legend, and of McCoy's reign as emperor of the cattle kingdom. He had boasted that he could deliver two hundred thousand cattle in his first decade. He was wrong. In the first four years he shipped over two million out of his stockyards. He was one of the rare American promoters whose production exceeded his propaganda. He was, they liked to say, "the real McCoy."

Obviously, a few cabins and some bare acres could not possibly cope with as many as five thousand cowboys paid off in a single night. McCoy did build some shacks and extra cabins. But mostly the cowboys slept out on the prairie and wheeled their chuck wagons into town, parking them in front of their favorite haunts—the saloons, the gambling joints, and the brothels. (The habit spread to other cow towns and coined the phrase "lunch wagon.") At the peak of the cattle trade Abilene was as rough as any town on the continent. Marshals came and went by the simple application of the six-shooter, until the arrival of one James Butler "Wild Bill" Hickok, who was not much like his heroic Gary Cooper impersonation. He was something of a desperado himself, a very sharp dresser and a murderous shot, who could skim a hat into the air and perforate the rim with a circle of bullet holes before it flopped to the ground. Happily, he chose to exercise his marksmanship by joining the law instead of fighting it. And the law in Abilene—and in many more mushrooming cow and mining towns—was a ball-and-cap six-shooter, developed in the Civil War, and very light. Before he came to Abilene Hickok had "registered" forty-three killings, and in the service of law and order he was to notch up a round hundred. He became the most feared mayor Abilene had ever had, and he said it all in one short sentence: "Talk about a rule of iron—we had it."

Through the 1860s and 1870s, the cow towns made the Wild West exactly that. Apart from their attraction for claim jumpers, hoodlums and fugitives from the law, they were the battleground between two natural enemies, the cattlemen and the sheep men. The romantic legend we have so lovingly polished through songs and movies has dolled up the truth of a harsh, sordid, and violent life. The death rate in these cow towns was proportionately ten or twenty times as high as that of New York City in its present turmoil. And out on the range, where never was heard "a discouraging word," but only the bellowing of poisoned cattle, all the feuds and sneaky murders were about three disputed necessities of life: Who owned the cattle, who had the grazing rights, who could secure the water holes?

As bad as the cow towns, and sometimes worse, were the mining settlements, where footloose bachelors hoped for gold or silver but mostly hacked away at copper, tin, or lead. And when they emerged like moles from their dust-choked tunnels, they took a deep breath and raised hell on the streets and in the brothels and saloons before the next descent. Their towns were as impermanent as their livelihood: a vein gave out, and a town would go to dust in a week. The miner, like the

---

Overleaf: A range hand cuts out a cow and her unbranded calf from an assembled herd. Photograph by Dane Coolidge dates from the 1890s.

cowboy, didn't domesticate anything. The homemaking—and the first codes of law to protect the homesteaders from the cowboys and their trampling herds—had to wait till the arrival of the first victims of the railroads' campaign to attract not birds of passage but settlers.

The railroad agents rattled around Europe looking for landscapes with failing crops and browbeaten minorities. But, in the early 1870s it was not just the poor and the persecuted who were drawn to the Western plains. There were some bizarre adventurers, none more odd than a party of upper-crust Englishmen who responded to the call of the West as a fashionable caper. One Sir George Grant advertised in the papers for a team of young bloods, perferably remittance men, to join him and found an English colony on a tract of land he had bought from the Union Pacific in western Kansas. Within two years he assembled his team, and they collected their hunting pinks and some horses, and a pack of Southdown sheep and some Aberdeen Angus cattle, and sailed away.

When Sir George got to St. Louis he bought a steamboat and was only slightly put out by the news that in western Kansas there was plenty of wind but no rivers worth the name. Nevertheless, these Englishmen had a fixed and beautiful and very confused picture of the West, which included riverboat gamblers, and buffalo hunts, and fox hunts, and endless nights of poker and faro, and a possible brush with wild Indians and with—who knows?—wild women.

The party dragged its steamboat two hundred miles across the prairie and found a creek. They dammed it up and made a little lake, navigable for eight or nine miles. Then they initiated the new life, which was great fun for a while. There were no foxes and no buffalo, so they shot jack rabbits and coyotes and barged up and down the lake and tended their cattle. This went on for four years. But the infernal summer heat and the withering winters got them down. There was a long drought. And the very few women available were not up to the legendary standard. So in the end the whole thing was, as one of them said, "a deuced bore." Sir George Grant had the satisfaction of seeing the village named Victoria, after Her Gracious Majesty. And he had introduced to the United States the Aberdeen Angus breed of cattle.

By then, only three miles to the north, there were interlopers, a band of Russians who had also answered a Union Pacific advertisement. They were, more correctly, Germans, for their forefathers had migrated to the Volga basin, at the invitation of Catherine the Great, to improve the farming. A century later these so-called Roosians jumped at the offer of a cheap passage and free lands in the dream world beyond the seas. Why should they settle fifteen hundred miles inland, in the empty center of America? Well, like most other immigrant farmers, they had an instinct for the familiar land. They would go where the soil was ready for the very crop that had been their staple, wheat. Each of them brought to America one bushel of their native strain, Turkey Red wheat. They were told that the hard prairie was bad for wheat, but they were a stubborn and superstitious lot and they stayed. Unlike the Englishmen, they could not leave of their own free will. If they failed, they were stuck. The wheat turned out to be a very tough and resistant strain, and it flourished. They called their town after *their* sovereign, Catherine. Twenty years from the time the "Roosians" arrived, Kansas had become the wheat bowl of America, and was to be the granary of the Allied armies in two world wars.

And there were many others, from many countries, who came to arid land and made it bloom. Perhaps they were too readily seduced by the railroads. But all of them were eager to make the most of what was, to any European, an astonishing law: the Homestead Act, passed by Congress in 1862, which decreed that anyone at all could have one hundred and sixty acres of public land free by simply agreeing to work it and produce a going crop within five years. The homesteaders, then, were the first true inhabitants of the plains. They introduced the new and stable element—the family. And they began a raw life with very raw materials. There were no trees on the prairie, so their houses were made of dried sod, whimsically known as "prairie marble," and for fuel they used the dung of the buffalo. Doctors were rare, and there was much sickness and many widowers. And many otherwise healthy women went mad, from the scrimping, the droughts, the burning summers and the polar winters, the loneliness, and the ceaseless wind—which was both the prairie farmer's curse and his blessing.

The windmill was one of the three things that made it possible for a homesteader to make a life. The second was a special plow. The typical iron plow simply could not cut through the heavy matted sod of the prairie, which bakes under a midsummer temperature of 100 degrees and is petrified in winter at 40 degrees below zero. Yet the soil was deep and rich and once it was seeded it was capable of supporting splendid crops. It was left to John Deere, a Vermonter who had moved to Illinois, to invent a plow with a revolving blade and a steel moldboard. It cut the sod and then turned it over.

The third thing, simpler still, was barbed wire. To us it is as dull and obvious as a brick or a sheet of paper, but a hundred years ago it saved the homesteader. He might get a crop and make a livelihood, but where there was no timber he had no way of fencing in his farm. So it was invaded, mostly by cowboys, whose herds stomped in and trampled down the crops. Barbed wire re-drew the domestic geography of a large part of the United States. For the first time it defined the prairie farmer's private property. And it incidentally killed off the cowboy—or, rather, by denying him settled land as open range eventually turned him into a rancher, with his own domain fenced in. The longhorn gave way to quicker-fattening breeds, the Hereford and the Angus. The cowboy rancher too, in time, became a family man, a mechanic, a salesman separating his product from the other man's with the identity of a brand. But at first the cowboys, scandalized by the invention of barbed wire, attacked the homesteaders' fences with wire cutters, and provoked endless battles, legal and bloody, with families whose bales of barbed wire ringed their farms like a protective wall. One whole town of homesteaders in Wyoming was raided by cattle thieves and every living person was wiped out—except a newspaperman, who escaped to tell the tale.

In the end the West was won, with a bleak absence of drama, by the homesteader and his woman, the mother of the first generation raised on the plains. She was mother, mistress, nurse, seamstress, doctor, cook, accountant, comforter, and teacher—and was known and usually treated, even by cowboys and miners, as the untouchable Madonna of the Plains. It was she who first acquired the symbols of respectability, the dignity of a pony and trap, a frame house, and such high-toned city amenities as wallpaper, carpets, pictures on the wall, an organ or a piano. By 1890 it was possible for a strict and pious mother to raise a proud family in a frame house even in Abilene. It was the mother who accompanied the family hymn singing and read books aloud, especially "the good Book," maintaining the frontier tradition, which lasted long—too long, perhaps—in American life; that culture belonged to the women. She made the clothes, and in her spare time the coverlets and counterpanes, and hooked the rugs. You can see the handiwork of such a mother, who went to Abilene in 1892, in a small, high-roofed house on a corner. She wove into a cushion still extant the names of her seven sons. One of them died in infancy, but six of them grew to manhood in this cramped house, and one of them, fifty years later, was able to lay down the law to a boy born in the marble halls of Blenheim Palace: Winston Churchill. The corner house is the boyhood home of General and President Dwight D. Eisenhower.

In the year he was born, the last big tract of Indian land was declared open for settlement, in Oklahoma. The claimants and the speculators mounted their horses and lined up like trotters waiting for a starting gun. The itchy ones jumped the gun and were ever after known as Sooners—as Oklahoma was thereafter called the Sooner State. They raced for the good land and the water holes, banged in their stakes, and hunted around in panic to file a legal claim, for in the previous twenty years much blood had been spilled over disputed land claims. Waiting to oblige them were men in suits and hats standing on boxes labeled "law

With wood rare and expensive, blocks of sod had to do for building on the Great Plains; with n doctors and high mortality rates, it was best to have plenty of children. This family settled in Kansas in the 1880s.

office," to offer early proof that behind every successful American is a good lawyer.

In less than thirty years after the Civil War, all across the "enormous gap" spanned by the railroad, the interior was being conquered and domesticated. The whole sequence had been completed, from bare ground to camp ground to shanty town to prosperous "home town." It was some sort of high-water mark of Western civilization when the Dodge City Amateur Dramatic Society put on *A Midsummer Night's Dream*. The perils of the West had faded so rapidly that soon the city fathers could dress up as cowboys and organize a town band available for weddings and picnics. The Wild West declined into the title of a traveling circus presided over by the veteran slaughterer of the buffalo, Colonel William Cody, now a prosperous impresario and owner of a troop of tame Indians trotted out as actors before large audiences at home and abroad. (They appeared once in the pop-eyed presence of Queen Victoria.)

And the Indians? How about the far-flung tribes that had never heard of Buffalo Bill? Did they just scatter and pine away? Not quite. After the Civil War the government sent commissioners out West to sign a final set of treaties with formerly warlike tribes, to confirm and celebrate their presumed new trust in the white man. They were rounded up in vast internment camps that covered anything from a hundred to a thousand square miles. If these reservations were yet too confining for the nomadic tribes, and if ever they thought of breaking loose, the army was on hand to contain them. Since by that time all the great wandering herds of buffalo had been slaughtered and their skins shipped East, the Indians were obliged to troop to their reservations for a regular ration of government beef. If they stayed away, they would simply starve. From then on they were harmless, if not hungry, wards of the government.

In 1876 the country had a stunning reminder that some of them were not ready to be cowed into a bread line. Out of the blue came the news that one third of the Seventh Cavalry, under the command of General George Armstrong Custer, had been massacred while searching for, and unfortunately finding, a Sioux encampment on the Little Bighorn, in Montana. In its fury and humiliation, the army mapped a series of campaigns to ensure that the Indian would never again be anything but a reservation prisoner. Even the great Sitting Bull, the Sioux leader at Little Bighorn, yielded, was given amnesty, and came home from a safe haven in Canada. (Later he too joined Buffalo Bill's circus.)

Late in the 1880s, however, the subjected Indians were suddenly heartened by news of a savior, an Indian John the Baptist whose heralds came out of the wilderness and went among the tribes offering a miraculous regeneration of their pride and a new and glorious indepen-

By the turn of the century, even the roughest cow towns had been tamed. This farm home in southwestern Kansas boasted all the amenities, from wallpaper to an upright piano.

dence. All they had to do was to perform a magical rite—a special Ghost Dance. If this were reverently done, the white man's bullets would be as harmless as hailstones, the white man himself would disappear, and the buffalo would be reborn again and populate the earth. The news of this pathetic ritual was enough to alert, and alarm, the military. Buffalo Bill Cody volunteered to parley, but he had no success—the authorities had sent him to talk with the wrong men. (It is quite possible that the army did not, or could not, know the "right" men. For throughout the white man's dealings with the Indian, there has persisted the balky problem of the Indians' complex and odd—to us—principle of authority. It varied enormously from tribe to tribe, and the Indians themselves were just as often the bloody victims of it. Most tribes have a variety of leaders, not always a hierarchy, and in parleying it is essential to know their separate jurisdictions.)

In any case, it seems certain that the army was spoiling for a showdown. A great many of the regulars, having survived the Civil War and seeing their careers coming to a humdrum end when the Indian wars were finished, went off to practice a random "extermination policy" of their own. The fourteen-year interval between the Battle of the Little Bighorn and the final massacre at Wounded Knee, South Dakota, is dark with mischievous examples of bodies of the military taking off on small expeditions to bait handfuls of Indians into hostility, to slaughter them, and earn a medal.

In the autumn of 1890, near the reservation town of Pine Ridge, South Dakota, the Seventh Cavalry, the same regiment chopped up at the Little Bighorn, mustered for the kill. This time they brought up cannon—they were taking no chances. Their jumpiness was aggravated by the news—false, as it turned out—that Sitting Bull had been shot, and the Seventh rode to seek out a band of suspected Sioux renegades. What they found were two hundred men, women, and children. Without a parley or any attempt to establish that this horde was a band of warriors, the Seventh annihilated them, and the next day dug the bodies from the snow and buried them in a common grave. This wretched episode was known to the white man, and still is, as the "battle" of Wounded Knee.

That was the end of it. Throughout three centuries, there had been, here and there, good, even magnanimous, relations with the Indians. But the ruthless continental fact is that wherever the Indians had something that the white man wanted, the Indians lost it—by expulsion, by warfare, by a raft of treaties signed and treaties broken. What the white man wanted, ultimately, was North America, and he took it. In J. Russell Smith's tart epitaph: "The white man banished the Indian to lands where no white man could possibly survive. The Indian fooled him. He survived." And so, after a fashion, he still does.

Today, in many a Western town, on the anniversary of its founding, a skittish annual ritual is performed. The men prance on rearing steeds to the music of a band. The women ride in covered wagons; and the Indians, wherever they are available, consent to get themselves up in the old battle finery and jog along to demonstrate their status as picturesque dependents. The yearning for the open spaces and the free buccaneering life still nags at the American male, as it haunted Huckleberry Finn and kept him in flight from the tendency of women to lasso a man and tie him down. "She was goin' to civilize me," moaned Huck, "[but] I had been there before." We have all been there before. So today the Westerner likes to do for show or sport what his grandfather did for survival. Yet, like you and me, he rides mainly on the Interstate. His hitching post is a gas station with a gift of green stamps. He is corraled in towns and wind-blown suburbs and, even in the old wilderness, is tethered by a mortgage, a parent-teachers meeting, by galoshes, car insurance, alimony payments, and the other ties of domestic bliss.

Overleaf: *Wearing a top hat and sitting at the wheel of a Locomobile touring car in 1905, the 76-year-old Apache chief Geronimo was a pathetic caricature of the warrior who had terrorized Arizona a quarter of a century before.*

8

MONEY ON THE LAND

In the early 1820s, only four or five years after Illinois had graduated from a territory into a state, an Englishman crossed the northern section and remarked on an obvious fact that never fails to strike the West Europeans: "The eye sometimes surveys the green prairie without discovering on the illimitable plain a tree or a bush, or any other object, save the wilderness of flowers and grass."

It was something that also struck, and intimidated, the first white settlers, who had moved out of woodland and hill country onto a flat plain with no woods and, therefore, with none of the familiar materials for the making of houses, fires, and fences. So in the beginning the *prairie* was left to the Frenchmen—to the trappers and the hunters —who had christened it. The Anglo-Saxons, and the early immigrants from northern Europe, built their houses along the river bottoms where there was sometimes timber. One of the first handbooks for intending immigrants laid down the necessities of life as "a pair of good horses, a wagon, a cow, a couple of pigs, several domestic fowl, two ploughs (one for breaking the prairie, and the other for tillage) together with a few other tools and implements. . . . A log house can soon be erected."

This prescription anticipated the farmer's usual life on unusually tough soil without suggesting, however, the special richness of a sort of land that has no trees. The prairie was looked on not as an asset but as an impediment, yet one that a patient and resourceful family might overcome. Such a family could learn, it could try at least, to exterminate the pestiferous prairie dog, or gopher, and then snatch a new food from the grouse known as a prairie hen, and even discover a useful medicine in "prairie bitters," a beverage made from a pint of water and a quarter of a gill of "buffalo-gall."

Yet even while these early settlers were battling the prairie as a large natural enemy, there were men alive who began to see what machines might do to reap its vast resources. And at the same time, there were other men who saw the possibilities of reaping fortunes not from the

Some of the greatest fortunes of the nineteenth century started in bleak storefronts like this one in the northwest Pennsylvania oilfields. Impressive name and all, however, the Central Petroleum Company has vanished.

crops that lay *on* the land but from the resources that lay *under* it.

If we retrace the steps by which America went from a wilderness to a giant of technology, there are less than fifty years from the homesteader growing his food on the quarter section (one hundred and sixty acres) that the government had given him, to mammoth factories processing and packaging food for this nation and other nations. Less than half a century from a village on the prairie to the "first city of the plains" —Chicago, the city that more than any other in the world has had its greatness mocked by the curse of a violent legend. To most of the world, it has been in turn the scene of a devastating fire, a stage set to accommodate the gang wars of Al Capone, and the natural setting for the ugly riots that defamed the Democratic Convention of 1968.

It is about eight hundred miles inland from the Atlantic and for countless centuries was known only to the Indians. Then it was a trading post for French fur trappers. It lies on the southwestern corner of Lake Michigan, which is something less than half the size of England. This was the first of four lakes—Michigan, Huron, Erie, and Ontario—that were linked with canals to the north and east, giving clear access all the way from the Atlantic, fifteen hundred miles away, to the western shore of Lake Michigan. At that point, at Chicago, there was a snag—literally, an obstacle that impeded navigation. Between a bend in the Chicago River and the lake there was a sand bar. Once they cut through it, Chicago had a harbor. This was done in 1833, when the place was a squatter settlement of two hundred souls.

When the canal opened, the usual horde swept in: disappointed factory workers from the East, refugee farmers from the rocky soil of New England, immigrants from Europe. Two years later, when the traffic of the Lakes was beginning to hum, a thirty-year-old hustler from New York State arrived. William Ogden was an orphan, but of comfortable means, who had got out of school as soon as he could and at fifteen was already dabbling in real estate. He fancied, he once said, "I could do anything I turned my hand to, and that nothing was impossible." He entered the New York State Legislature on an election promise to build the New York and Erie railroad. But a land company excited him with tales of the boom-to-be along the shore of Lake Michigan, and in 1835 he went to look over a patch of Chicago land his brother-in-law had bought. He was as exhilarated, at a distance, as the Northerners who were sold a slice of paradise in the Florida land boom of the 1920s. They found their plots were underwater and sometimes under the sea. He found a piece of unbroken marsh, and he was disgusted. But he roamed around the rude village and imagined a metropolis. It would have been absurd, had he not made it come true.

Within a couple of years Ogden had been elected mayor of a town of four thousand. He poured money, lots of it his own, into literally hundreds of bridges, sewage plants, water systems, parks, and hundreds of miles of streets that went nowhere. And having created the shell of a city, he now began to fill it. There weren't many carpenters, and there wasn't much time, either, for planing beams and fastening them with pegs. Ogden heard about a new sort of house, a"balloon frame"—a light frame of two-by-fours nailed together so that the strain goes against the grain—and he plumped it in thousands on the land. Today, three houses in four in America are built in this way.

Ogden gambled on the furious growth of the city and in 1841, six years after he'd arrived, the first bumper crop on the prairie paid him off. Wagons brought the crops and the livestock into Chicago; and steamboats, brigs, and schooners carried them to New York and then to Europe. In only nine years Chicago had gone from a marshy village of two hundred squatters to the largest grain market in the world. It became the reception center for all the harvests and the livestock of the prairie. It is still the stock exchange of the American farmer. Every Wednesday, on the floor of the Chicago Commodity Exchange, there is a deafening frenzy of bidding that will be filtered, at twilight, over thousands of radio stations, into a few laconic phrases: "Wheat up one point, corn down three eighths, soybeans steady."

After the Civil War, more ships cruised into Chicago than into the six busiest ports of America combined. But the lake and the river traffic alone would not have made Chicago the mammoth among inland cities. It was the coming of the freight train that did it. Chicago became the ideal junction between the harvests of the encircling prairie and the people, thousands of miles in all directions, who would eat and use them. Because Chicago was where it was when it was—bang in the middle of the prairie—it became the biggest railroad center in the world. It has been host to more than half the presidential nominating conventions. Nowhere have more animals and raw crops been so dramatically transformed. A cow went into Chicago as a cow and went out as a steak or a tennis racket.

The scope of this immense transport system, and the novel ease of it, spurred the prairie to produce far more than the ordinary homesteaders could possibly grow. The raw materials—the soil and the seed, the sun and the rain—were there over millions of acres, but not all the small farmers in the world could satisfy the giant maw of Chicago. Their livelihood, it now developed, was based on a false assumption about the basic American farm. The Founding Fathers, remember, had never left

Overleaf: *Between 1860 and 1900 more than 400 million new acres came under cultivation, in part because of such machines as Cyrus McCormick's reaper.*

the East. Their idea of an expanding American agriculture was Virginia or Massachusetts going on forever: parcels of land happily alternating pasture with woods and little rivers, farms that were self-sufficient and suited to a single family.

But the prairie was not like that. One man's quarter-section, of one hundred and sixty acres, the standard square homestead struck off in the thousands on landmaps back East, might have the luck of good soil, a creek, and a few shade trees. But another man's *sixteen* hundred acres might be as hard as cement and barren of all shade and water. Many, many families who went into the Midwest with high hopes of self-sufficiency got badly bruised. Their acreage was too arid or too tough to work, the weather—droughts, hailstorms, winters—had a savagery beyond anything they had known, or a railroad land agent armed with a dispossess notice came by to buy them out for a song. The disenchanted had a bitter rhyme: "In God we trusted, in Kansas we busted."

What Ogden foresaw, and Chicago confirmed, was that, if farming was going to prosper far into the heart of the continent, it would have to turn into an industry. The machines appeared, setting the now characteristic American rhythm of the new need and the new invention to meet it. Ogden invited to Chicago a young Virginian, Cyrus McCormick, to mass-produce the mechanical reaper he had been demonstrating in the East. Before McCormick they cut wheat by hand with a scythe and cradle. His machine did the work of five men, with obviously less fatigue. And so, suddenly, Pennsylvania and Ohio were no longer the big wheat states. The breadbasket moved a thousand miles west—and it was a lucky thing, because the population of the United States went in forty years from thirteen million to sixty million, and Mr. McCormick's mechanical reaper guaranteed that they would be fed. After the reaper, there came in tumbling succession the automatic wire-binder, and the twin binder, the threshing machine, the combine, mechanical corn planters and corn cutters, huskers, shellers, the cream separator, the potato planter, the hay drier. America discovered many decades before Europe that land can be seen as a gorgeous deposit of raw material ready for mass cultivation and shipping and processing and packaging.

This realized ideal of "the farm industry" was a far cry from the original American ideal of the sturdy independent small farmer who made all his own farming and building implements, made the tallow for the candles and the soap, raised a few crops and a few cattle, and tapped the trees for the family sugar. Yet, by a familiar human contradiction, the faster this ideal faded, the more it was mooned over. Millions of Americans bought prints of old farming scenes in the hope of asserting as a sacred fact of American life what was already becoming a memory: the idea of America as a continent without cities, a far-flung republic of yeoman farmers.

But it was not only the conversion of farming into an industry that produced new cities across the country, cities that received, processed, and shipped the crops that lay above the ground. The resources of America are as far-flung as its geography, and, in Western landscapes that had seen more snakes and gophers than pigs and wheat, other fortunes were suddenly discovered to lie under the ground, and in the 1860s and 1870s, throughout the Rockies and the Sierras, those fortunes were unearthed. In 1858 traces of gold were found in Colorado and one year later there was a city that had, first, a hotel and a jewelry store and then the crowning symbol of the miner's prosperity—the "Opry House." Lumber sold in Denver for $100 per thousand feet; and sugar, coffee, and tobacco for their weight in the only going currency—gold dust. In Nevada, in 1859, scratching gold miners cursed the "black stuff" that made the recovery of gold difficult—until they had the stuff assayed and discovered that it was silver of unbelievable richness. A camp site of miners living like tenting Indians could turn in three years into a city of thirty-five thousand with five newspapers and gas lighting on the streets.

By the 1870s, with the war long over and the railroads stretching wider, America began to spawn small cities like rabbits. They grew wherever the railroad loaded produce or unloaded food and necessities. They were places of humble comfort, whose inhabitants wore cowhide boots and sat on Windsor chairs on bare floors and filled the evenings with the wail of the harmonica and the jew's-harp. But as they prospered they started asking for things that it would have been foolish to dream about in their parents' time. Heat and light, news and conveniences, and more sophisticated kinds of entertainment—something better than the local dramatic society and (as Will Rogers liked to recall) the Saturday night excursion downtown "to watch haircuts." It's hard to say whether the prairie communities yearned for city amenities, or whether the amenities were thrust upon them. At any rate, the era inspired a rush of inventors and the heyday of the Ingenious American.

When Samuel Morse flicked the switch that passed out the first telegraph message, somebody said that Maine could now talk to Florida. In Boston Ralph Waldo Emerson remarked, "Yes, but has Maine anything to *say* to Florida?" It is a good question, and one worth asking again in an America that floods the television screen with words and pictures from dawn to dawn, mainly because the television screen is there. But, in the last quarter of the nineteenth century, New York and Chicago had lots to say to each other, and to Denver and San Francisco, and the whistle-stops in between. And just as the railroad and the McCormick reaper combined to spark a mass production system for the farmer, so there was one man more than another who was inspired to mass-produce conveniences for remote towns that either improvised them or had never heard of them.

This man was Thomas Alva Edison, born in 1847 in a small town in Ohio and brought up in Michigan. The extent of his education was three months in a public elementary school. At twelve he was a railroad newsboy, and at fifteen a telegraph operator in various cities. Like Eli Whitney, he had been born with an itch to take things apart and see how they ticked; Edison then tended to put them together again and make them tick louder and longer, at half the price. At nineteen he took out his first patent, for an electrical vote recorder. A year or two later, he was working on a telephone. And, knowing well enough what New York in a hurry would want to say to San Francisco, he invented the stock ticker.

By the 1870s Edison had laid out, and crammed with scientific gear and instruments, not exactly a workshop but in rudimentary form something that not even the universities had—the first scientific research laboratory. He was neither a tinkerer nor a pure scientist who disdains practical utility. His genius was of a quite different order. He put to himself the right question at the right time: how to make a scientific principle workable as a universal convenience. If Edison had discovered gravity, he would have wondered how gravity could help the farmer and the grocer. He could admire the delicate workmanship of a Swiss watch, but wonder, How do you make a dollar watch?

His extraordinary tenacity when he thought he was on to something was most dramatically illustrated by his famous ordeal with the incandescent lamp. In the 1870s the most advanced common form of lighting was gas. The arc light had been developed in various expensive and clumsy forms, but what Edison wanted was a cheap filament in a small bulb to provide an electric light for the ordinary householder. To most of his contemporaries, to the gas companies most of all, this was about as sensible as ordering up a cheap family-sized space ship.

Edison mobilized his small staff with the sense of mission of an explorer headed for the Arctic wastes. He expected from the team the same dedication—and routine insomnia—he imposed on himself. He tried all sorts of conductors—metals like irridium, chromium, platinum. They overheated, they required enormous current, they oxidized. Edison now started a trial of endless materials, plausible and preposterous. Fibers, papers, hemp, bark, cork, and lemon peel. One day he plucked a hair from a friend's beard. But everything kept failing. He needed a tiny, tough, high-resistance filament that would burn in a vacuum.

In the end, he picked up a shred of sewing cotton. He carbonized it, mounted it on the electrodes, pumped out the air to one millionth of an atmosphere and then started to feed the power through Bunsen batteries arranged in series, increasing the current as he went. It didn't overheat. It

With three friends, Thomas Edison (left) perched on an old mill wheel during an outing. The others were also men of note: John Burroughs, the famous naturalist; auto maker Henry Ford; and Harvey Firestone, whose rubber company was the largest in the world.

stayed cool and alive for forty-five hours, and he knew that a solution was in sight. Next day he found that cardboard worked, but not well enough to suit him. He then conducted a test of six thousand vegetable fibers, and eventually he found a Japanese bamboo that lasted a thousand hours. And for the first time the world was lit with electricity.

Edison's creation of the "permanent" electric light swept the headlines, but some of its early users were scared by it. Mrs. Vanderbilt, the Fifth Avenue hostess, went into hysteria when two crossed lines started a fire. City governments were slow to take any risks with this hazardous gadget, though factories, and even ranches, started to install Edison's "lighting plant." And so did theaters. An attractive thing about Edison was that, until he was convinced of success beyond all reasonable, or unreasonable, doubt, he assumed total responsibility for his inventions. He was present at the first theatrical performance to be lit by electricity, a production of *Iolanthe.* After the intermission the lights began to waver and dim and go red. Edison dashed down to the cellar, stripped off his dress clothes, and started shoveling coal in to maintain the steam pressure. He went on shoveling throughout the banquet that was being given upstairs in his honor.

He rarely paused to wallow in the oceans of flattery that surrounded him. He always had thirty or forty ideas in his head, and before he died, at eighty-four, he had blitzkrieged the government with over a thousand patents. He would come into his lab in the morning, pat his pockets, sort through a wad of little notes, and toss one to an assistant. One day he left a scrap of paper on the bench of a man named Kruesi. It contained a drawing so primitive that it looked like a comic-strip joke. In the bottom corner was the note: "Kruesi, make this. Edison."

"What," asked the puzzled Kruesi, "will it do?"

"It will talk back," he replied.

It did. Edison had come on the simple, revolutionary discovery that a steady needle engraving in depth on a revolving cylinder of tinfoil can record the reverberations of the human voice—and that they can then be played back and amplified by the same horn that had received the original sounds. It was the start of the phonograph.

In the thirty-five years between the end of the Civil War and the end of the century, the golden time of American inventiveness, the United States Patent Office granted more than half a million patents. Alexander Graham Bell produced the miracle of the telephone; George Eastman, the handy family camera, a marvel known in all languages as simply a Kodak. And there was the home sewing machine, and the typewriter

Accompanied by the usual phalanx of lawyers (and several delighted messenger boys), John D. Rockefeller leaves a New York court after testifying in an antitrust suit.

(invented, oddly, fifty years before it caught on), and an immense improvement in dynamos and motors. And, capping this great age—which declined as the loner in the woodshed gave way to teams of technologists in labs—was the achievement of Orville and Wilbur Wright with the heavier-than-air flying machine.

At the very start of this machine age there was something else, not an invention but a discovery, which helped transform this country from a farming republic into an industrial colossus. It began by a river in the Alleghenies, in western Pennsylvania. For a century or more Pennsylvania farmers had found their streams muddied by a kind of black glue. It turned up with good soil. First, the farmers cursed it, and then, on an old tip from the Indians, they bottled it and sold it as medicine. As early as 1849, the owner of a salt well put out the "black glue" in pocket-sized bottles with his own printed label: "Genuine petroleum. None genuine without the signature of Samuel Kier." Kier's petroleum was touted far and wide as a cure for asthma, rheumatism, gout, tuberculosis, cancer, and fallen arches. (We do know that, as early as the Revolutionary War, it was a sure remedy for constipation.) A man then discovered that it made a pretty good, though smelly, lighting fluid. After that came a distillation process that produced a purer liquid, almost odorless when burned —kerosene. And in 1859 came the bonanza.

The owner of a tract of land that ran along Oil Creek decided that somewhere underground there must be a primary source for the scum from the creek that Mr. Kier had bottled so profitably. The landowner hired a middle-aged railroad conductor, one Edwin L. Drake, locally given the honorific of "Colonel," who was similarly inquisitive and had tried tapping wells by pick and shovel. He found an ooze of oil, but, after his men had nearly drowned when an underground spring erupted into the shaft, Drake concluded that oil lies deeper than water. He got a blacksmith, who was used to digging salt wells, to sink a seventy-foot shaft by a steam-drill process, and on a sweltering afternoon in August 1859 the black glue bubbled into a flood. The blacksmith jumped on his mule and jogged into Titusville crying: "Struck oil! Struck oil!" He had indeed hit on the first petroleum well. Everybody and his cousin descended on Titusville with mules and shovels and drills and moving platforms, and oil towns sprouted like weeds. Within thirty years, in a sprawling mass of shanty towns along Oil Creek, they were producing thirty-one million barrels in a single year.

There was no central system. It was Everyman for himself, in the well-established American tradition: discover a new resource—a turpentine forest, a seam of coal, a vein of silver, a gusher of oil—work it to exhaustion, ravage the land, and move on. And most of these first oil towns produced their fill and then went back to the grass and the wind.

What the oil business needed was organization.

The organizer was a prim, methodical twenty-one-year-old from Cleveland, Ohio, a smart bookkeeper who had saved his pennies and become a junior partner in a produce commission firm. The year after Colonel Drake's strike, a group of money men in Cleveland sent John Davison Rockefeller off to Oil Creek to look the situation over and report on the long-range possibilities of the gushers. He was not well received by the wildcats, one of whom called him "that bloodless Baptist bookkeeper." Another was to say later that he not only had foresight but "could see around the corner." After his first survey he went home and blandly reported to Cleveland that oil had no commercial future. It is clear that he didn't believe this; his report was more likely an early sign of his gift of protesting a lack of evidence while holding back "something for the lawyers."

He had sensed or been told that the black glue was not necessarily an end in itself. It was still oil for lighting, but Rockefeller guessed it might become oil for heating, for steamships, for lubrication, for power. He had heard the new word "refinery," a word that appealed to a neat young city man, as the crude wells and their cruder owners had not. He and his partner heard of a candlemaker who had refined lard oil and was moving on to petroleum. His responsibility to the Cleveland money men at an end, Rockefeller and his partner pooled their savings and invested all of $4,000 in the candlemaker's refinery. Very soon, Rockefeller got richer men to build more refineries, and richer men still. Since his habits were more austere than theirs, he absorbed them. And then he sat back and he dreamed a dream. He was of the type of Columbus, and Fray Marcos, but with a gift for double-entry bookkeeping. There really wasn't anything to stop him making his refinery business in Cleveland the biggest in Ohio, the biggest in the Midwest, in America. Why not the world? When he was thirty, he formed the Standard Oil Company of Ohio and bought twenty-five refineries.

Rockefeller built a monopoly by means both genteel and ruthless, and it was rudely hinted that he had in the palm of his hands the best state legislatures and United States Senators that money could buy. He not only got the railroads to give him secret low rates because of the colossal business he could throw their way; they secretly guaranteed him a bonus from the regular rates that all the small producers had to pay. When the arrangement leaked, it provoked a national outcry. But Rockefeller rode out the railroad scandal by the well-known expedient of sitting back and letting himself become a beneficiary of the lapse of time. He was only

---

Overleaf: *Thomas Anschutz painted this scene outside a steelworks in the 1880s. It was his only famous painting and it sold for a record-breaking $250,000 at auction in 1972.*

thirty-three when he owned ninety percent of all American refineries and all the main pipelines and oil cars of the Pennsylvania Railroad. Within a few years he was the first billionaire in history.

He lived most of his life more simply than most stockbrokers, like a frugal Scandinavian monarch. By his bedside in his New York house he had always on hand his Bible, though it lay on top of his bedside safe. At sixty, penitence set in. He was very much a Victorian in his capacity to rationalize his energy as the engine of God. And, as happened with many more of the money barons, the coming on of arthritis convinced him that he had made all his money for the public good. So, with complete sincerity, he disbursed it. Through a foundation created in his own name, he gave $530,000,000 for worldwide medical research. I must say that he is the only philanthropist I can think of who gave away his fortune with no strings binding its use. He was photographed everywhere doing folksy things—attending a county fair, teetering on the putting green, marrying off a couple of midgets for charity—to prove that even Rockefeller was as mortal as the rest of us and that, though he was a kind of monarch, he had the common touch.

As he moved into his nineties people began to doubt his mortality, but the news that he was restricted to a gruel and Graham cracker diet brought some consolation to the poor and healthy. When he died, at the age of ninety-eight, it was as if an emperor had gone. Certainly, by 1937, the era of the money barons was long gone, and Franklin Roosevelt —who was born when Rockefeller was forty-two—was baiting and besieging the "economic royalists" during the longest and worst depression in American history.

There were not many men like Rockefeller, but it didn't take many to constitute a cabal of real national, continental power that overshadowed the elected power of the Presidents of the United States. There was Henry Clay Frick, who turned coke and iron ore into gold, and E. H. Harriman, who collected railroads the way other men collect stamps. There were Harriman's rival, James J. Hill, and his ally, J. P. Morgan, whose specialty was money itself. And there was Frick's sometime friend and sometime enemy, Andrew Carnegie.

Carnegie had three specialties: steel, making money, and giving it away. The son of a poor weaver, he was born in a stone cottage in Dunfermline, Scotland, in 1835, at a time of such depression that in the revolutionary year of 1848 the family took off for America and for a squalid house in a grimy town called Pittsburgh. The father went back to weaving and the mother went back to stitching shoe leather; it was not much of a New World for them. But their twelve-year-old boy was as shiny as an apple and as lively as a squirrel, and he went hopping up the golden ladder rung by rung: from bobbin boy to telegraph messenger to railroad clerk, to superintendent to director. Until iron entered his career, if not his soul, and finally steel.

At the turn of the twentieth century he wrote an article that ended with the heroic phrase: "Farewell, then, Age of Iron; all hail, King Steel!" He was really proclaiming his own coronation, because he foresaw before anybody the infinite possibilities of steel, for bridge building and steamships, for elevators and knives and forks. Make steel, and make it cheap, and you could own the industrial empire of the new century. Before he was thirty, he had bought a large tract on Oil Creek but soon turned from oil to building, and buying up, iron and steel mills and their tributary coal and iron fields, and then the railroads that brought their products to the Great Lakes docks, and a steamship line that took them on to Europe. His monopoly of steel helped him to weather the depression of 1892, and nine years later he graciously permitted the United States Steel Corporation—formed for the purpose—to buy him out for $250,000,000. And then he abdicated, or retired, to a castle in the eastern highlands of Scotland. He was sixty-five and he had eighteen years yet to live. And he now began the career of lavish philanthropy that made his name known around the world.

Carnegie exemplifies to me a truth about American money men that many earnest people fail to grasp—which is that the chase and the kill are as much fun as the prize, which you then proceed to give away. Carnegie was odd in having a whole philosophy about the need, even the duty, to scatter his wealth. He didn't even come to count his millions until he began to disperse them. He wrote a best-selling sermon called "The Gospel of Wealth," which as a piece of dialectic will hardly compare with *The Wealth of Nations* or *Das Kapital*, but it deeply impressed some rather impressive people, including William Ewart Gladstone, and the chief rabbi of the United Hebrew Congregations of Britain, and the Archbishop of Westminster. "The problem of our age," it said, "is the proper administration of wealth." Carnegie went on to list, in descending order of importance, the proper beneficiaries of "the wise trustee of surplus wealth." They were universities, free libraries, hospitals, parks, public auditoriums, swimming baths, and churches. (Just after the birth of his son, Carnegie's father had heard a brimstone sermon on infant damnation. Choking with rage, he rose during the service, damned the minister, and broke forever with the Calvinist Church. He never let his son forget it.)

Carnegie's "gospel" is, however, alive with ringing little phrases that made him greatly admired, even revered, in his old age: "the kept dollar

---

Overleaf: *Encased in boiled shirts and vine leaves, wealthy New Yorkers carouse. "Hell," said Diamond Jim Brady, "I'm rich. It's time I had some fun."*

is a stinking fish"; "the man who dies rich dies thus disgraced." He started to disembarrass himself of his huge fortune, we should not forget, before the government would have saved him the embarrassment by taking it anyway. And, by an irony that galled him, he began with a church organ. A Scottish Presbyterian church had written and asked him for a pipe organ. It seemed a small thing, and before much could be made of it he provided it. But the gift was hailed first in the Scottish newspapers, and then in the American and the overseas press. In the next forty-odd years he found himself donating, around the world, over seven thousand pipe organs. And because, as a boy, he had had the first apprentice's card to a free public library in Pennsylvania, he gratefully presented over three thousand public libraries in America, Britain, Europe, Africa, and Fiji.

Of his attested $400,000,000, $350,000,000 went to public benefactions, another $20,000,000 to an endowment for peace, and the remaining $30,000,000 to support his old tenants, crofters and servants, and innumerable old friends (including $10,000 a year to David Lloyd George). He pensioned off the widows of former Presidents of the United States. (Congress blushingly caught up with him a little later.)

"The man who dies rich dies thus disgraced." By his lights, Carnegie was not disgraced. He left to his widow and daughter a trust fund that would keep them in considerable comfort, but only through their lifetime, for he maintained that the most evil possible use of money was to leave it to your own family. "I would as soon," he wrote, "leave my son a curse as the Almighty Dollar." Never having had a son, he was saved from risking this malediction.

As he sat in his castle and looked out over the splendid hills and the still lochs, he liked to think of himself as a simple Scottish laird who had given to America more than he took. It wasn't, however, a bad place to be when his steel workers—determined to organize in a union—were shooting it out with an army of strikebreakers hired by Frick. Carnegie was stung by the suggestion of a United States Senator from Indiana that he was "skulking in his castle," and, when the British press took him up on the killing and wounding at his Homestead plant, Carnegie made the mistake of publicly wallowing in self-pity. He swore he had received a telegram from his workers beginning "Kind master," and seeking to know only his wishes. The telegram was never found in his papers. The press of two continents rounded on him as a sanctimonious fraud. The St. Louis *Post-Dispatch* wrote:

Count no man happy until he is dead. Three months ago Andrew Carnegie was a man to be envied. Today he is an object of mingled pity and contempt. . . . [He ran] off to Scotland out of harm's way to await the issue of the battle he was too pusillanimous to share. . . . Say what you will of Frick, he is a brave man. Say what you will of Carnegie, he is a coward. And gods and men hate cowards.

The Glasgow Trades (Union) Council formally proclaimed him "the new Judas Iscariot." He was never quite the same again, and his stifled guilt undoubtedly built up some of the pressure that burst, nine years later, in a shower of philanthropy.

But his feeling against inherited wealth was genuine enough. The people he truly despised were the pack of self-aggrandizers, the sons and daughters of the new fortunes in coke and tin and copper and iron and streetcars and railroads who wanted only to flaunt their wealth in some private Versailles. They found it on the rocky coast of New England, at Newport, Rhode Island. Newport had once been a haven for religious dissenters out of Massachusetts and later a capital port of the slave trade. One hundred years after the Declaration that "all men are created equal," there began to gather in Newport a colony of the rich, determined to show that some Americans were conspicuously more equal than others. They became, in a manner of speaking, dukes and princes by buying or reproducing the trappings of the old dukes and princes of France and Italy. To display these trophies, they built summer houses of the appropriate style and scale. And if you needed a bloodline, Tiffany's of New York would improvise a suitable coat-of-arms. These first- or second-generation rich built what they always called, by a typical affectation of the day, "summer cottages," a name that would have been suitable only if they had been flanked by Blenheim or the Taj Mahal.

The "cottage" of the Vanderbilts, a massive Renaissance palace, was built by the mentor of the Newport colony, the third generation of a fortune originally assembled by the captain of a ferry boat that plied between New York and New Brunswick. From this humble craft Cornelius Vanderbilt developed a fleet of freighters and then a transatlantic steamship line. In his sixties he went into railroads, and before he died this formidable old codger, who read little and could not write very well, had the satisfaction of founding a university. When he died he left his son $94,000,000, which the son doubled in ten years. The Vanderbilt house was built by the ferry-boat captain's grandson and daughter-in-law. On the shell, the house, they spent a mere $2,000,000, and $9,000,000 on the furnishings. And they opened it on a hot August night in 1892 with a ball held in a golden room such as few Newporters had ever danced in before or since. This baroque splendor produced its own baroque style of neurosis: "Nothing," a candid girl once said, "but gaiety—and grief." On a famous night, the Vanderbilt ballroom glittered with the uniforms of a historic British regiment and the decorations of the diplomatic corps. There were no soldiers or diplomats present. They were an army of actors hired by a devoted wife whose husband had gone quietly mad and believed himself to be the Prince of Wales.

The colony's houses were opened for only about seven weeks in the summer, but during that time the inmates packed a royal lifetime in formal picnics and luncheons, in dinners and polo and yachting and fancy-dress balls. It could cost up to $200,000 to throw a fancy-dress ball. There was one lady who set aside each summer $10,000 for what she would later itemize as "mistakes in my clothes." When the brother-in-law of Czar Nicholas II went to Newport, he confessed he had never even imagined such luxury. He had certainly never seen horses bedded down on linen sheets embossed with the family monogram. It was unlikely, too, that he had ever seen a man fling a Persian carpet on his lawn and order an army of gardeners to reproduce the intricacies of the pattern and colors in a mosaic of flower beds. There was a dinner at which the centerpiece was a long, thin sandbox implanted with tiny pails and shovels of sterling silver. The guests were invited on a given signal to dig for favors—for rubies, sapphires, and diamonds.

The ultimate whimsy was achieved by one Harry Lehr, an acknowledged court jester, who issued invitations to a hundred dogs and their masters. It was to be a "bow-wows' banquet." Unfortunately, a reporter had managed to crash the party, and the next morning the story went out over the wires that the banquet menu had consisted of stewed liver and rice, fricassee of bones, and shredded dog biscuit. Thanks to the telegraph and the telephone, the newspapers and then the pulpits of big and little towns throughout the country shook with warnings about the fate of Sodom and Gomorrah.

It was a bad time for such goings-on to be advertised at all outside Newport. This pitiful frivolity simply put the match to a charge that had been gathering for a decade out on the farms and the cities of the prairie. Out of a deflation through the 1880s, out of farm prices falling and credit tightening, out of strikes in steel mills and hunger riots in several cities, there arose a farmers' People's Party demanding support for their cheapened crops and the free coinage of silver. These issues might have sounded drearily academic in the East, but they were stoked with emotion by tales, true and fantastic, about the greed of the so-called Robber Barons, and the ostentation of the society they had nurtured.

And while the Newport millionaires bent for rubies with their little sterling silver shovels, children in New York bent over sewing machines sixteen hours a day, for industry had produced something that was supposed, in the not so long ago, never to happen in America—a permanent factory population. It began to see itself as the slave of the trusts and the money men. In the year that the Vanderbilts threw open their golden doors, there was a coal miners' strike, a national railroad

---

Like other Newport plutocrats, William K. Vanderbilt called his Marble House a "cottage". It cost $11 million to build and furnish. This is the dining room.

strike, and a sweat-shop march, most of them aggravated by armies of strikebreakers and broken either by the state guard or by federal troops.

But it was out on the prairie that the people felt most cheated and disheartened. They had gone out to realize the dream of free men and free soil. They had been conned, first by the railroads and their land grants, then by the farm machines and their makers. For the price of those beautiful machines was a mortgage on the land. And thanks in part to the machines' productivity, the value of the dollar had trebled in twenty years. So the homesteaders were now in hock to the money makers, who had beguiled them into feeding two continents, and doing it too well.

In an angry time, America usually finds—and not always for her own good—an angry man. It found him, at the beginning of the 1890's, in Lincoln, Nebraska, in the heart of the prairie. His name was William Jennings Bryan. A handsome, farm-bred boy from Illinois, Bryan was a fairly unsuccessful lawyer who got into Congress with the help of the railroad and the liquor interests. That was a wry touch to his career, for he came to champion the defeated farmers against just such men.

Bryan had one consummate talent. He was the best, the most resounding breast-beater in the nation. He had a voice of bronze, and with it he expressed the most brazen beliefs of the cheated farmers. To roaring audiences he would chant: "The farmer who goes forth in the morning and toils all day is as much of a businessman as the man who goes upon the board and bets upon the price of grain." He was a massive Baptist, Anglo-Saxon to the bone, the new Moses of the Midwest. The East he called "the enemy country," the home of the gold standard and the money changers.

To Bryan, truth lay only in holy scripture, and scripture comprised two books: the Bible and the Constitution of the United States. The Bible talked about driving the money changers from the temple, and the Bible spoke truer than John D. Rockefeller. The Founding Fathers had laid it down that the basis of a sound national currency was gold *and* silver, and the Founding Fathers knew better than Carnegie or Morgan. So he had a solution to the depression and the deflation that was God-sent for the prairie. What could be simpler when you are short of money than to make it? Abolish, then, the accursed single gold standard and allow the free coinage of silver. Silver became holy water to Bryan, and the Democrats rushed to their convention in 1896 and bathed in it. And Bryan swept the convention and the Democratic presidential nomination with one speech—or, rather, with two final sentences that rolled around the nation: "You shall not press down upon the brow of labor this crown of thorns. You shall not crucify mankind upon a cross of gold."

It took the nation, but it didn't quite take all the votes. Plenty of farmers went for him. But the railroad tycoons and the steel owners and the oil companies were actually assessed hundreds of thousands of dollars, by the chairman of the Republican National Committee, to assist in Bryan's defeat. And though he lived on for thirty more years and ran for the Presidency twice again, and lost both times, his first great triumph in Chicago was really his last. The silver crusade collapsed within a few years, when they began extracting gold from low-grade ore.

But there was more to the killing off of William Jennings Bryan than that. He went on speaking for the lonely farmer when three Americans in four lived in towns or were moving to them. He wound up, in 1925, in a much-publicized trial in a small Tennessee town, prosecuting a young schoolteacher for teaching the theory of evolution. So to the end he was the advocate of rural America, of its habits, its bigotries, its nostalgias, and the bitterest of its lost causes—a republic of yeoman farmers. Just as his silver crusade was bypassed by a simple scientific process, so his rude Old Testament idea of the dignity of man was made to look foolish by the awesome figure of Charles Darwin. Not until 1968 did Tennessee abolish its anti-evolution law and decide that Man, even the small farmer, is a mammal.

But even by the turn of the century, the small farmer, "God's finest creation," was beginning to be a primitive relic of a nation that was given over to the combine, the ore freighter, the oil tanker, the grain exchange, to the factories and the assembly line and, for better or worse, to the cities.

9
THE HUDDLED MASSES

Aboard a ferry from Ellis Island, an Italian immigrant family gazes in hope and trepidation at the bustling reality of New York City, 1905.

"We call England the Mother country," Robert Benchley once remarked, "because most of us come from Poland or Italy." It's not quite as drastic as that, but today the chances of an American being of wholly English stock are, outside the South, no more than one in four. Only the English visitor is still surprised by this palpable fact. When a German makes his first trip across the Atlantic, he can go into almost any large city between southern Pennsylvania and the Great Lakes, and on across the prairie into the small towns of Kansas, and he will find himself among people whose physique is familiar, who share many of his values and his tastes in food and drink. The Scandinavian will be very much at home with the landscape and the farming of Minnesota, and he will not be surprised to hear that the state is represented in Congress by men named Langen and Olson and Nelsen. A Polish Catholic would easily pass as a native among the sandy potato fields, the lumbering wooden churches, and the Doroskis and Stepnoskis of eastern Long Island.

For three quarters of the population that hears itself so often hailed as "the American people" are the descendants of immigrants from Asia and Africa and, most of all, from the continent of Europe. They brought over with them their religions and folkways and their national foods, not least their national prejudices, which for a long time in the new country turned the cities of the Northeast and the Midwest into adjoining compounds of chauvinists, distrustful not only of immigrants from other nations everywhere but too often of their neighbors three or four blocks away.

But even the most clannish of them sooner or later had to mix with the peoples already there and learn among other things a new kind of politics, in which the dominant power went to men who knew how to balance the needs of one national group against another. The American delicatessen became an international store for the staples that the old immigrant could not do without. Few American children, certainly in the cities, need to be told that goulash comes from Hungary, liverwurst from

273

Germany, borscht from Russia, and lasagne from Italy. And even Gentiles who never tasted the combination probably know that lox—smoked salmon—and the doughnut-shaped rolls called bagels are as inseparable, in Jewish households of any nationality, as an Englishman's—and an Anglo-Saxon American's—bacon and eggs.

I remember once, during a strike in New York when the salmon wasn't coming in, there seemed to be a glut of bagels in the Jewish bakeries. In a whimsical moment I sent a cable to my editor warning him that I was about to put a piece on the wire to be entitled, "Lox Lag Brings Bagel Boom." He cabled right back: "Your message hopelessly garbled it reads lox lag brings bagel boom." A small but telling sign that many Englishmen, beneath the surface admission that Americans have developed their own civilization, still think of Americans as Englishmen gone wrong. If so, the deterioration set in long ago. The American population, like the American diet, began to lose its exclusive Anglo-Saxon elements as long ago as the 1840s, with a wave of immigration that swelled to a flood, and then to a tidal wave in the thirty years between about 1885 and the First World War.

Why did they come? Why do they still come? For a mesh of reasons and impulses that condition any crucial decision in life. But the most powerful was one common to most of the immigrants from the 1840s on—hard times in the homeland. They chose America because, by the early nineteenth century, Europeans, especially if they were poor, had heard that the Americans had had a revolution that successfully overthrew the old orders of society. Madame de Staël could tell a Boston scholar, in 1817, "You are the advance guard of the human race." And Goethe, ten years later, wrote for anybody to read: "Amerika, du hast es besser als unser Kontinent" (which may be loosely translated as: "America, you have things better over there.") He was thinking of the freedom from the binding force of "useless traditions." But people who had never heard of Madame de Staël and Goethe picked up the new belief that there was a green land far away preserved "from robbers, knights and ghosts affrighting." Whenever life could hardly be worse at home, they came to believe that life was better in America.

In Ireland in the middle 1840s human life had touched bottom. Ironically, two causes of the Irish plight came *from* America. The rising competition of American agriculture made thousands of very small farmers (300,000 of Ireland's 685,000 farms had less than three acres) shift from tillage to grazing, on barren ground. And the potato blight, which was to putrefy vast harvests in a few weeks, had crossed the Atlantic from America in 1845. Within five years the potato famine had claimed almost a million Irish lives, over twenty thousand of them dropping in the fields from starvation.

The young Queen Victoria was informed that the state of Ireland was "alarming" and that the country was so full of "inflammable matter" that it could explode in rebellion. So she paid a royal visit, serenely admired the beauty of the scenery, and was relieved that the people "received us with the greatest enthusiasm." Nevertheless, at Kingston and at Cork she noted: "You see more ragged and wretched people here than I ever saw anywhere else." One of those ragged people could well have been a bankrupt farmer from Wexford County who had gone to Cork. Most such, with any energy left over after the famine, retreated to the towns and either joined sedition societies or headed for America. This one chose America, and, like very many of the Irish who came after, his destination was chosen for him by the simple fact that Boston was the end of the Cunard line. His name was Patrick Kennedy, great-grandfather of the thirty-fifth President of the United States. He was one of the 1,700,000 Irish—a little less than one quarter of the whole population when the famine began—who left for America in the 1840s and 1850s.

Hunger, then, was the spur in Ireland. There were other, equally fearful incentives. In the single year of 1848 political storms swept across Europe—in Austria, an abdication, arrests, and executions; in Italy, a revolution and a declaration of war by the Pope against Austria; in Sicily, an uprising against the King of Naples; in Germany, a liberal revolution that failed. Both then and throughout the rest of the century and on into our own, in any troubled country, whether or not its mischief could be laid to known culprits, there was always the ancient scapegoat of the Jew. In eastern and central Europe the ghettos had long been routine targets for the recruiting sergeant and the secret police, and their inhabitants were acquainted from childhood with what one of them called "the stoniest sound in the world: the midnight knock on the door." It would be hard to calculate but easy to guess at the millions of American Jews whose forefathers were harried and haunted by these persecutors. It is something hardly thought of by most of us who came here by free choice, or were born here without ever having to make a choice.

In some cities of Europe, Jews were permitted to practice their religion in compounds. But in many more places, where the Jews had been systematically vilified for fifteen hundred years, authorities considered their rituals to be as sinister as black magic, and the more daring or devout worshiped in stealth. In America, they had heard, they could worship openly in their own fashion, Orthodox, Reform, Conservative — or, as radical Reconstructionists, they could look to the United States as a permitted rallying ground on which to muster the faithful for the return to Palestine. I dwell on the Jews because, in the great tidal wave of the late nineteenth- and early twentieth-century immigration, they were

275

Irish immigrants disembark at the Battery in New York about 1855. The Chinese junk was the artist's invention, though a few years later a junk did visit the city.

the most numerous of those who saw America as the Land of Canaan; because their story offers the most dramatic and arduous exercise in the struggle to assimilate; and because, as much or more than other peoples, they created the American polyglot metropolis against which, in 1924, the Congress protested with restrictive legislation that tried, too late, to restore the United States to its northern European origins.

So late as 1880, there were only a quarter of a million Jews in the United States. By 1924 there were four and a half million, the product of a westward movement that started in the early nineteenth century with their exodus from the ghettos of eastern Europe into the new factories of western Europe. They had moved in that direction earlier throughout the Thirty Years War and then after the later Cossack massacres and peasant revolts. But the factory system provided them with a legal right to flee from their inferior citizenship in Germany and from pogroms in Russia, Poland, and Romania. In the last quarter of the nineteenth century, both city and rural Jews were the willing quarry of emigration agents from America carrying glowing broadsides from house to house about the high wages, good clothes, abundant food, and civil liberties available in the New World. The sweet talk of these promoters might be sensibly discounted, but not the bags of mail containing "America letters" from relatives who had made the voyage and whose more practical accounts of an attainable decent life were read aloud in cottages, markets, and factories.

The word spread beyond the factories and the ghettos to the farmers of southern and central Europe. And whereas before 1890 the immigrant stream had flowed out of Scandinavia, Germany, Ireland, England, and Canada, in the next thirty years the mass of immigrants came from Italy, Austria-Hungary, Russia, and again and always Ireland.

The Germans formed a strong and special current in the mainstream of immigration. There were already a quarter of a million of them in the United States at the time of the Declaration of Independence, and in the thirty years between 1860 and 1890 they contributed more refugees than any other nation, among them more varied social types, more professionals, and more scholars than the others. They also settled far and wide. The German Jews, beginning as small merchants, prospered more conspicuously and founded many of the great banking families of New York. Wherever the Germans went, they tended to establish themselves, both by superiority of talent and a marked gift of clannishness, at the head of the social hierarchy of Jewry. The Sephardic Jews and the German Jews were at the top, and at the bottom were the Lithuanians and the Hungarians, elements in a social system that discouraged intermarriage between its upper and lower strata the defiance of which has probably caused as much snobbish anguish as the love matches of Jews and Gentiles in other immigrant families.

All told, in the first two decades of this century, an unbelievable fourteen and a half million immigrants arrived. They were mostly the persecuted and the poor, "the wretched refuse of your teeming shore" apostrophized by Emma Lazarus, a wealthy and scholarly young lady whose poetic dramas and translations of Heine are forgotten in the thunder of five lines inscribed on the Statue of Liberty. These unlettered millions were, for the most part, to become the "huddled masses" who, in the tenements of the American cities, would have quite a time of it "yearning to breathe free." They had never heard of Thomas Jefferson or George Washington. But they were the easy victims of the absurd myth that the streets of America were paved with gold—not much, perhaps, but enough to offer striking proof, in sepia photographs sent back to Poland or Hungary, of well-fed families who looked you in the eye, of a father or a cousin wearing a suit and shiny shoes, just like a doctor or a merchant in the old country.

Long before they arrived at the ports of embarkation—Constantinople, Piraeus, Antwerp, Bremen—emigrant trains had started deep inside Russia. Most of them were linked box cars, sometimes with benches, the men in one car, the women and children in another. Every few hundred miles the train would be shunted on to a siding in order to pick up other new armies, of Austrians, Hungarians, Lithuanians, and finally a troop of Germans, before they came to, say, Hamburg. There they were corralled and checked to see if they had the three essential passports to America: an exit paper, twenty-five spare dollars to prevent their becoming a public charge, and the price of the passage. By the 1890s lively rate wars between steamship lines had halved the steerage fare from about twenty dollars to ten. In an enclosure outside Hamburg they would be bathed, de-loused, and fed, and their baggage and clothes fumigated. Then they were ferried out to the big ship and stowed aboard, as many as nine hundred in steerage.

In the floating commune of the emigrant ship, the status symbols were few but well defined. A suitcase, however battered, was most likely the mark of a city man. To a poor peasant, a wicker basket was elegance enough. Most people tied everything up in a blanket or a sheet. They had brought with them what they thought to be indispensable to a decent life afloat. First, the necessity of a pillow, goose-feather, if they were lucky—a point of pride, a relic, and a symbol that some families kept throughout their lives. Village girls took along their only certain dowry, a special extra petticoat and, for formal occasions, a corset. Many of the young women were engaged to men from the home town on the other

side of the Atlantic. It was well understood that the ambitious male, engaged or already married, went on ahead to stake out the fortune, which was more often the bare living that could sustain a family. Many of these engagements were broken once for all on the way over by the rude proximity of the males in steerage.

Like all travelers, both simple and sophisticated, they were deeply suspicious of the other nation's food. It was a common thing to take along a cooking pot, a few raw vegetables, and a hunk of sausage or some other final reminder of the favorite snack. The religious invariably took with them the tokens of their faith, a cross or a prayer book or phylacteries; and a member of a closely-knit family would cherish an heirloom yielded up in the moment of parting. It could be nothing more pretentious than a brass candlestick or a lock of hair.

For two weeks or eight days, depending on the size of the ship, they sewed, played cards, sang to harmonicas or tin whistles, counted their savings, continually checked their exit papers, complained about the atrocious food and the ubiquity of the rats. The ones who could read, probably less than half the flock, recited the cheering promise of the emigrant agents' broadsides and pamphlets. The young women nursed the elders and the chronically seasick and resisted, or succumbed to, the advances of spry bachelors. There was no possibility of privacy in the swarm of steerage.

But as America came nearer, some of them suffered from nervous recall of the stratagems that had got them this far. Bright youngsters who had carefully failed their high school examinations in order to prove their unfitness for military service. Oldsters who began to mask a fever with massive doses of medicine. Embezzlers, petty criminals, and betrothed men skipping breach-of-promise suits who had obviously had the wit to fake an exit pass or steal the passage money. A lot of people had a lot to hide.

Far down in the lower bay of New York City, they crowded to the rail to eye their first Americans in the persons of the immigration inspectors, two men and a woman in uniform clambering up a ladder from a cutter that had nosed alongside. The captain was required to note on the ship's manifest the more flagrant cases of contagious disease, for only seventy years ago they were still on the lookout for yellow fever and leprosy. The unlucky victims of such ailments were taken off in a quarantine boat to a special island to be deported as soon as possible.

The harbor was sometimes choked with ships at anchor. In the early 1900s there could be as many as fifteen thousand immigrants arriving in

Sprawled on deck at the end of their journey in 1902, immigrants wait to disembark at Ellis Island, where new buildings could "process" 8,000 a day.

one day, and the ships had to drop anchor and wait. But eventually the engines would rumble again, and there, like a battleship on the horizon, stood what the song calls "Manhattan, an isle of joy." Closer, it grew into a cluster of pinnacles known as skyscrapers. And then the midtown skyscrapers topped the ones first seen. It was unlike any other city, and to the European it was always audacious and magical, and threatening.

Soon the newcomers would be on the docks sorting their bundles and baggage in a babble of languages, and when that was done they were tagged with numbers. Until 1892 they were cleared for entry at Castle Garden, once a fort, then a theater and a public amusement place down at the Battery. However, the volume of immigrants grew so great, and so many of them managed to disappear into Manhattan before being "processed," that a larger and more isolated sorting point had to be found. So, from 1892 on, once the immigrants had been tagged with numbers they were shipped aboard a ferry or a barge to what was to be known in several languages as "the isle of tears," the clearing station, Ellis Island.

It had been used by the early Dutch as a picnic ground. Much later its three acres were increased by landfill into twenty-seven, and it became a government arsenal. Today, it looks like a rather imposing college recently gutted by fire. It is totally derelict, a frowzy monument to the American habit of junking and forgetting whatever wears out. But wandering through its great central hall and tattered corridors, seeing the offices with their rusting files, the broken lavatories, and upturned dining tables, one can imagine the bedlam of its heyday, when the milling swarm of strangers was served and interrogated by hundreds of inspectors, wardens, interpreters, doctors, nurses, waiters, cooks, and agents of immigrant aid societies; and all the while a guerrilla army of con men, land swindlers, and hackmen passed out fresh broadsides boosting the heavenly prospects of the inland towns and unheard-of settlements on the prairie.

The newcomers crowded into the main building and the first thing they heard over the general bedlam were the clarion voices of inspectors bellowing out numbers in Italian, German, Polish, Hungarian, Russian, and Yiddish. According to assigned numbers they were herded into groups of thirty and led through long tiled corridors up a wide staircase into the biggest hall most of them had ever seen. Its dimensions, its pillars, its great soaring windows still suggest the grand ballroom of some abdicated monarch. Once they were assembled there in their thousands, the clearance procedure began. I recently pressed an aged immigrant to describe it. "Procedure?" he squealed incredulously. "Din, confusion, bewilderment, madness!"

They moved in single file through a stockyard maze of passageways and under the eye of a doctor in a blue uniform who had in his hand a

Around the turn of the century, public health nurses on Ellis Island conduct medical examinations of immigrant women. On the far wall is a chart for checking eyesight — using the Cyrillic alphabet.

piece of chalk. He was a tough instant diagnostician. He would look at the hands, the hair, the faces and rap out a few questions. He might spot a panting old man with purple lips, and he would chalk on his back a capital "H" for suspected heart disease. Any facial blotches, a hint of gross eczema brought forth a chalked "F," for facial rash. Children in arms were made to stand down to see if they rated an "L" for the limp of rickets or some other deficiency disease. There was one chalk mark that every family dreaded, for it guaranteed certain deportation. It was a circle with a cross in the middle, and it indicated "feeble-minded."

Next they moved on to two doctors dipping into bowls of disinfectant and snapping back the eyelids of suspects, usually with a buttonhook. They were looking for a disease very common then in southern and eastern Europe, trachoma. If you had it, an "E" was chalked on your back, and your first days in the New World were surely your last.

About eight in ten survived this scrutiny and passed to the final ordeal, the examination before an immigration inspector standing with an interpreter. Not noticeably gracious types, for they worked ten hours a day, seven days a week, they droned out an unchanging catechism: Who paid your passage? How many dependents? Ever been in prison? Can you read and write? (There was for a long time no legal obligation to be able to do either.) Is there a job waiting for you? (This was a famous catch, since a law called the Contract Labor Law forbade immigrants from signing up abroad for any work at all.) Finally, your name was checked against the ship's manifest. Many people were lucky to emerge into the new life with their old name. An Irish inspector glancing down at what to him was the gobbledygook of "Ouspenska" wrote on the landing card "Spensky." A Norwegian with an unpronounceable name was asked for the name of the town he had left. It was Dröbak. The inspector promptly wrote down what he thought he'd heard. Another Norwegian standing nearby philosophically realized that his own name was just as unmanageable and decided that what was good enough for his friend was good enough for him. To this day the progeny of both families rejoice in the name of Robeck.

But a new identity was better than none, and it gave you a landing card. With it you were now ready to pay a visit to a currency booth to change your lire or drachmas, or whatever, into dollars. This exchange could entail prolonged haggling and not a few fist fights with the cashiers, who for many years were short-change artists. But at last you were handed over to the travel agent or the railroad men, if you were going far afield, or you sought the help of an aid society or a beckoning politician, if New York was to be the end of the line. Most immigrants could speak hardly a word of English except the one they had memorized as the town of their destination. A man would unfold a scrap of paper and point to a block-printed word: "Pringvilliamas." Maybe he eventually arrived in Springfield, Massachusetts, and maybe he didn't. But at this point the immigrants' only concern was to get off Ellis Island. All of them looked in relief for the door that was marked "Push to New York." And they pushed.

Now, after another ferry ride, they set foot on the earth of the land that was paved with gold. I once asked a successful but unfailingly cynical immigrant if the reality hadn't meant a shattering disillusion. "But there *was* gold," he said, "to us. There were markets groaning with food and clothes. There were streetcars all over town. You could watch the automobiles. There was no military on horseback and no whips. The neighbors were out in the open, trading and shouting, enjoying free fights. And to a boy like me it was a ball, a friendship club. The streets were an open road." Admittedly, here was a man who had always been able to cope.

There were probably many more who soon came to feel that, at best, they had traded a fearful time in the homeland for a baffling or brutal time in the slums of the cities. Such people went for help to the immigrant aid societies, which proliferated for the needy and the puzzled of the separate nations. The Jews of any nation gravitated to a newspaper office, that of the *Jewish Daily Forward*. It still survives, as the last Yiddish daily left in the United States. Starting in 1897 it attained a high circulation of two hundred and fifty thousand. Today, only seventy-five thousand New Yorkers need or choose to read the daily news in Yiddish. But the desperate immigrants didn't buy it for the news alone. Some went to its office clutching painfully written letters for publication in a daily feature that for nearly eighty years has served as a first-aid station to the immigrant. It is called the "Bintel Brief," and from the beginning the column advertised the various plights of the stranded and helped parted relatives to come together again. It was a blessing to many a wife yearning to find her husband. And, of course, it was a curse to many a husband yearning not to find his wife. But in the main it listened to and advised immigrant Jews who were exploited or bewildered by the polyglot society they had moved into.

DEAR EDITOR: I was born in a small town in Russia, and until I was sixteen I studied in *Talmud Torahs* and *yeshivas*, but when I came to America I changed quickly. I . . . became a freethinker. . . . When I go past a synagogue during these days and hear a cantor chanting the melodies of the prayers, I become very gloomy and my depression is so great that I cannot endure it . . . what is your opinion of this?

DEAR EDITOR: For a long time I worked in a shop with a Gentile girl, and we began to go out together and fell in love. We agreed that I would remain a Jew and she a Christian. But after we had been married for a year, I realized that it would not work. . . . Advise me what to do now. I could never convert and there's no hope for me to keep her from going to church.

DEAR EDITOR: In the name of all the workers of our shop, I write these words to you . . . we make raincoats. With us is a thirteen-year-old boy who works hard for the two and half dollars a week he earns. Just lately it happened that the boy came to work ten minutes late. This was a "crime" the bosses couldn't overlook and for the lost ten minutes they docked him two cents.

DEAR EDITOR: I am a girl from Galicia and in the shop where I work I sit near a Russian Jew . . . once, in a short debate, he stated that all Galicians were no good. . . . According to him the *Galitzianer* are inhuman savages . . . Dear Editor, does he really have a right to say this? I hope you will print my letter and give your opinion.

The files of the "Bintel Brief" ache with troubles: of parents grieved that the American-born son refuses to keep *kosher*; of students who quit chemistry or law books because they were told no Jew could graduate; of a son in a torment of conscience because he feels he must go back and defend his mother and sisters from a new pogrom; of the ignorance and brutality of sweatshop bosses; of the hopelessness of escaping from the bigotry of the neighborhood and the slights of the Gentile shopkeepers. Very many of these Jews found out what the Irish in New York had found out before them—that however much they felt imprisoned with their own kind, they were unwanted on the outside. After the first wave of Jews from southern and eastern Europe, the newspaper advertisements were dotted with new variations on the old warning, "No Irish need apply."

In the early years of this century, you could have gone down to New York's Lower East Side, and to similar parts of Pittsburgh and Chicago, and looked on the roaring maelstroms of any street scene as proof positive that the immigrants of many nations were already bubbling together in the melting pot. Yet, if you went closer and listened, you would know that they were all bustling within the confines of Little Italy or Little Russia. Mike Royko has pointed out that until as late as the 1950s Chicago

was a place where people stayed put for a while, creating tightly knit neighborhoods as small-townish as any village in the wheat fields. The neighborhood towns were part of larger ethnic states. To the north of the Loop was Germany. To the northwest Poland. To the west were Italy and Israel. To the southwest were Bohemia and Lithuania. And to the south was Ireland.

Painter George Bellows called this Hogarthian vision of New York's Lower East Side, where many immigrants settled, "The Cliff Dwellers."

Sooner or later, the ones with health and energy, and gumption or cunning, would want to break away altogether or at least to find some dependable link with the big alien society around them. They frequently found it in a character who haunted the docks and the employment agencies and the factories, a man whose headquarters was the local political clubhouse and whose daily beat was up and down the wobbly staircase of the tenements. The American neighborhood politician is a type not greatly admired by students of political science. Nonetheless, he was the lifeline between the castaway and the new society. In New York he was usually an Irishman or a Jew, a native American, but his parents or grandparents most likely had been immigrants, and he was well acquainted from birth with the primitive needs of people.

In exchange for your vote, a *quid pro quo* so elementary that it was only rarely hinted at, he would do his damnedest to get you a job, he would fish your son out of trouble, he would hound the landlord to repair the stove or the bathtub. You had a daughter dramatically plain—he would go to work on the marriage broker. In bad times he brought up coal and food. He knew when the baby was coming and he got the doctor. These were not casual good deeds. They were the daily grind of a system as subtle and firm as the lineaments of city geography that dictated it.

A front door was the entrance to a house of several families, and a house was connected with other houses to form a city block. So many blocks made up a precinct, serviced by political runners under a precinct captain, whose official salary was that of a fire inspector, a licensing agent of the city liquor board, or some other department of the city government. In turn, a precinct was a subdivision of a ward, patrolled by other far-ranging runners who could be brought to heel by the ward boss, the commander of the field force always in touch with other ward bosses and with such collateral officers of the dominant political party as county clerks, assessors, aldermen, state legislators, and Congressmen. The control of an election district was the prize, and the election was the payoff. From doorman to elected judge, the hierarchy of these offices was as exact as the ranks of an army—and in some cities it still is. Its responsiveness was always being tested from the top, where the ward boss might have a thousand Lithuanians dumped in his neighborhood, to the bottom, where the precinct worker or ward heeler was called on in the middle of the night to rustle up a loan, a bail bond, or a midwife.

For better or worse, it was the election district captains and the ward bosses who ran the cities. New York built the most durable (and periodically the most notorious) system in Tammany, the city's Democratic

By strength of numbers and organization, the Irish came to control the political machinery of several Eastern cities. Puck ran this cartoon in 1889.

PUCK.

organization. Named by the Irish after an Indian chief as a slap at the St. George societies of unrepentant Loyalists, it turned as early as 1800 into a political body under the leadership of Aaron Burr. Since then it has produced some admirable types, such as Fernando Wood, who left the city the legacy of Central Park, and Honest John Kelly, who was said to have "found Tammany a horde and left it an army." But, more often, it allowed some able scoundrel to exact, for big and little services rendered, fortunes well within the dreams of avarice. Men like William Marcy ("Boss") Tweed, whose colleagues conveniently made "clerical errors" in the city finances amounting to about $200,000,000, or Richard Croker, the exemplar of what he called "honest graft," who made enough to settle back in Ireland with a stable of thoroughbreds and a Cherokee Indian wife fifty years his junior.

One of the best-known practitioners of honest graft was a Tammany ward boss, George Washington Plunkitt, an Irishman and a butcher who deserted his trade for the care and comfort of his neighbors, and on the side made a fortune out of harbor transport and general contracting, when the second-generation Irish were coming to political power in the 1870s. He remains the model of the Samaritan politician and has left us a diary that contains an incomparable account of a day in the life of a ward boss of Tammany, which he called "the only lastin' democracy":

2:00 A.M.: Aroused from sleep by a bartender who asked me to go to the police station and bail out a saloon keeper who had been arrested for violating the excise law. Furnished bail and returned to bed at three o'clock.

6:00 A.M.: Awakened by fire engines. Hastened to the scene of the fire . . . found several tenants who had been burned out, took them to a hotel, supplied them with clothes, fed them and arranged temporary quarters for them.

8:30 A.M.: Went to the police court to secure the discharge of six "drunks," my constituents, by a timely word to the judge. Paid the fines of two.

9:00 A.M.: Appeared in the municipal district court to direct one of my district captains to act as counsel for a widow about to be dispossessed. . . . Paid the rent of a poor family and gave them a dollar for food.

11:00 A.M.: At home again. "Fixed" the troubles of four men waiting for me: one discharged by the Metropolitan Railway for neglect of duty; another wanted a job on the road, the third on the subway, and the fourth was looking for work with a gas company.

3:00 P.M.: Attended the funeral of an Italian. Hurried back for the funeral of a Hebrew constituent. Went conspicuously to the front both in the Catholic church and the synagogue.

7:00 P.M.: Went to district headquarters to preside over a meeting of election district captains, who submitted lists of all the voters in their districts and told who were in need, who were in trouble, who might be won over [to Tammany] and how.

8:00 P.M.: Went to a church fair. Took chances on everything, bought ice cream for the young girls and the children, kissed the little ones, flattered their mothers and took the fathers out for something down at the corner.

9:00 P.M.: At the clubhouse again. Spent $10 for a church excursion. Bought tickets for a baseball game. Listened to the complaints of a dozen pushcart peddlers who said they were being persecuted by the police. Promised to go to police headquarters in the morning and see about it.

10:30 P.M.: Attended a Hebrew wedding reception and dance. Had previously sent a handsome wedding present to the bride.

12:00 P.M.: In bed.

Where, no doubt, he fell asleep counting votes. And he got them. For while high-minded men might draw up blueprints of an ideal city, or sit among their friends and grow purple at the thought of Tammany's corruption, Mr. Plunkitt and his minions dealt with the realities of the city as they saw them. They did small things at inconvenient times for small people. They had their reward at the polls, which gave them a mandate to go on with their good works and the confidence, along the way, to milk the city's revenues. But they bred Americans out of foreigners.

Officially, you changed from a foreigner into an American citizen after filing naturalization papers, painfully boning up on a few elementary facts of American government, taking an indulgent verbal examination in these mysteries, and finally appearing before a judge to take the oath. But becoming an American was more complicated and for most more painful. It entailed at first the enormous obstacle of the language, and there are countless thousands of aged immigrants today who have managed with American life with the barest pidgin English.

On young families raising first-generation Americans, the pressure to learn the language was intense as the children grew and went through the public school, which, in immigrant neighborhoods, had the dual purpose of teaching the rudiments of mathematics and geography and also of Americanizing the small stranger within the gates. Then the children went home and saw their parents reading an Italian or Russian or Yiddish paper and they began to notice thick accents. They felt uncomfortable and then they felt ashamed. This slow but sure discovery that the parents were odd, and to the extent of their oddity figures of fun, is a great and tragic theme in American life and literature. And the parents' shameful awareness of it sent them off in droves to night school, to make the final capitulation to the new land by learning the language of their sons and daughters.

But it was by no means all humiliation and tragedy. There were other forces, other institutions, that dissolved the pain of strangeness. There was the burlesque theater, which in the beginning was exactly that—a place where the poor family could see farcical takeoffs of the operatic and other cultural heroes that the rich took seriously. But at the end of the nineteenth century it became a family theater, in which the immigrant saw the German comic, and the Irish, and the Italian, and the Jew play out the homely troubles that in life were no joke, translate into farce the immigrants' fears of American society and their mockery of each other. It was in the burlesque theater that they took it out on their common enemies: the slum landlord, the con man, the corner grocer, the money lender, the cop, most of all the judge, who was always irascible, outrageously unjust, and fatuously susceptible to a pair of pretty legs. He was often outsmarted by simple immigrants and he was always bribable, usually dismissing the case against a gorgeous defendant by arranging to meet her "around the corner at half-past eight." In other words, he was W. C. Fields and Groucho Marx, Jack Benny and Bert Lahr, Bobby Clark and George Burns and Phil Silvers. They were all cradled by burlesque.

By the time a generation or two of newcomers could relax into mimicry of each other's murderous ways with the English language, there appeared a humorous writer named Milt Gross, who tried to make over the immigrant into an American by retelling American history in the idiom of his readers from the Lower East Side. He wrote with galloping vivacity about "De Bettle from Bonker Heel," and "De Bustun Tip-potty" and "How It Got Inwanted Tenksgeeving Day." Here is his crisp and definitive account of Columbus's discovery:

So it sailed irrigodless Chreestopher Columbus hover de hocean wot he lended gradually by a lend wot it gritted heem dere radskeens—So dey said so—

"Hm, look, pale pipple!!! A leedle sissick no dot from de woyich is no—"
So Chrees sad:

"C. Columbus—dot's I'm—und de woild is rond—Dees is Hindia und I was told to look opp a guy entitled Gonga Dink . . . Ha wot—dees is wot—?? Dees is *America*—Yi Yi Yi—Queeck boyiss, hev preented on de beezness cods—'Countinants deescovered—while you wait—Eef you are plizzed tal de Quinn—If not tal oss.'"

I mentioned earlier that all you needed to get to America was an exit pass, twenty-five dollars, and reasonable health, but that what you were forbidden to have was a contract for a job in the new country. Toward the end of the Civil War, labor was so scarce that Congress made labor contracts signed abroad valid and protected by the courts. The subsequent rush into Europe of factory and railroad agents to sign up intending immigrants threatened a flood of cheap labor bound to industrial serfdom, and within four years the act was repealed.

In 1885 Congress decided to discourage unskilled immigrants by enacting a Contract Labor Law that prohibited the signing of foreigners to contract jobs, unless those jobs were professional or otherwise skilled. But the flood of the unskilled was not stopped, and the effect of the act was exactly the reverse of its intention. It meant that the really welcome immigrant was jobless, and in the high tide of immigration southern and central Europe was a bottomless pool of cheap labor. In the Midwest, they poured into the steel and coke factories and the railroad shops; in New York, into the garment factories. Among them were not only city people but peasants and poor farmers who had found themselves transplanted to a city block and were terrified of venturing further into the unknown Siberia of the countryside. Many thousands of them arrived just after the invention of such labor-saving devices as the sewing machine, which had been touted as a boon to the housewife, but was a curse to the seamstress. The labor that she had done for forty cents an hour was now being done by machines, and she had no choice but to stay on and work them for eight cents an hour.

The industrialists, the steel men, the iron and tin and railroad barons, came very easily to make the same large assumption about the inexhaustibility of cheap labor. But, as we have seen in Carnegie's troubles with his workers, the immigrant did not stay cowed forever. Henry Frick, Carnegie's bosom partner in his steel enterprises, was a fanatical opponent of labor unions, but he was quick to see that the latest wave of immigrants could be employed as strikebreakers. One year he employed Hungarians to break a strike. But within a year or two he had to hire Italians to break a strike of Hungarians, who by then were beginning to learn a specialty. In an irritable moment Frick got off a profound remark."The immigrant," he complained, "however illiterate or ignorant he may be, always learns too soon." Not soon enough, however, to deny these industrial tycoons their imperial hold on the raw materials of industry and, in the person of John Pierpont Morgan, on the national economy itself.

Overleaf: *A ten-year-old spinner in a North Carolina mill was photographed in 1909 by Lewis Hine for his appalling report on child labor in cotton mills.*

Time has been kind to these men who have been variously called, according to taste, giants of industry, the Potentates, and the Robber Barons. Carnegie is remembered for his libraries and philanthropies, Huntington for a great library, Frick for his lovely French house on New York's Fifth Avenue and its collection of exquisite paintings. Even their own offspring were hardly aware that the fortunes that could commission these palaces were built on the open shop, the seventy-hour week, and immigrant labor. When, a few years ago, a Pennsylvania historian wrote a biography of Frick that recounted the ruthlessness of his labor tactics, his daughter sued to stop publication. The figure drawn in this book was nothing like the adored and adoring father her memory cherished. The case went through the appeals court until, in the end, while American publishers trembled for the verdict, it was left to the United States Supreme Court to rule that the life of a public man is still in the public domain. The writing of biography in the United States was allowed to go on.

Eventually the government of the United States moved to arrest or restrict the power of the Barons over their industrial serfs. For a glimpse of the first of the protagonists in this inevitable showdown, you can begin by turning off New York's Madison Avenue onto a side street and going into a mansion for whose stones the architect Charles Follen McKim longed to use joints as tightly sealed as those in the walls of the Erechtheum.

"I would like," he told his client, "to follow their example, but it would cost a small fortune and no one would see where the additional money went."

"How much extra?" the client asked.

"Fifty thousand dollars," was the reply.

"Go ahead," said J. P. Morgan.

Today the Morgan Library is a treasure house of matchless bronzes, tapestries, enamels, porcelains, manuscripts from Milton to Dickens, one of the few surviving Gutenberg Bibles printed on vellum, all culminating in the first item of the catalogue, a ninth-century book of the four Gospels bound in gold and encrusted with precious stones. J. P. Morgan, it is worth remembering, spent millions on manuscripts and artifacts brought over from the lands of precisely those immigrants who could be bought in job lots for eight cents an hour.

Just to the right of the entrance is a red room known simply as Morgan's West Room. Here sat the only man alive who could afford to buy out Carnegie, and did so, and set up United States Steel, the first billion-dollar corporation. In this room the fate of industries and armies was decided, and the feeding of millions of European war refugees was financed. When the collapse of a trust company threatened a financial panic, Morgan locked up a posse of Wall Street bankers in this room and played solitaire in a corner until they came up with the money. Morgan alone redeemed the credit of the city of New York against the pressure of the London banks, and in his most majestic *beau geste* he saved the gold reserve of the United States Treasury by buying $65,000,000 worth of gold with bonds.

His supreme audacity was to form a single company to monopolize all transportation between the Great Lakes and the Pacific Coast. Since he had set up this company in New Jersey, he contended that he was ruled by New Jersey's laws alone. But the President of the United States recognized a monopoly outlawed by Congress. Morgan was summoned to the White House. "Mr. President," he said, "I'll get my lawyer and you get yours." The President got nine lawyers, the Supreme Court, in fact, and it ruled that "the Congress of the United States is not at the mercy of the state of New Jersey." It dissolved the monopoly.

The bridle on the power of such men was used very late. But once it had been used it was seldom thereafter relaxed. Morgan's improbable conqueror was a man who had been a sickly, shortsighted child anxiously pampered in the nursery of a Long Island country house. His childhood ambition was to be a taxidermist, and for a year or two he toddled around in a cloud of formaldehyde. His name was Theodore Roosevelt, a descendant of one of the old Dutch gentry of New York. To help him grow out of his embarrassing puniness, the family doctor ordered him to build up his muscles, according to the prescription then in favor, by doing strenuous setting-up exercises and throwing a medicine ball around. He obeyed with such alarming success that throughout his manhood he was famous as a hunter and explorer and came to drape the Long Island house with the pelts, horns, antlers, torsos, and heads of the denizens of three continents. In the long run, he became President of the United States and went gunning for the Robber Barons.

Roosevelt is affectionately recalled today as a half-heroic, half-comic figure, a bespectacled barrel of a man choking with teeth and jingoism; for at one time his obsession was to match the glory of the British Empire with an American dominion in the Caribbean and the Pacific. But though for a time Americans got a heroic bang out of the idea of empire, they were temperamentally averse to practicing it. President Taft might call on the country to think of the inhabitants of America's newly acquired overseas "territories" as "the little brown brother," but, in a country that had no taste for recruiting the soldiers and the civil servants, the work-horses of empire, the general sentiment was that of a Marine song: "He may be a brother of Big Bill Taft, But he ain't no friend of mine."

So Theodore Roosevelt liberated his imperial instincts in safaris at home and abroad, in assassinating moose and elephants, in disappearing

into the Brazilian jungle—bouts of muscle-flexing that celebrated his emergence from a frail childhood and vindicated his muscular Christianity.

That is the legendary Teddy Roosevelt. But there was another and splendid side to him. He was the first influential man of his time to see clearly that the United States was no longer a rural nation but an industrial giant run amok, whose keepers were not in the Congress or the White House but in Pittsburgh and Cleveland, and that West Room of Morgan's in New York City.

We have barely mentioned a President since Lincoln. This is not an oversight. For forty years after the Civil War the true national power lay with the oil monopoly, the steel trust, the railroad combines. They had all voted enthusiastically to elect Roosevelt Vice President. But when he got to the White House after McKinley's assassination, he looked at the ways, beginning with the standby stratagems of the holding companies, in which the Barons preserved their immunity from the law. He determined, if not to break them, to bring them under the control of Congress.

He had started, as Police Commissioner of New York, going after all the petty grafters who made life hell for the immigrants, and had achieved the feat of making Ellis Island decent and its inspectors able and courteous. As Governor of New York he went after the sweatshop owners and the tenement landlords. As President he charged up and down the social scale, flagellating everybody from food packagers to bankers, challenging them in the name of the federal government. The men who ran the trusts he called, in his squeaky but blazing fashion, "malefactors of great wealth." The trust he saw as an octopus whose longest tentacles bound the immigrants "as dwellers in a polyglot boarding house." His bravest mission was to try and see, through social legislation and new resources of education, that the immigrants should no longer be looked on as nationally identifiable pools of cheap labor. The country must stop talking about German-Americans and Italian-Americans and Polish-Americans: "We have room for but one language here, and that is the English language, for we intend to see that the crucible turns our people out as Americans." There must be no more "hyphenated Americans."

Roosevelt's aim was a double one: to liberate the immigrant from his daily grind in a polyglot compound, and to set him free from the hampering liabilities of his native tongue. The first aim did not begin to be achieved until 1911, when there was an appalling fire in New York's Triangle Shirtwaist Factory. It took a hundred and forty lives, roused the needle workers to go on strike and wakened the public conscience. And at the end of it, the airless sweatshop, with its two exits leading to one

Toothy and jovial as ever, Teddy Roosevelt met political disaster in 1912, when, having failed to secure the Republican nomination for President, he ran on the Bull Moose ticket and was roundly beaten.

rickety staircase, was abolished by New York State law. So was the peddling out of piecework to the immigrant's home. It took this trauma to start the Jewish garment workers organizing in unions for decent hours and tolerable wages, and it marked the fiery beginning of their emergence into New York politics. Within a year William Howard Taft would confide to reporters that "Jews make the best Republicans." (Forty years later, Adlai Stevenson, with equal conviction, confided that "Jews make the best Democrats.")

The liberation of the immigrant from his mother tongue was something that only time and two generations of American schoolchildren would achieve. By, say, the Second World War, it had been done. But in the past ten years or so there has appeared a new strain of ethnic pride, almost an insistence on reverting to hyphenated Americanism. The blacks who, arguing that "black is beautiful," refused to be assimilated in the white man's world may have led the way, but a similar pride in national origin is now being flaunted by immigrants old and new. As early as the first decade of the century, there were protests and small riots outside burlesque and vaudeville theaters against the caricaturing of German and Italian and Jewish traits. In the 1930s the motion picture industry devised a code to eliminate the representation of Greeks as conniving merchants, Italians as gangsters, Negroes as shiftless clowns. This new pride springs, I think, partly from a desperate desire of the underdog in the faceless cities to claim an identity, partly from the pragmatic aim of new immigrants—the Puerto Ricans after the Second World War, the Cubans after Castro's coup, the Hungarians after the Soviet invasion—to arrest at once their automatic consignment to the bottom of the labor market. They do not necessarily succeed, but at least they organize and agitate for the rights of equal pay and first-class citizenship.

Today the tenements are seventy years older than when the Poles and Italians and Lithuanians and Russians climbed into them, and they were old then. They are the crumbling homes of the newer refugees, and most of all of the native blacks who began sixty years ago to be refugees from the South and from the countryside everywhere. Today, in the cities, the masses are as huddled as ever, and they no longer come expecting El Dorado. More often than not they exchange a rural slum for a city hovel. They know it—and they hate it. And the threat of "the fire next time" is an ever-present one wherever the comfortable whites and the impoverished blacks grow farther apart.

But in the wake of the immigrant flood that we have been talking about, paupers became shopkeepers, and the sons and daughters of peasants bound for centuries to slivers of poor soil turned into clerks and nurses and accountants and schoolteachers and druggists and cab drivers and lawyers and doctors. Looking back on those sheepish legions, we should not pretend that they were ever rollicking characters in a musical comedy. But we should not forget, either, the millions who struggled for a decent and tidy life, and made it, and still do.

10
THE PROMISE FULFILLED — THE PROMISE BROKEN

At three o'clock in the morning of Monday, November 11, 1918, the State Department announced that Germany had surrendered and signed an armistice, and that all fighting in the World War would cease at 11:00 A.M., Continental Time. The twenty-eighth President of the United States, Thomas Woodrow Wilson, a slim bespectacled man with a long jaw and the contained self-assurance of a bishop, was up and at his desk. It was the middle of the night, no time to be clacking away at his usual typewriter (though within the hour a burst of whistles and sirens and pealing bells would drown out such a scruple), so he took out a sheet of White House stationery and wrote down in pencil: "Everything for which America has fought has been accomplished. It will now be our fortunate duty to assist by example, by sober, friendly counsel, and by material aid, in the establishment of just democracy throughout the world."

It is true that the Allies could not have defeated the Central Powers without the intervention of the United States in the last eighteen months of a war which was to record an atrocious pile of casualties: more than half of Russia's mobilized twelve million were killed or wounded; five and a half of France's eight million; more than a third of the nine million recruited by the British Empire and Commonwealth; one and a half million of Italy's five and a half million. When a whole generation of Europeans was maimed and faint with exhaustion, the United States had sent into the battlefields two million brash and lusty young men. American industry, already geared to a scale of productivity that Europeans could hardly grasp, poured arms and matériel across the Atlantic. American pride in a superior technology occasionally exceeded its performance: the Germans were meant to tremble before the firm promise of thousands of airplanes, though not a single American plane arrived in France in time to be used in the war. But the rude energy of the Americans, both in the flesh and in the factory, was decisive against an enemy whose people were pinched by starvation, whose cavalry horses had no reserves of feed, whose military transport in the last months rode on rubberless wheels.

Undoubtedly, Europe in the flush of victory was grateful to the last and most powerful of the Allies. But neither Britain and France nor the other Allies envisioned the peace settlement quite as Woodrow Wilson led the American people to see it, as a kind of moral Olympiad at which the United States would be the host nation. Soon after the Armistice, President Wilson began to draft in his mind a grand plan for "the establishment of just democracy throughout the world." The presumption of his rhetoric spread beyond the White House. "Now that the forces of Right have begun their reconstruction of humanity's morals," a newspaper proclaimed in November 1918, "the world faces a material task of equal magnitude." This purple passage came from an advertisement for steel window frames.

Between Wilson's self-assigned mission to preside over the peace and the advertising copywriter's celebration of America's industrial prowess, there is a link of moral and material pride that recalls the most rooted beliefs of the founders of New England: that a good Puritan, though living a life of the strictest piety, must yet live in the world and make God's will work through government, that material success or failure is not an aim in itself but a proof of God's pleasure. Now that America had saved old Europe, America would "reconstruct humanity's morals" and incidentally create unprecedented wealth. The twentieth century was to fulfill the promise of the Puritan fathers that goodness and success go hand in hand. And, so it seemed in 1919, America could not have had more providential luck than to find Woodrow Wilson in the White House. He was the perfect prototype of the seventeenth-century Puritan reincarnated. He would have been old John Winthrop's choice—and, with becoming modesty, his own—for President of the United States, if not of the world.

He was born in Virginia in 1856 and was steeped in Presbyterian blood down many generations, out of Scotland on the one side and Ulster on the other. His father was a Presbyterian minister, the son's lifelong model for high thinking and plain living. Moving from manse to manse, young Woodrow spent his boyhood in Georgia and South Carolina. From his earliest years, he was plainly intended to be a scholar, and he moved sedately down the groves of academe until, in his forty-sixth year, he became president of Princeton. His lectures, buoyant with high-toned and uplifting passages about corruption in government and greed in big business, were frequently published in magazines as philippics against Congress and the trusts.

But until he was fifty-five years old, which in 1911 was practically the twilight years, he was a theoretician. Then he was chosen by the Democratic bosses of New Jersey for the governorship as a highly respectable front—until he got to the governor's mansion and pained them with a state primary law, an employers' liability act, and other fumigating reforms. Within the year he had the luck to appeal to the elders of his party when they were more interested in defeating a Tammany-backed man for President than nominating their own. He would have had little chance of election if Theodore Roosevelt had not bolted the Republican party and set up his own, thereby splitting the Republican vote and permitting Wilson to walk serenely through the middle and become, two years after leaving Princeton, President of the United States.

There are three things about Woodrow Wilson that elevated him, for a dizzy year or so, to the status of a world savior, and in the end they brought him down: his unwavering high moral tone, his self-intoxicating eloquence, and his true concern for the dispossessed. From his college days on he saw himself as at least a favorite pupil of God, retained an absolute confidence in his own moral principles, and held a collateral belief that compromise is moral treason. Secondly, he was able to convey through the cloudy grandeur of his speeches, most of all when Americans were in the first flush of victory, the conviction that his righteous feelings were theirs.

The third thing was as rooted in his childhood as his piety but did him, in my opinion, a good deal more credit. He was nine years old when the Civil War ended, and he grew up in a wasteland of impoverished Southerners being treated as beaten aliens in their own country. When the World War was over, he was genuinely moved by the similar plight, on a huger scale, of the broken countries of central Europe. Then, as in an Old Testament dream, he had a revelation. He would go to Europe not simply as the chief American representative at the peace conference gathering in Versailles. He would draft, and hope to dictate, a new world order under a League of Nations pledged to universal peace. He would give to all small countries the right to govern themselves, "the right of self-determination." As he sailed for France, in December 1918, the first President to leave the country while in office, he said: "We are to be an instrument in the hands of God to see that liberty is made secure for mankind."

Also aboard was Robert Lansing, the Secretary of State. He confided to his journal: "The more I think about the President's declaration as to the right of 'self-determination,' the more convinced I am [that] . . . it is bound to be the basis of impossible demands on the Peace Conference . . . what misery it will cause." Lansing mooted his misgivings to

American painter George Luks saw Armistice Night, 1918, as an enormous outburst of flags, fireworks, and public enthusiasm.

Wilson, who coldly replied that it would not be a peace of "legalisms."

Wilson's vision had floated ahead of him to Europe, and to the dazzled crowds in Paris his coming was like the entry into Jerusalem. No President, no statesman of any country, had been so received as the deliverer who would lead us all into the promised land.

The disillusion in him was swift, and it came first in private to the Allied statesmen—to Lloyd George, Clemenceau, and Orlando, and their aides—who had expected a statesman and encountered a divine. It is not difficult to imagine the effect of this character, sitting coolly in the cloister of his own righteousness, on statesmen passionately drawing new frontiers, adjudicating the claims of millions of nationals for larger homelands, negotiating customs agreements, saying which country should control a river or a railway system, distributing the loser's colonies, most of all trying to thrash their way through the monstrous complexity of Europe's ethnic and nationalist jealousies, which a simpler offer of "self-determination" would only confuse rather than placate. At the end of it, the language of the treaty was artfully dressed up to hide from the President the honest realities he could not acknowledge, such as the French desire for some limits to the population of Germany and some economic restraints on her power to make another war. Wilson was placated by the smooth ambiguities of a super-subtle treaty. And he relaxed the one moral stand that reflected his courage: his steady suspicion that Germany was being asked to pay back, one way and another, more money than she could ever earn.

Wilson sailed for home amid a bedlam of criticism. The French press thought him pro-German. The British deplored his vague self-righteousness and lack of practicality. All the Allies began to fear, correctly, that they would be unable to repay the huge sums the United States had loaned them. (By 1967, fifty years after the United States had entered the war, France's original debt of just over 4.0 billion (i.e. 4,000 million) dollars had risen with unpaid interest to over 5.0 billion; Great Britain's 4.8 billion-dollar indebtedness was now at 7.3 billion, an interesting and forgotten figure never likely to be expunged from the books.)

Wilson received a formal welcome when he sailed into New York, but the domestic disillusion with him was cruelly swift. The Congress had no sure knowledge but a number of sharp suspicions about how much American sovereignty had been traded away to Wilson's precious League of Nations. The Senate would in time reject the Covenant of the League and so deliver the first world organization a body blow in its cradle.

While still president of Princeton University and not yet a politician, Woodrow Wilson sat stiffly for a portrait on the lawn of "Prospect," his home.

But "internationalism" had taken on an uglier popular meaning. It came to signify "international Communism," which had already over- thrown imperial Russia and terrified her neighbors. Within ten days of the Armistice, bands of soldiers broke up a Socialist rally in Madison Square Garden, and the next night a meeting of people who dared to call themselves "sympathizers" with the Russian Revolution was dispersed after some bloody beatings. While Wilson was at his lofty bargaining in Paris, the country was seized with the fear that the last great wave of immigrants had brought the revolutionary infection with them. Few ironies of the American experience are so exquisite or so sour as the predicament, in the dreadful year of 1919, of an American fresh from the battlefields of Europe—some soldier named, say, Polanski or Steinberg—who had once fled from persecution in the old country and was now persecuted in the new as a Bolshevik.

Every misfortune that normally follows in the train of a great war—the closing of munitions factories, a cutback in the working week, a slump in the price of crops that for four years had poured into the granaries of the Allies—could be interpreted as tactical triumphs of the Communist strategy to overthrow the American republic. The Mayor of Seattle, a stronghold of the radical Industrial Workers of the World and the scene of a city strike, received a bomb in the mail. So, in Atlanta, did the chairman of the Senate's Immigration Committee. The first law officer of the United States, the Attorney General himself, had his house in Washington blown up. He was A. Mitchell Palmer, a confessed Quaker but probably the most belligerent Quaker in the history of the faith.

Palmer's name should be memorized in schools as the archetype of the paranoid witch hunter with which the Republic is regularly afflicted whenever an unpleasant turn of history—a spy scare, a wave of violence, a dramatic plunge of the stock market, the "loss" of some foreign ally we never owned—cannot be logically explained or seems to be beyond the control of the government of the United States. He ordered or con- doned raids on magazine offices, public halls, private houses, union headquarters, meetings big and small of anyone—socialists, liberals, atheists, freethinkers, social workers—who could be identified or accused as Bolsheviks or rumored to be such by the nearest excitable citizen. Palmer's hysterical example led, among other horrors, to a drastic revision of the immigration laws. The flow of immigrants from eastern and southern Europe slowed to a dribble, and there was a time when more people were being deported from Ellis Island than were coming in. In the South and Midwest, the chauvinist fever took a virulent form all too common among Anglo-Saxons and Celts when they are touched by panic: it bred a bigot army, led by the Ku Klux Klan, dedicated to the harassment, beating, and occasional lynching of any "foreigner" who could not claim Anglo-Saxon Christian origins, that is to say the Jew, the Roman Catholic, and the Negro.

The returned soldiers and the released munitions workers had their legitimate grievances and added them to the general ferment. Veterans had been promised homes and found surburban boxes at extravagant rents. During the war, labor had willingly forfeited the right to strike. Now it was freed from that pledge, and its instinct, in the face of arbitrary layoffs and an alarming rise in the cost of living, was to strike. In 1919, one of the black years of this century, there was a national steel strike and a railroad strike and a police strike in Boston and race riots in twenty-three cities. For there was a new menace to the city worker's peace of mind—the black man and his family from the South, who had moved into the Northern industrial towns to do war work, and when the war was over stayed housed in what had once been lower-middle-class white neighborhoods.

In July 1919 a teen-aged black boy—"colored," as we should have called him then—was holding on to a railroad tie after a bout of swimming in Lake Michigan when he happened to drift over to the waters facing a beach reserved for whites. He was stoned from the white beach. Soon afterwards he was seen to lose his grip of the tie. Nobody ever knew for certain whether he had been hit, but he drowned—and his friends back on the black beach stormed over to the whites. This was the start of a riot that seized all the neighborhoods where Negroes had moved into the white fringes. For one week Chicago was a battleground for bombings, shootings, stabbings, fires, white forays into Negro slums, gang retaliations; and at the end of it twenty-three Negroes and fifteen whites were dead, and five hundred thirty-seven people were wounded.

A small footnote to the history of idealism is the fact that, throughout Attorney General Palmer's notorious "raids," throughout the sickness and violence of 1919, Wilson had only one thing in mind: to see the Treaty of Versailles passed unimpaired by the Senate. While the Senate was hedging the treaty with reservations that would exclude the United States from the League of Nations, Wilson resolved to talk the people into it. While in the Rockies, however, his health broke, and his train came home. He suffered a cerebral thrombosis and for seventeen months he lay or dozed in the White House, a sick shadow of the savior of Europe, quite beyond the management of his office.

He was not removed for disability. He was charitably ignored. Americans were already bored or disenchanted with Europe, a Europe haggling

---

Overleaf: *Lynch law flourished in the years after World War I; in 1919 alone, 70 Negroes were lynched. This grisly scene took place in Marion, Indiana in August, 1930.*

over colonies, sunk in famine, erupting into revolutions, haughtily lamenting the materialism and parsimony of the recent hero across the Atlantic. Americans were exhausted by their own troubles, many of which were put down to the chivalrous American intervention in Europe, and especially to the intervener himself. America suddenly wanted no part of Europe and ditched the League of Nations. She wanted to slide back into a bath of nostalgia for the good old days before the war and Wilsonian internationalism, for the nineteenth-century America that had obeyed its first Presidents and avoided all "foreign entanglements."

Very little is dependable in the politics of a going democracy except the people's conviction that one world-saver at a time is enough. After Lincoln, Andrew Johnson. After Lloyd George, Bonar Law. After Churchill, Attlee. After Roosevelt, Truman. Now, after an eight-year audience with an archbishop, America wanted nothing so much as a quiet, long drink with a crony. She looked around for a homespun leader—or, rather, the bosses of the Republican party found him—in a small Midwestern town, Marion, Ohio. The bosses had come to a deadlock in their nominating convention. Two factions were unalterably opposed to each other's candidate. So they met in a room in the Blackstone Hotel and there appeared unto them as in a vision the perfect compromise candidate: a small-town newspaper editor, now a Senator, a clubbable and genial buddy who had one supreme qualification for the Presidency usually lacking in its incumbents—he looked like a President ordered up by central casting, as massively handsome as an Indian chief. That would take care of the necessary façade and its popularity with the people. Behind it, however, there was no stuffing, nothing cantankerous or formidable. He was reliably weak, pliable, accommodating. He bore the resonant name of Warren Gamaliel Harding.

On the now famous night of decision, the bosses summoned Harding to their hotel room and asked him to go off into an inner room, to commune with himself and to think if there was anything in his past or present life that might, on disclosure, embarrass the office of the Presidency. It is a customary ritual, and it always receives the same modest confession of spotlessness. Harding went inside and thought. He must have thought very hard indeed. Considering what we know now, we should be staggered that he returned to the bosses within twenty minutes and said he had reviewed his life and could find no fault or flaw in it. He had, in fact, had a flaming extramarital love affair in Ohio, garlanded with a pile of letters still very much in existence. At that moment, he had a mistress who was to bear him a child and make a bestseller out of the experience when he was dead and gone. But the private life of a United States Senator was his own to hide, and by senatorial courtesy so was the private life of his worst enemy on the Senate floor. And in 1920 Senators and reporters alike observed the quaint tradition of silence.

Harding was elected by a landslide, and the 1920s began to bloom. His short reign basked in what he himself had called "normalcy." The word was at first accepted as a joke or a slip by a President whose inflated prose style was said, by one acid reporter, "to resemble nothing so much as a string of sponges."

Unfortunately, this welcome buddy had other buddies, including one Cabinet officer and other high officials of the government, who quietly pilfered the public treasury while Harding was promising to hunt down the "Reds" and deferring to the urging of the great corporations to fortify American production behind the highest tariff walls in her history. What the people never knew at the time was the scale and audacity of the crookeries of Harding's advisers. In 1923 the Senate investigated "irregularities" in the Veterans' Bureau. It had been defrauded of tidy sums by its chief, a friend of Harding's, and he went to prison for two years. But he was the only malefactor to be advertised during Harding's lifetime. While the President played poker or connived at he knew not what, the lobbyists he had brought in from Ohio made money while the going was good. His Attorney General tore up all his bank records when he came to trial years later. The Custodian of Alien Property milked his bureau and also went to jail. And so did Harding's Secretary of the Interior, bribed with $100,000 for secretly leasing government oil reserves to another buddy. The head of the FBI appointed a deputy chief who had been a convicted murderer and a German spy. The lesser fry who fed off the fatter fry were infinite in number.

The public knew nothing of all this until a Senate investigation during the term of Harding's successor opened up the snake pit. But Harding knew some of it, more of it as his three short years went by, and the dawning knowledge combined with his private amorous turmoil griped him with a bellyache that killed him. He was buried in his home town, in a splendid Doric memorial. There, in respectful ignorance, the American people mourned the passing of a great man. "He was not a bad man," said Teddy Roosevelt's daughter, "he was simply a slob." Harding himself said it more truly and touchingly: "I was a small-town editor, I could not grasp I was President of the United States."

It took a little time for the news of Harding's death in San Francisco to travel the three thousand miles east to a small town in Vermont where the Vice-President, Calvin Coolidge, was staying with his widowed father, a deputy sheriff locally known as the Colonel. But eventually a telephone operator eleven miles away got the message and it came first in the middle of the night to the old father. He called to his son, who woke

Mrs. Coolidge, and, in an episode that is now part of the folklore, the new President went downstairs, helped his father find a copy of the Constitution, and brought out the family Bible. By long custom, a new President is sworn in by the Chief Justice of the United States, who was in his bed five hundred miles away. Since Colonel Coolidge was a notary public, he risked performing the solemn ceremony himself. It was 2:30 in the morning of August 3, 1923. By the light of a kerosene lamp in the sitting room of a farmhouse Calvin Coolidge took the old oath to "preserve, protect and defend the Constitution of the United States."

The United States had a lord and master from a country store in Vermont, and he was to reaffirm the faith in country stores and the people bred in them, because Coolidge appeared to be the genuine rural article that Harding was soon seen to have debased. He looked and sounded like a throwback to the rude farmers who had fired the first shots of the Revolution. He was, in fact, an Amherst graduate who had gone into a comfortable small-town law practice, though he was very soon on the public payroll—first as a city solicitor, next as a state legislator, and in succession, a mayor, a state senator, and finally Governor of Massachusetts. A single sentence delivered as Governor, during a Boston police strike, probably did more than any political machination to guarantee his nomination for the Vice-Presidency: "There is no right to strike against the public safety by anybody, anywhere, at any time." The whole country memorized it as the consummation of a rule of public service devoutly to be wished. And when he became President the whole country saw him, not as a shrewd, substantial Massachusetts lawyer with a melancholy taste in humor, but as a Vermont farmer, a man canny as a Yankee drummer, wry as a crab apple, and full of dry, unplumbed wisdom. If people need a savior, they usually get him in the image they want.

When American life was getting to be very complicated indeed, what with a knotty tangle over war reparations abroad and labor strife at home, Coolidge was a man of few words who pointed simply at the country's prosperity and delivered himself of two dicta: he believed, with Jefferson, in as little government as possible, and he declared that "the business of America is business." Very soon America was reveling in what was to be known as the Coolidge prosperity, which had very little to do with him and everything to do with the historic fact that America, after the First World War, had vaulted into the position of the world's creditor nation; that its unscathed industries achieved miracles of production on the first great assembly lines; that it had the highest average income of any country; that it made more steel than Europe; and that Henry Ford built a motorcar for Everyman.

When Ford first sought financial backing, the very notion of farmers and shopgirls owning automobiles was so ridiculous that the House of Morgan told him to keep such daydreams to himself. Ford rented a brick shed, managed to scrape together $28,000 in subscribed capital, and settled down to his daydream with single-minded frenzy. He sold seventeen hundred of his first model, a two-cylinder, eight-horsepower car with a chain drive, and in the next five years he tried out eight more models. He was looking for a strong cheap metal, which he finally found in an imported piece of vanadium steel, and in 1909 he used it on his first Model T.

Ford, however barmy his politics or paranoid his later feelings about the Jews and trade unions, remains a giant of American history for one great reason: like Edison, he believed in supplying conveniences for the many rather than service for the few. It was a belief that led straight to paper towels and cafeterias and supermarkets and motels. Ford made his radical breakthrough by thinking first of the needs of hundreds of thousands of consumers. His original labor policies made him the American god to employees, and his volcanic flow of productivity made him a terrible titan to his competitors. In 1914 the national average wage was $2.40 a day. Ford paid a minimum of $5.00. His first touring Model T cost $850. By 1926, when he had quadrupled the average wage to nearly $10, the Model T sold for only $350 and had a self-starter. It must have been a galling day for old J. P. Morgan when, as early as 1915, Ford drove his one millionth car off the assembly line. By the end of the 1930s Ford had produced twenty-eight million cars.

It is staggering to consider what the Model T was to lead to in both industry and folkways. It certainly wove the first network of paved highways, subsequently the parkway, and then freeway and the interstate. Beginning in the early 1920s, people who had never taken a holiday beyond the nearest lake or mountain could now explore the South, New England, even the West, and in time the whole horizon of the United States. Most of all, the Model T gave to the farmer and rancher, miles from anywhere, a new pair of legs.

There was something else flourishing in the 1920s that was equally revolutionary to people who lived, say, a hundred miles from the nearest town. I recall an advertising tycoon, Bruce Barton, saying in the late 1940s, when we were in a dither about the Russians: "What we ought to do is to send up a flight of a thousand B-29s and drop a million Sears, Roebuck catalogues all over Russia." The mail-order catalogue arrived at the home of the farmer, cowboy, miner, and rancher, and they looked it over and realized that they had the world's biggest store in their mailbox. The farmer could simply send off for all his equipment, from wagons and road scrapers down to his jeans. His wife could riffle through sixty pages for clothes to buy and pick a cheap equivalent of what "smart" women

Sears, Roebuck and Co., Chicago

Spring and Summer - 1927
Index and Information Pages - 459 to 485

were wearing in New York and Chicago. And for ninety-five cents, her daughter could get the very hat that was worn by the "It Girl," Clara Bow, one of the first idols of the motion picture industry, which was beginning to serve a collateral function as the national store window for fashions of all sorts—bathing suits and hairdos and furniture and the cocktail habit and "companionate marriage" and many other fads and frivolities.

Hollywood grew to be the most flourishing factory of popular mythology since the Greeks. It is the main reason why the America of the 1920s that passed into the file of the world's memory is not an America of throbbing steel production, not the sudden flowering of a brilliant native literature, but a kind of mass idiocy and frivolity. Europe, drained of life and invention after the war, first jeered and then eagerly copied these hectic fads—cocktails, bobbed hair, the Charleston, and night clubs, and also the lyrical tunes of Richard Rodgers, the love-lorn waltzes of Irving Berlin, the bounce and poignancy of George Gershwin—as new signs of life.

America was top dog and knew it and was consumed with an itch for the superlative. Even so austere a figure as Justice Oliver Wendell Holmes sensed the mood at the end of the World War and generalized in a learned article on natural law what was to become a law of competitive life for Americans in the 1920s:

It is not enough for the knight of romance that you agree that his lady is a very nice girl—if you do not admit that she is the best God ever made or will make, you must fight. There is in all men a demand for the superlative, so much so that the poor devil who has no other way of reaching it attains it by getting drunk.

America had attained it by making Wall Street the world's money mart, and Hollywood the factory of the world's daydreams, and Tin Pan Alley the maker of the music it danced to. It seemed only right and proper that the first mother to swim the English Channel should be an American mother.

Given the national mood, it was only appropriate that suddenly, in 1927, the overnight hero of the world was an American. On a drizzly May morning, three airplanes lined up on a muddy, primitive runway on Long Island. They were all going for a shot at a $25,000 prize for a nonstop transatlantic flight. Of the three, one was both the strangest and the smallest: it was twenty-seven feet, three inches long, had no radio and no sextant, and its instrument panel was less pretentious than that of a 1927 automobile. It had cost $6,000, and every inch of its construction had been carefully watched over by the man who was going to fly it; unlike the others he was going alone, and he did not intend to hop islands or countries, he was going for the whole stretch—New York to Paris. He

By 1927 the Sears, Roebuck catalogue was running to nearly 1,100 pages containing 35,000 Bargains," and the company's sales exceeded $300 million a year. To customers and would-be customers, the catalogue was "The Great Wish Book."

319

At Long Island's Roosevelt Field, Charles Lindbergh stands beneath the wing of his monoplane. At right, New York welcomes him home with ticker-tape.

was a skinny, blond twenty-five-year-old from Minnesota, who had been a parachute jumper and an airmail pilot in the wildcat days.

The plane—which for balance carried all the gasoline it could in a cased-in cockpit up front, so that the pilot was literally flying blind—wobbled and bounced into the heavy skies, and that night forty thousand baseball fans in New York stood and prayed for its pilot. In Tokyo, at their midnight, people swarmed into the streets. The stock exchanges of London, Berlin, and Amsterdam interrupted regular quotations with the word—that there was no word. As the second night came on in Paris, an appeal went out to everybody who owned an automobile—which might be from seventy to eighty thousand, maybe—to head for a landing field at Le Bourget and line up in two files, switch the headlights on and thus create a visible shaft of white fog. Into it, thirty-three hours after just missing the telephone wires on Long Island, the strange plane trundled and stopped. It was engulfed by one hundred thousand Parisians. When they lifted the pilot out of the cockpit, if he had said he was Alexander the Great, they'd have believed him. All he said was: "I am Charles Lindbergh." He came home to naval salutes and a frenetic press, and a ticker-tape parade up Broadway.

The ticker-tape parade was to become New York's special accolade for a few carefully chosen national gods. Down the decades the biggest blizzards have been reserved for such returning heroes as General Eisenhower, General MacArthur, astronaut John Glenn, and, three years after Lindbergh, a sunny, firm-jawed, handsome lawyer from Atlanta, Georgia. A peculiar choice, but in him the 1920s was saluting an old ideal in the moment of its passing.

He was Robert Tyre Jones, Jr., a weekend golfer but the best golfer of his time, some people think the best of all time. But he had a grace and charm on and off the course that, curiously, made him the idol of two continents in a very brash time, and that to people who didn't know a putter from a shovel. His universal appeal was not as a golfer. What then? The word that comes to mind is an extinct word: a gentleman, a combination of goodness and grace, an unwavering courtesy, self-deprecation, and consideration for other people. This fetching combination, allied to his world supremacy in one sport, was what made him a hero in Scotland and England as much as in the Midwest and his native Georgia.

Once, in a national championship, he drove his ball into the woods. He went after it alone, and, in standing to the ball, he barely touched it. He came out of the woods, signaled his fault, penalized himself one stroke and by one stroke lost the championship. When he was praised for this and similar acts of sportsmanship, he was genuinely disgusted. "You might as well," he said, "praise a man for not robbing a bank."

In his middle forties he was paralyzed by a rare disease, and a friend asked him for the medical outlook. "I will tell you privately," he said, "it's not going to get better, it's going to get worse all the time, but don't fret. Remember, we 'play the ball where it lies,' and now let's not talk about this, ever again." And he never did. So what we're talking about is not the hero as golfer but something that America hungered for and found: the best performer in the world who was also the hero as human being, the gentle, chivalrous, wholly self-sufficient male. Jefferson's lost paragon, the wise innocent.

Innocence was something that most mothers wished very much their daughters had. For the 1920s brought on a drastic revolt against the prewar mores of gentility; and though the revolutionary symbols now seem trivial, they were sufficiently bizarre to alarm the middle-aged. Corsets were abandoned along with the Viennese waltz. Long skirts were scandalously abbreviated, and long hair was "bobbed." Young women smoked, and in public, and danced into the dawn to the sensual moan of the saxophone, an instrument forgotten for eighty years but now revived and condemned, by city fathers and magistrates on both sides of the Atlantic, as a siren sound beckoning young girls to a losing battle with a fate worse than death.

Not all of the parental anxiety was misplaced. Sexual "emancipation" was the watchword of the young, and it was lent a frightening authority by Dr. Sigmund Freud, whose theory and practice of psychoanalysis became a daring fashion. Not from Freud himself but from brisk newspaper and magazine popularizations, both young and old picked up a grotesque misunderstanding of Freud's theory of unconscious repression: which is what happens when people repress an instinct and don't know they're doing it. What everybody seemed to think he was saying was that consciously to *suppress* an instinct, any instinct, would make you break out in insanity or pimples. So sex drenched the magazines and the movies and the theater, until Robert Benchley, the drama critic of *The New Yorker*, was driven to write:

I am now definitely ready to announce that Sex, as a theatrical property, is as tiresome as the Old Mortgage . . . I am sick of rebellious youth and I'm sick of Victorian parents and I don't care if all the little girls in all sections of the United States get ruined, or want to get ruined, or keep from getting ruined. All I ask is: don't write plays about it and ask me to sit through them.

There was something worse than the saxophone or bobbed hair, if not sex, because it stimulated every vice—liquor, whose very illegality made it as precious as forbidden fruit. In the moral fervor of the First World War, Congress had passed a Constitutional Amendment that long-suffering wives of drunken husbands on the frontier had been demanding for half a century: the total national prohibition of the manufacture, transportation, and sale of alcohol. When the war was over, it was backed by law, and it was subsequently known as the Noble Experiment. It did not noticeably endow Americans with more nobility than they already had. On the contrary, it gave rise to a national underground industry, based in Chicago, that turned small-time safecrackers and brothel owners into millionaires.

Gangsters were not new in America, but Prohibition opened up the green pastures to men who organized their own breweries and transport, paid off the police, supplied rot-gut liquor to hand-picked clubs, and stuck the owners with a further protection fee in case, as occasionally happened, some underpaid police squad might forget itself and enforce the law. In time the gang leaders grew greedy, divided Chicago into rival territories, and fought each other for their control. But, in accordance with the old Roman code, they showed resolution in war and magnanimity in victory. There was, for instance, Dion O'Banion, an Irishman whose cover for his liquor empire was a florist's shop. He was double-crossed by an Italian, made a derisory remark about Sicilians, and was successfully disposed of by Al Capone and Johnny Torrio. His funeral casket was of bronze and solid silver. It was followed by the sorrowful Capone and Torrio, and by $50,000 worth of flowers contributed, in loving memory, by the opposition. The murderers were never found. Capone, however, had the sense to buy himself an armor-plated Cadillac.

The conspicuous gangsters of the 1920s have vanished. In our time, they have moved with masterly discretion into real estate, banking, the export-import trade in drugs, the control of supermarkets, hotels, big and little corporations—so that today nobody knows for sure where legitimate business ends and the syndicate takes over.

It took America thirteen years to concede that the Noble Experiment was a squalid disaster. While it flourished, the public momentarily shuddered at the gangland murders and the baroque funerals, then returned to its pleasures and its prosperity. These Chicago episodes were mere excrescences on the general health. A good man was in the White House, and business was booming. Church membership in the United States had never been higher, and the pulpits resounded with some of Winthrop's favorite texts: "Thou shalt remember the Lord thy God, for it is He that giveth thee the power to get wealth" .... "Blessed is the man that feareth the Lord.... His seed shall be mighty upon earth .... wealth and riches shall be in his house."

Some explanation of these providential blessings had to be found, and it came from another Chicagoan, appropriately a parson's son, who had

The best thing about Prohibition may have been its end. In 1933, a group of young ladies celebrated repeal for the benefit of a news photographer.

helped to found a giant advertising company. His name was Bruce Barton, and he wrote a book called *The Man Nobody Knows.* It could have carried the subtitle "The Puritan Promise Fulfilled." It sold close to a million. Like popular mystics before and since, Barton re-created God in the image of his time. He took a second look at the Carpenter of Nazareth and saw him as Jesus Christ, Supersalesman. From the book we learn that Jesus was an advertising genius and that copywriters would do well to copy the pith of his slogans: "Arise, take up thy bed and walk"; "What shall it profit a man if he gain the whole world and lose his own soul?"; "Render unto Caesar the things that are Caesar's." In another chapter, we learn also that Jesus was the founder of modern business, having taken "twelve men from the bottom ranks of business and forged them into an organization that conquered the world." Above all, says Barton, He made no distinction between business and "my Father's business." That is to say, between work and religion. And neither did Calvin Coolidge.

Did Coolidge have some foreboding of what was going to happen to this earthly paradise? He gave no hint of it. Nevertheless, in the spring of 1928 he abruptly announced that he was not going to run again for the Presidency. "There was a volcano boiling under him," wrote H. L. Mencken, "but he did not know it, and was not singed. When it burst forth at last, it was Hoover who got its blast, and was fried, boiled, roasted and fricasseed."

The volcano erupted on the floor of the New York Stock Exchange and burned corporations, banks, taxi drivers, farmers, janitors, and chorus girls, all those who had been riding high in what President Hoover had called "the final triumph over poverty." On October 24, 1929, blocks of shares went down the river in ten- and twenty-thousand lots. Five days later came the deluge, and it became clear years too late that the torrent of liquidation was caused, not so much by the big traders and bankers—who rushed in to try and plug the flood with twenty-five million dollars—but by legions of small-timers who had no margins to speak of. In other words, the Everest of the 1929 stock market was a mountain of credit on a molehill of actual money. Now, to the very Puritans who had seen the hand of God in the Coolidge prosperity, the crash was a punishment; and the pulpits now groaned with other, forgotten warnings from the Psalms: "They that trust in their wealth, and boast themselves in the multitude of their riches; none of them can by any means redeem his brother, nor give to God a ransom for him."

Other, more secular analysts saw—though admittedly by hindsight —other explanations. Today you cannot buy without meeting high margin requirements. In 1929 you could buy a dollar stock with ten cents in your hand; today it would have to be sixty to sixty-five cents. The federal government regulates investing, and insures brokerage accounts, as it also insures the smallest bank deposit. But none of these safeguards existed in the 1929 casino of the stock market. And the weekly theatrical trade journal *Variety* summed it up in five grim, sassy words: "Wall Street Lays An Egg."

Nowhere, in the following months and years, was the going so rough as in the idle factories, for this nation had been the first to transfer skill on a massive scale from the man to the machine. Yet, within three months of the crash, men who worked in big factories, small men who had merrily played the market, were warming their hands before scrap wood fires in the underpass beneath the Chicago Opera House (Samuel Insull, the man who had made a present of it to the city, saw some hungry and muttering mobs and quietly increased his bodyguard from two to thirty). But the Great Depression in America was not just a blow to the extremes of the millionaire and the coal miner. It blighted everybody, except the very poor who had nothing to lose. When steel stocks went from ninety down to twelve, the automobile manufacturers simply let half their workers go. There were skyscrapers just finished that lacked tenants. A secretary was a ridiculous luxury. There were truckers with nothing to truck, crops that went unharvested, milk that went undelivered to people who couldn't afford it. When I first arrived here, as a student in a college town, I couldn't go out in the evening to mail a letter without being stopped by nicely dressed men who had told their wives they were out looking for night work. So they were—they were out on the streets cadging dimes and quarters.

Somebody had to take the blame, and it fell on Coolidge's unlucky successor, President Herbert Clark Hoover, a world-famous engineer who had done mighty work ten years earlier organizing the feeding of starving Europe. He had been at Versailles, where John Maynard Keynes had called him the only man there who "imported into the councils of Paris . . . precisely that atmosphere of reality, knowledge, magnanimity and disinterestedness which, if they had been found in other quarters also, would have given us the Good Peace." But now Hoover was simply the football coach whose plays lost the big game, and his bitter memorial was the shanty towns of the unemployed down by the rivers of scores of cities.

Outside the cities were the bankrupt farmers who had fed the armies of Europe in the fat years and had known only collapsing prices ever since. (Harry Truman's Kansas City haberdashery went bust not in 1929 but in 1922, when "90 cent wheat would not buy $15 shirts.") The farmers had been the forgotten men of the Coolidge prosperity. The rural South had been forgotten or exploited since the Civil War and had overplowed its cotton land for generations till the topsoil crumbled and the hillsides were trenched with erosion. Out on the prairie and the Great Plains beyond, an unending drought through the mid-1930s and the steady west wind withered the wheatlands and buried farms to their windowsills in oceans of sand. And when, during two summers, the western sky billowed with the terrifying "black rollers," the farmers saw the punishment of the Old Testament God in "the whirlwind by day and the darkness at noon."

Long before the drought and the Dust Bowl, and long ignored by the prospering cities, was the nation's chronic poor relation—the South. For three quarters of a century Southern tenant farmers, white and black, had been very sad citizens, the victims of worn-out single crops, living off a diet of corn, fatback pork, and no green vegetables. They were not, as the Northern press made them out to be, shiftless people; they were exhausted from the twin diseases of malnutrition: scurvy, and pellagra.

Perhaps more than the rest of us, they were to find their redeemer in a man who lived a thousand miles away from them, and a million light-years from their experience of the life and death of an American family. He was the thirty-second President of the United States, the luckless Hoover's Democratic successor: Franklin Delano Roosevelt, mostly of English blood with a dash of Dutch. His father, already over fifty when the boy was born, was a dim, genteel country squire of substantial means. His mother was an adoring, imperious matriarch, who would surely have agreed with George Bernard Shaw: "Never fret for an only son, the idea of failure will never occur to him." It was a highly cushioned life young Roosevelt led in his birthplace, a two-winged Hudson River "bracketed villa" (later done over as a Georgian stone mansion) ninety miles north of New York City with a noble prospect over the river. Here Franklin Roosevelt led a charmed life, and all through his life he was a charmer. His mother didn't want to have him coarsened by contact with a rabble of other boys, so she brought in private tutors until he was ready for Groton. He wasn't much of a student but, being mad for boats, dabbled a little in naval history. (If the navy had been at the disposal of his mother, she would have given it to him for Christmas.)

After Groton he ambled socially through Harvard, married the niece of the former Republican President, Theodore Roosevelt, and then went to law school. He never graduated, but through his connections joined a prosperous law firm, got into politics, and in the First World War wangled the only job he wanted, Assistant Secretary of the Navy. In 1920 the glamour of the Roosevelt name was appropriated by the Democrats, and they ran him for Vice-President. He was buried in the Harding landslide, along with the other apostles of Woodrow Wilson, but twelve years later he was resurrected as a presidential candidate. He might be Governor of New York, but he was not the most acceptable

White House material. It was a heavy handicap for an American politician to have gone to Harvard and have an upper-crust accent. And there was another political liability: he was a mother's boy from the landed gentry. To compound his disabilities, he had been paralyzed by poliomyelitis in his fortieth year, and for the rest of his life he never had the use of his legs. Yet, throughout the twelve years of his Presidency, the press, including the inveterate smart alecks among the still and newsreel photographers, respected a convention unlikely to be honored today: they never photographed him in movement. I saw him once being lifted out of his car like a sack of potatoes, and put on his feet, and given two sticks and two helping hands, and his hat stuck on his head for him. This was not the Roosevelt the public saw. They saw the burly upper body, the bull-like neck, and the tossing head, the confident savior of the Republic in a dark time.

He was elected President in 1932 (not to mention 1936, 1940, and 1944, the only man to break the record of two terms in the White House). In the month before his inauguration, banks were failing every hour, and for two weeks gold and currency were being withdrawn at the appalling rate of $15,000,000 a day. The government, which had lent over $850,000,000 to the banks, now started to lend heavily to the railroads. On March 4, 1933, the day of his inauguration, Roosevelt hurled a thunderbolt at the headlines by closing—without any sure legal sanction—every bank in the country. He would decide which banks deserved federal support and which would have to go under. It was the day the money stopped; literally, you had to cadge a meal, live on the tab in places that knew you, pay with a check for a cab ride and once—I remember—for a shoeshine.

Roosevelt then asked Congress for emergency power "as great as the power that would be given me if we were in fact invaded by a foreign foe." Since there were twelve or thirteen million unemployed, he got it. Congress passed the legislation and he proclaimed something called the NRA (the National Recovery Administration), which practically appropriated the lawmaking power of Congress, suspended antitrust laws and sanctioned government by trade association by requiring employers to draw up a binding code affecting about seven hundred industries, fixing wages and prices and labor practices for everybody from steelworkers to burlesque strippers.

Roosevelt, having promised to give the government back to the states, had seized power at the center. For two dizzy years, America had a fling at National Socialism. Roosevelt was for all administrative purposes a dictator, but a benevolent one, and the country loved it. In time, however, it became too much for the "nine old men" of the Supreme Court. As so often happens with the Court, it took only a tiny pretext to destroy

a mighty power. In a decisive case the Court ruled that, if two brothers reared a sick chicken in New York State and sold it there, it was no business of the executive branch of the federal government—that, in short, the whole NRA "code" had stolen the constitutional lawmaking power from the Congress. The NRA was destroyed. Roosevelt fumed, but only for a while, because he was never down for long. He returned to his great gift for directing the gaze of the lawmakers at the dire plight of the whole continent, and Congress disbursed relief funds in floods. He had in the meantime shoved through Congress huge federal loans for public works, and at the same time he gave the industrial worker who had been hounded by company spies the right to organize and bargain. He handed out hard dollars to the unemployed and took three million youngsters off the streets to build highways and plant ten million trees. He mobilized actors in a federal theater and, in the happiest inspiration of the Works Progress Administration, hired unemployed scholars, writers, and local historians to produce several hundred volumes of guidebooks to the states. He stopped the automatic production of groaning farm surpluses, paid the Southern farmers to diversify their crops and built enormous dams to hold the flooding of the great river valleys—and then made the valleys flower through electricity and controlled irrigation. In all, he brought national relief to national unemployment; he conserved the soil of the worn-out South; he established once for all the federal government's right to plan economic and social welfare on a national scale, as the great corporations had done for their industries; he captured the ruling initiative from Congress and, like no President since Wilson, used the Presidency as the spokesman of the people's needs.

In effect, he signed a check in the government's name for several billion invisible dollars. What strikes me about him now is the triumphant contradiction between his genial, fluty manner and his extraordinary tough hide. He would make up to anyone he needed, a labor leader in one state, a conservative Republican in another. He would overlook the race bigotry of a Senator in a Southern state where he wanted to do something for the poor white farmers. And on behalf of what he called first "the forgotten man" and then "the little man," he allied himself with corrupt city governments, in Memphis, Jersey City, Chicago, because —as he once privately said—"they may be sons of bitches but they are our sons of bitches." Not since Lincoln had there been such an artful manipulator of the good, the bad, and the bewildered in between. I believe he saved the capitalist system by deliberately forgetting to bal-

With a cigarette holder at its customarily jaunty angle, Franklin Delano Roosevelt was photographed in 1939 in his hand-controlled Ford coupé.

ance the books, by transferring the gorgeous resources of credit from the bankers to the government, no matter what the national debt might be. A journalist of ferocious talent, Westbrook Pegler, who loathed Roosevelt for most of his later days, has written, I believe, his best epitaph:

As a social and political liver-shaker he has had no equal in our time in this country. Ornery, tricky, stubborn, wayward and strong as a bull. . . . He looked nice and dressy back there in 1932 . . . there was nothing in his past record to indicate what a cantankerous hide he would turn out to be. . . . Anyone who gentles Mr. Roosevelt is simply imposing a handicap on himself, for he won't gentle you back. . . . But never in our time have people been so conscious of the meanness which a complacent upper class will practice on the help, and of the government's duty to do something real and personal for the assistance of those who are so far down that they can't help themselves. He needs to be fought all the time, for he has an enormous appreciation of himself and of any idea which he happens to approve, but if the country doesn't go absolutely broke in his time, it will be a more intelligent and a better country after him.

Yet Roosevelt came in on a promise to do something that has balked governments of every ideological brand before and since—to guarantee full employment in peacetime. He didn't make it. In 1938 there were still ten million unemployed. In the next four years the number did indeed shrink—it went out of sight—but this was not Roosevelt's doing but Hitler's. Because the stacks of the steel mills barely began to belch smoke again until the first war orders came in from the British and the French.

The American artist Thomas Hart Benton began his mural, "America Today," in 1930, on a wall at the New School in New York. This panel is "The Changing West."

11

THE ARSENAL

On the day that the Second World War began, George Bernard Shaw wrote: "There will be only two winners: the United States and the Soviet Union." And so there were. For more than a quarter of a century the world has watched, sometimes with relief and often with dread, the increasing and competing might of the only two superpowers. It is assumed by most people everywhere under forty, I should imagine, that the United States of America has always been a military mammoth. On the contrary, one of the most dogged traditions of the United States through its first 160 years was a distrust of a large armed force, and in the beginning the actual prohibition of a standing army, navy, and marine corps. Until the Second World War Americans looked on war not as a profession but as an emergency disruption of life; once the war was over, the soldiers got out of uniform and all but the smallest stock of weapons was scrapped.

This strange tradition arose from the colonists' association of a national army with professional soldiers from abroad under the orders of their king. Once the king was defied and beaten, the colonies did not propose to create a substitute national force that might, on the orders of any national person or body, threaten the safety of the states and the *separate* militias that they maintained. "Maintained" is a strong word, for the militias were mobilized only in emergencies, and even then had no chain of command, no regular officers. In colonial times the only military establishment was a rifle by the fireside. Whenever there was a secessionist uprising, a trade or tax riot, or an Indian raid, it was the duty of the citizen to grab his rifle when the militia was mustered. Every farmer and mechanic knew in his bones, if not by heart, Adam Smith's precept: "Every man must in some measure join the trade of soldier to whatever other trade or profession he happens to carry on." When the trouble was over the rifle went back where it belonged, by the fireplace.

At the end of the Revolutionary War—we noticed earlier—the Continental Army, Navy and Marine Corps were dissolved; and the militias went home to their own states and disbanded. They had all had enough of the only national army they had seen, and their prejudices were

The first atomic bomb, code-named "Trinity," erupts into the predawn sky of southern New Mexico. Light rain, accompanied by thunder and lightning, had delayed the firing for 90 minutes. The blast, when it came, had the force of 20,000 tons of TNT.

reinforced by tales told by old men, or recent immigrants, about the brutal habits of press gangs and recruiting sergeants.

So the Constitution of the United States, in its Second Amendment, came to declare: "A well-regulated Militia, being necessary to the security of a free State, the right of the people to keep and bear Arms shall not be infringed." This famous sentence is commonly reproduced on plaques outside the headquarters of rifle associations. Or, rather, part of it: ". . . the right of the people to keep and bear Arms shall not be infringed." This is the part quoted as holy writ by the gun clubs, the hunters, and the sportsmen, not to mention some militant radicals and lunatics on the loose. The true import of the Second Amendment lies in the missing first part of the sentence, which insists on the need for a citizens' army, a "well-regulated militia." It is the only point the Constitution makes in sanctioning a citizen's right to bear arms. There is no constitutional right to go out and shoot an elk or a pheasant, let alone to stick up a neighbor or assassinate a President.

The new nation's decision to abolish all national armed forces seemed daring, not to say noble, to many people at the time. To the Europeans, however, disarmament offered an irresistible opportunity to annex America's trade by raiding her ships. The seas were no longer protected by the British navy, and all the produce of America that went to sea became a prime target for privateers, not least for the British navy itself. The situation was so alarming that the first two American Presidents, Washington and John Adams, had to pay off certain pirates with a couple of million dollars in protection. This was meant as a desperate holding operation while the Congress made up its mind to create a navy. It finally did so in 1794, enlarging a fleet of three ships to fifty-five in order to protect the American Mediterranean trade from the depredations of the British, French, and Spanish.

Four years later the United States Marines were created as an emergency force to help the navy battle French privateers in an undeclared war, mainly in the West Indies. Because of their oft-sung prowess in fighting the Barbary pirates, and later in patrolling and raiding the coasts of Mexico in the Mexican War, it was the marines who were to capture the popular imagination. So late as the 1920s and 1930s, whenever trouble brewed in the Caribbean, which Americans regarded as their southern safety zone, the cry was always: Send in the marines!

The creation of a national army was an accident. The Continental Army had been disbanded at the end of the Revolutionary War, but there were two caches of military stores, at West Point and Fort Pitt, which it seemed prudent to keep. Somebody had to guard them, and one company of artillery (Battery D, Fifth Field Artillery) was retained not as the nucleus of a national army but as a caretaker. That was all there was of an American army until, in 1791, Congress passed a law levying an excise tax on distilled spirits. Several counties of new settlers west of the Alleghenies rebelled (being Scots and Irishmen), and President Washington, having no national army, was embarrassed to have to borrow troops from the state militias to put down what became known as the Whiskey Rebellion. And when Indian uprisings in Ohio, Indiana, and Michigan merged into a large offensive, it was obvious that the new nation would have threats to its "domestic tranquillity" too serious to leave to willing locals. So the regular army was formed with one infantry regiment.

Throughout the nineteenth century its steady job—apart, of course, from forming the nub of the vast conscripted armies of the Civil War—was to put down regional uprisings and to be the prime protector from the Indians of the settlers on the frontier. This was essentially the job of the cavalry, and it was the cavalry that manned the forts the army built in Indian country or bought from such land pirates as Sutter. When the Apaches swooped down on a wagon train or, later on, a stagecoach or a small Western settlement, the cliff-hanging tension was relieved by the sound of a bugle and the arrival from Fort Riley or Fort Bliss of the contemporary Errol Flynn or John Wayne and a troop of cavalry with its colors flying. This is one movie legend that is true enough. For over fifty years the United States Cavalry was the traveling civilian's protector. It was the land force of the army, and more often than not its officers were Southerners. They had come from horse country in a horse culture, they had ridden and hunted since they were boys. For the first two years of the Civil War it was the Southern cavalry that held off the Northern forces. And yet, at the start of that war a famous old cavalry general declared that "since the invention of the rifled cannon, the day of the Cavalry is over."

They have been saying it ever since. And they said it for keeps when, early in 1942, the first American cavalry unit sent to the Pacific was captured and starved on Bataan in the Philippines. In that miserable February—when Japan was overrunning Malaya, the British were fleeing from Singapore, and German submarines off the coasts of New Jersey and Florida were picking off American freighters, I visited Fort Riley, Kansas. A few of us sat through a grim-lipped lunch while the bad news kept chattering in on the tickers from the Pacific. The horses, after a morning drill, were harrumphing outside the window. A young officer wondered aloud to the bandy-legged colonel if there was any future for horses in warfare. The colonel held a chicken leg, snapped at it, and put it back on his plate. Without looking up, he said, "They used them on Bataan. They ate them." Today, there are sixteen horses left in the cavalry. They are used for military funerals.

The U.S. Army remained small and inconspicuous until the Second

337

World War. I doubt that in any other country, except Sweden and Switzerland, was it so uncommon in peacetime to see soldiers in the towns or around the countryside. Sailors were something else. The navy became a permanent necessity, because America was a huge island of incomparable natural resources, and where there is much power there is much to defend. Since Britain obligingly owned and patrolled the Atlantic, the Pacific Ocean became America's protective moat. Long before the Second World War, there could never be any doubt of the fact in the minds of visitors to San Diego, San Francisco, and Seattle.

At the start of the Second World War, the first newsreels of American soldiers bustling around old cannon and tenting in small fields would—I imagine—have greatly amused Adolf Hitler. For he had already bypassed the old ways of war with the innovation of the blitzkrieg, which synchronized machines on the ground with machines in the air. The bombers razed whole cities, the tanks moved in against the armies on the ground, and the foot soldiers mopped up the pockets of resistance. While America was calling up the officers' training corps and handing out rifles to the first draftees, Hitler was mopping up Europe from Warsaw to the English Channel. Then the French surrendered, and the British were left alone to recognize very late that their eighteen miles of channel was no protection against the new war from the air. In the next years the British civilians, men and women, had to work in hundreds of old, small factories, scattered through Scotland, Wales, and England, to avoid the disaster of single great strikes from the air. But America provided a steady lifeline of supplies and, when Congress repealed its Neutrality Act, unloosed a flood of airplanes, tanks, guns, steel, food, freighters, everything—according to President Franklin Roosevelt—that would "enable them to fight for their liberty and our security. We have the men, the skill, the wealth, and above all the will. We must be the great arsenal of democracy."

It was not enough. Within eighteen months of the start of the war, and eight months after the French surrender, Britain had no money left to pay, or to offer as collateral, for the material she needed. At this point Roosevelt rammed through Congress an act to lend or lease Britain everything she wanted. It was an affront to the millions of Americans who did not share Roosevelt's prejudice that, if Britain were conquered and her navy captured, America would be the Nazis' next port of call. The country divided furiously and openly between those who were for intervention, or for the suspicious aim of "all aid short of war," and those America Firsters who quoted Jefferson's warnings about "entangling alliances" and urged isolation in what they called Fortress America. "We believe," said Charles Lindbergh, "that the security of our country lies in the strength and character of our own people, and not in fighting foreign wars."

It had been almost exactly two years since the British people had heard over the radio the toneless voice of Neville Chamberlain, their Prime Minister, saying that Germany had been told to withdraw her troops from Poland; but "I have to tell you that no such understanding has been received and in consequence, this country is at war with Germany." Roosevelt, there is little doubt, now longed to do the same. But no American President can tell the people they are at war. He has to ask the Congress to declare it. That, at least, is what the Constitution says. It gives Congress also the exclusive power to "raise and support armies" and for "a term no longer than two years." (In fact, Congress has made no declarations of war since the ones against Bulgaria, Hungary, and Romania in June 1942. Since Roosevelt, five Presidents have bypassed Congress by exercising a war power and then saying that it was an "inherent" power of the Presidency. And very necessary to claim, the Presidents' supporters have said, when a nuclear Armageddon might give you only fifteen minutes' notice.)

Roosevelt was harshly reminded that the Constitution still stood. But when Hitler overran the Netherlands and forced the surrender of France, Congress passed a law conscripting young men for a year's training. When, in August 1941, this draft act was about to expire, Roosevelt wanted it renewed. The isolationists raised a storm against him, partly from disillusion with the last American effort to "save the world for democracy"; partly from the conviction that to go into Europe again would, as one Senator put it, "plow under every fourth American boy"; partly from a deep resentment at Roosevelt's secret order to the Navy to convoy Allied merchantmen. The United States was, in truth, very nearly a secret belligerent. The Germans knew it, and so did the Congress. In August 1941 the House Armed Services Committee met to hold hearings on extending the draft and to bring the question of the war-making power to a showdown. Things were going very badly for the Administration till at last it brought up its big gun: the Army Chief of Staff, General George Catlett Marshall, a flinty lifetime soldier as impressive for his restraint under a bombardment of rhetoric as he was for the disheartening statistics he quoted. (It was Marshall who first publicly equated the American army with the standing army of Sweden.) It is probable that, without him, the United States would have found itself four months later with nothing but its small volunteer army. For, when the renewal act went to the floor of the House, it was passed by 203 to 202.

Then there came a Sunday afternoon, the first in December, a cold, brilliant jewel of a day. I had gone down to Washington to cover a monster rally of the America Firsters. But by that time the war was two years old, for most of that time Britain had been fighting alone, and it was hard to enchant British newspaper readers with reports of the strength of the American isolationist sentiment. Frankly, also, I for one, like most of the British correspondents in this country, was sick of rallies. Admittedly, the last one I had been to was something of a freak, but it was a powerful purge. It was a frightening tumult in Madison Square Garden, a rally of the German-American Bund, whose squat little leader goggled through thick lenses at his roaring flock and ranted up against three enormous floodlit portraits of George Washington, Abraham Lincoln, and Adolf Hitler.

I had another good reason on that Sunday afternoon to skip the familiar frenetic oratory of such as Lindbergh and Senator Burton Wheeler. Sunday afternoons in winter were an American institution: the New York Philharmonic piped from coast to coast its regular concert over the only mass medium we had, the radio. My Washington host, an official of the British Supply Council, easily persuaded me to settle in his living room as the orchestra started to tune up, and the strings and woodwinds went skittering up and down the scale. It was about to launch into a Shostakovich symphony when there was an abrupt halt and a crackle on the radio. A breathless voice said, "One moment, please," and then: "The Japanese have attacked Pearl Harbor, the United States naval base on Oahu Island in the Hawaiian Islands." The designation of "Oahu Island" instead of "Honolulu" was a small recognition of our vague sense, in those very far-off days, of Pacific geography. I suspect that not one American in a hundred, on that brilliant day, knew that Honolulu was the main base of the American Pacific fleet.

Most Americans up to that moment thought of Japan as a remote Asiatic nuisance, a friend of Hitler's, that had invaded China and Indochina and was now under the heel of a fire-eating general, Tojo. Reading through interminable single-column dispatches in *The New York Times*, it was possible to learn that for some weeks past Tojo and the Japanese military had been demanding American consent to the expansion of the Japanese empire through Southeast Asia. But Pearl Harbor was a bolt out of the blue.

On Monday December 8, Congress declared war on Japan, and the next day Roosevelt held a press conference. We expected to see a drawn, grave figure, but he rattled on with his usual buoyancy about a speed-up in production, and a shortage of metals, and he was wryly amused at the protests of one reporter that the army and navy had given him "the run-around." They pressed him on rumors that "a lot of leaves" had been granted at Pearl Harbor, that "someone slept." Roosevelt blew a riffle of

Oily smoke billows from the burning hulk of U.S.S. Arizona, one of eight battleships destroyed by Japanese carrier-based planes at Pearl Harbor on December 7, 1941.

smoke and smiled back. "How do I know? How do *you* know? How does the person reporting it know?"

But he already knew what we would not know until the going was good. The Pacific fleet had been pulverized. Of the fleet's eight battleships, one was blown up, three sunk, four crippled. Three destroyers gone, and 177 Army and Navy planes demolished on the ground. Perhaps Roosevelt's aplomb was not merely a brave cover-up for purposes of morale. Pearl Harbor to him was a political godsend. It deflated the isolationists with a single thrust. Only a year before, Roosevelt had appeared before a great rally in his third presidential campaign and had given a promise that brought heart's ease to the mothers of America (and votes to Roosevelt). "I shall say it again and again and again—your boys are not going to be sent into any foreign wars." Well, there was no more question of sending, or coaxing, American boys into foreign wars. This was an all-American war.

Disused factories lit up like firecrackers. America became a continental workshop, and quite safe—as Lindbergh had said and could now bitterly recall—from aerial bombing. Of course, by the 1930s everybody knew *ad nauseam* that the Americans were the masters of mass production. But of what? And of what quality? Air Marshal Goering assured Hitler that there was nothing to fear from American industry and technology. "The Americans," said Goering, "cannot build airplanes. They are very good at refrigerators and razor blades." Even friendly Europeans still harbored a strong prejudice against the products of the assembly line and a complementary prejudice in favor of high skill and craftsmanship.

I remember an optical plant in New Hampshire that, once America was in the war, received a contract for bombsights and the like. The place was suddenly flooded with semi-skilled young workers, and the old men—most of them foreign born—were loud in their lamentations over the slap-happy indifference of the young to precision and discipline. But to their dismay, new molds were cast, the assembling was done by newcomers, the product was stamped out in abundance, and it worked.

In the countryside outside Detroit there was a creek running through flat, sandy pastureland. Within six months of Pearl Harbor this bucolic scene had been transformed into what somebody called "the most enormous room in the history of man," half a mile long, a quarter of a mile wide. Raw materials were fed in at one end and were disgorged, an hour later, at the other end in the shape of a finished bomber, which was plucked by another assembly line and moved out for immediate testing on an airfield. From this room, at Willow Run, there emerged 8,760 planes a year. It was astounding, but it was not enough for Roosevelt. In a high-flown moment he had publicly promised the Allies 60,000 planes a

A nearly endless procession of Dauntless dive bombers takes shape on the Douglas Aircraft assembly line in California. In all, 5,000 of these planes were produced here.

year, a foolish boast that Charles Lindbergh dismissed as "hysterical chatter." By the end of 1942 Roosevelt had missed his mark by only 12,000. The following year American factories turned out 86,000 planes.

This starting orgy of mass production sent locomotives to Iran, trucks and tanks and aluminum to Russia, airplanes and ordnance and jeeps to every ally between Scotland and New Zealand. One year after Pearl Harbor the razor-blade manufacturer had outstripped the war production of Germany and Japan and the forced labor of their conquered countries. Hitler and mechanized warfare together confronted Americans with the sort of challenge to which they respond like catapults: a dare to beat the unbeatable, to choke the world's champ with massive doses of his own medicine.

Productivity was not the only triumph. There was a challenge for Americans to show their capacity for inventiveness in a new situation. They sent men off into the desert with new infrared counters to scan the rocks for minerals in a hurry. They developed the specialty of "dehydration chemists," who compounded a candy bar that could keep a man sustained in the jungle for a couple of weeks. They set the Forest Products Laboratory in Madison, Wisconsin, to testing out airplane wings made of sixteen-ply paper. They produced the Jeep and the first amphibious trucks. They tapped the cunning of an old Irishman down in New Orleans who had designed a maneuverable speedboat that was just the thing for Prohibition rumrunners. When the Navy put out a bid for a pursuit boat that could turn on a dime, Andrew Higgins adapted twenty years of extra know-how to a still more maneuverable speedboat. He appeared in Washington with a blueprint within forty-eight hours of the Navy's first request, and the bootlegger's secret weapon turned into a vast fleet of PT boats.

But shipping was another story. There was no miracle formula available to the shipbuilders, who were suddenly called on to provide transport and supplies for the Atlantic and now, also, for the huge Pacific. The government kept insisting on a miracle, however, and got it in the shape of a lumbering, undramatic tub called a "Liberty ship." In its final form it was the brainchild of Henry Kaiser, a bald bullfrog of a construction man who liked nothing better than the word of an expert that something couldn't be done. He had helped to build Boulder (now Hoover) Dam, on the Arizona-Nevada border, where the pouring of the cement spillway put no outrageous strain on mountain ridges as firm as steel. But when he drew plans to build the Grand Coulee Dam up in the rainy Pacific Northwest, he was warned by the army engineers that before the cement spillway could set, the soft mountainsides would crumble and send the Columbia River cascading death and destruction through the valley towns. Henry Kaiser received the official report, and, having learned how it couldn't be done, he settled down to do it. He built refrigeration tubes the width of city blocks and the height of a sky-scraper, planted them in rows, froze the mountains, poured the spillway, removed the tubes, and saw the Columbia River flow docilely along the channel he had prescribed.

He had never built a ship before. When the Liberty ships appeared they had no furnace plates, no emergency generators, no fire-detection devices. And as steel grew short they shortened the anchor chains. The crew, instead of being scattered below, lived in a single mid-ship house. But all the engine parts were interchangeable, and the sections were welded. These tubs were not intended as proud specimens of the shipbuilder's art—and Kaiser's rivals, among the old firms in New Orleans and San Francisco, were the first to shudder at them; they were great, galumphing, seagoing improvisations, and at the start some of them snapped and went to the bottom a thousand miles from the enemy.

I remember going into Kaiser's Richmond shipyard in California. The place was laid out like a gigantic chessboard, with cranes hovering overhead depositing parts, engines, and booms in alphabetically marked and numbered squares. Thirty thousand components came in in this way, and it was like something out of Disney: trolleys whizzing, and hooters honking and buzzing, a whole deckhouse moving to the ways upside down. It would then be upended while the welders descended on it like an army of woodpeckers. You'd have a stem and a keel and then part of plate A-1 would be welded to A-2, and S-13 to S-14, and so on. The workers knew even less about shipbuilding than Kaiser. Only one in two hundred had ever been in a shipyard. Kaiser himself talked about the "front" and "back" end of a ship. Roosevelt said, "I don't care what he calls them, provided he delivers." And he did; the first Liberty ship, built on the East Coast, took 245 days from assembly to launch. Kaiser's California models got this down to four days.

The best thing about the Liberty ships was their number. The early ones replenished the dwindling food stocks of Britain. The later ones replaced transport ships in the Pacific and offered the first guarantee of a continuous supply line across the English Channel—the missing link that made an Allied invasion of Europe impracticable for two and a half years.

This seemingly inexplicable delay in the mounting of a second front had enraged the Russians and depressed the British, whose populations had little or no understanding of the vast scope of the war in the Pacific—a quarter of the globe for a battleground. At first aircraft carriers were the only airfields along the six thousand-mile approach to Japan, the

---

Overleaf: *Waist-deep in the icy Channel waters, American troops from an LCT slosh toward Omaha Beach, Normandy. The hardest fighting of D-Day took place here.*

LOOSE TALK CAN COST LIVES

THE MARINES HAVE LANDED—!

APPLY TO NEAREST RECRUITING STATION

MILES OF HELL to Tokyo!

WORK WHERE YOU'RE NEEDED

CONSULT YOUR U.S. EMPLOYMENT SERVICE OFFICE

WAR MANPOWER COMMISSION

6 WAR LOAN

The Sky's the Limit!

KEEP BUYING WAR BONDS

enemy's homeland. Then for three and a half years Americans had to inch along the loose chain of the enemy's outer island bases, making contact with guerrillas, threading through jungle bush, in which, surprisingly, many Americans from the cities of the prairie and the East were at home. In 1941 they had learned jungle fighting in the swamps of Louisiana, in an enormous war game commanded by the then totally unknown Major (temporary Colonel) Dwight D. Eisenhower.

To the American soldiers, sailors, airmen, and marines in the Pacific, Hitler was on another planet, and so was the clockwork precision of a blitzkrieg. To the European who read daily of the tactical collision of great land armies on his own continent, there was something equally unreal and alien in the thought of the virile Americans being picked off singly along jungle trails, or trapped in batches in a clearing, or dying from obscure tropical diseases.

Yet the outcome of the Japanese war was not really decided in the Pacific. It was preordained a decade before by a pathological mistake of Hitler's: in general by his suppression of the intellectuals, in particular by his persecution of the Jews and the dispatch into exile of their most brilliant scientists. These men, whether they were German or neighbors of Germany, saw the handwriting on the wall and fled to America. Among them, Hitler might have trembled to think, if he had been a meditative man and not a mystic, were half a dozen or more of the world's leading physicists. There was Albert Einstein. There was Enrico Fermi, an Italian. There were Edward Teller, Leo Szilard, and Eugen Wigner, three Hungarians, so obscure that in the summer of 1939 they had to enlist Einstein's help—and he, in turn, the help of a banker—to reach President Roosevelt with word of the dire consequences that might follow from the secret news that Germany had forbidden all exports of uranium ore from Czechoslovakia. Since the State Department had at the time not the slightest suspicion of the military significance of uranium, Einstein's letter—written in August but not delivered till October—probably baffled Roosevelt more than it disturbed him. At any rate, the Secretary of War did not hear the strange words "uranium" and "fission" until the fall of 1941, and the President's decision to form a small committee and put some substantial money into the project the refugees had been urging on him was not taken until the day before Pearl Harbor.

Hundreds of posters exhorted Americans to help the war effort — by working in defense plants, avoiding rumors, buying bonds, collecting scrap metal and rubber, keeping up morale.

In the spring of 1943 a very small dribble of odd-looking tourists arrived in Santa Fe, New Mexico, the first capital of New Spain in North America. They came one at a time, and they never met together as a group in public. They were under instruction not to call each other by their professional titles, either doctor or professor. They were a secret team of refugees and native American and British scientists who had gathered at Santa Fe before being driven off thirty miles northwest to Los Alamos. There, in the loneliness of the desert, they would brew the Apocalypse.

Today their retreat looks like some old silver miner's cabin or the relic of a long-vanished road gang. It is all that is left of the base camp of this band of eminent men who built a primitive laboratory and lived and worked for two years in a secret society. They carried false driving licenses and went under assumed names. Fermi was Henry Farmer. Niels Bohr, a Dane, was Nicholas Baker. Their leader was a forty-year-old American, Dr. Robert Oppenheimer, known as Oppy. They were allowed no personal contact here with their families, who could write only to a post-office box number. They lived in tar-paper shacks. The cleaning women and the other routine job workers were chosen for their illiteracy, in case they came on an engineering tool or a formula on a scrap of paper. A United States Senator whose investigating committee had achieved some fame for exposing fraud and extravagance in war costs was forbidden by President Roosevelt even to question the huge expenditures on this mysterious project or to find out what it was all about.

It was about, of course, the atomic bomb. This team had worked for eighteen months or so on the theoretical construction of the bomb, and at Los Alamos they spent another two years making it. Until the end they didn't know whether it would go off, or, if it did, whether they could absolutely control the nuclear chain reaction. They were 99.9 percent sure, but between the theory and the proof there was one tenth of one percent possibility of the end of all of us. The test site had to be as far as possible from settled country. It had to be a flat horizon to minimize the effects of the blast. It had to have reliably fine weather and only light winds. It had to be close enough to Los Alamos to be within an easy day's ride, but far enough away to discourage conjecture that the bomb and the secret work at Los Alamos were connected.

The chosen place was over two hundred miles due south from Los Alamos on a part of the Alamogordo bombing range in a blinding stretch of desert. The team's waking misgivings were not pacified by the Spanish name for this country, which was where disabled Spanish wagon trains could expect no help and were left to die. Three hundred years earlier the Spaniards' route across this country had been dubbed the *jornada del muerto*, the "journey of death."

The final assembly of the bomb began on July 12, 1945, in an old ranch house. Two days later, they had it mounted on a hundred-foot tower. They locked in the central core of the bomb, and by the night of the fifteenth they were ready. There then blew in a tremendous storm of thunder and crashing hailstones, a final explosion of defiance of the elements they could not control. But at last the thunder rumbled away and the rain stopped, and before dawn on the sixteenth they retreated to observation shelters of reinforced concrete built ten thousand yards south, west, and north of the firing point. Trucks stood by for an emergency retreat, to be conducted by drivers who knew the desert roads by night.

As the countdown started they stretched face down on the ground, with their feet towards the blast, and they covered their eyes. In one of the shelters Oppenheimer was seen to hold to a post to steady his shaking body.

At 5:29 and 45 seconds in the morning on July 16, 1945, there was an immense flash of light, brighter than any they had ever seen, shocking all the color out of the sage and the red soil and the mountains. There was a single thunderclap, and at the site itself an inferno of flames was sucked into a rising pillar of smoke, which then billowed into a vast mushroom and slowly dissipated in the high winds.

The prostrate scientists were stunned out of all professional pride. Oppenheimer could think only of a line from a Hindu poem: "I am become Death, the shatterer of worlds." Three weeks later, the shattered city of Hiroshima began to count one hundred thousand dead, and three days after that Nagasaki received the second bomb.

The decision to drop the bomb was made on the fearful calculation that an invasion of Japan might confront five million defenders and five thousand suicide aircraft and cost up to two million American lives. That decision was made by the man who had been permanently forbidden to look into the atomic project, by that one-time Senator who, when Roosevelt dropped dead in April 1945, was now President Truman. So the Second World War ended in a flash "brighter than a thousand suns." When the Japanese were led aboard the battleship *Missouri* in Tokyo Bay to surrender, the American commander in the Pacific, General Douglas MacArthur, said it in four resonant words: "These proceedings are closed."

The proceedings in Europe had been closed, too, by conventional bombing and artillery that in one city, Dresden, had been more lethal than Hiroshima. The Germans camped out amid the ruins of the Third Reich, which had lasted only twelve of the thousand years that Hitler had promised. But the cost of liquidating him was thirty million lives and the devastation of Europe.

It was a good time to remember Winston Churchill's old recipe of "magnanimity in victory." Within two years the United States devised a grand plan, the Marshall Plan (whose true author was Under Secretary of State Dean Acheson), which asked western Europe what it needed to rebuild itself. The largesse poured out from an act of Congress, the European Recovery Program—in the main to Britain, France, Germany, and Italy—and the railroads were rebuilt, the factories and farms subsidized, international trade reborn; the simple, breathtaking aim was, in Dean Acheson's words, "to restore the fabric of European life." This creative gesture of generosity, which cost the American people between ten and fifteen billion dollars, has not been matched in modern history; a truth only slightly dimmed by the need to convince Congress that it was a plan of resistance to the Soviet Union's takeover of eastern Europe.

Not only Germany and Japan had been mortally weakened. Half the world was wounded, and the fifty victorious nations swore to heal it through a new League of Nations. In April 1945 the United Nations was born in San Francisco. In the quarter century since its founding, scattered teams of quite selfless and denationalized people have repaired the health, agriculture, and economies of innumerable poor countries. Apart from this vast and successful humanitarianism, which was and is little advertised, there was one thing more than another that the United Nations was set up to do. It was, in the words of its charter, "to save succeeding generations from the scourge of war."

If it was to be done, it would be done in the chamber of the U.N. Security Council. This was the body that would consider all threats to peace. If it agreed on a given threat, it would vote to order action—which meant, in the last resort, military action. The Council was the core of the United Nations. It consisted of several elected nations and the permanent presence of the five big powers—the United States, Britain, France, the Soviet Union, and China—although there were, in fact, only two big powers, the superpowers of America and Russia. Because of their overwhelming strength at the end of the war, it was thought useless to draw up a charter that could override the will of these two and the lesser three. In other words, the charter made the large presumption that the wartime alliance would last. Unless the so-called Big Five agreed, nothing could be done, for any of them could veto an otherwise unanimous vote for action.

But when the Council got down to regular meetings, it was obvious that it was paralyzed not so much by the veto as by the growing conflict between the United States and the Soviet Union that prompted its use. The Russians reacted defensively to the American bomb and the spreading network of American strategic bases from the Sea of Japan to Greenland. The Americans reacted in anger to the Russians' absorption of Romania, Poland, and then Czechoslovakia. The Western world echoed the clanging sentence of Churchill, which was nothing more than an old reporter's blunt report: "From Stettin in the Baltic to Trieste in the Adriatic, an iron curtain has descended across the continent."

The United Nations did in time stop wars in Indonesia, Kashmir, the Congo, and the Middle East, and its Security Council voted unanimously to conduct a war against the northern invaders of South Korea. But that vote was unanimous only because the Soviet Union happened at the moment to be boycotting the Council. On the fateful weekend when the Council met, there were no jet planes to wing a man from Moscow to the meeting in time. The Russians have never stayed away since.

The Korean War was the first United Nations war. It was to be the last in which the Americans would carry the brunt of the fighting. After two years they had had enough of it, and a year later General—by now President—Eisenhower stopped it. This was almost certainly done by a secret threat to use tactical atomic weapons, a move not reported until thirteen years later. It began to dawn on the old practitioners of *real-politik* at the United Nations that it was not the Security Council that kept the peace but America's possession of the atomic bomb—and, now, of the hydrogen bomb. There ensued a fearful period in which a new kind of spy appeared. Atomic spies had been caught in Canada, the United States, and Britain, and it led in this country to a terrified hunt for spies in the government, and frequently to the hounding of officials big and little who wouldn't have known the difference between a secret code and a quadratic equation. It took us several years to learn that the secrets of nuclear energy are as open as the laws of gravity. Today schoolchildren may troop through a government museum in Albuquerque, New Mexico, and inspect the whole range of America's nuclear arsenal.

But there is a somber contradiction in the possession of these terrible weapons. At one time, the Spanish galleon was the ultimate weapon, and it built an empire and cowed Europe. In the nineteenth century the strength of the British navy dictated the Pax Britannica. But the first use of a nuclear bomb on Japan caused a worldwide moral revulsion against its further use. And so the United States became the first supreme power that could not use its ultimate weapon. Its impotence was disguised for several years by the gigantic virility of its war machine. In fact, America's dominion was very brief, from 1945 to 1949, when the Russians exploded *their* bomb. But throughout the 1950s and well into the 1960s, the triumphant feeling persisted that America could dictate a Pax Americana.

At the high and icy noon of his inauguration, President John F. Kennedy delivered himself of a sentence as gallant and resounding as anything in the Gettysburg address. It was not, on examination, much more realistic. "Let every nation know, whether it wishes us well or ill, that we shall pay any price, bear any burden, meet any hardship, support any friend, oppose any foe, to assure the survival and the success of

---

Overleaf: *At the centerpoint of power—in the Oval Office of the White House—President John F. Kennedy takes a call as his brother Robert, the Attorney General, stands by.*

liberty." A staggering commitment of life, liberty, comfort, food, automobiles to *any* nation that asked America to give her all. Yet, in the euphoria of owning the best and biggest bombs, the United States concluded treaties of protection with forty-three nations; offered to play St. George to forty-three possible dragons. And in this brief Samaritan glow, America—which forty years before had renounced Europe forever—now had her President go there and proclaim West Berlin as America's front line against the Communist world: "'There are many people in the world who really don't understand, or say they don't, what is the great issue between the free world and the Communist world. Let them come to Berlin! . . . Today, in the world of freedom, the proudest boast is—'Ich bin ein Berliner!'"

This was heady stuff. Though the bomb could not be dropped, it fostered the dangerous conviction that nations with different ideologies and different needs could, in Woodrow Wilson's phrase, be made "safe for democracy." In the result, America was seen to have given a worldwide pledge to leaders of all sorts of ideologies who would fight their conventional wars and use the bait of the American pledge to oblige America to join in. In the Kennedy days there was little question about whether America was willing to help little nations put down their aggressors (assuming one could always identify the aggressor) because there was no question at all that America was able. The appearance of thirty-five hundred American marines along the Mekong River had frightened the Pathet Lao much as the arrival of a British battleship in the Mediterranean used to frighten Greece or Turkey.

This easy victory set a fatal precedent. For after Laos came Vietnam, a suppliant in the night, asking only advisers and technicians and arms. But it didn't work. There followed more technicians, and "paramilitary" groups, and more arms, and in the end continuous and massive aerial bombing. For ten years the American elephant could make the earth tremble, but it couldn't conquer the ants who lived on it. The wildest nightmares of three Presidents were realized in the dispatch of half a million men, more than had gone to Korea, suffering more casualties than Korea.

Many Americans, especially the young who would have seen a villain in Hitler and fought him, could see no vital American interest in Southeast Asia. They saw the villains closer at home—in successive administrations that sustained the war, and also in universities committed to research in the technology of nuclear and biochemical warfare. These rebels were reacting to something already a quarter century old but of which most people have become aware only in the last decade: the monumental break in the history of warfare known as R and D—Research and Development. It began quietly during the Second

World War, when a few scientists started meeting in a modest hotel in California to develop the technology of conventional war. They were innocently initiating the process of research and development, which in our day presumes the full dependence of the military on scientists "thinking the unthinkable." The unthinkable is, of course, the technology of nuclear annihilation. This is what rattled the students and other academics, because many of the thinkers were university teachers on government grants.

But the moral problem is trickier than it first seemed. At Los Alamos today, the primitive lab that created the atomic bomb has been replaced by a gleaming compound that developed the hydrogen bomb and is now involved half in weapons research and half in pure nuclear research. The trouble is that you never know which is going to turn into which. The man who invented the wheel never imagined it would carry artillery. And Albert Einstein, when he devised his famous formula about the nature of energy, never remotely guessed that $E = mc^2$ would come to equal Hiroshima. There are, at Los Alamos, generators whose job is to test the ability of nuclear warheads to withstand hostile environments. But they may also discover a beam that could search out and destroy cancer cells.

Of course, it is no comfort to the conscience to say that a lethal weapon might also do good. The men who work at Los Alamos have to make an initial moral commitment: they are there in the main to work on weapons research, but they are also alert to the stirring possibility that as a by-product of their regular research they may be able to offer to our cities all the clean power they will ever need. Nonetheless, Congress, remembering that the Russians, too, are thinking the unthinkable, has tended to appropriate eight or nine times as much money for weapons research as for the peaceful development of nuclear energy.

Looking back to the place we started, the "increasing and competing might of the only two superpowers," someone is bound to reflect that all this ought to be the main problem not of America or Russia but of the United Nations. What has *it* done to dissolve the nuclear rivalry? Well, in 1945 the first fifty members of the United Nations signed a charter that contained a clause that a simpleton, or a man from Mars, might take to be the keystone of the U.N.'s power. It is Article 43, and it binds the member nations to make available to the Security Council "on its call and in accordance with a special agreement or agreements, armed forces, assistance and facilities, including rights of passage, necessary for the purpose of maintaining international peace and security." These agreements were to be "negotiated as soon as possible." Nearly thirty years have gone by, but they have never been negotiated because the United Nations has never had the force to assert the authority it claimed. No member nation is willing to accept an international verdict, let alone the overwhelming power to enforce it, against its own national interests.

We are left with the humbling admission that, if the United Nations has failed, it is because it is no better than the humans who comprise it. Consequently, the United Nations must be, and has long been, discounted as a force able to match or control the superpowers. They go their independent ways, probing the mysteries of technological warfare, vying with each other in building stockpiles of nuclear weapons that could destroy the world many times over. And other, smaller powers, out of fear or an insensate view of prestige, are hastening to develop their own "nuclear capability"—the capability, that is, of helping along the destruction of this planet. In all former times the piling up of armaments has in itself ensured that one day they would go off. We are now told that, on the contrary, they offer us the comfort of "a balance of terror."

So what, three hundred years after the trusty rifle by the fireside, is our shield? It is one room, in Nebraska, a central switchboard that can tap the energy released at Alamogordo in missiles disposed around the world. And this room is under the control of one human being, the President of the United States.

The ultimate defense of the United States, of her NATO and other allies, is spread around forty-six world bases. But they and all their nuclear weapons are under the instantaneous control of a Strategic Air Command headquarters planted underground in Omaha, Nebraska, 1,150 miles inland from the Atlantic, deep in the bowels of the Midwest. Here teams of controllers, working in shifts around the clock, hold at the ready never less than a thousand missiles, any one of which packs the destructive force of all the bombs dropped in the Second World War. One other nation at least has similar missiles, and it follows that this underground headquarters could be the supreme target of an enemy. It is not indestructible. But if it were destroyed the control of the missiles would pass to alternative commands. One of them is a fleet of aircraft in which each plane reflects the total command capability of the huge underground post and is therefore called the Looking Glass. One plane is always in the air, as the active unit of a fleet on perpetual ground alert.

The Looking Glass carries a flight crew of four, as well as three radio operators, two maintenance men, and behind them a "battle staff" of eleven. Since a man might need a snack to sustain him even through Armageddon, there is also one steward. The front section of the Looking Glass is a room no larger than fifteen feet by five, which can command all the bases, all the submarines, all the airborne forces. It can signal the launch for all the missiles the United States owns anywhere in the world. It is in direct touch at all times with the President, with the Chiefs of

Staff, and with the others who comprise the National War Command. Installed on one wall along the port side is the holy of unholies, a red box. It is under constant surveillance, and if any unauthorized person tries to open its wooden lid, it lets off an alarm calculated to galvanize the drowsiest member of the crew. It contains the President's secret orders, to which only two men on the plane have access. One is the chief of the Airborne Battle Staff, and he sits close by the box. The other, sitting farther up front, is the General Officer.

The President's sealed orders arrive regularly by courier under armed escort. They are locked in the box. The President has always at his side, no matter where he is at home or abroad, an inconspicuous aide who carries a code. It changes unpredictably, but it always corresponds with the code that is used in the sealed orders. They may direct something as humdrum as the shift of a bomber force, they can be the order for total war. If that signal came, each of the two sole responsible officers would take out his own key. No one man can open the box or launch a missile. Everywhere, in this command post and in the missile sites, it takes two keys. Having opened the box, they would take out the orders, break the seal, decode, and check to see that the verbal order corresponded with the orders in the box. Then, and only then, in the last extremity, would they move to a special telephone, the counterpart of the red telephone underground, and—by simply lifting it—give the war alert to all the silos, and the Polaris subs, and the B-52 bombers with their nuclear payloads.

For many years now—and while you are reading these words—there have been loaded B-52 bombers en route to predetermined points well short of enemy territory but headed in his direction. They automatically return to base unless they receive a checked and rechecked war alert. They can fly ten thousand miles without refueling, and their crews average a seventy-four-hour week, eating and sleeping at all times close by the aircraft.

It is a Saturday morning. Two automobiles arrive and park outside the ground entrance to a very simple, even shabby-looking, shack. Two young men get out. They are the new shift, and they are as casual as a gas-station mechanic relieving his buddy. They show a wad of identification cards at the inner gate.

They are worth a long look, for they are specially trained to keep what is surely the loneliest, and could be the last, vigil of human warfare. Yet these doomsday warriors look no more like soldiers than the soldiers of the Second World War looked like conquistadors. They would have

---

Overleaf: *Squatting in the late afternoon sunlight, elements of a Safeguard antiballistic missile complex near completion on the North Dakota plain.*

amazed Eisenhower and deeply pained MacArthur. For as the technologists have taken over, the professional soldiers have shed their fine feathers and their once impressive physique. The more expert they become, the more they look like lab assistants in small colleges. You see the type in small variations everywhere, manning the consoles of Omaha, commanding submarines that resemble nothing so much as an IBM plant. They may have capacious bow-window bellies or be reedy as beans. They can wear glasses. They stand around, at sea, at a ground base, or deep in a missile silo, and they "program" their incomprehensible jargon into consoles, dictating out of large manuals, throwing switches, watching a run of lights, announcing with all the dramatic flair of an inventory clerk that the first missile is "away" and presumably about to destroy Moscow or Peking. The Revolutionary War's first minutemen must have looked by contrast like grenadiers. Today, the marines are the last physical soldiers.

Our two young men are waiting for a subterranean voice to say that the old crew is ready to ascend. They lean against the gate and exchange small talk about their interests.

They have families, they play pool or go bowling on their off nights, they do carpentry and gardening, they follow the football scores. One of these two looks to the day when his tour is up and he'll be free to plant trees in New Hampshire.

They go down in the elevator, tramp along a corridor, and wait for a safety door to open. They come to the small control room and are greeted by the officer going off duty. The ensuing dialogue is as spare as that of a bored exchange in a Noel Coward play, but duller—a catechism about the "status" of the alert team, the panel switch, the flight area, the launch switch. Check, check, check.

They have had thorough psychiatric tests, which are periodically repeated. Each is responsible for watching the other. If one of them breaks down and seems likely to go berserk, it is the other's duty to shoot him.

They go through the last motions of the changeover by proving that they know the combination of the red box. They check the authenticity of the keys, which would need to be turned simultaneously before a presidential order to fire a missile could be carried out. All that remains is for them to take over the guns of the retiring crew. Then they are locked in, for a twelve-hour stretch.

The whole system—from the White House through the National War Command, through Omaha and the bombers to the farthest nuclear sub—is fortified with checks and counterchecks against both human and technological error. But, in the end, someone will have to decide whether these soldiers will remain simple family men or the triggers of

Armageddon. Who is it to be? America? Russia? China? The rapidly qualifying new members of the nuclear club? We are assured on all sides that the true deterrent will be a human one, and that even a President of the United States dare not and could not make the irrevocable decision without the consenting knowledge of other men.

Still, there is a special danger about the new technological warfare. Its jargon is as dense and impersonal as the computers that plot it; but the thing itself has an infernal and seductive fascination. In the first week of June 1963 I had the doubtful privilege of being helicoptered out into the Pacific, with the rest of the White House press corps, to watch day and night exercises from the bridge of the aircraft carrier U.S.S. *Kitty Hawk.* The daytime performance was brilliant enough: sleek missiles whooshing from below and vanishing in a plume of smoke; the Phantoms skimming across the bow and lost to sight in ten seconds; the little jets, a hundred or more of them, rising on elevators to the main deck, unfolding their wings and whizzing off over the blue water till they were recalled and came hurtling back at one hundred and fifty miles an hour to be retrieved with a jolt by the snaking catapult cables.

But at night the performance had a pure and unholy beauty. The great ship is almost immovable in the sailless Pacific. The night silence is punctured from time to time by a series of horns and buzzing sounds punched out by coordinators on an immense console winking in the darkness of the upper bridge. In response to these orders, small armies of figures in phosphorescent orange and emerald uniforms advance and retreat across the deck like bright clockwork midgets. At intervals, there is a rumble as of underground steam pressure, and a huge missile explodes out of the ship's belly, mounts like a flying submarine and is suddenly a cinder expiring on the horizon. And always the Phantoms are tearing off and returning. Another long silence and again a few well-modulated orders on the bridge. And again the ghastly and beautiful missiles soar off over the sea, or leap out of it like dolphins at play in the Apocalypse. I recalled, with shameful exhilaration, Donne's terrible line: "What if this present were the world's last night?"

Let us hope that among the men who will have to face the irrevocable decision will be enough battle-worn veterans like General Sherman, who have had enough of war to despair of it. For the greatest danger is that the technology of the unthinkable war will enchant its practitioners, growing so subtle and mighty as to acquire a momentum all its own, which mere men will be powerless to subdue.

Overleaf: *In fog at Khe Sanh, a godforsaken firebase just below the DMZ, two bored Marines stand guard. A classic Vietnam war picture by David Douglas Duncan.*

Epilogue

THE MORE ABUNDANT LIFE

Studded with swimming pools, a Southern California suburb exudes prosperity and a sense of life lived in the most pleasant surroundings possible.

William Empson once defined the obvious as "what seldom gets said." It is what all historians should be striving for, but it manages to evade them when they look at their own time, for the funny but shrewd reason that Dr. Johnson could not see how a bicycle would go: "You ride yourself and the machine as well." The mind is not working on a removed object but on objects that are also part of the mind at work. Hence the enormous amount of invective and special pleading that go into the writing and discussion of contemporary history. One danger a historian faces when he tries to apply his knowledge of the past to the present is the temptation to draw analogies—in which, unfortunately, what is new may be more significant—and hurt more—than what is familiar. Another is the professional's love for a complete story. He cannot bear what is unresolved.

Before I came to the end of this work, I went through a score of books written in the late 1940s, some of them modest, some of them strident, which told us what our problems were and how we ought to solve them. They make discouraging reading today. None of them anticipated the breakup of the British and French empires, or the Russian—let alone the Chinese!—penetration of the Middle East and Africa. None of them foresaw the decision of the subject peoples of Africa and Asia—and, for that matter, of the American Negro— to act on the grand promise of the Declaration of Independence that "all men are created equal." To hedge all bets, most of these savants promised troubles in every quarter of the globe, but they were not the important troubles that happened, except for what was beginning to happen—the Russian lunge toward the domination of Europe.

We ought not to gloat over the failings of our own clay. But if the reader is still unconvinced, except by the commentators who share his prejudices (the normal definition of a good commentator), he should look back to the people who were doing the prophesying in the 1920s, to celebrated pundits like Bernard Shaw, H. G. Wells, Bertrand Russell,

Count Keyserling. I was brought up on such pontiffs, and learned from them that marriage was on its last legs; that world government was just around the corner, since another world war would promptly extinguish the human race in a cloud of poison gas; and that eugenic breeding was as inevitable as it was right. None of these things has happened. Eugenic breeding, as naïve a fetish as ever obsessed the intelligentsia, has now to be looked up in books of social history that record the rise and fall of flagpole-sitting, the Yo-Yo, and Major Douglas's social credit.

It is a record to instill caution if not humility. We do not know what is crucial and what is not about the palpable problems of crime, corruption in government, America's sensible role in the world, the status of the blacks, a cure for inflation, not to mention the new problems of pollution, pesticides, drugs among the young, the need to revise the democratic view of every stage of public education. Many things happening in America today have happened before. This epilogue looks at some of them, and at their roots, while preserving the right of an author coming to the end of a four hundred-year retrospect to say as clearly as possible where he thinks this nation has arrived. So let us now consider what Americans hoped for from Roosevelt's promise of "the more abundant life," and what they got.

Something between a quarter and a fifth of America, half the West, is semi-desert. For centuries much of it has been at the mercy of the Colorado River, which is either a trickle that leaves the land parched or a torrent that floods it with silt. The desert is not infertile. "Spit on the desert," the old-timers used to say, "and a flower will grow." On the Arizona-Nevada border is one of the great works of man: Hoover (formerly Boulder) Dam, which bottles the fourteen hundred-mile flow of the Colorado and teaches it to spit accurately and often on a quarter million acres of dry land. Backed up behind the Dam is a reservoir, a man-made lake one hundred and twenty miles long, which holds five thousand gallons of water for every man, woman, and child alive. The dam took five thousand men twenty-one months to build, and, to get to the bottom of the spillway, you have to go down what would be a fifty- or sixty-story skyscraper. Hoover Dam was built early in the 1930s, during the Depression, before the age of plastics and synthetic lavatory tile, so it had to fall back on the beautiful strong materials of the old order—aluminum and steel, copper and brass. Men drove tunnels through the canyon bedrock and held the river in them while the spillway was poured: 700 feet high, 4,440,000 cubic feet of concrete. They planted great icing tubes to hasten the cooling; left to Nature, it would have taken a century to set.

Merely to recite these feats and figures recalls the cadences of

Deuteronomy and the triumphant prescription for the Promised Land. To tame the Colorado and make the desert bloom was the stated aim of President Roosevelt when he dedicated the dam on September 30, 1935. And Roosevelt did seem then to millions of Americans to be their Moses. Only his enemies—the "money changers who have fled from their high seats in the temple of our civilization"—would have mocked if he had raised his soaring tenor and cried: "My doctrine shall drop as the rain, My speech shall distil as the dew, As the small rain upon the tender herb, And as the showers upon the grass." After Boulder, Roosevelt was consumed with a passion for more dams: for the world's largest, Grand Coulee, to harness the Columbia River; and then for the forty dams of the Tennessee River, to revive its ruined valley and send power to homes, farms, stores, mines, and factories over a region almost as large as the United Kingdom. The "interests" might howl, as an irritable New York Congressman did, that there was no one to sell power to "except rattlesnakes, coyotes, and rabbits" in the "vast gloomy tablelands" of the Pacific Northwest; and the private utility companies might foresee "galloping Socialism," as Wendell Willkie, their able lawyer, did, in the shocking plan to make hydroelectric power a public resource to be piped through federal transmission lines. But it was all part of Roosevelt's revised version of Lincoln's assertion that "this country with its institutions belongs to the people who inhabit it." An old countrywoman in New Hampshire spoke for the inhabitants: "We feel that our country has been given back to us."

The dam may be taken as a symbol of Roosevelt's New Deal, a majestic exemplar of the doctrine that hydroelectric power was the essential handmaiden of "industrial democracy" and that through it the Southwest would blossom into a fruit and vegetable bowl (which it did), that farmers would multiply (which they didn't), and that industry would burgeon to the great good of everybody. More electricity, more power, was to be the guarantee of what Roosevelt called "the more abundant life."

But a vast expansion of power made the desert and much else of America bloom in ways that Roosevelt never had in mind. If it hadn't been for Hoover Dam, Las Vegas might still be the dusty Western town of a few thousand where I first bedded down in a "tourist home" with a couple of cockroaches the size of mice—a town whose water came from an artesian well, whose chamber of commerce was a one-story stuccoed building, whose baseball park seated seven hundred, whose cottonwoods shaded still the relics of its old Mormon stockade. But it is now the capital and the archetype of the new pleasure cities of America. Platoons of billboards offer screaming solicitations to people driving through to stop and stay and enjoy themselves. Before the sun goes down, the huge signs pierce the eyeballs as cruelly as Broadway by daylight. But when the twilight comes on, and the distant mountains harden into a cardboard cutout against a sky going from turquoise to purple, Las Vegas settles into a large shape and style that is nowhere but America in the 1970s. By night, at thirty thousand feet, it looks as if all the Vatican and Crown jewels had been piled on a strip of blue velvet. A single downtown hotel consumes as much electricity as the houses in a town of sixty thousand. It composes a night-time image of Babylon in the desert.

But it is Everyman's cut-rate Babylon. Not far away there is, or was, a roadside lunch counter and over it a sign proclaiming in three words that a Roman emperor's orgy is now a democratic institution. It says: "Topless Pizza Lunch." And in the pleasure domes of Las Vegas people line up for hours to register into motels and indulge the pleasures that once were reserved at Baden Baden for Edward VII and King Farouk. Outside is the open oven of the desert, inside is the wet slap of air-conditioning and the mechanical chatter around the clock of "one-armed bandits" in every motel lounge, drug store, and supermarket. There are the supper shows, with electrically amplified bands disciplining lacquered nudes to the precision of a guards regiment. Everywhere there are the spinning roulette wheels and the green-baize tables bathed in glowing circles of light, and around the tables a jungle of colored Lurex pants and polyester jeans and peacock shirts and fish-net see-throughs, and a mob of faces, more often out of Norman Rockwell than out of Daumier. For the stakes can be as high or low as you like. It is the big time on a low budget.

Nevertheless, though it was made possible by the generators at Hoover Dam, it would be the understatement of the century to say that this was not what Franklin Roosevelt meant by "the more abundant life." Las Vegas in the 1970s is only one example of a revolution in middle-class American values, and it is perhaps the starkest historical contrast between the old American Dream and the new American reality. Certainly this is a civilization, and maybe a decadence, away from the New World for which the newcomers, after their first harvest, rose and gave thanks.

America was settled by a large variety of characters, but whether they were pious or shifty, they had also to be tough and patient and make the most of a few rude staples. Today food in mountainous quantities groans and gurgles from coast to coast in variations both succulent and frivolous. America used to be the land of boundless space. Today, except for the lonely bombing ranges of the West and the impenetrable mountains, boundless space is available only to such as the traffic reporter in his helicopter instructing the earth-bound midgets how to thread their way home. America reveled at the beginning of the century in the latest

In their dressing room at a Las Vegas club, where a floor show offers gamblers a break from the serious business of losing money, showgirls check their makeup and exiguous costumes before going on stage.

ingenuities of the glorious Industrial Revolution. Today we have reaped that whirlwind. America was the magic word and the better life for millions of Europeans penned in ghettos. Today the magic has faded but the tenements remain.

Such contrasts exist everywhere in the world. But they always seem more depressing and dramatic in America because America didn't inherit a nation—it invented one that was supposed to be better than everything that had gone before. Europeans in particular take a mean delight in pointing out the gap between the advertised ideal and the reality. Morally, Americans know as much as any of them about the seven deadly sins. And, because we expected more, we know more about disillusion. But materially, what was new about the American experiment was the attempt to deny special privilege and bring well-being to the masses. Over thirty years ago a presidential candidate, that same Wendell Willkie who fought Roosevelt over the prior rights of public and private power, came back from a postwar tour around the world and said: "The American economy is not going to be able to prosper after this war unless Americans regard as necessities what other people look on as luxuries."

This impulse was at work far earlier than most of us would guess. Take, as a dramatic example, Frederic Tudor, the son of George Washington's Judge Advocate General, an upper-crust Bostonian, the very last type you would expect to become the first tycoon, the founding father of the art of salesmanship, or the inspirer of anything so democratic as an ice-cream parlor. He was born in 1784. His three brothers went to Harvard, but he wanted to be up and doing, so he quit school at thirteen. He became a merchant, and an inventor with so many mad ideas that didn't pay off that a whimsical brother wondered why he didn't break up the ice on the Boston ponds and ship it to the tropics. The youngest Tudor ignored the crack and seized on a brain wave. He shipped one hundred and thirty tons of ice to Martinique. It melted in six weeks. Insulation was the big problem, and with the fanaticism of Edison in pursuit of a filament, Tudor tried everything from straw to blankets and he beat it in the end with sawdust. To procure uniform blocks of ice, he got a friend to design an ice cutter with two parallel runners made of iron with saw teeth. They were pulled across the ponds by horses. Within fifteen years he had collared title to the New England ponds, got monopoly rights on building icehouses in Havana and New Orleans and Charleston and had his own fleet shipping ice in thousands of tons to the West Indies, Persia, India, and Europe.

The foreigners were delighted with the product but slightly bemused about what to do with it. Tudor responded by anticipating two centuries of salesmanship and advertising. He realized that the golden rule of merchandizing is to create an appetite for something you didn't even know you wanted. He sailed around half the globe convincing dazed clients that iced drinks were the elixir of health, that a hospital without ice was ready for the plague, that a meal without ice cream was a cannibal's snack. Pretty soon malaria victims were dabbing ice on their foreheads, and fashionable houses in London, Cairo, and Casablanca were serving ice cream.

Fashionable people were all right but they were not a mass market. Tudor undercut his competitors, made simpler ice houses, offered bargains in bulk and, in the end, sold his ice for a penny a pound. He made ice a necessity, even—at the end of the Second World War—in England.

Tudor was the brilliant forerunner of the American businessman and advertiser at their most characteristic. A century before the first assembly line, he anticipated its great aims: to entice not clients but a horde of customers, to convert luxuries into necessities, to give the mass of people the illusion, at least, that they could buy at a discount the services formerly reserved for the rich. A month after the Duchess of Windsor was photographed in her wedding gown, a New York department store had cheap and plausible copies of it available, at a tenth of the price, for the high school June bride. In the new suburbs, row houses have swimming pools, little ones that mimic the large swimming pools of the rich. And a single worldwide chain of American motels provides for the ordinary family on tour a standard air-conditioned bedroom, with a color television set, a telephone, a bureau, a desk, a dressing room, a bathtub, free ice, and the services on tap of a laundry, a dry cleaner, a baby-sitter, a doctor, a dentist, and a parson. If the general pride in these middle-class values appears to outsiders to be excessive, it ought to be said that it took excessive sweat and labor in one century to hew out of the prairie and the forest this comfort and these values, which in the next century the great-grandchildren could afford to despise.

But to maintain these habits of conspicuous prosperity, the American family has taken over the policy the government adopted in the Depression: deficit financing. Without the credit card, the mortgage, and the bank loan, it is doubtful whether the affluent society would stay affluent through the enormous broad span of the middle class. Since the Second World War, the crumbling centers of the cities have been replaced more often by skyscraper office buildings for banks and loan insurance companies than for housing. The central land is now too expensive for housing, a fact that ought to make us think again about the priorities human beings set for themselves. The old city types, the so-called solid citizens, tend more and more to depart for the country and the new suburbs. In one of those mass movements that follow every war, several millions arrived in California after the Second World War to make it the most populous state in the Union. Young men from the dingy parts of Pittsburgh and Chicago and East St. Louis and a score of other cities had found themselves, in the early 1940s, sailing out of San Francisco or San Diego or performing amphibious training along the beaches of Santa Barbara and Malibu. They spread the word that California was the place where there were no slums, where the valleys were fruitful, the sun a constant companion, and where the living was easy. The San Fernando Valley, when I first knew it, was a latter-day relic of the landscape of New Spain, with tiled houses, corrals, large ranches, files of eucalyptus trees marching through green pastures to the horizon. Bing Crosby sang a song, "Make the San Fernando Valley Your Home," and a million and a half people took him up on it. What has turned a thousand green valleys into a thousand choking suburbs is the coincidence of a postwar leap in population with the easy escape-hatch of the automobile. The automobile and the installment plan have obliterated the old distinction between town and country and, incidentally, stripped the approach to the cities of their regional identity.

Nowhere has this vast spread of anonymity so buried the original character of a town and its surroundings as in what we must regard as the first of modern cities—Los Angeles. It was once called "twenty suburbs in search of a city." It is now forty or fifty subdivisions of a metropolitan sprawl. It never felt called upon to develop the usual network of public transportation because, in a country where there is one car for every two people, Los Angeles has three and a half million automobiles for a population of roughly three million. It was the first city built for the automobile. Between a quarter and a third of the city's land area is now monopolized by the automobile and its needs—by freeways, highways, garages, gas stations, car lots, parking lots. And all of it is blanketed with anonymity and foul air.

In America there are two things that people choose to do about the automobile problem: to try to cure it, or to escape from it. There are always the traditional watchdogs of the Congressional investigating committees, which have the power to subpoena practically everyone but the President, to hear the complaints of any citizen with a plausible case, and to make even such giant corporations as General Motors make an apology (for having *him* investigated) to a private investigator who had charged them with subordinating safety, in the design of their cars, "to the tyranny of the cost accountant." But frequently these committees take down millions of words of testimony that are never acted on—for they are, in the end, only as effective as the people are moved to be roused by them. And at some undetermined point in the past two decades, a point that may one day be seen as a historic turning point in the morale of the American people, the revelations of Congressional

What the automobile hath wrought: "The Speedway" in Tucson, Arizona. The mayor of the city considers this to be the ugliest street in America.

committees bored the people more than they stirred them. What was worse, through the late 1960s and early 1970s, the old honorable American figure of the muckraking journalist produced shocking disclosures of corruption in the Congress itself that quite simply failed to shock anybody. (Not until the spring of 1973 were the whole people galvanized out of their cynical torpor by the revelation that inside the White House itself a group of the President's senior advisers had organized a politburo using secret methods of spying and burglary that appeared to flout both the legislative power of Congress and the most fundamental guarantees of the Constitution.)

By the early 1970s moral indifference seemed to have overcome the two ancient political parties, and the people's trust in them—and in such subsidiary bodies of the Establishment as the armed forces, the bankers, the churches, and even the doctors—was reported in national polls and surveys to be very little. It was left to such knights of the consumer as Ralph Nader and his followers to nag on our behalf or, in many places, to do-it-yourself watchdogs to swab up with their pocket handkerchiefs the ocean of social decay. There is, for instance, in Los Angeles a Mrs. Ellen Harris, who posts herself by the telephone in her bedroom in the hope of becoming the terror of the city fathers. She reports poor sewage disposal, the decibel volume of airplanes, the smog density, the violations of power plants and refineries, the stench and pollution that now befoul the California beaches. There are some politicians who have come to believe that the distance from Washington to the ailing borough or town is too far for any hope of a cure, and that the next great movement of reform must come from people willing to regard their own neighborhoods as the first English settlers regarded their palisaded villages—as the only manageable units of society. In this belief, there is at once the hope of alert citizenship and the danger of vigilantism.

But the mass of city dwellers do not seem willing to trust either the authority of Washington or the power of their own municipal governments. In the past twenty years millions of them have abandoned the city and its afflictions altogether and gone to new suburbs in open country. These too have quickly taken on the city's monotonous order and copied its addiction to drugs and its random violence.

All of this has led a generation of the idealistic young to reject the city and the suburb both, and the whole caboodle of values of what it calls Middle America. These people have retreated into deeper country to do what the first Puritans did, to build their own houses, to start their own society from the ground up. There is one such commune in New Hampshire where the members—all university graduates—grow their own food, do their own baking and churning and mending, and perform all the chores of a rural, self-sufficient society. Or nearly self-sufficient. For, not to seem to scorn their country cousins, they help the locals cut their hay, they buy their grain in bulk from a cooperative. They share all the tasks of their common life, take regular turns minding the children and come together only at the evening meal. There they sit down gravely and, as in some primitive seventeenth-century print, they hold hands and a young woman recites a grace: "Calm down, little brother. Time heals all wounds. No matter how much one is weeping, the moon always follows the sun. Eat your bananas and fresh leaves and don't cry any more, because ever and ever the moon will follow the sun. We thank thee, Lord, for happy hearts, for rain and sunny weather. We thank thee, Lord, for this our food, and that we are together. Amen."

At this writing they have been there three summers. It remains to be seen whether what they represent will last. Communes come in many shapes and styles, dedicated to innumerable creeds, to neo-Buddhism, to The Process, to vegetarianism, to free love. California especially has long been the spiritual home of imported religions from yoga to instant serenity, and health cults from yogurt to high colonic irrigation. The idea of a community of purists or malcontents in retreat is almost as old as the Republic—which was, after all, founded by malcontents.

The classic model of the American commune was one created in 1825 in Indiana, on the banks of the Wabash, by Robert Owen. Born in Wales, Owen was a prosperous, self-made mill owner who first introduced humane reforms in his own factories and then headed for America to found "an empire of good sense" on thirty thousand acres he had bought in a place he renamed New Harmony. He bought up the dormitories of the Rappists, a failed religious colony, and attracted intellectuals, Swiss educators, scientists—nine hundred eager disciples. His experiment excited political reformers and philosophers all over Europe, most notably Friedrich Engels.

Owen's principles were lofty. There was to be total equality of the sexes. All property was to be held in common. There was to be "absolute freedom of action for the individual." This last prescription alone should have served as a warning that political sagacity, or for that matter common sense, had been mislaid. Good sense, indeed, seems to have been the last thing that ruled them. For the leaders had in common that strain of pure asininity that runs through the most earnest idealists. Children, for example, were to have a special place in society. They were to be "the tender, privileged guests of society." Too often they turned out to be children.

Overleaf: *On a commune "somewhere in the woods," a young couple reads a bedtime story. Commune members call themselves "the Family" and live in tepees.*

Equality of labor was another thing. Everybody was to demonstrate the dignity of labor by doing the humblest chores, whether they were able or not. Owen offered and started to do the baking, and was implored to desist only when general indigestion set in. And, like many another fervent advocate of equal rights, *he* laid down the rules. Three years was enough for the hardiest of his followers. Freedom, it turned out, meant the freedom to be a wealthy hanger-on or a poor incompetent. The farmers complained that the musicians got equal wages for just fiddling around. Some man coveted another man's wife. Some woman had an awful laugh.

In short, these dedicated purists made the maddening discovery that they had more than a taint of human nature. They found that living with nine people, or nine hundred, could be more of a strain than living with a million. By the end of its fourth year, the empire of good sense was dissolved. It had cost Owen four fifths of his fortune. It left behind a band of scholars, the germ of some excellent social reforms having to do with education and the social status of women, and a few sturdy physical relics, including, every spring, a perennial reminder of the first high hopes in the blossoming of the golden-rain tree, which was imported from China by Owen's best friend and his partner in the original deal. But the most solid memento of the doomed experiment stands on the banks of the Potomac: the Smithsonian Institution, founded by a steady campaign in Congress of Owen's son.

But the communes of our day, wise or freakish, are minority protests. The unrepentant majority has other solutions, and, if it has the money to escape from the dangerous city and the satellite suburbs, it may now depart for its own Middle America communes, for idyllic enclaves in the country designed on the drawing board and financed by an insurance company, a bank, or a steamship line. They may be planted on a thousand acres, on a natural or artificial island, and here they build their own schools, churches, golf course, boat dock, riding stables, craft shops, community center, and a galaxy of clubs—the Brownies, the PTA, the hospital guild, the garden club, the choral society, the Senior Citizens. They are bucolic retreats for the comfortable, but they are well aware of the hostile world outside. For whereas their city counterparts, the large condominium fortresses, have closed-circuit television keeping watch in elevators and garages, in the country there is a patrol, a guarded entrance gate, and perhaps a lake as a serviceable moat. Spaced obstacles arise along the path of the stranger attempting to enter. He is greeted by a friendly sign: "Welcome to Paradise Island"—which bears, however, the thoughtful reminder: "See Security Officer for Your Pass."

Yet in the context of over two hundred million Americans, all three of these solutions—the commune, the protected bucolic suburb, the condominium fortress—are the same. They are, indeed, no solution at all of social conflict but evasions of it. They all seek to substitute for the real world an ideal, safe microcosm. And they are surely doomed. For they simply ignore the sick and destructive element of society that sooner or later will have to be dealt with: the city poor, most of all the ever-growing and derelict population of the blacks.

The question of what to do with the blacks is one of the oldest and guiltiest of America's problems. The fifth President, James Monroe, thought that the blacks could have no happy future in the land they'd been sold to. He gave his blessing and his name to the capital of Liberia, Monrovia, founded in Africa by high-minded whites as a haven for ex-slaves. It was never a probable solution, for black labor was too precious to export, and the Negroes were powerless to organize a general exodus even if they had wanted to. In the century and a half between Monroe and our own time, Abraham Lincoln spoke most frankly for most Americans when he said: "Neither my own feelings nor those of the mass of whites will admit of making them social and political equals. . . . The only preventive of amalgamation is a separation of the races."

And the word "separation" became a talisman. In the 1880s Negroes began to claim the protection of one of the last of the Reconstruction laws, namely the Civil Rights Act of 1875, when they were kept out of hotel dining rooms, the dress circle of an opera house, the ladies' car on a train. The Supreme Court held the act unconstitutional, and the Southern states passed a flurry of laws decreeing separate passenger cars on trains. In 1892 one Homer Adolph Plessy challenged such a law in Louisiana and lost. The Supreme Court froze the social mobility of the Negroes for sixty years by ruling that henceforth they were to be granted "separate but equal" rights. The snag was that they were rarely equal.

Monroe's solution was revived just before the Second World War when a Senator from Mississippi, Theodore Bilbo, offered a bill for federal aid to Negroes wanting to settle on Liberian lands that had all this while been held in trust for them. In spite of a considerable file of Negro signatures to a petition, the idea seemed at the time to be reactionary madness, and the Senate turned it down. The next step was provoked by the heavy Negro representation in the armed forces of the Second World War (though it was the American Indian who served out of all proportion to his numbers). It led to the end of separate Negro regi-

Overleaf: *Accompanied by armed National Guardsmen, young blacks head nervously into Mississippi aboard a Greyhound bus during a 1962 demonstration.*

ments and President Truman's civil rights campaign in the election of 1948.

But 1954 was the year that sparked the black revolution of our day, and the innocents who lit the charge were Oliver Brown, of Topeka, Kansas, and his eight-year-old daughter, in whose behalf the father sued the city school board for forbidding her to go to a white school a few blocks away, forcing her instead to cross railroad yards to take a bus twenty-one blocks away. The Supreme Court ruled in her favor, overthrew the Plessy doctrine of sixty-two years before, declared that to separate whites and blacks in public education deprived children of "the equal protection of the laws guaranteed by the Fourteenth Amendment," and ordered the integration of public schools "with all deliberate speed." The majority opinion was written by Chief Justice Earl Warren, whom President Eisenhower had appointed to the Court in the awareness that he had once been a genial, sound, conservative old district attorney. The apotheosis of Earl Warren was something that baffled Eisenhower till the day he died.

For several years the Southern legislatures wriggled through a mesh of loopholes in their state constitutions to reassert the right of segregation. And since "deliberate speed" moved no faster than a turtle, the Negroes began their own mass protests, against many of the old offenses, first with laborious marches in the company of white sympathizers. Everyone anticipated trouble in the South, and that's where the first sporadic violence came. But no one guessed at the tenacious resistance of the whites in the cities of the North. The word "confrontation" emerged from the dictionary with a new and menacing air—in Little Rock, Arkansas; in Oxford, Mississippi; in Dallas, Texas; in Watts, California; in Detroit, Newark, Baltimore, and Washington. The subsequent turmoil is a part of all our lives.

Today the mass of blacks is not much better off, except —surprisingly —in local government in small Southern towns. Yet on college campuses and in training schools, there are blacks learning professions and businesses that they will practice in the white world. There are blacks who want no part of the white world, who want a black Establishment, even lands or separate states of their own. And there are blacks who want any number of alternatives in between.

In the universities, schools of African studies are reteaching the history of America and erecting a pantheon of forgotten heroes—Nat Turner, a Virginia slave who led an insurrection and was hanged in 1831; Marcus Garvey, a Jamaican who started a Negro nationalist movement in New York in 1917 to develop independent Negro nations in Africa and who was jailed for supposedly misusing the funds subscribed for the steamship line that would carry the colonizers back to Africa—and contemporaries who were to turn into murdered martyrs, Malcolm X and Martin Luther King. For the first time the black population of America, the submerged one ninth, has developed a philosophy and is acting on it. In 1972 the first wholly black political convention was held. But however much we may feel that the violence of the 1960s is a terror that has passed, the pressures that sparked it are with us still.

Speaking for myself, I believe that Monroe's and Garvey's solution—which Lincoln approved with wistful hindsight—might have been wise in 1820. But it is a century and a half too late. I do not know what the realistic solution is. I do know (and there are many disenchanting episodes in American history to prove it) that few things are more mischievous to good government and to "domestic tranquillity" than splendid rhetoric that doesn't pay off. There is certainly the smell of such rhetoric in the Establishment's reassurances and also in what the active majority of black leaders are asking: the rehousing of one ninth of the population; the chance of free education through college; the strangling of the international and national drug traffic at its roots; a radical integration of the police forces; and the overhauling of the prisons, the jury system, and the courts. This is no more than standard liberal, even conservative libertarian, doctrine, but it would call for prodigies of goodwill. It would also call for a massive subsidy of taxes, white taxes, beyond the experience or the known tolerance of the whites to bear.

As a historian I'm not sure that an integrated society will work. As an old reporter I suspect that the blacks will not get more than Lincoln's "mass of whites" is willing to give them. The best hope, the only sensible hope, is that the mass of whites have greatly changed since Lincoln's day, or will change. So that the blacks, whether inside or outside white society, can become an equal race separately respected.

Our confusion about what the blacks want and what they are likely to get may not be praiseworthy, but it is understandable. Nearly thirty years ago the best available statesmen, historians, soldiers, and politicians sat down in San Francisco to try and gauge the probable future and to direct it. They failed completely to anticipate the two universal movements of our time: the urge of the colored peoples everywhere to be their own rulers; and the urge of country people everywhere to decamp to the cities and the suburbs.

These two coinciding movements have produced a general sense of fear and frustration that once affected—when the American Republic was founded—only a brooding minority of French and English philosophers: the feeling that their own society was overcome by tragic failure, that America was less than the advertised paradise, and that the only pure society existed in some distant island inhabited by noble savages. In the eighteenth century these idealists couldn't sail away there. They could only feed their fantasy on the wishful thinking of explorers. They believed, because they wanted to, in a Brazil where splendid naked women dwelled in perfect amity with men seven feet tall who lived to be one hundred and forty years old. They yearned for "natural religion and natural morality" embodied in creatures innocent of the vices of Christendom; and to their delight, the French explorer Bougainville confirmed the wish with a delirious account of Tahiti. From that moment the idealist trek was on, back to unspoiled nature as the cure for all our woes.

Today we live with more relentless pressures—from crime outside our homes to the specter of the final war. It is no accident, I think, that ours is the great age of tourism, so much so that something less than half the member countries of the United Nations live by it. The promotional come-on is not so fanciful, but just as unreal, as the invitation to Florida held out four hundred years ago by another Frenchman, Jacques Lemoyne, in the first professional painting known to be done in America. The jet plane offers Nirvana and El Dorado in an economy family package. "Getting away from it all," if only for a month, a week, is something all of us can indulge at bargain-basement prices. Computers slot us into available flights. Other computers in travel offices and hotels assign us to a room and private bath on islands we have never seen.

Yet the mirage of the earthly heaven has retreated farther and farther afield. Today, probably for more millions than will ever get there, it is—as it was for the grouchy dreamers of eighteenth-century France—an island in the Pacific. And where more insulated from the madding world than a tiny chain of islands at the exact center of an ocean lapping four continents—Hawaii?

Here, in the winter that George Washington and his ragged army fought to survive at Valley Forge, the first white man stepped ashore and was greeted by the natives as one of their four gods come down to earth. The promise of the tourist literature is that you, too, will feel like Captain Cook. For here are rain forests, and waterfalls, and Bougainville's memento, the bougainvillea; and the dreamy bonus of beautiful, nubile maidens. Such a scene exists on the island of Maui.

But half an hour's flight from Maui is Honolulu, the capital of the fiftieth state. At first glance this city seems a happier and more permanent melting pot than any we have on the mainland. The Polynesians have intermarried freely with most other strains. One notices casually the issue of a Chinese father and an island mother; of a Filipino and a Scot; of a white American father and a Polynesian or Japanese mother. And so far the blacks appear to be more relaxed. Maybe this is the ultimate hope, the next stage in the human family.

But the people of Honolulu are in the same stew as the rest of us. Eighty percent of the islanders have chosen to jam into this city. Planters burn sugar cane for real estate and fill the air with smoke and ash. Surf riders, noticing the signs—"Warning: Polluted Water"—pick out the clean waves. There is choking traffic and urban sprawl and suburban density, and towering skyscrapers, and—"Stop For Guard Check"—the new fear of one's neighbor. Hawaiians had a strong original culture and now preserve a microcosm of it on the east coast of Oahu as a poor Hawaiian's Williamsburg. The more entertaining elements—the music, the flower festivals, the hula, the native drinks—have been diluted and bottled for the tourists who invade the islands in order to feel carefree and safe in the last of the states. Hawaii, far away in the middle of the Pacific, is yet another Western problem. There is no place to hide. And it is time to sum up.

What is fiercely in dispute between the Communist and non-Communist nations today is the quality and staying power of American civilization. Every other country scorns American materialism while striving in every big and little way to match it. Envy obviously has something to do with it, but there is a true basis for this debate, and it is whether America is in its ascendant or its decline.

I myself think I recognize here several of the symptoms that Edward Gibbon maintained were signs of the decline of Rome, and which arose not from external enemies but from inside the country itself. A mounting love of show and luxury. A widening gap between the very rich and the very poor. An obsession with sex. Freakishness in the arts masquerading as originality, and enthusiasm pretending to creativeness. These symptoms are shared by western Europe, though they seem to be milder there only because America has a livelier tradition of self-criticism.

In the past decade America has demonstrated the Roman folly of exercising military might in places remote from the centers of power, and of finding herself so frustrated by the stamina of primitive peoples on their own ground as to fall back on the Roman conclusion that "nothing could reconcile the minds of the barbarians to peace unless they experienced in their own country the calamities of war."

There is, too, the general desire to live off the state, whether it is a junkie on welfare or an airline subsidized by the government: in a word, the notion that Washington—Big Daddy—will provide. And, most disturbing of all, a developing moral numbness to vulgarity, violence, and the assault on the simplest human decencies.

Yet the original institutions of this country still have great vitality: the Republic can be kept, but only if we care to keep it. Much of the social turmoil in America springs from the energy of people who are trying to apply those institutions to forgotten minorities who have awakened after a long sleep.

As for the rage to believe that we have found the secret of liberty in general permissiveness from the cradle on, this seems to me a disastrous sentimentality, which, whatever liberties it sets loose, loosens also the cement that alone can bind any society into a stable compound—a code of obeyed taboos. I can only recall the saying of a wise Frenchman that "liberty is the luxury of self-discipline." Historically those peoples that did not discipline themselves had discipline thrust on them from the outside. That is why the normal cycle in the life and death of great nations has been first a powerful tyranny broken by revolt, the enjoyment of liberty, the abuse of liberty—and back to tyranny again. As I see it, in this country—a land of the most persistent idealism and the blandest cynicism—the race is on between its decadence and its vitality.

There are the woes, which we share with the world, that you can see from your window: overpopulation; the pollution of the atmosphere, the cities, and the rivers; the destruction of nature. I find it impossible to believe that a nation that produced such dogged and ingenious humans as Jefferson and Eli Whitney, John Deere and Ford, Kettering and Oppenheimer and Edison and Franklin, is going to sit back and let the worst happen. There is now a possibility, at least, that nuclear energy can help us to cure incurable diseases, to preserve our food indefinitely, and through breeder reactors, which renew more power in the act of spending it, can actually clean the cities and, let us pray, the oceans. And that would take us over a historical watershed that none of us has ever conceived.

Very often when I was on the road and writing or pondering all this, I found that many old American maxims and idioms, snatches of songs and sententiae floated from the back of my mind into the front of it. When you climb down a rocky cleft in the Great Smokies to a trailblazer's cave or lean into the slamming winds of the prairie, it is not hard to see why "Root, hog, or die" became a warning watchword for several generations. At other times, coming on the records of pioneer husbands who had abandoned their families and joined a railroad gang or headed for the mining country, I found myself spoiled for a choice of their proper epitaph, between "Westward the course of empire," "Pike's peak or bust," or "I love my wife but oh, you kid!" And traveling past the rickety cabins of the black man's back country, and through his scabrous city slums, there often seemed to be only one American theme song: "Sometimes I'm up, Sometimes I'm down, And sometimes I'm almost to the ground."

More often than I care to admit, one of the oldest of American chestnuts seemed newly roasted. It is that line of the Italian immigrant asked to say what forty years of American life had taught him: "There is no free lunch." By now it is a facetious truism, but it is also a profound truth forgotten by the Founding Fathers in the ecstasy of promising everybody life, liberty, and the pursuit of happiness—and it is forgotten again today when committees of Congress imply that transferring $40,000,000 of tax money from the defense budget to revenue sharing will fix everything.

It is a bitterly, and sometimes rousingly, complicated place, this land thrashing over such incessant contradictions as control and permissiveness, the radical young and the conservative middle, the limitlessness of civil rights and the limitations of presidential power. The Swedish sociologist Gunnar Myrdal helped make sense of the constant commotion with his remark to the effect that, while the American tradition is a conservative one, what it has struggled to conserve are often very radical principles indeed.

A still more timely reminder that the government of a free people is meant to be argued about comes from the most famous of American jurists. It gives me, at least, some hope in the outcome of our present conflicts, for it embraces the notion of healthy life as a continuing conflict and strongly suggests that the comfortable impulse to submit and yield to one view of American life or a single instrument of government is an impulse of decay. It is that tremendous line of Justice Oliver Wendell Holmes: "A Constitution is made for people of fundamentally differing views."

Overleaf: *Painted by Jacques Lemoyne, who accompanied a French expedition to Florida in 1564, this bizarre scene purported to show Indians worshipping a column bearing the arms of the King of France. What it really shows is the familiar shape of an old dream — the infinite and readily available abundance of the New World.*

To Acknowledge

So many hundreds of people helped me that naming them would make a book in itself. From the moment the idea of the television series was conceived, one producer (Michael Gill), four directors (Gill, Ann Turner, David Heycock, and Tim Slessor), and two or three camera crews did their best over two years to see that it was safely delivered and got on its feet. I have listed them all at the end of this note, though a roll call is a poor mark of gratitude for so much unflagging devotion, technical skill, and good humor.

Along the way—which means, along the hundred thousand miles or so we traveled—we received the unstinting help by day and sometimes far into the night of innumerable curators, house historians, librarians; foresters and rangers of the National and State Park services; soldiers, sailors, marines, atomic scientists (Harold Agnew more than anybody); keepers of archives, policemen, janitors, and bystanding citizens from the First Lady to the last of the cowboys. Everywhere, the local citizenry leaped to be of service; on the prairie, especially, they added warm hospitality.

My debt to many historians is something harder to isolate, since down forty years or so it becomes more difficult all the time to know which influences you took in through your pores and which through a well-remembered name. But there are one or two commanding figures to whom I owe a great deal. Sir Denis Brogan was the man who, more than any other, got me fascinated by American history, first in print and then, through a long friendship, in the flesh. He broke, for me, the academic mold and demonstrated what many lesser historians fearful of their pedagogic standing would not do even if they had the wit: he would add a gloss from Cole Porter to a text from Chief Justice Marshall, or recall a sage bit of advice from James A. Farley to puncture some swollen volume by a professor of political science who had never been closer to a precinct captain than the university library. In other words, Brogan saw, and sees, that history is all around us and is no preserve of scholars. I was consequently delighted when he undertook to be the historical consultant on the television series. When his judgment differed from mine, he would often write: "But this is your business, not mine," a very welcome change from a pedant who squealed at a critical adjective about his pet and sent me a fast note saying: "The characterization of Mr. J. will not do." On quite simple matters of fact, both Sir Denis and I nodded from time to time, and I have hastened to correct these errors in the waking hours.

Of all the standard historians, both classical and revisionist, I have been most grateful most often to that venerable Admiral of the Ocean Sea, Samuel Eliot Morison, who threw me a lifeline when I was floundering in whirlpools of competing "facts" and theories. Of later men, Daniel Boorstin whipped up my interest in many vital, though little-noticed, movements. I am specially indebted to him for putting me on to William Ogden, the first mayor of Chicago, and to Frederic Tudor, the first tycoon. And I ought to mention the pleasure and profit I have taken for many years from the works of John Bartlet Brebner, Henry Steele Commager, J. Russell Smith, Mark Sullivan, Frederick Lewis Allen, Gerald Johnson, and J. Frank Dobie, and, more recently, particular volumes by Edmund S. Morgan, James MacGregor Burns, Alvin Josephy, and Merlo J. Pusey. The five volumes of James Truslow Adams' *Dictionary of American History* are a wonderful sheet anchor to have at one's elbow, and both at one's elbow and deep in the hinterland I have learned many things from the incomparable Federal Guides to the States that cannot be found in any other books. I am also grateful to many correspondents between Hawaii and Scotland who questioned or amended or otherwise cleared up statements made in the television series. Among these I am happy to thank Morris Ernst, James Thomas Flexner, J. R. Pole, Audrey Williamson, Peter Farrar, Sheridan A. Logan, John Byrne Cooke, and, especially, Leon J. Salter, an erudite anthropologist who enlightened me (too late, alas, for the film) about "the Bering Strait myth."

None of these worthies is responsible for the errors and frailties that no doubt still burden the text. I must also add the names of several people who are normally excused from a favorable citation, because it is simply supposed to be their daily job to get a television series on the air or a book into the stores. Peter Robeck, of *Time-Life* Films, Inc., was the earliest laborer on the television commodity exchange and finally landed Xerox, the only sponsor I know willing to let a fifty-minute program run fifty minutes without wrenching intervals for the contemplation of the transverse colon or a fluid with the cleaning properties of sulphuric acid. C. Peter McColough, David Curtin, and Robert N. Stahl are to be saluted here.

Once the series was filmed and done with, my next labor was this book, and here there were other people who moved in to match the devotion of the film crews. First among equals is Peter Campbell, who laid out the splendid illustrations of Lord Clark's *Civilisation* and began the same service for me. He was aided at once by Mr. Knopf's indefatigable Anthony Schulte and subsequently by Charles Elliott, Mary Jenkins, and the ever-willing Ann Turner (who should have had enough by the time she had finished directing two of the films). It is not possible to do more than hint here at the encouragement I have taken for a quarter of a century from the friendship and the blunt integrity of the maestro himself, Alfred A. Knopf.

My secretary, Ingrid Luce, bore up with Teutonic phlegm through three years of my unpredictable comings and goings. Finally, it would be churlish to overlook the unsleeping watchfulness over both the film and the book projects of "Justice" Irving Cohen, to whom my debt is payable but insufficient.

No doubt I have omitted, and therefore wounded, some invaluable Mr., Mrs., Miss, or Ms. I claim exemption from a sentence for contempt on the grounds well stated by a learned judge: "Justice is a splendid thing, but you must not expect justice from this life."

The BBC "America" crews:

PRODUCER: Michael Gill.

DIRECTORS: Michael Gill, Ann Turner, Tim Slessor, David Heycock.

CAMERAMEN: Kenneth MacMillan, A. A. Englander, Phil Meheux, John Wyatt.

ASSISTANT CAMERAMEN: Colin Deehan, David Evans, John Walker, Michael Spooner.

SOUND RECORDISTS: Malcolm Webberley, Ron Brown, Colin March, Graham Rodger.

ELECTRICIANS: Stan Palmer, Ken Aylett, David Gorringe, Geoffrey Appleyard, Joe Cooksey, Alan Muhley.

FILM EDITORS: Allan Tyrer, David Thomas, Dan Rae.

ASSISTANT FILM EDITORS: Rosina Pedrick, Derek Towers, Jonathan Crane, Dick Tumbleson, Clive Bell.

DUBBING MIXERS: Alan Dykes, John C. C. Hale.

RESEARCH ASSISTANTS: Joy Curtiss, Sally Evans.

PRODUCERS' ASSISTANTS: Barbara Cannell, Ruth Roberts, Diane Sullivan.

MUSIC ADVISER: Charles Chilton.

MUSIC ARRANGER: Alfred Ralston.

STILLS PHOTOGRAPHER: Roynon Raikes.

ROSTRUM CAMERAMAN: Ivor Richardson.

PICTURE CREDITS

INDEX

Abilene, Kans., 229, 232–3, 238
abolition, 134, 200, 218
Acheson, Dean, 351
Acton, Lord, 122
Adams, Daniel, 168
Adams, John, 100, 104, 107, 109, 110, 121, 126, 127, 153, 336
Adams, Samuel, 104, 132
Ali, Muhammad, 12
Allen, Ethan, 130
Allen, Fred, 15
Andrews, Charles M., 81
Anschutz, Thomas, 259
anti-Communism, 310, 315
Antietam, Battle of, 204, 206, illus. 210–11
anti-evolution laws, 271
armed forces, 335–8
army, 336–8
Articles of Confederation, 130–4, 137
assembly line production, 342, 344, 345
Astaire, Fred and Adele, 9
atomic bomb, illus. 335, 349–51, 353
Attlee, Clement, 314
Attucks, Crispus, 101

barbed wire, 237–8
Barry, Commodore John, 131
Barton, Bruce, 317, 324, 326
beaver trade, 170–1
Bell, Alexander Graham, 256
Bellows, George, 286
Benchley, Robert, 273, 323
Benton, Thomas Hart, 332
Bering, Vitus, 24
Berlin, Irving, 319
Bermuda, 73
Bierstadt, Albert, 185
Bilbo, Sen. Theodore, 381
Bill of Rights, 147, 150
Blake, William, 133
Body, W. S., 155
Bohr, Niels, 350
Boone, Daniel, 156, 158, 160
Booth, John Wilkes, 216
Boré, Jean Étienne, 193
Boston Massacre, 101
Boston Tea Party, 104–5
Bougainville, Louis Antoine de, 386

Bow, Clara, 319
Boyd, Dr. William, 24
Braddock, Edward, 95, 111, 156
Bradford, William, 76, 78
Brady, Diamond Jim, illus. 263
Brady, Matthew, 214
Brewster, William, 76
Brown, John, 200
Brown, Mather, 153
Brown, Oliver, 384
Bryan, William Jennings, 270–1
buffalo, 155, 179
Buffalo Bill, see Cody, Col. William
Bull Run, Battle of, 204
Burke, Edmund, 104
burlesque theaters, 292
Burr, Aaron, 290
Burroughs, John, illus. 254
Byrd, William, 69

Cabot, John, 31
Capone, Al, 248, 324
Carnegie, Andrew, 262–3, 266–7, 293, 296
carpetbaggers, 219
Carroll, Charles, 121
Cartier, Jacques, 46, 47, 52
Catherine the Great, 236
cattle, 232, 236, 238
cavalry, 337
Chamberlain, Neville, 339
Chancellorsville, Battle of, 206, illus. 212–13
Charles I, 79
Charles II, 88
Charles III (Spain), 43
Charlestown Company, 178, 179, 183
Chicago, founding of, 248–9, 252
Chichester, Sir Francis, 12
Chinese laborers, 228–9
Chisholm Trail, 229, 232
Churchill, Sir Winston, 67, 218, 238, 314, 351, 352
Cíbola myths, 36–8, 39
civil rights legislation, 381, 384
Civil War, 200, 201, 202–4, 206–7, 214, 216, 218–19, 223, 226
Clark, Gen. George Rogers, 131, 163
Clark, Meriwether, see Lewis and Clark expedition

Clark, William, 163, 166
Clay, Henry, 200
Clemenceau, Georges, 308
Cleveland, Grover, 226
Cody, Col. William, 240, 242
coinage, 270–1
Columbus, Christopher, 23, 25–6, illus. 27, 28–35, 62
Committees of Correspondence, 104, 105, 106, 132
communes, 223, 376–7 and illus., 380
Communism, 310, 315
Concord, Battle of, 107
Confederacy, 202–4, 206–7, 214, 216, 218–19
Congressional investigations, 374, 376
Constitution, 7, 14, 125, 141, 143, 144–7, 150, 216, 336, 339
Constitutional Convention, 132–4, 136–7, 140–1, 143–4
Continental Congress, 104, 110, 111, 114, 116, 130
Contract Labor Law, 284, 293
Cook, Capt. James, 386
Coolidge, Calvin, 78, 116, 315–16, 326
Coolidge, Dane, 233
Cornwallis, Lord, 125
Coronado, Francisco, 36–42
Cortés, Hernando, 24, 35, 46
Cosa, Juan de la, 32
cotton gin, 192–3, 196
Cotton Kingdom, 190–1
cowboys, 232–3
Crèvecoeur, Jean de, 91
Croker, Richard, 290
Crosby, Bing, 374
Cumberland Gap, 156, 158
Custer, Gen. George Armstrong, 240

dams, 368–9
Darwin, Charles, 271
Declaration of Independence, 116, 120–1, 130, 132, 367
Deere, John, 237, 388
deficit financing, 373
De La Warr, Lord, 66
De Smet, Fr. Pierre Jean, 45
De Soto, Hernando, 36

Dickens, Charles, 156, 190
Dixon, Jeremiah, 93
Donnaconna (Huron chief), 47
Douglas, James, 160
Drake, "Col." Edwin L., 258
Drake, Sir Francis, 35, 61
Drayton, Michael, 63–4, 66
Du Lhut, Sieur, 58
Duncan, David Douglas, 363
Dust Bowl, 328

Earp, Wyatt, 110
Eastman, George, 256
Edison, Thomas, 254 and *illus.*, 256, 388
Einstein, Albert, 349, 357
Eisenhower, Dwight D., 238, 322, 349, 353, 362, 384
El Dorado myths, 38, 47, 62, 156
Elizabeth I, 61
Ellis Island, N.Y., *illus. 281*, 282 and *illus.*, 284–5, 299
Emancipation Proclamation, 218
Emerson, Ralph Waldo, 253
Engels, Friedrich, 377
Estebán, 37
European Recovery Program, 12, 351–2

Fairbanks, Douglas, 9
Fairfax, Lord Thomas, 105
farmers and farming, 252–3, 268, 270–1, 327–8
Ferdinand (king), 30, 31, 62
Fermi, Enrico, 349, 350
Firestone, Harvey, *illus. 254*
First World War, 303–4
Five Nations, 51
Floyd, William, 121
Ford, Henry, *illus. 254*, 316–17, 388
Fort Duquesne, 95, 156
Fort Pickens, Fla., 202
Fort Sumter, S.C., 202
Fort Ticonderoga, N.Y., 95, 131
Fort William, Wyo., *illus. 171*
forty-niners, 177–9, 182–3, 185
Founding Fathers, 132–3, 270
Francis I, 46–7
Frankfurter, Justice Felix, 147
Franklin, Benjamin, 116–17, 120, 121, *illus. 122*, 134, 136, 153, 388
Frazier, Joe, 12
French and Indian Wars, 58, 94–5, 98–9, 111, 140, 156, 158, 162
French-Canadians, 170
French explorations, 46–7, 50–2, 54–5, 58–9
French Revolution, 133, 150
Freud, Sigmund, 323
Frick, Henry, 262, 266, 293, 296
fur trade, 43, 50–2, 83, 170–1

Gage, Gen. Thomas, 105, 107
Gardner, Alexander, 210–11, 216
Garvey, Marcus, 384, 385
George III, *illus. 93*, 94, 100, 125–6, 137
German immigrants, 278

Geronimo (Apache chief), *illus. 243*
Gershwin, George, 319
Gettysburg, Battle of, 204, 206
Gettysburg Address, 214
ghettos, 285–6
Gibbon, Edward, 110, 387
Gladstone, William Ewart, 125, 263
Glenn, John, 32, 322
Goering, Hermann, 342
Goethe, 274
gold rushes, 35, 155, 171, 174–6, 177–9, 253
gold standard, 270
Gorges, Sir Ferdinando, 63
Grand Coulee Dam, 344–5, 369
Grant, Sir George, 236
Grant, Ulysses S., *illus. 209*, 216, 219
Great Depression, 225, 327–8, 329, 373
Great Plains, 247–9, 252, 328
Greene, Gen. Nathaniel, 191, 196
Gross, Milt, 292

Hakluyt, Richard, 62, 66
Hamilton, Alexander, 14, 126, 137, 140, 143, 144, 153
Hammarskjöld, Dag, 136
Hancock, John, 120–1
Harding, Chester, 156
Harding, Warren G., 314–15, 328
Harlan, Justice John Marshall, 146
Harriman, E. H., 262
Harris, Mrs. Ellen, 376
Hart, William S., 7
Hawkins, Sir John, 35, 61
Heap Wolves (Comanche chief), *illus. 23*
Henry, Patrick, 106–7, *illus. 109*, 132, 143
Henry IV, 50
Henry VIII, 31
Hersey, Tim, 232
Hickok, "Wild Bill," 110, 233
Higgins, Andrew, 344
Hill, James J., 262
Hine, Lewis, 293
Hitler, Adolf, 332, 338, 339, 340, 342, 344, 349
Holmes, Justice Oliver Wendell, 146, 207, 214, 309, 389
Homestead Act, 237
homesteading, 15, 18, 237–8, 240, 248, 270
Honolulu, Hawaii, 340, 386–7
Hoover, Herbert, 326, 327
Hoover Dam, 344, 368–9, 370
House of Burgesses, 67–8
House of Representatives, 143
Hughes, Chief Justice Charles Evans, 146
Huguenots, 58
hydroelectric power, 368–9

immigration, 273–5, 278–9, 281–2, 284–6, 288, 290–3, 299–301, 310
incandescent lamp, 254, 256
Independence Hall, 137, *illus. 143*

Indians, *illus. 23, 38, 39, 42, illus. 48–9*, 51, *illus. 52*, 55, *illus. 56–7, illus. 64*, 66, 78, 84, 95, 158, 163, 166 and *illus.*, 168, 170–1, 232, 240, 242–3 and *illus.*, 337
Industrial Revolution, 197–8, 370, 372
Insull, Samuel, 327
Intercolonial Committees, 104, 105, 106, 132
inventions, 253–4, 256, 258
Irish immigrants, 274–5, 278, 288, 290
Iroquois League, 51
Isabella, Queen, 30, 31, 62
isolationists, 338, 339–40

Jackson, Andrew, 166, 168 and *illus.*, 170
James I, 63, 66, 77
Jamestown settlement, 63–4, 66–9
Japan, 337, 340, 342, 345, 349, 351, 353
Jefferson, Thomas, 58, 68, 78, 94, 100, 106, 107, 111, 120, 121, 122, 133, 145, 147, 150–1, 153 and *illus.*, 156, 160, 162–3, 166, 185, 189, 190, 198, 279, 316, 323, 338, 388
Jennison, Pvt. Edwin Francis, 204
Jesuits, 51
Jewish immigrants, 275, 278–9, 285–6, 300, 349
Johnson, Andrew, 314
Johnson, Lyndon B., 216
Jones, Bobby, 9
Jones, Robert Tyre, Jr., 322–3
Jonson, Ben, 62
judicial review, 144–5

Kaiser, Henry, 12, 344–5
Keaton, Buster, 7
Kefauver, Estes, 12
Kelly, Honest John, 290
Kennedy, John F., 216, 275, 353 and *illus.*, 356
Kennedy, Patrick, 275
Kennedy, Robert F., *illus. 353*
Kettering, Charles Franklin, 388
Keynes, John Maynard, 327
Keyserling, Count, 368
Kier, Samuel, 258
King, Martin Luther, Jr., 385
Korean War, 353
Ku Klux Klan, 310–11

Lafayette, Marquis de, 100
Lansing, Robert, 305, 308
La Salle, Sieur de, 50–5, 98
Las Vegas, Nev., 369–70
Law, Bonar, 314
Lazarus, Emma, 279
League of Nations, 131, 305, 308, 311, 314
Leakey, Dr. Louis S. B., 23
Lee, Robert E., 204, 207, 214 and *illus.*, 216, 219
Lehr, Harry, 268

Lemoyne, Jacques, 386, 389
Lend-Lease Act, 338
León, Ponce de, 36
Levin, M. G., 24
Lewis and Clark expedition, 59, 163, 166, 226
Liberia, 381
Liberty ships, 344, 345
Lincoln, Abraham, 185, 202–3, 216 and *illus.*, 218, 314, 340, 369, 381, 385
Lindbergh, Charles, 9, 319, *illus. 320–1,* 322, 338, 340, 342, 344
Little Bighorn, Battle of, 240, 242
Livingston, Philip, 121
Livingston, Robert, 121, 162–3
Lloyd George, David, 266, 308, 314
London Company, 63, 66, 67–9, 73
longhorn cattle, 232
Looking Glass (operation), 358–9
Los Angeles, Calif., 374
Louisiana Purchase, 161–3, 166
Loyalists, 107, 109, 126–7
Luks, George, 306
lynching, *illus. 311*

MacArthur, Gen. Douglas, 322, 351, 362
Madison, James, 14, 132, 140–1, 143, 144–5, 153
mail-order catalogues, 317, 319 and *illus.*
Malcolm X, 385
Malvern Hill, Battle of, 204
Marbury, William, 145
Marcos, Fray, 37–8, 66
marines, 336, 362
Marshall, Gen. George Catlett, 339
Marshall, James Wilson, 174, 185
Marshall, Chief Justice John, 145, 146, *illus. 147,* 170
Marshall Plan, 12, 351–2
Marx, Karl, 175
Mason, Charles, 93
Mason, George, 14, 134, 140, 143, 147
mass production, principles of, 196–7, 342, 344, 345
Massachusetts Bay Colony, 76–9, 81, 83, 85, 86–7
Mayflower, voyage of the, 76, 77–8
Mayflower Compact, 78
McCarthy, Joseph, 12
McClellan, Gen. George Brinton, 204
McCormick, Cyrus, 252
McCoy, Joseph, 229, 232–3
McKim, Charles Follen, 296
McKinley, William, 299
Megarini, Fr., 45
Mencken, H. L., 143, 326
Mendoza, Don Antonio de, 37, 38
Mercator, Gerhardus, 18
Mexican War, 175, 198, 207, 336
Mexico Territory, 171, 174; *see also* New Spain
Middle Colonies, 88, 90, 110
militias, 335–6
Miller, A. J., 155, 171

mining towns, 233, 236
Mississippi River, 8–9, 52, 54–5, 161–2, 193, 196, 202
Missouri Compromise, 198, 202
Mitchell, S. Weir, 206
monopolies, 297, 299
Monroe, James, 162, 163, 381
Monticello, Va., 151, 153, 189
Morgan, John Pierpont, 262, 293, 296–7, 299, 317
Morison, Samuel Eliot, 83, 86, 161
Mormons, 23, *illus. 223,* 223–6
Morse, Samuel, 253
motion picture industry, 319
Mount Vernon, Va., 111
Myrdal, Gunnar, 389

Nader, Ralph, 374, 376
Napoleon Bonaparte, 116, 162, 163
National Recovery Administration (NRA), 329, 331
National War Command, 359, 362
navy, 336, 338
Negroes, 69, 72, 111, 120, 134, 189, 190–1, 198, 200, 202–3, 206, 218, 300, 311 and *illus.*, 367, 381, 384–5, 388; *see also* slaves
Nelson, Thomas, 121
Neutrality Act, 338
New England Company, 81
New France, 50–2, 54–5, 58
New Spain, 35–9, 42, 99
Nobs of San Francisco, 183, 185
North, Lord Frederick, 100, 105
nuclear weapons, 356–9, 362–3

Oakley, Annie, 110
O'Banion, Dion, 324
Ogden, William, 248–9, 252
Ohio Company, 140
oil discoveries, 258–9
Old South Meeting House (Boston), 101, 104
Oñate, Don Juan de, 42
Oppenheimer, Dr. Robert, 350, 388
Oregon Trail, 171
Orlando, Vittorio E., 308
Otis, James, 104, 107
Owen, Robert, 377, 380

Paine, Thomas, 58, 132–3
Palmer, A. Mitchell, 310, 311, 315
Palmerston, Viscount, 218
Paul III (pope), 37
Pearl Harbor, 340 and *illus.,* 342
Pegler, Westbrook, 332
Penn, William, 88, 160
People's Party, 268
Perez Juan, 31
Persac, Adrian, 193
Peter the Great, 24
philanthropists, 262, 263, 266
Philip II, 42
Pickford, Mary, 7
Pilgrims, 73, 76–9
pioneers, 160–1, 175, 177–9, 182–3, 185
Pitt, William, 100, 110

Plessy, Homer Adolf, 381
Plunkitt, George Washington, 290–1
Pocahontas, 66
Point, Fr., 45
Pole, J. R., 134
political organizations, 288, 290–1
Polk, James Knox, 175
Polo, Marco, 32, 33
Pope, Alexander, 122
Popham, Sir John, 63
Portolá, Capt. Gaspar de, 43
Prando, Fr., 45
Princeton, Battle of, 111
Prohibition, 323–4
Promontory Point, Utah, *illus. 230–1*
Provincial Convention, 106, 107
Puritans, 73, 76–9, 81, 83, 86–8, 304

race riots, 311
railroads, 226 and *illus.,* 228–9, *illus. 230–1,* 249, 253
Raleigh, Sir Walter, 73
Raleigh Tavern, 106
Ramírez, Fr., 39
Ravalli, Fr., 45
religious dissenters, 88, 90
research and development, 356–7
Revere, Paul, 101
Revolutionary War, 93, 94–5, 98–100, 101–7, 109–11, 114, 116–17, 120–2, 125, 126–7, 335
Ridgefield, Battle of, 107, 109
robber barons, 259, 262–3, 266–7, 293, 296–7, 299
Robespierre, 133
Robinson, John, 76
Rockefeller, John D., *illus. 256,* 259, 262
Rodgers, Richard, 319
Rogers, Will, 253
Rolfe, John, 66
Roosevelt, Franklin D., 12, 262, 314, 328–9, *illus. 330–1,* 331–2, 338, 339, 340, 342, 344, 345, 368, 369, 370, 372
Roosevelt, Theodore, 13, 297, 299 and *illus., 305, 328*
Rousseau, Jean-Jacques, 58, 160
Royko, Mike, 286
Rush, Benjamin, 121
Russell, Bertrand, 367

Sacajawea, 163, 166
salt and salt licks, 158, 160, 161
Salter, Dr. Leon J., 24
Sandys, Sir Edwin, 76, 77
scalawags, 219
Scott, Dred, 202
Sears, Roebuck catalogue, 317, 319 and *illus.*
Second World War, 332, 335, 337–40, 344–5, 349–52, 356–7, 381
sectionalism, 141
segregation, 381, 384
Senate, 143
Separatists, 76–7
Serra, Fr. Junípero, 43, 45

sharpshooters, 109–10
Shaw, George Bernard, 328, 335, 367
Sherman, Robert, 121
Sherman, Gen. William, 218, 363
Shiloh, Battle of, 204, 206
shipbuilding, 344, 345
silver: mining, 253; coinage, 270–1
Sitting Bull (Sioux chief), 240, 242
slavery, 69, 72, 111, 120, 134, 189, 190–1, 198, 200, 202–3, 206, 218; *see also* Negroes
Smith, Adam, 335
Smith, J. Russell, 242
Smith, Capt. John, 64, 66
Smith, Joseph, 224, 225
Smith, Sir Thomas, 63
Smithsonian Institution, 380
Spanish explorations, 26, 30–3, 35–9, 42–3, 45–6; *see also* New Spain
Spice Islands, 26
Staël, Mme de, 274
Stamp Act, 99–100, 120
Standard Oil Company of Ohio, 259
Stanford, Leland, 229
steamboats, 193, 196
steel industry, 263
Stevenson, Adlai E., 300
stock market crash (1929), 326–7
stockyards, 232
Strategic Air Command, 358–9, 362–3
suburbs, 373–4, 376
Supreme Court, 144–7, 200, 202, 216, 296, 297, 329, 331, 381, 384
Sutherland, Justice George, 146
Sutter, Johann August, 171, 174–6, 331
Szilard, Leo, 349

Taft, William Howard, 297, 300
Talleyrand, Charles, 162–3
Tammany organization, 288, 290, 305

taxation of the colonies, 99–101, 104–5
Tecumseh (Shawnee chief), 168
telegraph, invention of, 253
Teller, Edward, 349
Thoroughgood, Adam, 69
Tippecanoe, Battle of, 168
tobacco, 66–7
Tocqueville, Alexis de, 18, 19, 197
Tojo, Gen. Hideki, 340
Torrio, Johnny, 324
Toussaint L'Ouverture, Pierre, 162
Townshend, Charles, 100
Tracy, Marquis de, 51
transcontinental railroad, 226, 228–9
Triangle Shirtwaist Factory, 299–300
Truman, Harry, 216, 314, 327, 351, 384
Trumbull, John, 114
Tudor, Frederic, 372–3
Turkey Red wheat, 13, 237
Turner, Nat, 384
Twain, Mark, 9
Tweed, William Marcy "Boss," 290

United Nations, 131, 352–3, 357–8, 386
United States Steel Corp., 263, 296
Ustinov, Peter, 90

Valley Forge, Pa., 114, *illus. 118*, 386
Vanderbilt, Cornelius, 267
Vanderbilt, William K., 268
Verrazano, Giovanni, 46, 47
Versailles, Treaty of, 305, 308, 311
Vespucci, Amerigo, 25
Victoria (queen), 151, 236, 240, 275
Vietnam War, 356
Vinci, Leonardo da, 30
Voltaire, 58

wagon trains, 177–9, 182–3, 185
Walker, Thomas, 156
War of 1812, 168
Warren, Chief Justice Earl, 147, 384

Warren, Joseph, 104
Washington, George, 95, 100, 110–11, 114 and *illus.*, 116, 127, 131, 132, 133–4 and *illus.*, 136, 137, 141, 168, 207, 279, 336, 337, 340, 386
Washington, Martha, 111, 114
Wells, H.G., 367
Wheeler, Sen. Burton, 340
Whiskey Rebellion, 337
Whitman, Walt, 223
Whitney, Eli, 191–3, 196, 197, 388
Wigner, Eugen, 349
Wild West, 233, 236–8, 240, 242–3
Wilderness Campaign (1864), 209
Wilderness Road, 158
Williamsburg, Va., 67, 105–6
Willkie, Wendell, 369
Wilson, Woodrow, 136, 214, 303, 304–5, 308 and *illus.*, 310–11, 328, 331, 356
Winthrop, John, 79, *illus. 81*, 83, 86–8, 304, 324
Winthrop, John (grandson), 94
witches, persecution of, 87
"witch hunters," 310, 311, 315
Witherspoon, John, 121
Wood, Fernando, 290
Work Projects Administration (WPA), 13, 331
World War I, 303–4
World War II, 332, 335, 337–40, 344–5, 349–52, 356–7, 381
Wounded Knee, Battle of, 242
Wright Brothers, 258
Writers' Program (WPA), 13, 331
Wythe, George, 121

Yeardley, Sir George, 67
York, Sergeant, 110
Yorktown, Battle of, 125
Young, Brigham, 224–5